The Annotated Bibliography of Canada's Major Authors

The Annotated Bibliography of Canada's Major Authors

Volume Two

Edited by Robert Lecker
and Jack David

ECW PRESS

Canadian Cataloguing in Publication Data

Lecker, Robert, 1951-
  The annotated bibliography of Canada's major
authors.

Includes index.

ISBN 0-920802-08-7 (set) ISBN 0-920802-02-8 (v.1)
bd. ISBN 0-920802-04-4 (v.1) pa. ISBN 0-920802-38-9
(v.2) bd. ISBN 0-920802-40-0 (v.2) pa.

ISBN 0-8161-8491-7 [American Distribution, v.1]
ISBN 0-8161-8552-2 [American Distribution, v.2]

1. Canadian literature - Bibliography. I. David,
Jack, 1946-   II. Title.

Z1375.L43   016.81   C79-094602-5

Published with the assistance of the Association for Canadian
Community Colleges and The Canada Council.

Printed in Canada by The Porcupine's Quill, Inc.,
and typeset by Erin Graphics, Inc.

Cover: "Canada Tree II," by John K. Esler.

Distributed in Canada by
  ECW PRESS
  356 Stong College, York University
  Downsview, Ontario M3J 1P3

Distributed outside Canada by
  G.K. Hall & Co.
  70 Lincoln Street
  Boston, Massachusetts 02111

For Paula and Sharon . . .

. . . and to the dedicated work of
Alan Horne, Bruce Whiteman,
George Wicken, Lila and Raymond
Laakso, and Marianne Micros.

Contents

Introduction

This is Volume II of an ongoing, multi-volume series entitled *The Annotated Bibliography of Canada's Major Authors (ABCMA)*. The series is designed to be the first collection of comprehensive, annotated bibliographies of works by and on Canada's major French and English authors from the nineteenth and twentieth centuries. In its entirety, *ABCMA* contains ten projected volumes, five of which will be devoted to prose, and five to poetry. Each volume, in turn, will include five discrete, annotated bibliographies of works by and on specific writers.

The composition of authors included in individual volumes has been determined according to two criteria: current bibliographical needs shared by readers, and critical groupings reflecting common literary aims. This volume, for example, attempts to meet the demand for solid bibliographical information on five of Canada's most respected poets. Future volumes in the series will continue the attempt to meet the bibliographical requirements of scholars in a format which facilitates critical comparison. As each volume in the series appears, a developmental perspective covering the range of Canadian literature will emerge.

Although no bibliography can compensate for individual research, *ABCMA* does provide both the scholar and the general reader with two unique tools. First, the series presents full listings of all works by the major Canadian authors covered in each volume. These listings cover books, manuscripts, contributions to books and periodicals — including poems, short stories, essays, audio-visual material, miscellaneous works, and a selection of reprinted anthology contributions. This comprehensive presentation of primary sources includes all book editions and indicates where and when material has been reprinted, revised, excerpted, or retitled. Second, the series contains a complete, annotated list of works on the author — including books, sections of books, articles, audio-visual material, theses and dissertations, interviews, literary awards and honours, plus book reviews (on the author's individual works) selected according to such criteria as critical importance, regional response, idiosyncratic perspective, and non-Canadian evaluation. The annotations in the sections devoted to critical writings are designed to furnish an informed but objective analysis of the arguments advanced in each secondary source. Throughout the series, the sections devoted to primary and secondary works are organized chronologically so as to provide the reader with a sense of the relation between creative output and shifting critical response. This relation is examined in a brief introduction which precedes each bibliography.

As the above description suggests, *ABCMA* aims to present comprehensive, dependable bibliographies on major Canadian writers. To this end, the editors have directed the compilers to obtain complete information regarding primary and secondary material up to December 31, 1979. This goal has been achieved, with the exception that book reviews have been selected according to the criteria outlined above and discussed in more depth below. The editors recognize that the comprehensiveness of *ABCMA* may only be determined after a considerable period of time; they also acknowledge the fact that bibliographies on living authors must be subject to constant scrutiny and revision. To allow for the introduction of supplementary information and new entries listing primary and secondary material published after 1979, updates to *ABCMA* will be issued periodically.

The bibliographical principles which have been applied to the series are those established by the Modern Language Association as set forth in *MLA Handbook* (New York: Modern Language Association, 1977). The bibliographical style of *ABCMA* is, therefore, compatible with the most widely accepted form of bibliographical citation used in North American literary scholarship. The parts and sections of each bibliography are organized chronologically; in the case of chronological duplication, alphabetical ordering is employed.

Each bibliography contains the following basic components:

Table of Contents

Introduction

Part I

Works by the Author

A   Books and Manuscripts

B   Contributions to Periodicals and Books: Poems, Short Stories, Articles, Reviews, Letters, Audio-Visual Material, Miscellaneous Works, and Selected Anthology Contributions

Part II

Works on the Author

C   Books, Articles and Sections of Books, Theses and Dissertations, Interviews, Audio-Visual Material, and Awards and Honours

D   Selected Book Reviews (plus selected reviews of audio-visual works where applicable)

Index to Critics Listed in the Bibliography

The organization of each component is more fully described as follows.

Table of Contents: The table of contents lists the components of each bibliography and indicates the pages on which these components are to be found.

Introduction: The Introduction begins with a brief chronological survey of the critical perspectives which have been offered on the author. This is followed by a discussion of the existing state of bibliography on the author and includes a summary of any bibliographical problems or limitations encountered by the compiler.

Part I: Part I of each bibliography is devoted to works *by* the author. These works are listed chronologically under the subsections and headings described below.

A. Books and Manuscripts: This section contains a complete list of all books published by the author (organized chronologically according to date of publication), as well as a list of the author's manuscripts held privately or by institutions (ordered according to the extensiveness of the manuscript collection). When an author has published in one genre only, the section devoted to books and manuscripts contains only two separate headings; however, when an author has published books in several genres (e.g., criticism, drama, travel books) or has edited books or anthologies, separate subheadings indicating each kind of work are presented within the section. These too are organized chronologically.

Insofar as the specific means of citing primary titles is concerned, the following procedure has been adopted: the *original title* of the first edition is followed, consecutively, by the *place of publication*, the *name of the publisher*, the *date of publication*, and the *number of pages* in the edition. (In the case of simultaneous publication in several places, alphabetical ordering is employed.) After this initial entry, the same information is provided for all subsequent editions and translations of the original work, with the exception that in non-translated editions the original title is understood to remain constant. Translated titles are, therefore, cited in full, while the *absence* of a title after the intial citation indicates that the edition in question bears the title of the first edition. When an edition contains a critical introduction or foreword, this fact is noted in the entry. Within this section, annotations are also provided to indicate features particular to a given edition.

The section devoted to manuscripts is meant to establish a description of the contents in manuscript collections, and to provide information as to where those collections may be found. The full address of the location of each collection is therefore specified. The location is followed by a short list of the contents comprising the collection. This list alters according to the extent that manuscript materials have been catalogued. The data are accompanied by an annotation which comments on the comprehensiveness of the collection. The compiler has listed the material in the collection according to the manner in which the manuscripts are stored; thus the identification of the contents ranges from a list of all manuscripts (organized in relation to the system employed by the cataloguing institution), to an extensive summary of previously unidentified material contained in boxes, folders, files, and the like. In all cases the compilers have sought to convey the scope of any given manuscript collection.

B. Contributions to Periodicals and Books: This section provides a comprehensive listing of poems, short stories, articles, reviews, letters, audio-visual material, and miscellaneous material by the author which has been published in books, periodicals, and anthologies. Needless to say, the nature of the authors' contributions to these sources differs; consequently, the headings in this section also differ according to the nature of the contributions. Generally speaking, however, the organization of headings in this section corresponds to the works' degree of importance (as reflected by critical opinion indicated in Part II). Thus, when an author's contributions to periodicals, books, and anthologies are primarily poems, the section opens with a description of published poems, followed by the next most important area of contribution, and so on. The section also includes (when applicable) a listing of audio-visual materials published by the author. Once again, the citations which appear under each heading are organized chronologically.

This section also provides details on material which has been reprinted, revised, retitled, excerpted, or reprinted in one of the author's own books. When an item has been reprinted, full information as to publication data pertaining to the reprint is given. The fact that an original publication has been reprinted in *revised* form is indicated parenthetically thus: Rpt. (revised). When a work has been *reprinted and retitled*, the new title is indicated in quotation marks: Rpt. ("New Title"). When a work has been *reprinted, revised, and retitled*, the entry reads: Rpt. (revised—"New Title"). *Excerpted*

reprints are indicated as: Rpt. (excerpt). Finally, the fact that a work reappears in one of the author's books is indicated at the end of the entry by an abbreviation which refers to the title of the author's book. A full list of abbreviations precedes all citations. Audio-visual work is ordered according to date of release. Such technical information as duration, film size, tape speed, and contents is provided.

This section also includes a list of the author's works which have been reprinted in selected anthologies. The anthologies are arranged in chronological order, while the author's contributions are alphabetized to expedite identification. This compilation is included for the information of readers who wish to gain some sense of the works which have been most widely anthologized, and some idea of how the selections made by various editors have altered over time. Full publication data regarding these selected anthology contributions are to be found in the preceding citations.

Part II: Part II of each bibliography is devoted to works *on* the author. These works are listed chronologically under the subsections and headings described below.

C. Books, Articles and Sections of Books, Theses and Dissertations, Interviews, Audio-Visual Material, and Awards and Honours. As in Section B, the actual headings in Section C vary according to the nature of the critical works which exist on each author. Every entry in this section of the bibliography is annotated with a description of the critical viewpoints expressed in each secondary work. Full-length books devoted to the author's work obviously receive the most extensive annotations. However, annotations may be equally extensive for articles, interviews, or theses and dissertations which are deemed to be of outstanding critical importance. Full publication data are given for all secondary sources. This coverage extends to include publication data pertaining to critical works which exist in reprinted forms. The format governing the citation of these reprints is identical to that described in Section B of Part I above. Theses and dissertations are identified according to the year they were completed and the institutions at which they were presented. Literary awards and honours are listed chronologically, as are interviews with the author and audio-visual material on the author's work.

D. Selected Book Reviews: This section contains a list of selected book reviews on the author's books listed in Part I, Section A. The sub-headings in this section correspond to the title of each work. Beneath each title heading is presented, in chronological order and with annotations, a representative cross-section of reviews. The book reviews have been chosen according to the following criteria: a) critical excellence (reviews which offer significant critical insights), b) regional response (reviews which assess the impact of the book from the viewpoint of a particular region), c) idiosyncratic appeal (reviews which offer unconventional interpretations or which display engaging critical biases), and d) non-Canadian evaluation (reviews which attempt to place the work in a literary context extending beyond Canada).

Index to Critics Listed in the Bibliography: This index provides an alphabetical cross-reference to the names of critics listed in Part II.

* * *

The editors welcome the submission of corrections, additions, and queries. Correspondence should be addressed to the publisher.

Future volumes of *ABCMA* will include the following authors:

Milton Acorn	John Metcalf
Hubert Aquin	W. O. Mitchell
Gérard Bessette	Susanna Moodie
Earle Birney	Alice Munro
Marie-Claire Blais	Emile Nelligan
Nicole Brossard	John Newlove
Ernest Buckler	bpNichol
Morley Callaghan	Alden Nowlan
Bliss Carman	Michael Ondaatje
Roch Carrier	P. K. Page
Robertson Davies	Thomas Raddall
Louis Dudek	Charles G. D. Roberts
F. P. Grove	Sinclair Ross
Anne Hébert	Saint-Denys-Garneau
Hugh Hood	F. R. Scott
A. M. Klein	A. J. M. Smith
Raymond Knister	Raymond Souster
Robert Kroetsch	Robert Stead
Irving Layton	Catharine Parr Traill
Stephen Leacock	Michel Tremblay
Dennis Lee	Miriam Waddington
Dorothy Livesay	Rudy Wiebe
Eli Mandel	

Margaret Atwood
An Annotated Bibliography
(Poetry)

Alan J. Horne

Introduction

In *From There to Here* Frank Davey wrote that "Margaret Atwood has enjoyed a spectacular climb to the summit of Canadian letters"; and in *The Canadian Novel in the Twentieth Century* George Woodcock observed that a consideration both of Atwood's prose writings and of her poetry shows "the versatility with which her intelligence plays over the horizons of her perceptions.... No other writer in Canada of Margaret Atwood's generation has so wide a command of the resources of literature, so telling a restraint in their use."

In many ways, Margaret Atwood is regarded popularly as well as academically as one of the brighter stars of the Canadian literary scene. She is one of those writers who have greatly improved the stature of Canadian literature at home and abroad. She is heard on the radio, seen on television, read about in *Chatelaine* and *Toronto Life*. Her books are known and read by the general public. Her name and her writings are recognized in the United States and Britain. Her books are taught at school. However, like most living writers still in the flood of production, Atwood must suffer changes in the critical esteem in which she is held. Some people feel that Atwood has done too many different things too well. She writes poetry and fiction, criticism and drama; she writes for adults and she has now ventured into writing for children; she even illustrates her own books.

In addition to her novels and short stories, Margaret Atwood has published seven major poetry collections. The essential feature both of her fiction and poetry has been described as a search for a personal and national identity. Survival is a central theme throughout her works, as is the quest for self unity.

The Circle Game, Atwood's first important collection, was enthusiastically received. The imagery, the language, and the poetic discipline were all noted and praised by reviewers, one of whom wrote that Atwood's craft was deceptively simple and displayed sureness of touch. Hugh MacCallum in *The University of Toronto Quarterly* claimed that Atwood's vision was one in which ritual and pattern create a charmed circle of art that imprisons the mind, from which the poet endeavours to escape. Imprisonment and the need for escape, the search for identity, and above all, the struggle to survive were all seen as themes of *The Circle Game*. Gary Ross in *Canadian Literature* (and other critics as well) treats *The Circle Game* as a poetic sequence which deals with isolation and human alienation and the need to break out of this "circle" and to enter into positive relations with others.

The Animals in That Country was seen as a continuation of Atwood's exploration of the principles of identity and of the experience of alienation. Tom Marshall found her poems "a little inhuman" but another reviewer felt that they represented a real progression from the severely personal poetry of *The Circle Game*; and even F. M. Macri in his critical review in *Modern Poetry Studies* in 1974 claimed it as the best collection to that date.

The Journals of Susanna Moodie and *Procedures for Underground* were published in the same year. Robin Skelton, in reviewing both, felt they exhibited Atwood's strong sense of place and ambiguous feelings about Canadian culture. Carolyn Allen in *Essays on Canadian Writing* in 1977 found "transformation" to be one of the major themes in Atwood's poetry, reflected particularly in *The Journals of Susanna Moodie* and the later *You Are Happy*, where Atwood created women who were willing to break out of mythic or social moulds. Another reviewer felt that *Procedures for Underground* continued in the same vein as earlier collections but displayed a variety of subjects and concerns, and these poems offered a more visible attempt to maintain contact with another human being.

Power Politics, the most personal of Atwood's collections, was very well received, though some reviewers found the expressed emotions raw and intense and the relationship described as too destructive for comfort. As George Bowering wrote: "A beautiful book of poetry—it hurts." And as Gloria Onley observed in *West Coast Review*, the power structure is patriarchal, so that a woman's energies and self "have no existence except as defined and canalized by the colonizing, victimizing male." Onley extended her study of the sexual politics behind *Power Politics* in an article in *Canadian Literature*, where she describes the theme as "role-engulfment."

The poems in *You Are Happy* are much calmer, and end with a kind of coming-to-terms with the world of man-woman relationships. Robert Fulford wrote that the poems drag the reader along "on a kind of forced march through the intricate sensibility of one of our most remarkable writers." As another writer expressed it, *You Are Happy* "moves beyond the problem of individual survival and begins as exploration of what's to be found in a life of comingled feeling."

Margaret Atwood is undoubtedly an important figure in the Canadian literary scene, but before 1974, when a preliminary version of this bibliography appeared in *Canadian Library Journal*, virtually no bibliographic work on her had been published. The first "Checklist" was revised for the special "Atwood Issue" of *The Malahat Review*, January 1977. The present publication contains considerable revisions and additions, in an attempt to provide an accurate and useful record of Atwood's continuing output and of critical writings on her.

Bibliographic work on a living writer as active in so many fields as Margaret Atwood is difficult. Apart from using standard periodical indexes and the somewhat inadequate annual lists of critical works which are published in such journals as *Canadian Poetry: Studies, Documents, Reviews*, one depends to a large extent on the careful and persistent perusal of as many relevant periodicals as one may find. In addition, items are reported by interested friends and colleagues and by the writer herself. Some discoveries even seem to be made quite by chance. However, I wish to acknowledge in particular the usefulness of the bibliography included in Andrew Scott's M.A. Thesis, "Margaret Atwood: A Critical Appreciation," and the continuing assistance of Jerry Rosenberg, who is working on a book on Atwood. Help was also gained from Carol Fairbanks' *Margaret Atwood: A Bibliography of Criticism*, which appeared in *Bulletin of Bibliography*, 36, No. 2 (April-June 1979), 85-90, 98.

Certain omissions from the bibliography are deliberate; in particular, no attempt has been made to include all newspaper articles or reviews. Similarly, the listing of anthologies which include Atwood's work is selective.

Part I

Works by Margaret Atwood

(For prose works by Atwood see *ABCMA*, Vol. I)

A   Books (Poetry, Children's Book, Broadsides, Libretto) and Manuscripts

Poetry

A1   *Double Persephone*. Market Book Series, Book 1. Toronto: Hawkshead, 1961. 16 pp.

A2   *The Circle Game*. Bloomfield Hills, Mich.: n.p., 1964. 18 leaves.
     Printed in a limited edition of fifteen copies designed, printed, and illustrated with eight colour plates by Charles Pachter.

A3   *Kaleidoscopes Baroque: A Poem*. Bloomfield Hills, Mich.: n.p., 1965. 15 pp.
     Printed at the Cranbrook Academy of Art in a limited edition of twenty copies, with colour illustrations by Charles Pachter.

A4   *Talismans for Children*. Bloomfield Hills, Mich.: n.p., 1965. 6 leaves.
     Printed in a limited edition of ten copies with colour illustrations by Charles Pachter.

A5   *Expeditions*. Bloomfield Hills, Mich.: n.p., 1966. 10 leaves.
     Printed in a limited edition of fifteen copies, with colour illustrations by Charles Pachter.

A6   *Speeches for Doctor Frankenstein*. Bloomfield Hills, Mich.: n.p., 1966. 29 pp.
     Printed at the Cranbrook Academy of Art in a limited edition of fifteen copies, designed, illustrated, and printed by Charles Pachter.

A7   *The Circle Game*. Toronto: Contact, 1966. 80 pp. Toronto: House of Anansi, 1967. 80 pp.
     One hundred copies of this House of Anansi edition were published in cloth with a slipcase, and signed by Atwood.
Introd. Sherrill Grace. Toronto: House of Anansi, 1978. 90 pp.

A8   *The Animals in That Country*. Boston: Little, Brown [1968]. 69 pp.
Toronto: Oxford Univ. Press, 1968. 69 pp.

A9   *The Journals of Susanna Moodie*. Toronto: Oxford Univ. Press, 1970. 64 pp.
     Illustrated. "The collages and cover design are by Margaret Atwood."

A10   *Procedures for Underground*. Boston: Little, Brown [1970]. 79 pp.
Toronto: Oxford Univ. Press, 1970. 79 pp.

A11   *Power Politics*. Toronto: House of Anansi, 1971. 58 pp.
New York: Harper and Row [1973]. 56 pp.

A12   *You Are Happy*. New York: Harper and Row [1974]. 96 pp.
Toronto: Oxford Univ. Press, 1974. 96 pp.

A13   *Selected Poems*. Toronto: Oxford Univ. Press [1976]. 240 pp.
New York: Simon and Schuster [1978]. 240 pp.
     Contains a selection from six books of poetry: *The Circle Game, The Animals in That Country, Procedures for Underground, The Journals of Susanna*

Moodie (in full), *Power Politics*, and *You Are Happy.*

A14 *Two-Headed Poems.* Toronto: Oxford Univ. Press, 1978. 112 pp.

Children's Book

A15 *Up in the Tree.* Toronto: McClelland and Stewart [1978]. 28 pp.
   Written and illustrated by Atwood for children.

Broadsides

A16 *What Was in the Garden.* Santa Barbara, Cal.: Unicorn, 1969. 1 leaf.
   A broadside with colour illustrations by Charles Pachter. One of twelve broadsides by Canadian poets in *Unicorn Folio Series 3, Number 1, A Canadian Portfolio.*

A17 *Dreams of the Animals.* N.p.: n.p. [1970?]. 1 leaf.
   The poem, later published in *Procedures for Underground,* is here printed from an original drawing by Atwood, in the form of a broadside.

A18 *Marsh, Hawk.* Toronto: Dreadnaught [1977]. 1 leaf.
   A broadside, illustrated by Suzanne Mogensen; one of fifty-two broadsides printed as a collection entitled *52pickup.*

Libretto

A19 *The Trumpets of Summer.* [Toronto]: n.p. [1964]. 15 pp.
   Choral suite for mixed chorus, four soloists, male speaker, and six instruments; commissioned by the CBC for the Shakespeare Quatercentenary. Music by John Beckwith, text by Margaret Atwood. First performed in Montreal, November 29, 1964. The text only printed here.

Manuscripts

A20 Thomas Fisher Rare Book Library
University of Toronto
Toronto, Ontario

The University of Toronto Library is the major depository of Margaret Atwood's manuscripts. The material is housed in boxes and an outline of their contents follows.

Box 1:
Correspondence; miscellaneous items including biographical notes, an essay entitled "My Poetic Principles," dated October 29, 1962; announcements of poetry readings; typescript of *Trumpets of Summer,* with working copy, printed libretto, correspondence with John Beckwith. Also some unpublished poems.

Box 2:
Prose—short stories and *The Edible Woman.*

Box 3:
Prose—*The Edible Woman* (continued).

Box 4:
Poetry, including *The Animals in That Country*; an unpublished play in verse, "Thus Parts the Hero."

Box 5:
Poetry—early manuscripts circa 1958-63.

Box 6:
Poetry—early manuscripts (continued); and material written in Vancouver in 1964-65.

Boxes 7-9:
Poetry—later work.

Box 10:
Page proofs of *The Edible Woman.*

Box 11:
Negative microfilm and paper copy of Charles Pachter's thesis for the degree of Master of Fine Arts, Cranbrook Academy of Art, Bloomfield Hills, Michigan.

Boxes 12-15:
Vocal score of *Trumpets of Summer*; manuscript and typescript of "Oratorio for Sasquatch, Man and Two Androids"; various drafts of *Surfacing*; an unpublished novel, "Up in the Air So Blue"; *The Journals of Susanna Moodie*; *Procedures for Underground*; *Power Politics*; and manuscript of "Rhyming Cats" (written circa 1948-50).

B   Contributions to Periodicals and Books (Poetry, Selected Anthology Contributions), Audio and Audio-Visual Recordings, and Published Graphic Work

(For Atwood's prose writings see *ABCMA*, Vol. I)

Note: When an item is reprinted in one of Atwood's books, this fact is noted in the entry through one of the following abbreviations:

The Circle Game (A7) .... *CG*
The Animals in That Country .... *TAITC*
The Journals of Susanna Moodie .... *JSM*
Procedures for Underground .... *PFU*
Power Politics .... *PP*
You Are Happy .... *YAH*
Selected Poems .... *SP*
Two-Headed Poems .... *THP*

Poetry

B1   "The First Brush-Cut." *Clan Call* [Leaside High School], 1, No. 6 (1954-55), 29.

B2   "The Mind." *Clan Call*, 2, No. 1 (1956-57), 37.

B3   "The Conversation." *Acta Victoriana*, 83, No. 1 (Nov. 1958), 11.

B4   "Spratire." *Acta Victoriana*, 83, No. 2 (Dec. 1958), 22.

This poem is one of several contributions by "Shakesbeat Latweed" which, according to Margaret Atwood, is the "joint author" pseudonym under which Atwood and Dennis Lee wrote while students at Victoria College.

B5 "Knell and Nativity." *Acta Victoriana*, 83, No. 4 (Feb. 1959), 19.

B6 "Fruition." *The Canadian Forum*, Sept. 1959, p. 130.

B7 "Confessional." *Acta Victoriana*, 84, No. 1 (Dec. 1959), 8.

B8 "Small Requiem." *The Canadian Forum*, Dec. 1959, p. 202.

B9 "Paeon." *The Sheet*, No. 1 (Jan. 1960), p. 7.

B10 "Hanging Garden." *Acta Victoriana*, 84, No. 2 (March 1960), 10. Rpt. in *The Canadian Forum*, Aug. 1960, p. 114.

B11 "Inscription." *Acta Victoriana*, 84, No. 2 (March 1960), 13. Rpt. in *The Canadian Forum*, Aug. 1960, p. 115.

B12 "Mausoleum." *Acta Victoriana*, 84, No. 2 (March 1960), 12. Rpt. in *The Canadian Forum*, Aug. 1960, p. 115.

B13 "Pharos." *Acta Victoriana*, 84, No. 2 (March 1960), 12. Rpt. in *The Canadian Forum*, Aug. 1960, p. 115.

B14 "Pyramid at Sunrise." *Acta Victoriana*, 84, No. 2 (March 1960), 13. Rpt. in *The Canadian Forum*, Aug. 1960, p. 115.

B15 "Sculpted Zeus." *Acta Victoriana*, 84, No. 2 (March 1960), 11. Rpt. in *The Canadian Forum*, Aug. 1960, p. 114.

B16 "Small Colossus." *Acta Victoriana*, 84, No. 2 (March 1960), 10. Rpt. in *The Canadian Forum*, Aug. 1960, p. 114.

B17 "Temple of Artemis." *Acta Victoriana*, 84, No. 2 (March 1960), 11. Rpt. in *The Canadian Forum*, Aug. 1960, p. 114.

B18 "The Bottled Woman." *Varsity*, 79, No. 68 (18 March 1960), 6. Rpt. in *The Tamarack Review*, No. 21 (Autumn 1961), p. 21.

B19 "The Expelled." *Varsity*, 79, No. 68 (18 March 1960), 6.

B20 "The Triple Goddess: A Poem for Voices." *Acta Victoriana*, 85 (sic) [84], No. 3 (April 1960), 8-13.

B21 "Harvesters." *The Canadian Forum*, June 1960, p. 60.

B22 "Towered Woman." *The Canadian Forum*, June 1960, p. 60.

B23 "The Girl Too Early." *The Sheet*, No. 2 (Sept. 1960), p. 3.

B24 "Reflection." *The Sheet*, No. 2 (Sept. 1960), p. 3.

B25 "The Kollege Koffee Krowd...a Pome." *The Strand* [Victoria College], 14 Oct. 1960, p. 3.
     Published under the pseudonym "Shakesbeat Latweed."

B26 "From the Island: Three Small Songs." *Acta Victoriana*, 86 (sic) [85], No. 1 (Nov. 1960), 13.

B27 "A Hymn to VCU." *The Strand*, 11 Nov. 1960, pp. 3-4.
     Published under the pseudonym "Shakesbeat Latweed."

B28 "To the Strand, on Demand." *The Strand*, 25 Nov. 1960, p. 3.

Published under the pseudonym "Shakesbeat Latweed."

B29 "Event." *The Sheet*, No. 3 [1961?], p. 3.

B30 "News from Nowhere." *The Sheet*, No. 3 [1961?], p. 3.

B31 "Pastoral Elegy." *The Sheet*, No. 3 [1961?], p. 4.

B32 "Childhood under Glass." *Acta Victoriana*, 86 (sic) [85], No. 4 (March 1961), 1.

B33 "Eye." *Acta Victoriana*, 86 (sic) [85], No. 4 (March 1961), 1.

B34 "The Field of Souls." *Acta Victoriana*, 86 (sic) [85], No. 4 (March 1961), 2.

B35 "Island, Fall." *Acta Victoriana*, 86 (sic) [85], No. 4 (March 1961), 1.

B36 "We and Our Lost Souls." *Acta Victoriana*, 86 (sic) [85], No. 4 (March 1961), 2.

B37 "Seaweedy." *The Strand*, 10 March 1961, pp. 2-3.

Published under the pseudonym "Shakesbeat Latweed."

B38 "Proserpine." *Jargon*, No. 2 (Spring 1961), p. 4.

B39 "The Triple Woman." *Jargon*, No. 2 (Spring 1961), p. 3.

B40 "Wind in Weeds." *Jargon*, No. 2 (Spring 1961), p. 4.

B41 "Woman by the Water." *The Canadian Forum*, April 1961, p. 5.

B42 "Invasion." *Delta*, No. 15 (Aug. 1961), p. 19.

B43 "Lover." *The Tamarack Review*, No. 21 (Autumn 1961), p. 21.

B44 "Woman on the Subway." *The Tamarack Review*, No. 21 (Autumn 1961), p. 20.

B45 "Etc." *Alphabet*, No. 3 (Dec. 1961), p. 74.

B46 "Garden." *The Canadian Forum*, July 1962, p. 92.

B47 "The Interior Decorator." *The Sheet*, No. 5 (Sept. 1962), p. 7. Rpt. in *The Tamarack Review*, No. 27 (Spring 1963), p. 33.

B48 "The Whore and the Dove." *Alphabet*, No. 5 (Dec. 1962), pp. 48-49.

B49 "The Witch and the Nightingale." *Alphabet*, No. 5 (Dec. 1962), pp. 44-45.

B50 "The Apotheosis of Guinivere." *The Fiddlehead*, No. 55 (Winter 1963), pp. 12-13.

B51 "The Betrayal of Arthur." *The Fiddlehead*, No. 55 (Winter 1963), p. 11.

B52 "Elaine in Arcadia." *The Fiddlehead*, No. 55 (Winter 1963), p. 11.

B53 "The King." *The Fiddlehead*, No. 55 (Winter 1963), p. 13.

B54 "The Kings." *The Fiddlehead*, No. 55 (Winter 1963), p. 10.

B55 "The Recollections of Vivien." *The Fiddlehead*, No. 55 (Winter 1963), p. 10.

B56 "The Rider." *The Fiddlehead*, No. 55 (Winter 1963), p. 12.

B57 "The City Girl." In *Poésie/Poetry 64*. Ed. Jacques Godbout and John Robert Colombo. Montréal: Les Editions du Jour; Toronto: Ryerson, 1963, pp. 107-08.

B58 "Houses." In *Poésie/Poetry 64*. Ed. Jacques Godbout and John Robert Colombo. Montréal: Les Editions du Jour; Toronto: Ryerson, 1963, p. 113.

B59 "The Lifeless Wife." In *Poésie/Poetry 64*. Ed. Jacques Godbout and John Robert Colombo. Montréal: Les Editions du Jour; Toronto: Ryerson, 1963, p. 110.

B60 "The Slideshow." In *Poésie/Poetry 64*. Ed. Jacques Godbout and John Robert Colombo. Montréal: Les Editions du Jour; Toronto: Ryerson, 1963, p. 111.

B61 "The Somnabulist." In *Poésie/Poetry 64*. Ed. Jacques Godbout and John Robert Colombo. Montréal: Les Editions du Jour; Toronto: Ryerson, 1963, pp. 110-11.

B62 "The Cold Philosopher." *The Tamarack Review*, No. 27 (Spring 1963), p. 30.

B63 "The Dwarf." *The Tamarack Review*, No. 27 (Spring 1963), p. 32. Rpt. in *Manitoba Law School Journal*, 1, No. 2 (1963), 146.

B64 "The Little Sister." *The Tamarack Review*, No. 27 (Spring 1963), p. 29.

B65 "What Happened to the Idiot Boy." *The Tamarack Review*, No. 27 (Spring 1963), p. 31.

B66 "Little Nell." *Alphabet*, No. 6 (June 1963), p. 54.

B67 "Mad Mother Ballad." *Alphabet*, No. 6 (June 1963), p. 53. Rpt. in *The Canadian Forum*, June 1963, p. 70.

B68 "The Mad Mother." *The Canadian Forum*, June 1963, p. 70.

B69 "My Leper Lover." *The Canadian Forum*, June 1963, p. 71.

B70 "The Orphan from Alberta." *Alphabet*, No. 6 (June 1963), p. 51.

B71 "Poor Tom." *Alphabet*, No. 6 (June 1963), p. 52.

B72 "The Idiot Boy Unborn." *Evidence*, No. 7 (Summer 1963), p. 90.

B73 "Pig-Girl." *Delta*, No. 22 (Oct. 1963), p. 28.

B74 "Exhibition Rides." *Volume 63*, No. 1 (Dec. 1963), pp. 59-60.

B75 "The Acid Sibyl." *The Fiddlehead*, No. 59 (Winter 1963), p. 60.

B76 "The Double Nun." *The Fiddlehead*, No. 59 (Winter 1963), pp. 61-62.

B77 "Fall and All." *The Fiddlehead*, No. 59 (Winter 1963), p. 58.

B78 "The Revelation." *The Fiddlehead*, No. 59 (Winter 1963), pp. 60-61.

B79 "The Revenant." *The Fiddlehead*, No. 59 (Winter 1963), pp. 58-59. Rpt. in *Kayak*, No. 14 (April 1968), p. 9. *TAITC*.

B80 "The Siamese Twins." *The Fiddlehead*, No. 59 (Winter 1963), p. 60.

B81 "The Witch's House." *The Fiddlehead*, No. 59 (Winter 1963), pp. 62-63.

B82 "A Failure of Spells in the Necropolis." *Canadian Poetry*, 27, No. 2 (Feb. 1964), 29-30.

B83 "Voices: Ancestors." *Canadian Poetry*, 27, No. 2 (Feb. 1964), 30-31.

B84 "Descent as Dissection." *The Canadian Forum*, March 1964, p. 280.

B85 "He/She/It." *Queen's Quarterly*, 71 (Spring 1964), 40-41.

B86 "In My Ravines." *Queen's Quarterly*, 71 (Spring 1964), 42-43. *CG*.

B87 "Willow Pattern Plate." *The Canadian Forum*, April 1964, p. 23.

B88 "After the Flood, We." *The Canadian Forum*, Sept. 1964, p. 131. *CG; SP*.

B89 "A Meal." *The Canadian Forum*, Sept. 1964, p. 131. *CG*.

B90 "Office Lady." *The Canadian Forum*, Sept. 1964, p. 131.

B91 "Against Still Life." *Kayak*, No. 2 [1965?], pp. 6-8. Rpt. in *Ellipse*, No. 3 (Spring 1970), pp. 70, 74, 76. Rpt. (trans.) in *Ellipse*, No. 3 (Spring 1970), pp. 73, 75, 77. *CG*.

B92 "Boar." *Evidence*, No. 9 (1965), p. 14.

B93 "Epithalamion." *Evidence*, No. 9 (1965), pp. 12-13.

B94 "Evening Trainstation before Departure." *Kayak*, No. 2 [1965?], pp. 4-5. *CG*.

B95 "Pink Lady (Sea Anenome, Stanley Park.)" *Evidence*, No. 9 (1965), pp. 11-12.

B96 "This Is a Photograph of Me." *Kayak*, No. 2 [1965?], p. 3. Rpt. in *English*, 16, No. 94 (Spring 1967), 142. Rpt. in *Ellipse*, No. 3 (Spring 1970), p. 54. Rpt. (trans.) in *Ellipse*, No. 3 (Spring 1970), p. 55. *CG; SP*.

B97 "The Commuters." *Edge*, No. 4 (Spring 1965), p. 83.

B98 "The Mountain Climbers." *Edge*, No. 4 (Spring 1965), p. 84.

B99 "On the Streets, Love." *Edge*, No. 4 (Spring 1965), pp. 82-83. *CG*.

B100 "Camera." *Kayak*, No. 4 (1965), pp. 49-50.

B101 "The Impossibility." *Kayak*, No. 4 (1965), pp. 48-49.

B102 "A Pair of Complements." *Kayak*, No. 4 (1965), pp. 46-47.

B103 "The Stamps." *Kayak*, No. 4 (1965), pp. 45-46.

B104 "The Explorers." *Prism International*, 5, No. 1 (Summer 1965), 28-29. *CG; SP*.

B105 "Gardens." *Literary Review*, 8, No. 4 (Summer 1965), 513-14.

B106 "The Settlers." *Prism International*, 5, No. 1 (Summer 1965), 29-30. Rpt. in *Ellipse*, No. 3 (Spring 1970), pp. 50, 52. Rpt. (trans.) in *Ellipse*, No. 3 (Spring 1970), pp. 51, 53. *CG; SP*.

B107 "Talismans for Children." *The Canadian Forum*, July 1965, pp. 86-87.
See A4.

B108 "Descents." *English*, 15, No. 90 (Autumn 1965), 216-17.

B109 "Migration: C.P.R." *Alaska Review*, 2, No. 1 (Fall 1965), 27-31. *CG; SP.*

B110 "A Messenger." *Kayak*, No. 7 (1966), pp. 7-8. *CG.*

B111 "Part of a Day." *Kayak*, No. 9 (1966), p. 12. *TAITC.*

B112 "The Shadow Voice." *Kayak*, No. 9 (1966), p. 11. *TAITC.*

B113 "The Soldiers." *Kayak*, No. 9 (1966), p. 14.

B114 "Where Are You." *Kayak*, No. 9 (1966), p. 13.

B115 "The Listener." *Quarry*, 15, No. 3 (March 1966), 7-8.

B116 "Man with a Hook." *Quarry*, 15, No. 3 (March 1966), 9. *CG.*

B117 "Private Life of Mr. Z the Detective." *Quarry*, 15, No. 3 (March 1966), 6-7.

B118 "Una Voz." *Parva* [Mexico], No. 5 (May-June 1966), pp. 8-9.
A Spanish translation of "A Voice" from *The Animals in That Country.*

B119 "More and More." *Talon*, 4, No. 3 (1967), 4. Rpt. in *Ellipse*, No. 3 (Spring 1970), p. 68. Rpt. (trans.) in *Ellipse*, No. 3 (Spring 1970), p. 69. *TAITC; SP.*

B120 "Roominghouse, Winter." *Talon*, 4, No. 3 (1967), 2-3. *TAITC; SP.*

B121 "Chronology." *Prism International*, 6, No. 3 (Spring 1967), 39-40. Rpt. in *Ellipse*, No. 3 (Spring 1970), pp. 56, 58. Rpt. (trans.) in *Ellipse*, No. 3 (Spring 1970), pp. 57-59.

B122 "An Icon." *Prism International*, 6, No. 3 (Spring 1967), 38-39. *TAITC.*

B123 "Provisions." *Prism International*, 6, No. 3 (Spring 1967), 40. Rpt. in *Ellipse*, No. 3 (Spring 1970), p. 44. Rpt. (trans.) in *Ellipse*, No. 3 (Spring 1970), p. 45. *TAITC.*

B124 "At the Tourist Centre in Boston." *Saturday Night*, June 1967, p. 49. *TAITC; SP.*

B125 "It Is Dangerous to Read Newspapers." *Poetry Australia*, 3, No. 16 (June 1967), 6. *TAITC; SP.*

B126 "I Was Reading a Scientific Article." *Poetry Australia*, 3, No. 16 (June 1967), 5. Rpt. in *Other Voices*, 3, No. 3 (Nov. 1967), 17. *TAITC; SP.*

B127 "Arctic Syndrome: Dream Fox." *The Tamarack Review*, No. 44 (Summer 1967), pp. 34-35. *TAITC.*

B128 "Astral Traveller." *The Tamarack Review*, No. 44 (Summer 1967), pp. 38-39. *TAITC.*

B129 "A Fortification." *The Tamarack Review*, No. 44 (Summer 1967), p. 38. *TAITC; SP.*

B130 "A Foundling." *The Tamarack Review*, No. 44 (Summer 1967), p. 36. *TAITC; SP.*

B131 "The Green Man." *Quarry*, 16, No. 4 (Summer 1967), 6. *TAITC.*

B132 "Interview with a Tourist." *The Tamarack Review*, No. 44 (Summer 1967), pp. 32-33. *PFU.*

B133 "Poem." *The Tamarack Review*, No. 44 (Summer 1967), p. 39. Rpt. in *Ellipse*, No. 3 (Spring 1970), p. 42. Rpt. (trans.) in *Ellipse*, No. 3 (Spring 1970), p. 43. *TAITC* ("Axiom: You Are a Sea"); *SP* ("Axiom").

B134 "Progressive Insanities of a Pioneer." *Quarry*, 16, No. 4 (Summer 1967), 8-11. *TAITC*; *SP*.

B135 "The Reincarnation of Captain Cook." *The Tamarack Review*, No. 44 (Summer 1967), p. 37. *TAITC*; *SP*.

B136 "The Surveyors." *The Tamarack Review*, No. 44 (Summer 1967), pp. 33-34. *TAITC*.

B137 "A Voice." *Quarry*, 16, No. 4 (Summer 1967), 12. *TAITC*; *SP*.

B138 "What Happened." *Quarry*, 16, No. 4 (Summer 1967), 13. *TAITC*.

B139 "I Contain Death." *West Coast Review*, 2, No. 2 (Fall 1967), 33.

B140 "The Animals in That Country." *Other Voices*, 3, No. 3 (Nov. 1967), 16. Rpt. in *Ellipse*, No. 3 (Spring 1970), pp. 44, 46. Rpt. (trans.) in *Ellipse*, No. 3 (Spring 1970), pp. 45, 47. *TAITC*; *SP*.

B141 "Attitudes towards the Mainland." *Other Voices*, 3, No. 3 (Nov. 1967), 16. Rpt. in *Ellipse*, No. 3 (Spring 1970), pp. 48, 50. Rpt. (trans.) in *Ellipse*, No. 3 (Spring 1970), pp. 49, 51. *TAITC*.

B142 "The Gods Avoid Revealing Themselves." *Other Voices*, 3, No. 3 (Nov. 1967), 17. *TAITC*.

B143 "Notes from Various Pasts." *Other Voices*, 3, No. 3 (Nov. 1967), 16-17. *TAITC*.

B144 "A Pursuit." *Other Voices*, 3, No. 3 (Nov. 1967), 18. Rpt. in *Adam*, 32, Nos. 314-315 (1967), p. 46. Rpt. in *Ellipse*, No. 3 (Spring 1970), p. 78. Rpt. (trans.) in *Ellipse*, No. 3 (Spring 1970), p. 79. *TAITC*.

B145 "Sundew." *Other Voices*, 3, No. 3 (Nov. 1967), 18. *TAITC*.

B146 "Backdrop Addresses Cowboy." *Kayak*, No. 14 (April 1968), pp. 6-7. *TAITC*; *SP*.

B147 "The Trappers." *Kayak*, No. 14 (April 1968), pp. 7-8. *TAITC*.

B148 "Closet." *Pluck*, 2, No. 1 (Fall 1968), 4-5. Rpt. in *Spectrum: The Richmond Tri-Annual Review*, 5, No. 2 (Winter 1969-70), 45-46.

B149 "Cyclops." *Catalyst*, 2, No. 1 (Fall 1968), 19. *PFU*; *SP*.

B150 "Two Versions of Sweaters." *Catalyst*, 2, No. 1 (Fall 1968), 18. *PFU*.

B151 "National Film Board: Shorts before Features." *Saturday Night*, Oct. 1968, p. 30.

B152 "The Creatures of the Zodiac." *Kayak*, No. 18 (1969), p. 60. *PFU*.

B153 "Death of an Unidentified Insect: Atonement and Apotheosis." *Kayak*, No. 18 (1969), p. 61.

B154 "Earth Dances in a Bad Area." *Kayak*, No. 18 (1969), p. 62.

B155 "Game after Supper." *Merry Devil of Edmonton*, No. 1 (1969). Broadside. Rpt. in *Field*, No. 2 (Spring 1970), p. 19. *PFU*; *SP*.

B156 "Hypothesis: City." *Kayak*, No. 18 (1969), p. 63.

B157 "A Night at the Royal Ontario Museum." *Atlantic*, Jan. 1969, p. 93. *TAITC*.

B158 "We Don't Like Reminders." *Merry Devil of Edmonton*, No. 1 (1969). Broadside. *PFU*.

B159 "Even Here in the Cupboard." *Canadian Author & Bookman*, 44, No. 3 (Spring 1969), 23.

B160 "Carrying Food Home in Winter." *Poetry*, 114, No. 1 (April 1969), 38. *PFU; SP*.

B161 "Dream: Bluejay or Archeopteryx." *Poetry*, 114, No. 1 (April 1969), 35-36. *PFU*.

B162 "For Archeologists." *Poetry*, 114, No. 1 (April 1969), 34. *PFU*.

B163 "Projected Slide of an Unknown Soldier." *Poetry*, 114, No. 1 (April 1969), 39. *PFU; SP*.

B164 "Three Desk Objects." *Poetry*, 114, No. 1 (April 1969), 37. *PFU; SP*.

B165 "Easter 1968; 84th Street, Edmonton." *Black Moss*, 1, No. 2 (May 1969), 19-20. *PFU*.

B166 "Dreams of the Animals." *Edge*, No. 9 (Summer 1969), pp. 114-15. *PFU; SP*.

B167 "3 Moons." *Maclean's*, Aug. 1969, p. 8.

B168 "Ancestors." *Spectrum: The Richmond Tri-Annual Review*, 5, No. 1 (Fall 1969), 19-20.

B169 "Three Delayed Messages." *Quarry*, 19, No. 1 (Fall 1969), 9-11.
First section — i. "As We Sat by the Shore" — rpt. as "Delayed Message" in *Procedures for Underground*.

B170 "Time Trap." *Spectrum: The Richmond Tri-Annual Review*, 5, No. 1 (Fall 1969), 21.

B171 "Automatic Pension." *Duel*, No. 1 (Winter 1969), p. 66.

B172 "Fragments: Beach." *Imago*, No. 13 [1970?], pp. 27-29.

B173 "He Is a Strange Biological Phenomenon." *Kayak*, No. 23 (1970), p. 41. *PP*.

B174 "He Is Last Seen." *Kayak*, No. 23 (1970), p. 42. *PP*.

B175 "In Restaurants We Argue." *Blewointment*, Fascist Court Issue (1970), p. 33. *PP* ("They Eat Out"); *SP*.

B176 "Lying Here, Everything in Me." *Armadillo* (1970), p. 58. *PP; SP*.

B177 "Oratorio for Sasquatch, Man and Two Androids." In *Poems for Voices*. Toronto: CBC, 1970, pp. 14-28.
The first eleven lines are not by Atwood; the CBC later produced an erratum slip apologizing for this.

B178 "Untitled One." *Kayak*, No. 23 (1970), p. 38. *PP* ("I Look Up, You Are Standing"); *SP*.

B179 "Untitled Three." *Kayak*, No. 23 (1970), p. 40. *PP* ("This Year I Intended Children").

B180 "Untitled Two." *Kayak*, No. 23 (1970), p. 39. *PP* ("My Beautiful Wooden Leader"); *SP*.

B181 "You Mean You Can't Fly and See." *First Encounter* (1970), p. 36.

B182 "Dancing Practice." *The Tamarack Review*, No. 54 (Winter 1970), pp. 45-46. *PFU*.

B183 "A Dialogue." *The Tamarack Review*, No. 54 (Winter 1970), pp. 40-41. *PFU*.

B184 "Girl and Horse." *Atlantic*, Jan. 1970, p. 70. *PFU*; *SP* ("Girl and Horse, 1928").

B185 "Magician as Junkman." *The Tamarack Review*, No. 54 (Winter 1970), pp. 43-44.

B186 "Poem: Nov. 22." *Merry Devil of Edmonton*, No. 2 (Jan. 1970).
Broadside.

B187 "Procedures for Underground." *The Tamarack Review*, No. 54 (Winter 1970), pp. 39-40. *PFU*; *SP*.

B188 "A Spell for the Director of Protocol." *The Tamarack Review*, No. 54 (Winter 1970), pp. 41-42. *PFU*.

B189 "Woman Skating." *The Tamarack Review*, No. 54 (Winter 1970), pp. 42-43. *PFU*; *SP*.

B190 "Fishing for Eel Totems." *Field*, No. 2 (Spring 1970), p. 20. *PFU*; *SP*.

B191 "Habitation." *Prism International*, 9, No. 3 (Spring 1970), 85. *PFU*; *SP*.

B192 "Highest Altitude." *Prism International*, 9, No. 3 (Spring 1970), 84. *PFU*; *SP*.

B193 "Midwinter, Presolstice." *Ellipse*, No. 3 (Spring 1970), p. 70. Rpt. (trans.) in *Ellipse*, No. 3 (Spring 1970), p. 71. *PFU*; *SP*.

B194 "A Morning." *Prism International*, 9, No.3 (Spring 1970), 82. *PFU*; *SP*.

B195 "Pre-Amphibian." *Ellipse*, No. 3 (Spring 1970), pp. 64, 66. Rpt. (trans.) in *Ellipse*, No. 3 (Spring 1970), pp. 65, 67. *CG*; *SP*.

B196 "Resurrection." *Ellipse*, No. 3 (Spring 1970), p. 62. Rpt. (trans.) in *Ellipse*, No. 3 (Spring 1970), p. 63. *JSM*; *SP*.

B197 "River." *Ellipse*, No. 3 (Spring 1970), p. 60. Rpt. (trans.) in *Ellipse*, No. 3 (Spring 1970), p. 61. *TAITC*.

B198 "Return Trips, West." *Prism International*, 9, No. 3 (Spring 1970), 80-81. *PFU*; *TAITC*.

B199 "A Soul, Geologically." *Prism International*, 9, No. 3 (Spring 1970), 82-83. *PFU*; *SP*.

B200 "You Are the Sun." *New*, No. 12 (April 1970), p. 22. Rpt. in *It Ain't Me Babe*, 1, No. 10 (23 July 1970), 16. *PP*; *SP*.

B201 "You Fit into Me." *New*, No. 12 (April 1970), p. 23. *PP*; *SP*.

B202 "You Too Have Your Gentle." *New*, No. 12 (April 1970), p. 23. Rpt. in *PP* as Section 2 of "Small Tactics."

B203 "Buffalo in Compound: Alberta." *The Canadian Forum*, April-May 1970, p. 20. *PFU*; *SP*.

B204 "Chrysanthemums." *The Canadian Forum*, April-May 1970, p. 57. *PFU*.

B205 "The Small Cabin." *The Canadian Forum*, April-May 1970, p. 4. *PFU*; *SP*.

B206 "Descent." *New Yorker*, 27 June 1970, p. 50.

B207 "Christmas Tree Farm: Oro Township." *The Malahat Review*, No. 15 (July 1970), pp. 97-98.

B208 "The Shrunken Forest." *The Malahat Review*, No. 15 (July 1970), p. 96. *PFU*.

B209 "6 a.m., Boston, Summer Sublet." *The Malahat*

Review, No. 15 (July 1970), p. 95. *PFU*.

B210 "Younger Sister, Going Swimming." *The Malahat Review*, No. 15 (July 1970), pp. 94-95. *PFU*; *SP*.

B211 "You Refuse to Own." *Blewointment*, Occupation Issue (Aug. 1970), p. 1. Rpt. in *Poetry*, 117, No. 2 (Nov. 1970), 107. *PP*; *SP*.

B212 "I See You Are a Fugitive, Stumbling across the Prairie." *Vigilante*, No. 2 (Fall 1970), p. 3. *PP*; *SP*.

B213 "Yes at First You." *Vigilante*, No. 2 (Fall 1970), p. 3. Rpt. in *Mademoiselle*, July 1972, p. 156. *PP*; *SP*.

B214 "Hesitations outside the Door." *Poetry*, 117, No. 2 (Nov. 1970), 100-06. *PP*; *SP*.

B215 "He Discovers It Is No Longer a Dignified Profession." *Seven* [1971?], p. 23.

B216 "Sleeping in Sun-." *Blewointment*, Oil Slick Speshul [1971?], p. 7. *PP*.

B217 "After the Agony in the Guest." *The Canadian Forum*, March 1971, p. 420. *PP*; *SP*.

B218 "Beyond Truth." *The Canadian Forum*, March 1971, p. 422. *PP*; *SP*.

B219 "For Stones, Opening." *The Canadian Forum*, March 1971, p. 420. *PP*.

B220 "He Reappears." *The Canadian Forum*, March 1971, p. 420. *PP*.

B221 "It Is a Trap." *Tuatara*, No. 4 (March 1971), p. 17.

B222 "I Walk the Cell, Open the Window." *The Canadian Forum*, March 1971, p. 420. *PP*.

B223 "Not the Shore but an Aquarium." *The Canadian Forum*, March 1971, p. 420. *PP*.

B224 "Spring Again, Can I Stand It." *Tuatara*, No. 4 (March 1971), p. 18. *PP*.

B225 "There Are Better Ways of Doing This." *The Canadian Forum*, March 1971, p. 420. *PP*.

B226 "These Days My Fingers Bleed." *The Canadian Forum*, March 1971, p. 420. *PP*.

B227 "They Were All Inaccurate." *The Canadian Forum*, March 1971, p. 422. *PP*; *SP*.

B228 "Waiting for News of You." *The Canadian Forum*, March 1971, p. 420. *PP*.

B229 "We Hear Nothing These Days." *Saturday Night*, March 1971, p. 8. *PP*; *SP*.

B230 "What Is It, It Does Not." *The Canadian Forum*, March 1971, p. 422. *PP*; *SP*.

B231 "Near the High Bridge with Traffic." *Moving Out*, 2, No. 2 (1972), 84.

B232 "You Are Happy." *Manna*, No. 2 (1972), p. 55. *YAH*; *SP*.

B233 "First Prayer." *Di-al-og*, Passover Issue (1972), p. 46. *YAH*.

B234 "Singing and Dancing: Near Lake Ontario." *Toronto Life*, June 1972, p. 12.

B235 "Last Prayer." *Unmuzzled Ox*, 1, No. 3 (Summer 1972), 57.

B236 "Your Back Is Rough All." *Mademoiselle*, July 1972, p. 180. *PP*.

B237 "First Element." *Blackfish*, No. 3 (Summer 1972), pp. 24-28. Rpt. in *Vanderbilt Poetry Review*, 1, No. 2 (Fall-Winter 1972), 21-22.

B238 "You Try Undressing Me." *Edge* [New Zealand], No. 4 (Aug. 1972).

B239 "Head against White." *Vanderbilt Poetry Review*, 1, No. 2 (Fall-Winter 1972), 24-26. Rpt. in *Exile*, 1, No. 1 (1972), 40-42. *YAH*; *SP*.

B240 "Newsreel: Man and Firing Squad." *Vanderbilt Poetry Review*, 1, No. 2 (Fall-Winter 1972), 22-23. *YAH*; *SP*.

B241 "I Knew What I Wanted." *Unmuzzled Ox*, 1, No. 4 (Autumn 1972), 21.

B242 "Tricks with Mirrors." *Aphra*, 3, No. 4 (Fall 1972), 16-19. Rpt. in *Is.*, No. 14 (Summer 1973), pp. 22-25. Rpt. in *Miss Chatelaine*, Fall Fashion Issue (1974), p. 19. *YAH*; *SP*.

B243 "A Return." *Northern Journey*, No. 2 (1972-73), pp. 77-78.

B244 "Book of Ancestors." *Impulse*, 2, Nos. 3 & 4 (1973), 19-21. *YAH*; *SP*.

B245 "Variations for the Termite Queen." *Kayak*, No. 32 (1973), p. 3.

B246 "Late August." *New York Times*, 21 Jan. 1973, p. 17. *YAH*; *SP*.

B247 "There Is Only One of Everything." *Nation*, 29 Jan. 1973, p. 151. Rpt. in *Boundary 2*, 3, No. 1 (Fall 1974), 6. *YAH*; *SP*.

B248 "Paradigm #3." *Applegarth's Folly*, No. 1 (Summer 1973), p. 104.

B249 "Audience." *Ariel*, 4, No. 3 (July 1973), 38-39.

B250 "Marsh, Hawk." *Nation*, 22 July 1973, p. 22. *THP*. Also published separately, see A18.

B251 "Digging." *Stooge*, No. 9 (Fall 1973), n.p. Rpt. in *Boundary 2*, 3, No. 1 (Fall 1974), 4-5. *YAH*; *SP*.

B252 "Here Are the Holy Birds." *Field*, No. 9 (Fall 1973), p. 8. *YAH*.

B253 "It Was Not My Fault, These Animals." *Field*, No. 9 (Fall 1973), p. 5. *YAH*.

B254 "Repent." *Stooge*, No. 9 (Fall 1973), n.p. Rpt. in *Pocket Poetry Monthly*, 1, No. 2 (July 1975), 11. *YAH*.

B255 "There Must Be More for You to Do." *Field*, No. 9 (Fall 1973), p. 6. *YAH*.

B256 "When You Look at Nothing." *Field*, No. 9 (Fall 1973), p. 7. *YAH*.

B257 "Four Evasions." *Nation*, 15 Oct. 1973, p. 374. Rpt. in *Branching Out*, 2, No. 1 (Jan.-Feb. 1974), 27. *YAH*.

B258 "War Movie II." *Times Literary Supplement*, 26 Oct. 1973, p. 1294.

B259 "Chaos Poem." *Branching Out*, Preview Issue (Dec. 1973), p. 22.

B260 "Four Auguries." *Blewointment*, What Isint Tantrik Speshil Issue (Dec. 1973), pp. 20-21. *YAH*; *SP*.

B261 "Life Mask." *Branching Out*, Preview Issue (Dec. 1973), p. 23.

B262 "Not You I Fear." *Atlantic*, Dec. 1973, p. 121. *YAH*.

B263 "Fishbowl." *New*, Nos. 22 & 23 (Fall-Winter 1973-74), p. 30.

B264 "Circe Mud Poems." *Unmuzzled Ox*, No. 3 (1974), pp. 30-32. *YAH*; *SP*.

B265 "Songs of the Transformed." *Poetry*, 123 (Feb. 1974), 257-67. *YAH*.

B266 "I Am Not a Saint or a Cripple." *Branching Out*, 1, No. 1 (March-April 1974), 13.

B267 "Love Is Not a Profession." *Branching Out*, 1, No. 1 (March-April 1974), 13.

B268 "Too Much Rain This Year." *Mademoiselle*, May 1974, p. 136.

B269 "For G. Making a Garden." *Craft Horizons*, 34, No. 3 (June 1974), 14.

B270 "Paradigm #1." *Craft Horizons*, 34, No. 3 (June 1974), 17.

B271 "Silence." *Craft Horizons*, 34, No. 3 (June 1974), 31.

B272 "I Made No Choice." *Arts in Society*, 11, No. 1 (Spring-Summer 1974), 150. *YAH*.

B273 "We Walk in the Cedar Grove." *Arts in Society*, 11, No. 1 (Spring-Summer 1974), 151. Rpt. in *The Malahat Review*, No. 41 (Jan. 1977), p. 133. *YAH*.

B274 "November." *Atlantic*, Nov. 1974, p. 97. Rpt. in *Books in Canada*, Nov. 1974, p. 17. *YAH*; *SP*.

B275 "Marrying the Hangman." *Capilano Review*, No. 7 (Spring 1975), pp. 17-19. Rpt. in *Ms. Magazine*, Oct. 1978, pp. 58-59. *THP*.

B276 "The Santa Claus Trap." *Weekend Magazine*, 25 Dec. 1976, pp. 7-9.

B277 "Five Poems for Dolls." *Exile*, 4, Nos. 3 & 4 (1977), 5-9. *THP*.

B278 "Threes." *The Malahat Review*, No. 41 (Jan. 1977), p. 152.

B279 "Untitled." *Parnassus: Poetry in Review*, Spring-Summer 1977, pp. 10-11. *THP* ("Two Miles Away").

B280 "Once I Could Move." *Mademoiselle*, July 1977, p. 142.

B281 "Night Poem." *Field*, No. 17 (Fall 1977), p. 38. *THP*.

B282 "Two-Headed Poems." *This Magazine*, 11, No. 5 (Oct. 1977), 18-21. Rpt. in *American Poetry Review*, 8, No. 5 (Sept.-Oct. 1979), 26. *THP*.

B283 "The Man with a Hole in His Throat." *Waves*, 6, No. 2 (Winter 1978), 30-31. *THP*.

B284 "Dust." *Field*, No. 18 (Spring 1978), pp. 80-81.

B285 "Nasturtium." *Field*, No. 18 (Spring 1978), pp. 78-79. *THP*.

B286 "The Woman Makes Peace with Her Faulty Heart." *Field*, No. 18 (Spring 1978), pp. 76-77. *THP*.

B287 "The Woman Who Could Not Live with Her Faulty Heart." *Field*, No. 18 (Spring 1978), pp. 74-75. *THP*.

B288 "All Bread." *The Canadian Forum*, June-July 1978, p. 22. *THP*.

B289 "Another Night Visit." *The Canadian Forum*, June-July 1978, p. 20.

B290 "Footnote to the Amnesty Report on Torture." *The Canadian Forum*, June-July 1978, p. 21. *THP*.

B291 "Four Small Elegies." *The Canadian Forum*, June-July 1978, pp. 21-22. Rpt. in *American Poetry Review*, 8, No. 5 (Sept.-Oct. 1979), 26. *THP*.

B292 "Today the Lawn Holds." *The Canadian Forum*, June-July 1978, p. 22. *THP* ("Today").

B293 "You Begin." *The Canadian Forum*, June-July 1978, p. 22. *THP*.

B294 "The Puppet of the Wolf." *Acta Victoriana*, 102, No. 2 (Fall 1978), 7. *THP*.

B295 "Solstice Poem." *Meanjin*, 37, No. 2 (July 1978), 186-88.

B296 "Foretelling the Future." *American Poetry Review*, 8, No. 5 (Sept.-Oct. 1979), 23. *THP*.

Selected Anthology Contributions

B297 "The Dwarf." In *Best Poems of 1963*. Palo Alto: Pacific Books, 1964, p. 9.

B298 "August Still Life," "Bring with You," "Eventual Proteus," "The Explorers," "Returning to the Room," "The Settlers," "Summer Again." In *Modern Canadian Verse in English and French*. Ed. A. J. M. Smith. Toronto: Oxford Univ. Press, 1967, pp. 401-11.

B299 "Interview with a Tourist," "The Reincarnation of Captain Cook," "A Voice." *Best Poems of 1967*. Palo Alto: Pacific Books, 1968, pp. 9-11.

B300 "The City Planners," "Descents." In *New Voices of the Commonwealth*. Ed. Howard Sergeant. London: Evans Brothers, 1968, pp. 42-44.

B301 "After the Flood We," "A Night in the Royal Ontario Museum," "The Animals in That Country," "Astral Traveller," "At the Tourist Centre in Boston," "Backdrop Addresses Cowboy," "Elegy for the Giant Tortoises," "The Green Man," "Journey to the Interior," "The Landlady," "Playing Cards," "This Is a Photograph of Me." In *Five Modern Canadian Poets*. Ed. Eli Mandel. Toronto: Holt, Rinehart and Winston, 1970, pp. 56-71.

B302 "The Animals in That Country," "Death of a Young Son by Drowning," "Further Arrivals," "Game after Supper," "The Immigrants," "The Islands," "A Night in the Royal Ontario Museum," "Procedures for Underground," "Progressive Insanities of a Pioneer," "Some Objects of Wood and Stone," "Younger Sister Going Swimming." In *15 Canadian Poets*. Ed. Gary Geddes and Phyllis Bruce. Toronto: Oxford Univ. Press, 1970, pp. 163-80.

B303 "After the Agony in the Guest," "I Can Change My—," "In Restaurants We Argue," "Lying Here, Everything in Me," "This Year I Intended Children," "We Are Standing Facing Each Other," "Your Back Is Rough All," "You Refuse to Own," "You Want to Go Back." In *New American and Canadian Poetry*. Ed. John Gill. Boston: Beacon, 1971, pp. 9-16.

B304 "The City Planners," "It Is Dangerous to Read Newspapers," "Man with a Hook." In *Live Poetry*. Ed. Kathleen Sunshine Koppell. New York: Holt, Rinehart and Winston, 1971, pp. 7-10.

B305 "The Accident Has Occurred," "A Dialogue," "Dream: Bluejay or Archeopteryx," "Eden Is a Zoo," "He Is Last Seen." In *40 Women Poets of Canada*. Ed. Dorothy Livesay. Montreal: Ingluvin [1972?], pp. 15-20.

B306 "The Animals in That Country," "Death of a Young Son by Drowning," "Dream 1: The Bush Garden,"

"Dream 2: Brian the Still-Hunter," "They Travel by Air," "Three Desk Objects." In *The Oxford Anthology of Canadian Literature*. Ed. Robert Weaver and William Toye. Toronto: Oxford Univ. Press, 1973, pp. 7-13.

B307 "The Animals in That Country," "Chronology," "Dreams of the Animals," "Journey to the Interior," "Procedures for Underground," "There Is Only One of Everything," "They Eat Out," "You Refuse to Own." In *Canadian Poetry: The Modern Era*. Ed. John Newlove. Toronto: McClelland and Stewart, 1977, pp. 21-31.

Audio and Audio-Visual Recordings

B308 *The Journals of Susanna Moodie*. Canadian Poets 2. [Toronto]: CBC, 1969.
A twelve inch phonodisc 33 r.p.m. Read by Mia Anderson.

B309 *The Twist of Feeling*. [Toronto]: CBC, 1971.
An audio-tape, cassette and reel-to-reel, thirty minutes duration. Margaret Atwood discusses the ideas and emotions behind her poems in *Power Politics* and reads some of the poems.

B310 *Margaret Atwood*. [Toronto]: High Barnet, 1973.
A cassette audio-tape, sixty minutes duration. Atwood reads from *The Circle Game*, *The Animals in That Country*, and *Procedures for Underground*.

B311 *Progressive Insanities of a Pioneer*. [Willowdale, Ont.]: Universal Education and Visual Arts, n.d.
A sixteen mm. colour film, duration five minutes. A film interpretation of the poem.

B312 *The Journals of Susanna Moodie*. [Willowdale, Ont.]: Universal Education and Visual Arts, n.d.
A sixteen-mm. black and white film, duration fifteen minutes. A film interpretation of the volume of poetry.

B313 *The Poetry and Voice of Margaret Atwood*. [New York]: Caedmon, XC 489, 1977.
A twelve-inch phonodisc 33 r.p.m. Atwood reads a selection from *The Animals in That Country*, *Procedures for Underground*, *Power Politics*, and *You Are Happy*.

Published Graphic Work

B314 Programme cover design for "The Pirates of Penzance." Produced by Victoria College Music Club, Feb. 1959.

B315 Programme cover design for "The Big F." Produced by Victoria College Bob Review, Nov. 1959.

B316 Programme cover design and sketches for "The Mikado." Produced by Victoria College Music Club, Feb. 1960.

B317 Programme cover design and posters for "Epicoene; or, The Silent Woman." Produced by Victoria College Dramatic Society, Dec. 1960.

B318 Programme cover design and sketches and posters for "The Yeomen of the Guard." Produced by Victoria College Music Club, Jan.-Feb. 1961.

B319 Cartoons in *The Strand*. 10 March 1961.
See B27 and B28.

B320 Collages for *The Journals of Susanna Moodie*. Toronto: Oxford Univ. Press, 1970.
See A9.

B321 "Kanadian Kultchur Komics."
Published under the pseudonym of "B.G." (Bart Gerrard). A comic strip which has appeared in every issue of *This Magazine* since Vol. 8, Nos. 5-6, (Jan.-Feb. 1975).

B322 "Portrait of the Artist As a Young Cipher." *Graduate*, 5, No. 1 (Sesquifall Issue 1977), 8-9.

    A comic strip written and drawn by Atwood.

B323 "Hairdo." *Weekend Magazine*, 4 Feb. 1978, pp. 6-7.

    A comic strip written and drawn by Atwood.

B324 *Up in the Tree*. Toronto: McClelland and Stewart, [1978].

    Written and drawn by Atwood. See A15.

Part II

Works on Margaret Atwood

(For works specifically about Atwood's prose writings, see *ABCMA*, Vol. I.)

C   **Books, Articles and Sections of Books, Theses and Dissertations, Interviews, and Awards and Honours**

    Books

C1   Sandler, Linda, ed. *Margaret Atwood: A Symposium*. (*The Malahat Review*, No. 41, Jan. 1977.) Victoria: Univ. of Victoria, 1977. 228 pp.

    Contents: Linda Sandler, "Interview with Margaret Atwood," pp. 5-27; Rosemary Sullivan, "Breaking the Circle," pp. 30-41; Jane Rule, "Life, Liberty and the Pursuit of Normalcy—The Novels of Margaret Atwood," pp. 42-49; George Woodcock, "Transformation Mask for Margaret Atwood," pp. 52-56; Rick Salutin, "A Note on the Marxism of Atwood's 'Survival,'" pp. 57-60; Al Purdy, "An Unburnished One-Tenth of One Per Cent of an Event," pp. 61-64; Margaret Atwood, "An Album of Photographs," pp. 65-88; Tom Marshall, "Atwood Under and Above Water," pp. 89-94; Robert Fulford, "The Images of Atwood," pp. 95-98; John Hofsess, "How To Be Your Own Best Survival," pp. 102-06; Robin Skelton, "Timeless Constructions—A Note on the Poetic Style of Margaret Atwood," pp. 107-20; Margaret Atwood, "Worksheets," pp. 121-33; Rowland Smith, "Margaret Atwood: The Stoic Comedian," pp. 134-44; Margaret Atwood, "Threes," p. 152; Eli Mandel, "Atwood

Gothic," pp. 165-74; Margaret Atwood, "The Resplendent Quetzal," pp. 175-88; Jerome H. Rosenberg, "On Reading the Atwood Papers in the Thomas Fisher Library," pp. 191-94; Alan J. Horne, "A Preliminary Checklist of Writings by and about Margaret Atwood," pp. 195-222.

This special issue of *The Malahat Review* is a collection of critical essays and appreciations. Sullivan's article attempts to show how Atwood, in her poetry and fiction, tries to disengage from history, from time, from the inheritance of human nature, to break out of the "circle game" of language and logic. Like the narrator in *Surfacing*, she comes to terms with the past and refuses to be a victim, but has not achieved spiritual regeneration. Rule describes *The Edible Woman* as a farce about the pursuit of normalcy; to the narrator in *Surfacing*, normalcy is terrifying and important; in *Lady Oracle*, the "pursuit of normalcy, down all the misleading by-ways of language, is controlled by Margaret Atwood [who] . . . has written a satire of the first order." Marshall points to Atwood's search for a personal and a national identity, in both the poetry and the fiction, as the essential feature of her work. Skelton suggests that Atwood, in many of her poems, uses a structure he calls "modular," and cites Pound, Stevens, and Yeats as precedents. Modular poetry is about states of being rather than events. Smith examines Atwood's fiction as observations of the grotesqueries of middle-Canadian life. Mandel sees Atwood's repetitive use of reduplicating images (mirrors, photographs) and her totemic animal imagery as owing much to the traditional patterns of gothic horror. The "Album of Photographs" is a fascinating chronological record.

C2   Grace, Sherrill. *Violent Duality: A Study of Margaret Atwood*. Montreal: Véhicule, 1980. 154 pp.

Certain themes and forms persist in Atwood's writing. "Duality, the tension between art and life, the dilemma of the artist, problems of role-playing, victimization, the fallibility of human perception, and of course, portrayal of the Canadian landscape" are the dominant themes. Of the books of poetry, *The Journals of Susanna Moodie* is "Atwood's major poetic achievement to date." As for the novels, "If *The Edible Woman* is an anti-comedy and *Surfacing* is a ghost story, then *Lady Oracle* must be an anti-Gothic . . . ." In terms of other Canadian writers, "Her nearest of kin . . . are James Reaney and, possibly, Jay Macpherson."

Atwood's formal poetic strengths include "a cool, acerbic wit, ironic eye and laconic phrase. . . . [T]he combination of detachment and irony coupled with cut-off line and duplistic form dominates her poetry." Her novels employ "first-person narrators, ironic self-reflexive narratives, and symbolic or even mythic structures . . . ." She also draws on the Canadian tradition which emphasizes "the past and the individual's need to be part of a social context. . . ." It is in her poetry that Atwood "is truly distinctive and commanding." Thus, except for *Surfacing*, "Atwood fails to sustain in her fiction the eerie, disembodied voice that rivets our attention in her poetry." "For Atwood the dynamic of violent duality is a function of the creative act. . . . [S]he has continued to explore the inescapable tension between art and life, the two immortalities . . . and of the need to accept and work within them. To create, Atwood chooses violent dualities, and her art re-works, probes, and dramatizes the ability to see double."

Articles and Sections of Books

C3   Marshall, Tom. "Les animaux de son pays: Notes sur la poesie de Margaret Atwood." *Ellipse*, No. 3 (Spring 1970), pp. 81-86.

Claims the principal themes of Atwood's poetry are imprisonment and the need to escape, the search for identity, and above all, the struggle to survive. These were expressed in her first book, *The Circle Game*; in the second, *The Animals in That Country*, there is some optimism but also the fear that we may destroy what we need to live with, such as the country itself. Lack of form and lack of structure are real threats.

C4   Brown, Rosellen. "The Poetry of Margaret Atwood." *Nation*, 28 June 1971, pp. 824-26.

Finds Atwood's poems exemplary as the testimony of a woman who bears with her "the curse of the underground" but who appears very rational. Sees Atwood as a haunted, quietly functioning woman, who writes of her primitive vision of stone, water, and animals as our grandfathers and ourselves.

C5   Waters, Katherine E. "Margaret Atwood: Love on the Dark Side of the Moon." In *Mother Was Not a Person*. Comp. Margret Andersen. Montreal: Content Publishing and Black Rose Books, 1972, pp. 102-19.

Explores the sexual politics of the man-woman relationship in Atwood's poetry. The poet uses the personal as a particularization of the socio-political and this in turn becomes a metaphor for the universal. Atwood does this from a feminist viewpoint. "The man-woman relationship is symptom and symbol of the unsolved riddles of her humanity."

C6   Woodcock, George. "Margaret Atwood." *Literary Half-Yearly*, 13, No. 2 (July 1972), 233-42.

Identifies three essential characteristics of Atwood's poetic character: the sharp, ironic inversion; the movement from the metaphorical to the literal use of images; and the combination of visual sensibility with intellectual discipline. The identity of her poems and her first novel is very close—both are about the distances and defences between human beings. Atwood's experience in handling images and myths in her poetry is reflected in the craftsmanship of *The Edible Woman*. In addition, this is a "social novel of high perceptiveness." Atwood does for her own generation what Jane Austen did for hers. *The Journals of Susanna Moodie* shows Atwood as poet conscious of a sense of history and of the land, but there is also a "kind of transference," which extends links between what is perceived and the perceiver.

C7   Ayre, J. "Margaret Atwood and the End of Colonialism." *Saturday Night*, Nov. 1972, pp. 23-26.

"Nationalist radicals" like Atwood believe that the older writers such as Callaghan and Richler "are locked into alienated colonialist attitudes, persisting in their belief that cultural standards are set in New York or London." Because of her intense feelings about this, Atwood spent the last year spreading her ideas about Canadian literature and national identity. Some biographical details follow and some perceptive comments about her writing—she "plays the role of psychic iconoclast, pulling the categories of existence apart and presenting a broken, confused reality that her readers must often put back in order for themselves."

C8   French, William. "Icon and Target: Atwood As Thing." *The Globe and Mail*, 7 April 1973, p. 28.

A summary of Atwood's speech to the Empire Club in April 1973. She realizes that she has become a sort of symbol of Canadian national cultural aspirations, a "Thing" rather than a celebrity. The answers a "Thing" gives are listened to but are shot at as well as worshipped. Serious cultural nationalists want a distinctive culture and are unafraid to measure it against international standards.

C9   Webb, Phyllis. "Letters to Margaret Atwood." *Open Letter*, 2nd Ser., No. 5 (Summer 1973), 71-73.

A personal response to Atwood and her work inspired by the publication of *Survival*.

C10   Piercy, Marge. "Margaret Atwood: Beyond Victimhood." *American Poetry Review*, 2, No. 6 (Nov.-Dec. 1973), 41-44.

A long general article covering the two novels,

five books of poetry, and *Survival*, which Atwood had then written. The author admires Atwood and hopes that, as she has come to identify herself in the tradition she has defined as literature of a victimized colony, she will "help consciously define another growing body to which her work in many of its themes belongs: a women's culture."

C11   Davey, Frank. "Margaret Atwood." In *From There to Here: A Guide to English-Canadian Literature Since 1960*. Our Nature—Our Voices, Vol. II. Erin, Ont.: Porcépic, 1974, pp. 30-36.

A short, positive survey of Atwood's work, of which her poetry is claimed as her most accomplished and important. In *The Circle Game*, Atwood's world is full of danger and the surfaces are unstable. "The 'circle game,' the self-deception most people practise to convince themselves there is stability and order, is ultimately for Atwood the most insidious aspect of this environment; since ... it threatens her psyche." Later volumes amplify this conception—man attempts to impose order and form on ever-changing "space" only thus to bring about his alienation from nature. *Power Politics* is much more obviously personal. The first two novels elaborate on the themes expressed in the poetry and make them more explicit without expanding them. The usefulness of *Survival* has been in provoking interest in Canadian writing. Atwood claims the themes of victimization and survival dominate the literature, but she can only do this by being very selective in choosing her texts.

C12   Onley, Gloria. "Breaking through the Patriarchal Nets to the Peaceable Kingdom." *West Coast Review*, 8, No. 3 (Jan. 1974), 43-50.

Contrasts Shadbolt's blurred and neo-romantic poetry, as seen in *Mind's I*, with the sharply visual and laconic quality of Atwood's. In *Power Politics*, her perception and emotion struggle in the role-playing prompted by the need for order in personal relation-ships. Characterizes her poetry as primarily "showing a woman's mind unable to live with the structures imposed on it by her culture," a culture based and fed on power. The power structure is the patriarchy: the woman's energies and self "have no existence except as defined or canalized by the colonizing, victimizing male." When this structure is broken, the problem of identity becomes central.

C13   Onley, Gloria. "Power Politics in Bluebeard's Castle." *Canadian Literature*, No. 60 (Spring 1974), pp. 21-42.

A study of the sexual politics evidenced in Atwood's work. The theme of *Power Politics* is "role-engulfment"—romantic love, a devastating mode of existence. Sexual love is imaged several times as a shattering of the ego; the body is described as a mechanism remotely controlled by the head. These themes are repeated in *Surfacing*, where sex is linked with mechanization, coercion, and death. A link between depersonalized sex and modern technology was suggested by George Steiner in his *In Bluebeard's Castle: Notes Towards a Redefinition of Culture*, and there is also expressed the view that syntax is an active mirroring of systems of power and order. In *Surfacing* language is seen as a means of imposing psychological power structures; and in *Power Politics* language is described as turning from tool to weapon. Language itself is Bluebeard's castle. Atwood suggests that the end of sexual politics might come only with the end of civilization as we know it. Her works are "frighteningly precise image structures, iconoclastic keys to getting mentally outside Bluebeard's Castle."

C14   Rogers, Linda. "Margaret the Magician." *Canadian Literature*, No. 60 (Spring 1974), pp. 83-85.

The writer's response to Atwood's poetry is an intensely personal one. She is fascinated by the language but finds "there is no dialogue on any level.... Atwood, the magician, hypnotizes with the brilliant image which dazzles without illuminating."

C15 Ross, Gary. "The Circle Game." *Canadian Literature*, No. 60 (Spring 1974), pp. 51-63.

A detailed criticism of *The Circle Game* as a poetic sequence and not as a collection of individual poems. From the beginning the haunting sense of isolation is associated with geographical wilderness; but urban "civilization" means human alienation—it obliterates humanity. "The Circle Game" is the pivotal poem—it confirms these previous themes; evaluates human relationships as destructive; and above all crystallizes the feeling of imprisonment. The previously unquestioning acceptance of the poet's predicament is now changed—she wants to break the circle. From now on, the wilderness becomes less intimidating and she sees relations with others more positively. A love relationship, however, is threatening to her individuality, and we face the problem of how to escape from isolation without losing our separate wholeness. Some sort of reconciliation is achieved—as physical landscape reflects the inner state of the perceiver, the poet's recognition of affinities with others, the terror of landscape disintegrates.

C16 Glicksohn, Susan Wood. "The Martian Point of View." *Extrapolation*, 15, No. 2 (May 1974), 161-73.

This article claims that Atwood's poetic vision is that of a contemporary individual trying to comprehend an alien world and of an unworldly creature revealing the reality beneath the civilized surface of this world. In her poetry humans are changed into non-human shapes; the everyday world becomes a nightmare landscape; the self is literally as well as figuratively submerged. The horror is the more chilling because the poet expresses it so calmly. The language and imagery of science and technology, particularly in *Power Politics*, contribute to the feeling of alienation and horror. Science fiction themes and concepts such as time travel enable her to describe the exploration of her own human complexity.

C17 Jones, D. G. "Cold Eye and Optic Heart: Marshall McLuhan and Some Canadian Poets." *Modern Poetry Studies*, 5, No. 2 (Autumn 1974), 170-87.

Jones claims that three Canadian poets—P. K. Page, Margaret Avison, and Margaret Atwood—tell us to look at the world with our heart and not our head. For Atwood, sight threatens to let us see only the surface of things and not the reality beneath. In Atwood's "photograph" poems, the speaker is not visible in her own photograph, for she has, as it were, retreated under the surface of the film. She proposes that if our vision is faulty, we should close our eyes and may thus recover our other senses.

C18 Macri, F. M. "Survival Kit: Margaret Atwood and the Canadian Scene." *Modern Poetry Studies*, 5, No. 2 (Autumn 1974), 187-95.

A most critical survey of Atwood's poetry, whose imagery and themes are claimed to be transparent and continually repeated. "There are slight variations, but these are few and so infrequent as to give little feeling of artistic merit." *The Journals of Susanna Moodie* repeats already familiar imagery and repeats all the poet has said previously. In Macri's opinion, the critical acclaim accorded this book by Canadian reviewers is due more for its historical persona than for its poetry. *Procedures for Underground* reiterates the images, compounds the schizophrenia, and intensifies the paranoia. More of the same in *Power Politics*, though the poetry deals directly with the problems of male-female cohabitation. *The Animals in That Country* is the best collection. Atwood's technique is surgical, her verse line concise, and the trick of taking a thought and turning it inside out is repeated and transparent. A reading of her prose works, particularly *Survival*, helps one appreciate better her creative talents. However, the exposition of themes, motifs, and recurrent patterns adds up to a theory of Canadian literature which may confuse a whole generation into seeing victims everywhere.

C19　French, William. "The Women of Our Literary Life." *Imperial Oil Review*, 59, No. 1 (1975), 2-7. Rpt. in *Canadian Author & Bookman*, 51 (Spring 1976), 1-6.

A brief survey of women fiction writers in Canada from Frances Brooke, whose novel *The History of Emily Montague* was published in 1769, to the present day. French describes Atwood as "the best-known and most versatile" of the leading women writers today.

C20　Norris, Ken. "Survival in the Writings of Margaret Atwood." *CrossCountry*, No. 1 (Winter 1975), pp. 18-29.

A reading of Atwood's work which finds the theme of survival central to her fiction and poetry. Many of the early poems express the perspective of the pioneer. There is also the question of survival in love relationships — whether to remain cold and essentially uninvolved or whether to give oneself to a relationship and lose one's individual personality. In *You Are Happy* ("a brilliant collection") Atwood shows herself able to form a relationship without having to sacrifice any part of herself. "Perhaps what is most impressive about *You Are Happy* is that it moves beyond the problem of individual survival and begins an exploration of what's to be found in a life of commingled feeling."

C21　Woodcock, George. "Margaret Atwood: Poet as Novelist." In *The Canadian Novel in the Twentieth Century: Essays from* Canadian Literature. Ed. George Woodcock. New Canadian Library, No. 115. Toronto: McClelland and Stewart, 1975, pp. 312-27.

This article, dated 1974, was constructed from two previously published articles which appeared in the *Literary Half-Yearly* (see C6) and *Ariel*, 4, No. 3 (July 1973), 16-28 ("Surfacing to Survive: Notes on the Recent Atwood" which is devoted to her prose writings [see *ABCMA*, Vol. I, C10]). Woodcock's conclusion is that a consideration both of Atwood's prose writings and of her poetry shows "the versatility with which her intelligence plays over the horizons of her perceptions.... No other writer in Canada of Margaret Atwood's generation has so wide a command of the resources of literature, so telling a restraint in their use."

C22　Frankel, Vivian. "Margaret Atwood: A Personal View." *Branching Out*, 2, No. 1 (Jan-Feb. 1975), 24-26.

Apart from offering an interesting picture of Atwood reading to university audiences in Montreal, this is a simplistic article. It relates some misconceptions which have arisen about the "Atwood legend" — that she is hostile to men, and finds them threatening; that she is a menacing pessimist. It asserts that Atwood knows what is important to her and what is not. Contains good photographs.

C23　Conlon, Patrick. "Margaret Atwood: Beneath the Surface." *Toronto Life*, Feb. 1975, pp. 44-51.

A good, professionally journalistic article, mostly biographical. It provides some interesting insights into Atwood's relations with the public, her friends, and the reviewers.

C24　Ladousse, Gillian. "Some Aspects of the Theme of Metamorphosis in Margaret Atwood's Poetry." *Etudes Canadiennes*, No. 2 (1976), pp. 71-77.

The author claims that the theme of metamorphosis in Atwood's poetry is obsessive. Her vision is one of perpetual mutation which provides a means of access to a different kind of reality where form is abolished. Two kinds of metamorphosis are identified — the Protean aspect and the change from man to animal (the Circe myth).

C25　MacGregor, Roy. "Mother Oracle." *The Canadian*, 25 Sept. 1976, pp. 15-18.

An interview-style article which describes Atwood's private life and how the public intrudes. She feels that she has become a "Thing" — "people make up what you are, then praise or attack you for it." As for her work, MacGregor claims she is telling Canadians about themselves rather than about herself. A study of Survivalwoman in the comic strip "Kanadian Kultchur Komics," written and illustrated by Atwood, will produce a good picture of what she is like today. Well illustrated with colour photographs.

C26   Allen, Carolyn. "Margaret Atwood: Power of Transformation, Power of Knowledge." *Essays on Canadian Writing*, No. 6 (Spring 1977), pp. 5-17.

One of the major themes in Atwood's poetry is "transformation." In *The Journals of Susanna Moodie* and the Circe/Mud poems in *You Are Happy*, she creates women who are willing to break out of mythic or social moulds, and create themselves.

C27   Dilliott, Maureen. "Emerging from the Cold: Margaret Atwood's 'You Are Happy.'" *Modern Poetry Studies*, 7, No. 1 (Spring 1977), 73-90.

A generally favourable and detailed review article which finds that after the stridency and monotony of some poems in the second section, and ideas and images which are not new, the book opens out in the last section. There the themes and imagery used earlier are woven into "warmer, more lyrical verses than any Atwood has yet produced." Some of these last poems are "the best that Atwood has ever written."

C28   Davey, Frank. "Atwood's Gorgon Touch." *Studies in Canadian Literature*, 2, No. 2 (Summer 1977), 146-63. Rpt. in *Brave New Wave*. Ed. Jack David. Windsor: Black Moss, 1978, pp. 171-95.

Davey maintains that Atwood's poetry is preoccupied with a struggle between time and space. She expresses the human need to transcend time, using such devices as mythology, art, and imagination, but these "must be recognized as either weapons or crutches used by the weak in the face of mutability." Her poems construct a catalogue of evasions that are all

extensions of the human need to believe "nothing can change." But appearances are deceptive: "the appearance of stasis conceals process; the appearance of solidity conceals liquidity; the appearance of order conceals chaos; the appearance of predictability presages surprise." From *Double Persephone* to *You Are Happy*, Atwood's poems express her efforts as an artist to escape the static aesthetic of space and enter time, process, and mortality. Yet the irony is that for Atwood art itself seems inevitably to possess the "gorgon touch": "like a mirror [the poet] creates art at the expense of [her] own participation in reality."

C29   Foster, John Wilson. "The Poetry of Margaret Atwood." *Canadian Literature*, No. 74 (Autumn 1977), pp. 5-20.

Atwood's poetry is concerned with the self's inhabitation of spaces, and with the physical space of Canada, both past and present. The pioneer experience is a metaphor for the psychic journey towards acceptance of forms, spaces, and roles at once inescapable and constantly to be resisted. Atwood's inward journey is an exploration of the self and its relationships.

C30   Landsberg, Michele. "Late Motherhood." *Chatelaine*, Oct. 1977, pp. 44-46, 119-23, 125.

A fairly superficial article based on interviews with some of Canada's most celebrated women who had babies later than usual. Atwood is able to relax and enjoy her baby—if she had become a mother in her twenties "it would have been a catastrophe...a very destructive thing to do."

C31   Stevens, Peter. "Explorer/ Settler/ Poet." *Univeristy of Windsor Review*, 13, No. 1 (Fall-Winter 1977), 63-74.

A discussion of the poetry of Atwood, Newlove, Purdy, and McNeil which uses the figures of early pioneers to construct a sense of a Canadian literary consciousness. Dealing at length with "The Journals of Susanna Moodie," Stevens finds that Mrs. Moodie fits admirably into the theme of explorers and settlers as embodiments of the search for poetic language to express Canadian myths.

C32   Grace, Sherrill E. "Introduction ." In *The Circle Game*. By Margaret Atwood. Toronto: House of Anansi, 1978, pp. 9-15.

The writer believes that certain fallacies arose in reviews of these early poems when first published that have tended to follow Atwood — that her poems are autobiographical, that she is a "mythopoeic poet" of the Frye school, that she is a feminist and a Canadian nationalist. Fewer than half of the poems appear in the *Selected Poems* so that the sense of pattern formed by the sequence of the poems is missing. In *The Circle Game* Atwood is exploring the fallibility of human perception — we distort and delimit life; freedom is both necessary and dangerous.

C33   Mallinson, Jean. "Ideology and Poetry: An Examination of Some Recent Trends in Canadian Criticism." *Studies in Canadian Literature*, 3, No. 1 (Winter 1978), 93-109.

An examination of three separate instances of ideological criticism of Canadian poetry, criticism which is doctrinaire and baleful because it misinterprets the poetry that exists and prescribes certain attitudes and poetic modes as desirable. The three critics dealt with are John Bentley Mays, Frank Davey, and George Amabile. After a brief mention of Davey's criticism of *Power Politics* — "the flashily contrived wit of most of the poems parallels the 'castrating bitch' manipulativeness of the persona" — Mallinson concentrates on Amabile's review of *You Are Happy* in *CV/II* (see D51) where he finds reasons for not admiring the poems because he does not like what he thinks they are saying. His interpretation may be rooted in the social and psychological expectations which he, as a male, has about attitudes he believes are appropriate to women. Mallinson concludes with her own sympathetic reading of the poems.

C34   Bilan, R. P. "Margaret Atwood's 'The Journals of Susanna Moodie.'" *Canadian Poetry*, No. 2 (Spring-Summer 1978), pp. 1-12.

This article claims that the book is tightly organized and tied to a chronological sequence showing the growth of the central character. To understand it fully one must take full account of the structure. The poems are also linked by the repetition of a number of key images: trees, fire, light, and darkness. "As in much of Atwood's poetry, the exploration of a new land is also a psychological exploration of the self." The arrangement of the poems in "Journal II" makes untenable a simple reading of Moodie's relationship to the land as becoming consistently more positive. While she begins to recognize the reality of her new country, she is still struggling to come to terms with it. At the end, she prefers the land to society, but it is only in death that she can become one with the land.

C35   Sillers, Pat. "Power Impinging: Hearing Atwood's Vision." *Studies in Canadian Literature*, 4 (Winter 1979), 59-70.

A review article dealing with Atwood's *Selected Poems*. The style of the poems is almost ascetically direct and to the point; even when the language seems dull, its opacity transmits significance. Nearly all the poems are preoccupied with pictures, viewpoints, landscapes — but in order to hear what the poet is saying, the reader also is implicated. The poems are specifically addressed to an audience and are so reader-involving, using rhetoric to achieve power and force.

Theses and Dissertation

C36   Yeo, Margaret E. "The Living Landscape: Nature

Imagery in the Poetry of Margaret Atwood and Other Modern Canadian Lyric Poets." M.A. Thesis Carleton 1969.

One of the concerns frequently expressed in modern Canadian poetry is the impact of the power, energy, and indifference of the landscape upon man. A desire to belong to the land, and the problems it creates, are tied to the search for a Canadian identity. The poetry of Atwood offers one approach to the problems Canadians find in coming to terms with their violently powerful environment.

C37 Power, Linda Laporte. "The Reality of Selfhood: A Study of Polarity in the Poetry and Fiction of Margaret Atwood." M.A. Thesis McGill 1973.

Explores the relationship between the concept of polarity and the quest for the reality of selfhood in selected works by Atwood. It examines the structure, methodology, and the chronological development of the quest from its first appearance in her early poetry to its definitive form in *Surfacing*, while simultaneously analyzing the patterns of polarity which inform the selected works.

C38 Regan, Nancy. "The Geography and History of the Mind: An Analysis of the Works of Margaret Atwood." M.A. Thesis Rhode Island 1975.

Discusses the relation between environment and history in selected works by Atwood.

C39 Scott, Andrew. "Margaret Atwood: A Critical Appreciation." M.A. Thesis New Brunswick 1975.

A critical examination of Atwood's work published up to 1974. Evaluates significant themes and images, and examines Atwood's use of myth and her possible alignment with a group of Canadian mythopoeic poets. Some basic archetypal rhythms and symbolic patterns are identified.

C40 Parks, Claudia Susan [now Ingersoll]. "The Solitary

Dancer: Isolation and Affirmation in the Poetry of Margaret Atwood." M.A. Thesis Memorial 1976.

Explores Atwood's themes and imagery and traces a growing movement away from alienation toward hope, discovery, and individual potential.

C41 Gronvigh, Joanne. "Thematic Development in the Work of Margaret Atwood." M.A. Thesis Dalhousie 1977.

Gronvigh comments on the themes of survival and male-female relationships as they emerge through Atwood's prose and poetry. A wide-ranging study.

C42 Packer, Miriam. "Beyond the Garrison: Approaching the Wilderness in Margaret Laurence, Alice Munro and Margaret Atwood." Diss. Montreal 1978.

Analyzes the way in which Atwood's and Munro's protagonists transcend the so-called garrison mentality. Particular attention is given to linguistic analysis and comparison.

Interviews

C43 Halpenny, Francess. *A Dialogue with Margaret Atwood*. Toronto: Univ. of Toronto, Faculty of Library Science.

A cassette audio-tape, forty-five minutes duration. Not published. A general interview before a class at the Faculty. October 18, 1972.

C44 Levenson, Christopher. "Interview with Margaret Atwood." *Manna*, No. 2 (1972), pp. 46-54.

A rather defensive interview. Deals mostly with her poetry—writers who influenced her, what poetry attempts to do, how she starts writing (from images rather than from ideas), how to read poetry aloud. Two interesting comments—poetry does not express emotion but evokes emotion from the reader; and she wrote *The Journals of Susanna Moodie* as separate poems.

C45   Gibson, Graeme. "Margaret Atwood." In *Eleven Canadian Novelists*. Toronto: House of Anansi, 1973, pp. 1-31.

One of a series of interviews first taped for broadcasting on the CBC. Matters discussed include the difference between writing poetry and fiction; what the novelist's role is; the Canadian tradition in writing; the problems of getting published and of being a woman writer; and answers to detailed questions about *The Edible Woman* and *Surfacing*.

C46   Miner, Valerie. "Atwood in Metamorphosis: An Authentic Canadian Fairy Tale." In *Her Own Woman: Profiles of Ten Canadian Women*. Ed. Myrna Kostash. Toronto: Macmillan, 1975, pp. 173-94. Rpt. (condensed) "The Many Facets of Margaret Atwood. " In *Chatelaine*, June 1975, pp. 32-33, 66-70.

A useful interview in the biographical details it provides of Atwood's childhood and the influence of her parents. About her childhood she said "The only thing I regard as important was the moment I realized I wanted to be a writer.... I stopped writing from age eight to grade 12. I consider it my sterile period." Describes the complexity of her personality and her reluctance to talk about some aspects of her personal life.

C47   Swan, Susan. "Margaret Atwood: The Woman as Poet." *Communiqué*, No. 8 (May 1975), pp. 8-11, 45-46.

An interview which concentrates on the changing image that a female poet has with the public at large and with other writers. It contains some insights into Atwood's views about women's relationships with men. In French and English.

C48   Van Varsveld, Gail. "Talking with Atwood." *Room of One's Own*, 1, No. 2 (Summer 1975), 66-70.

Deals with Atwood's attitude towards feminism in literature. She does not feel she should be "propagandist" in her writings; and talks about the development of a separate female mythology, about magazines for women only, and about sexual discrimination in reviews.

C49   Kaminski, Margaret. "Interview with Margaret Atwood." *Waves*, 4, No. 1 (Autumn 1975), 8-13.

A rather scrappy interview—Atwood discusses *The Edible Woman* and considers it not a feminist novel; the story is not autobiography but fiction. Then on to poetry, and the effect of reviews. Atwood feels that a lot of interest in *You Are Happy*, as in *Power Politics*, is mythological.

C50   *The Education of Mike McManus: Margaret Atwood*. Ontario Educational Communications Authority, 1976.

Videotape, colour, thirty minutes duration. A television interview.

C51   Gibson, Mary Ellis. "A Conversation with Margaret Atwood." *Chicago Review*, 27, No. 4 (Spring 1976), 105-13.

Atwood describes what she attempted to do with *Survival*—"It's not an academic book ... it gives you a way into the literature"—and how the literary and publishing scene in Canada has changed drastically over recent years.

C52   Slopen, Beverley. "Margaret Atwood." *Publisher's Weekly*, 23 Aug. 1976, pp. 6-8.

An interview given just after publication of *Lady Oracle*. Provides some interesting biographical details including those which relate to incidents in the novel.

C53   Slinger, Helen. "Interview with Margaret Atwood." *Maclean's*, 6 Sept. 1976, pp. 4-7.

Fairly superficial, dealing with what it is like to have a baby and with Atwood's views on the awakened interest in Canadian literature, and on Canadian politics.

C54 Schiller, William. "Interview with Margaret Atwood." *PWP*, 2, No. 3 (Fall 1976), 2-15.

An interesting interview which concentrates on Atwood's poetry. She talks of the poets who influenced her early work. She does not subscribe to theories— "Theories are useful to poets only insofar as they can make poetry out of them." Says that it is difficult to interview poets about their own work: "I have some difficulty recalling what processes were going on." Feels that reviewers often tend to write about a book of poetry as though reviewing the book that came out before it.

C55 Struthers, J. R. (Tim). "An Interview with Margaret Atwood." *Essays on Canadian Writing*, No. 6 (Spring 1977), pp. 18-27.

A stimulating interview which touches on many topics; serious but not solemn. It deals both with the poetry and the fiction, with some emphasis on *Lady Oracle*. There is discussion about the Canadian tradition in fiction and poetry, and its influence on Atwood; comments on her response to good and bad reviews; and about women writers.

C56 Oates, Joyce Carol. "An Interview with Margaret Atwood." *New York Times Book Review*, 21 May 1978, pp. 15, 43-45.

Provides some biographical background information. Atwood explains her interest in the Gothic and in supernatural fantasy, and gives her views on writing—"For me, every poem has a texture of sound which is at least as important as the 'argument'"; "If you can think of writing as expressing 'itself' rather than 'the writer,' this makes total sense" (that is, that the disciplines of prose and poetry evoke an almost totally different personality). Finally there is a discussion about writing not necessarily being auto-biographical; and in answer to the question, why do you write? she answers "Why doesn't everyone?"

C57 Davidson, Jim. "Margaret Atwood." *Meanjin*, 37, No. 2 (July 1978), 189-205.

An interview in Australia which deals with Atwood's views on Canadian nationalism and Quebec cultural nationalism. She compares the Canadian and Australian consciousness of time — "There's nothing lost in the mists of history, because history, as we know it, is not misty." The importance of women writers and the victimization of women are discussed. There is an interesting contrast between the "survivor" in Canadian literature and the "failed hero" or "loner" in Australian literature.

C58 Kappler, Mary Ellen, and Mike Zizis. "An Interview with Margaret Atwood." *Intrinsic*, No. 7/8 (Spring 1979), pp. 91-95.

A lightweight interview with few revelations.

C59 Hammond, Karla. "An Interview with Margaret Atwood." *American Poetry Review*, 8, No. 5 (Sept.-Oct. 1979), 27-29.

An important interview in which Atwood gives her views on such matters as the emergence of Canadian nationalism, feminism, myths, and the nature of poetry.

C60 Whiten, Clifton. "*PCR* Interview with Margaret Atwood." *Poetry Canada Review*, 1, No. 4 (Spring 1980), pp. 8, 10.

Atwood discusses comma splices, interviews, literary prizes, and the creative act.

Awards and Honours

C61 E. J. Pratt Medal (1961).

C62 President's Medal, Poetry, University of Western Ontario, London, Ontario (1965).

C63 Governor-General's Award for Poetry for *The Circle Game* (1966).

C64 The Centennial Commission Poetry Competition, First Prize for *The Animals in That Country* (1967).

C65 The Union Poetry Prize from *Poetry* (Chicago) for five poems from *Procedures for Underground* (1969).

C66 Writer-in-Residence, University of Toronto (1972-73).

C67 D. Litt., Trent University, Peterborough, Ontario (1973).

C68 The Bess Hokins Prize from *Poetry* (Chicago) (1974).

C69 LL.D., Queen's University, Kingston, Ontario (1974).

C70 The City of Toronto Award for *Lady Oracle* (1976).

D   Selected Book Reviews

Double Persephone

D1 Scott, Peter Dale. "Turning New Leaves." *The Canadian Forum*, Feb. 1962, pp. 259-60.
　　Includes a brief note of *Double Persephone*, which the reviewer finds serious and thoughtful, but too derivative, too contrived. It does show precision and rhythmic economy.

D2 Mandel, Eli. "Seedtime in Dark May." *Alphabet*, No. 4 (June 1962), pp. 69-70.
　　A mention only: the poems exhibit the paradoxical contrast of the stillness of life and the dance of art.

D3 Wilson, Milton. Rev. of *Double Persephone*. *University of Toronto Quarterly*, 31 (July 1962), 448-49.
　　Finds the gloss and precision startling.

The Circle Game (1964)

D4 MacCallum, Hugh. Rev. of *The Circle Game*. *University of Toronto Quarterly*, 35 (July 1965), 383.
　　A mention only of the early Atwood/Pachter version, which finds the poetry and pictures well matched.

The Circle Game (1967)

D5 Rutsala, Vern. "An Authentic Style." *Kayak*, No. 12 (1967), pp. 63-65.

The realization at the heart of the book is that the surface world exists to keep people apart. Something else fundamental separates people, a sort of animal fear. The "circle" is never broken and perhaps never will be—to "get inside" a person is usually impossible. The poet is wise and resigned, and the poems are relentless and skilful.

D6   Gibbs, Robert. Rev. of *The Circle Game*. *The Fiddlehead*, No. 70 (Winter 1967), pp. 69-71.

The poems exhibit the world as at once both over-civilized and savage. They reflect the endless human lot of quest and disappointment, and the only occasional escape from isolation.

D7   Harrison, Keith. Rev. of *The Circle Game*. *The Tamarack Review*, No. 42 (Winter 1967), pp. 73-74.

The simplicity and lightness of Atwood's style and language are foils for a darker undertone of meaning. Her control is detached and witty.

D8   Ondaatje, Michael. Rev. of *The Circle Game*. *The Canadian Forum*, April 1967, pp. 22-23.

Ondaatje finds the poems full of Atwood's own personal mythologies, and private and traditional worlds blend into one. She pits herself against the too-ordered world of "civilization." "Exceptional imagery and discipline survive each other."

D9   Stevens, Peter. "On the Edge, on the Surface." *Canadian Literature*, No. 32 (Spring 1967), pp. 71-72.

The landscapes of Atwood's vision are uncertain and stunted and there is a subterranean menace. We must travel and explore this—and explore ourselves—even though "the expression of these discoveries may be a self-defeating notion." The relationships between human beings offer little hope and there is little real communication. In spite of its lack of variation in tone, *The Circle Game* "is a volume well worth reading."

D10   Seaman, Roger. Rev. of *The Circle Game*. *Quarry*, 16, No. 4 (Summer 1967), 40-42.

The poet tries to break out of the "circle," which is many things—isolation, convention, the ordinary senses of our bodies which provide limited percep-tions. What succeeds in breaking the circle are "metamorphoses of the body," but many of these transformations are frightening and touched by horror. Perhaps there is no form nor central pattern, but there is love and there are words.

D11   MacCallum, Hugh. Rev. of *The Circle Game*. *University of Toronto Quarterly*, 36 (July 1967), 357-59.

"Fastidious and evocative poetry" which explores the forms by which the mind shapes experience into patterns. Atwood's vision is one in which ritual and pattern create a charmed circle of art that imprisons the mind and feeling, from which the poet endeavours to escape.

D12   Thompson, Eric. Rev. of *The Circle Game*. *The Fiddlehead*, No. 75 (Spring 1968), pp. 76-77.

Finds the poems elaborately structured and preoccupied with self. Atwood's craft is deceptively simple and "displays a sureness of touch which enables her to clarify ... the myth-real relationships." But her experience is small and she is unwilling to investigate the foregrounds of consciousness.

D13   Moon, Samuel. "Canadian Chronicle." *Poetry*, 112 (June 1968), 204-05.

The world of *The Circle Game* is one of conventionality and propriety, a "circle" from which it seems impossible to escape, producing frustrations, cruelty, and self-pity. There is no liberation from the allegories of myth and tradition, and although there is a loss of "self," the poet must continue the search.

D14   Garnet, Eldon. "For the Poets, the Landscape Is the Great Canadian Myth." *Saturday Night*, Feb. 1970, pp. 31-33.

The reviewer deals generally with how the land tradition is of essential importance to the Canadian poet who is able to project his personality into it and see it as a metaphor for his life condition. "The Canadian poet has transformed the land into a myth."

The Animals in That Country

D15 Gasparini, Len. Rev. of *The Animals in That Country. The Canadian Forum*, Dec. 1968, p. 212.

The poems in this book demonstrate the split between two worlds, one of the present, of beauty, material gain, and power, the other of the spirit. No transitions from one to the other are possible. "Her animals are human."

D16 Barbour, Douglas. Rev. of *The Animals in That Country. The Dalhousie Review*, 48 (Winter 1968-69), 568-70.

The reviewer finds this book represents a real progression from the severely personal poetry of *The Circle Game*. Her persona is an isolated character, locked in, trapped. In this collection the danger of love is the danger of delight and of beauty.

D17 Purdy, Al. "Poet Beseiged." *Canadian Literature*, No. 39 (Winter 1969), pp. 94-96.

Atwood's poems make complicated things simple as the human animal has the same simple motivations as other animals. The imagery in the poems amounts to the poems themselves. The poems are "black" — the poet is besieged by her own inner perceptions.

D18 Helwig, David. Rev. of *The Animals in That Country. Queen's Quarterly*, 76 (Spring 1969), 161-62.

Highly disciplined poems, astringent and centred on certain obsessive images. Atwood is concerned with forms, especially form as limitation.

D19 Marshall, Tom. Rev. of *The Animals in That Country.*

Quarry, 18, No. 3 (Spring 1969), 53-54.

"Her poems are beautifully made and always intelligent, but a little inhuman." They express the search for ways in which to define oneself, but her poetic form seems "too tight."

D20 MacCallum, Hugh. Rev. of *The Animals in That Country. University of Toronto Quarterly*, 38 (July 1969), 343-44.

A continuation of Atwood's exploration of the principles of identity. The one constant feature is the experience of alienation.

D21 Van Duyn, Mona. "Seven Women." *Poetry*, 115 (March 1970), 432-33.

One of seven books reviewed. The reviewer sees the compulsive theme of the poems as distrust of the surface world, of man, even of the poem itself. But ambivalence is displayed when Atwood expresses fear of a time before man, of the subterranean. The love poems express the same ambivalence: she wishes to assimilate both the world and her lover, but fears love will consume them.

The Journals of Susanna Moodie

D22 Bowering, George. "To Share the World or Despair of It." *The Globe and Mail*, 2 May 1970, p. 16.

"An extended lyric held together by some sort of frame." Atwood's voice finds a sense of place — she wants to share the world rather than possess it.

D23 Barbour, Douglas. Rev. of *The Journals of Susanna Moodie. The Canadian Forum*, Sept. 1970, pp. 225-26.

"Firmly establishes Margaret Atwood as one of our most important young poets." Atwood's Moodie is a mythic creation of the poet's mind but it is this persona we hear, not the poet.

D24 Purdy, Al. "Atwood's Moodie." *Canadian Literature*,

No. 47 (Winter 1971), pp. 80-84.

Atwood writes of Moodie's life in Canada as an experience of a kind of alienation, or "as if Atwood were from Mars and Moodie an English woman of 'gentle' birth." The poems all have a consistent and distinctive tone. There is little humour other than satire and little love of anything. There is however a "hard cold look at the human condition." There are many qualities of fictional biography in the book — an undeniably historical personage takes over. Atwood's Moodie is conveyed to us as a real person, but contains a lot of Atwood. By the end "the Atwood-Moodie persona becomes some kind of primitive corn-mother-spirit that sits in a modern bus along St. Clair Avenue in Toronto, embodying the ghostly citified barbarism of this country."

D25 Skelton, Robin. Rev. of *The Journals of Susanna Moodie*. *The Malahat Review*, No. 17 (Jan. 1971), pp. 133-34.

Also reviews *Procedures for Underground*. Both exhibit Atwood's strong sense of place and ambiguous feelings about Canadian culture. The Canada she portrays is a state of mind — "She has constructed from local and inimitable materials a vision which crosses all territorial boundaries." She has demonstrated a capacity to create a coherent poetic system capable of continual development and enrichment.

D26 Doyle, Mike. "Made in Canada?" *Poetry*, 119 (1972), 360-62.

A "catch-all" review of thirty-five volumes of Canadian verse, which mentions *Journals of Susanna Moodie* and *Power Politics*, and notes the tension in both books is the outcome of a desire to merge and a terror of being consumed.

D27 Stephen, Sid. Rev. of *The Journals of Susanna Moodie*. *White Pelican*, 2, No. 2 (Spring 1972), 32-36.

The reviewer sees the poems as providing a sort of "self portrait" of the poet. The tension in the book results from the struggle between two powerful voices, that of the pioneer and of the poet. Duality is present in much of Atwood's work and in many ways it is the duality which is central to Canadian myth. The reality of the harsh Canadian landscape and of the violence and horror of life is hidden under the pretence of a genteel "civilization."

Procedures for Underground

D28 Barbour, Douglas. Rev. of *Procedures for Underground*. *The Dalhousie Review*, 50, No. 3 (Autumn 1970), 437, 439.

Continues in the same vein as earlier collections, but displays a variety of subjects and concerns. In these poems there is a more visible attempt to maintain contact with another human being. Every poem — "and there is not a bad poem among them" — offers further evidence of the strength and value of Atwood's vision and craft.

D29 Maddocks, Melvin. "That Consuming Hunger." *Time*, 26 Oct. 1970, p. 116 (p. 82 in Canadian edition).

"She convincingly suggests that the overcivilized and the barbarous are one." Yet hope and despair follow each other in a cycle like life itself, and lyricism keeps thrusting through.

D30 Gibbs, Jean. Rev. of *Procedures for Underground*. *The Fiddlehead*, No. 87 (Nov.-Dec. 1970), pp. 61-65.

The ordering of the poems in this book is important — the book must be treated as a poetic unit rather than as a collection of recent poetry. The poet's private world of the first third of the book is a world gone mad. There is childhood innocence but also there are nightmares and alienation. The world of myth and the ideal is rejected, and the second section reaffirms this by the recurring patterns of the imagery. In the third and final section the poet arrives at some sort of a reconciliation, which is only possible through love.

D31 Wainwright, Andy. "Margaret Atwood's Drowned World." *Saturday Night*, Dec. 1970, pp. 33, 35.

Shows a greater wisdom and an acceptance of her position beneath the surface in a drowned world. Her world is "one of stopped time, of startling reversals, of landscapes and objects that might belong in a Dali painting." The poet is able to commune more calmly with the male-lover, another figure in the Atwood vision. The fear and mistrust of her earlier work is replaced here by "a kind of primordial quiet."

D32 Harcourt, Joan. Rev. of *Procedures for Underground*. *Quarry*, 20, No. 1 (Winter 1971), 52-53.

The nightmare quality of the poems is created by the intermingling of sinister and bleak otherworldly images with calm statements of physical life. Atwood, with her strange landscapes and images of time, produces "pioneer poetry in a science-fiction setting."

D33 Hornyansky, Michael. Rev. of *Procedures for Underground*. *University of Toronto Quarterly*, 40 (Summer 1971), 378-79.

A brief comment in which the reviewer notes two qualities in the poetry—"an imagination that pinpoints items in a sharp everyday landscape, then moves through and under them into unknown country; and a tight rein, a sureness of control that makes every word count." Her vision is "so exactly matched by her craft that neither can be judged separately."

D34 Stevens, Peter. "Dark Mouth." *Canadian Literature*, No. 50 (Autumn 1971), pp. 91-92.

Despite surface similarities to *The Circle Game*, this book expresses a promise of "breaking out." Words may break the inhibitions that fetter us—there is a progression towards a fundamental belief in the prerogatives of poetry in a threatening world.

Power Politics

D35 Stevens, Peter. "Deep Freezing a Love's Continual Small Atrocities." *Globe Magazine*, 24 April 1971, p. 16.

A mixed review. The coldness and sparseness of the language give a sense of unconcern. There is technical skill but the poetic sequence is somewhat repetitious.

D36 Jonas, George. "Cool Sounds in a Minor Key." *Saturday Night*, May 1971, pp. 30-31.

Atwood explores our instincts for love and aggression. Like her earlier works, this should be read as a sequence. The book is controlled, incisive, intelligent, and free from self-pity.

D37 Harcourt, Joan. Rev. of *Power Politics*. *Quarry*, 20, No. 4 (1971), 70-73.

The poems, angry and sometimes savage, deal with the intrinsic separateness of two people bound together by a relationship. There is a pause in the self-defeating, bitter, and scientific analysis of love only when the poet has a moment of doubt, that perhaps the shadowy "you" of the poems is the necessary victim of the other's tortured consciousness.

D38 Bowering, George. "Getting Used to It." *Canadian Literature*, No. 52 (Spring 1972), pp. 91-92.

"A book of beautiful poetry"—"It hurts." These two views are expressed by the reviewer. It is a sequence of lyrics rather than a collection of individual poems. Love is seen as a political struggle: the destructive relationship is the only man-woman relationship there is.

D39 Hornyansky, Michael. Rev. of *Power Politics*. *University of Toronto Quarterly*, 41 (Summer 1972), 334-35.

A "rave" note: Atwood's poetry shifts to a sardonic account of a love relationship.

D40 Allen, Dick. "Shifts." *Poetry*, 120 (July 1972), 239-40.

"A top-flight sequence of poems about a love affair, written with intensity of feeling, careful craft and harrowing imagery."

D41 McCombs, Judith. " 'Power Politics': The Book and Its Cover." *Moving Out*, 3, No. 2 (1973), 54-69.

A long review article which finds the book about the head or mind's ability to see, to reason, and to control, as well as a critique of love and of human power games. In the poems the irrational as well as the rational, the creative as well as the corrupt, are seen imposing their own distortions upon whatever they touch. Atwood parallels feminist ideas; *Power Politics* is a psychological study of self and process. The poet's achievement in this book is "to witness and create and understand a complex human reality: her vision is generic, modern, human: ... a tougher sanity which incorporates the truth and lies of the insane."

D42 Larkin, Joan. "Soul Survivor." *Ms.*, May 1973, pp. 33-35.

Describes *Power Politics* as "a small group of extraordinary lyrics" which explore the theme of victimization while describing the disintegration of an affair. It is not the product of the Women's Movement. Atwood's cold voice demystifies love and exposes how human beings do violence to one another in its name.

D43 Vendler, Helen. "Do Women Have Distinctive Subjects, Roles and Styles?" *New York Times Book Review*, 12 Aug. 1973, pp. 6-7.

"A true sequence, a death-struggle between man and woman." A very favourable review, noting the plain, explicit poetry, the terse, bright, and sure images, and the vivacity of the fantasies.

D44 Pritchard, William H. Rev. of *Power Politics*. *Hudson Review*, 26 (Fall 1973), 586-87.

Much of the book is fragmentary and some of it is pretentious; but Atwood's poems, like Eliot's, "truly germinate in an 'obscure impulse' and have no choice but to work themselves out."

You Are Happy

D45 Fulford, Robert. "Atwood's New Poetry an Exhilarating Trip." *Toronto Star*, 14 Sept. 1974, p. H7.

A most favourable review. The book has a kind of wholeness, moving from discomfort and resentment through magic and mythology to a kind of resolution, ending with a kind of coming-to-terms with the world of man-woman relationships. It "drags the reader along on a kind of forced march through the intricate sensibility of one of our most remarkable writers."

D46 Pearson, Alan. "A Skeletal Novella in Plain Diction. A Bestiary under Iron Grey Skies." *The Globe and Mail*, 28 Sept. 1974, p. 33.

An unsympathetic review with idiosyncratic comments on some of the poems. Some are praised but "The Songs of the Transformed" section puzzles the writer and "Siren Song" appears to be totally misunderstood. Atwood's language is so plain as to be "puritanical in its abstractness" and she risks using poetry "as a receptacle for the disposal of emotional refuse."

D47 Sandler, Linda. "Gustafson and Others." *The Tamarack Review*, No. 64 (Nov. 1974), pp. 92-93.

A comment only: Atwood's vision is most convincing in the two mythical sections of the book.

D48 Lauder, Scott. "We Are Not So Happy." *The Canadian Forum*, Nov.-Dec. 1974, pp. 17-18.

In the first four sections, "the familiar Atwood persona moves on through the lurking horrors which litter the landscape." The poems of the final section are generally positive. Her images are precise and her conceits frequently ingenious. Her faults and strengths are as interesting for what they reveal of the poet as for what they suggest about her ability. Despite Atwood's productivity, the reviewer is still uncertain of her standing.

D49 Jacobs, Anne. Rev. of *You Are Happy*. *The Dalhousie Review*, 54, No. 4 (Winter 1974-75), 790-92.

The reviewer claims this book is "a refinement of Atwood's earlier books of poetry." The poet explores a wider range of emotions and records this exploration, ending with the idea of reunification, of wholeness regained.

D50 Matson, Marshall. "Seize the Day and the Axe." *Books in Canada*, Feb. 1975, p. 24.

Different from *Power Politics* in that the language is more direct and love is finally regained. There is a more human expression of sexual conflict "and a varying of sharp aphorism and slow meditation with occasional prose poems."

D51 Amabile, George. "Consciousness in Ambush." *CV/II*, 1, No. 1 (Spring 1975), 5-6.

An unfavourable review which finds the poems "defiantly even arrogantly bad." Despite too much intellectualism and obscurity mingled with prosiness, verbosity, and an abundance of clichés, there are some fine, subtle passages, startling lines, and admirable discoveries.

D52 Scott, Andrew. "The Poet As Sorceress." *Essays on Canadian Writing*, No. 3 (Fall 1975), pp. 60-62.

Finds that Atwood here continues to explore themes like the politics of sex and the search for mythic roots with which to define a national consciousness. The reviewer suggests that, with her grasp of the techniques of both poetry and prose, Atwood might be tempted towards some experimental fusions of the two genres.

D53 Trueblood, Valerie. "Conscience and Spirit." *American Poetry Review*, 6, No. 2 (March-April 1977), 19-20.

Like her other books, this exhibits a female sense of kinship with the natural world. People are unhungry consumers, killing animals and plundering the land, but the land survives patiently. "Her poetry has the steady unrelenting pace of conscience. But...Atwood makes blessings of her exquisite cold landscapes and of the animals...and of the struggle of some of her characters to be humane." For Atwood words are the only totems left—for her, to name a thing is to propitiate it. "First Prayer" is the best poem in the book and "one of the most accessible and the most pervaded by the mysticism Atwood everywhere resists and makes ironic."

Selected Poems

D54 Colombo, John Robert. "There Is a Delight in Exposing Little Secrets." *The Globe and Mail*, 24 April 1976, p. 39.

A positive review which outlines her literary work, prose as well as poetry. *Selected Poems* celebrates "the remarkable achievement of a writer still in her thirties."

D55 Fulford, Robert. "Atwood's Poems Show Strength and Anger." *Toronto Star*, 24 April 1976, p. H6.

A very favourable review: "A reading of the *Selected Poems* produces a fresh appreciation of her very individual talents.... Her new book is a seamless whole."

D56 Bobak, E. L. Rev. of *Selected Poems*. *The Dalhousie Review*, 56, No. 2 (Summer 1976), 404-06.

This selection shows how peculiarly sensitive Atwood is to contemporary psychological attitudes. Her "underground," the metaphor central to her work, is precisely suited to the "urban, secular and inward-looking individual in our society who finds it difficult to connect either with other people . . . or with his natural surroundings, but who continues trying." The selection tends to favour the poet's more recent work, but the imbalance is slight.

D57 Geddes, Gary. "Now You See It . . . Now You Don't; An Appreciation of Atwood and MacEwen, Two Grand Illusions." *Books in Canada*, July 1976, pp. 4-6.

Atwood is a poet who evokes a response from the reader rather than one who describes her own emotions. Her sincerity is in her technique. This book allows the reader an opportunity to analyse her craft which makes her poetry fascinating and effective.

D58 Sandler, Linda. "The Exorcisms of Atwood." *Saturday Night*, July-Aug. 1976, pp. 59-60.

A favourable review which comments on the different collections from which this selection is made.

D59 Woodcock, George. "Playing with Freezing Fire." *Canadian Literature*, No. 70 (Autumn 1976), pp. 84-86.

"Establishes [Atwood] as a major poet in the Canadian tradition." The book displays the unity of her work and the consistency of her themes, revealed also in her prose writings.

D60 Struthers, J. R. (Tim). "Margaret Atwood Has Surfaced: The Fist Is Now a Hand." *London Free Press*, 22 Jan. 1977, p. 31.

Sees in *Selected Poems* a cyclical development in Atwood's poetry, an ascent from the depths of harshness to the warmth and humanity evidenced in the latest poems. The reviewer sees a matching parallel development in technical brilliance.

D61 Forsche, Carolyn. Rev. of *Selected Poems. New York Times Book Review*, 21 May 1978, pp. 15, 42.

"A chronicle of Atwood's preoccupation with surfaces." In a disturbing way, the poet romanticizes the Canadian landscape, the wilderness, and madness too, the uncharted territory of the self. "She seems to suspect that perhaps the disembodied being locked within her flesh . . . knows something she does not know." The reviewer regrets that "her voice so often indulges itself, meandering through these narratives with a stridency and submission to intention that preclude any power of language itself to issue its mysteries."

D62 Wood, Gayle. "On Margaret Atwood's *Selected Poems*." *American Poetry Review*, 8, No. 5 (Sept.-Oct. 1979), 30-32.

A review which charts the changes in Atwood's feelings about love and hate as expressed in "The Circle Game" through to "You Are Happy." The poems are disturbing, shocking, and brilliant. Occasionally when Atwood is being academic and clever, she is also tiresome. The poems which "deserve reading" provide a portrait of contradictions.

Two-Headed Poems

D63 Mays, John Bentley. Rev. of *Two-Headed Poems. The Globe and Mail*, 16 Sept. 1978, p. 39.

A strange and ambiguous review, which sees the poems as providing a political commentary on the present state of the nation. "A hateful unity, a fatal separation; all the rest, cant or sentimental hogwash: are these the only options so earnest a patriot as Atwood can come up with?" The poet's technical skills are noted but they do not save her from a drastic over-simplification of the situation. "Though joined at the head, Atwood and Canada must be separated, or at least distinguished, lest the despair of the first kill all hope in the body of the second."

D64 Matson, Marshall. "Yoked By Violence." *Books in Canada*, Jan. 1979, pp. 12-13.

Finds these poems, which tell of life on the land and of the land itself, sadder and more wintry than those in "You Are Happy." The poems reflect no seasonal progress but rather a repetition of winter. The "two-headed poems" are specifically the political ones in the middle of the book; elsewhere the "two-mindedness" reflects the differences of man and woman.

D65   Barbour, Douglas. Rev. of *Two-Headed Poems*. *The Fiddlehead*, No. 121 (Spring 1979), pp. 139-42.

The poems speak of broader vistas and greater hope than Atwood has previously expressed. Though there is still present the terror and force of conflicting forces, whether it is in the man-woman relationship or in Canada's political situation, the reviewer finds the collection successful because of the "affirmations" which it articulates.

D66   Hornyansky, Michael. Rev. of *Two-Headed Poems*. *University of Toronto Quarterly*, 48 (Summer 1979), 341-42.

A short, favourable review which, though it finds Atwood's poems do not make exhilarating reading, feels this collection presents a more mellow tone.

D67   Rosenberg, Jerome. "'For of Such is the Kingdom...': Margaret Atwood's *Two-Headed Poems*." *Essays on Canadian Writing*, No. 16 (Fall-Winter 1979-80), pp. 130-39.

Although this collection seems to be a repetition of earlier books, in fact it demonstrates "a new philosophic strength and a continued mellowing of her traditionally caustic tone." *Two-Headed Poems* also indicates Atwood's variation on Julian Jaynes's *The Origin of Consciousness in the Breakdown of the Bicameral Mind*. "Atwood achieves with clarity a tone of compassion and of love that surpasses all her prior attempts to engage her readers in such emotions."

Up in a Tree

D68   Landsberg, Michele. "A Gentle Plot with Good Humored Charm in Red, White and Blue." *The Globe and Mail*, 1 April 1978, p. 36.

A very favourable review which praises both the illustrations and the text as well designed for pre-schoolers.

Index to Critics Listed
in the Bibliography

Leonard Cohen
An Annotated Bibliography

Bruce Whiteman

Introduction

Despite the high profile which Leonard Cohen has achieved for himself as a writer, it is perhaps fair to say that his work has yet to find its true critic. The first two books (*Let Us Compare Mythologies* and *The Spice-Box of Earth*) fit easily into a romantic tradition that stretches back to W. B. Yeats, through him to Baudelaire and the Symbolistes, and eventually to Poe. (It is surprising that no one has ever written about Cohen and Poe.) By Cohen's time, this approach to poetry, with its overlapping senses of magic and despair, and its manipulative use of language to create certain effects of ambiguity that Pound described as "blurry [and] messy," was, if not discredited, at least out of fashion among many of his contemporaries in Canada and the United States. It is not unlikely that Cohen was aware of the new American school; as a friend and student of Louis Dudek he would undoubtedly have come into contact at an early stage with Pound's poetry, and would likely have been informed as well of the work being done by Charles Olson and the other writers who looked to Pound for direction. Cohen, however, has never interested himself in this side of Modernism. His influences are Yeats, A. M. Klein, and certain other Jewish writings, and the figure he strikes is the Rimbaldian one. (Had Rimbaud gone on to publish after *Les Illuminations*, might it not have been such a book as *The Energy of Slaves*?) It is perhaps significant that it is the "late romantic" phase of Cohen's work which has had the greatest success with both reviewers and the public alike.

With *Flowers for Hitler* (1964), Cohen's work began to move in a new direction. More and more, beneath the continued surface involvement with established themes (Judaism, violence, sex, etc.) Cohen's main subject came to be the nature and role of the artist himself. This concern had played a major part in his first novel, but by all appearances it was Cohen's increasing success and popularity as a writer, and then as a pop singer, that served to bring this theme to the fore. The publication in 1968 of both his *Selected Poems* and his first recording marked an important point in this development. Cohen began increasingly to devote his time to composing and recording, and the fact that he chose to publish a volume of selected poems at this time suggests that he considered a certain phase in his career as a poet to have come to an end.

When *The Energy of Slaves* was published in 1972, six years had elapsed since Cohen's last book of poems (excepting the *Selected Poems*), but the voice bears very little resemblance to the one found in the previous volume (*Parasites of Heaven*). Yet critics who thought *The Energy of Slaves* unpoetic, uninteresting, unCohenesque even, had forgotten or chosen to ignore certain poems in *Flowers for Hitler*, and the "New Poems" included at the end of the selected volume. *Slaves* was almost universally dismissed as Cohen dumping his notebooks indiscriminately on a previously converted public, and most critics on the one hand rejected the work as prosaic and boring, and on the other hand read and accepted Cohen's confessions at face value ("I am no longer at my best practising / the craft of verse / I do better / in the cloakroom with Sara"). Missing in *Slaves* is any sense of the poet as magician; instead we find a view of art as basically fake, or worse, as betrayal (this is a view which *Beautiful Losers* ultimately espouses as well). The coldness of the poems (which, if they are songs at all, are so in the manner of Ives's "The Cage") suggests not so much that Cohen has lost his touch as that he will no longer have any part of the concerns and clichés of that tradition dubbed "black Romanticism."

The Energy of Slaves is the only book of Cohen's poetry that might be said to be post-modern. With the recent publication of *Death of a Lady's Man*, *Slaves* now appears to have been an even more logical step in Cohen's progress as a writer. Where he used to use women and violence as mirrors in which to observe the hidden processes of his own life, more and more he seems to be discarding these in favour of an object, an actual mirror. Women are still in the room, of course, but the poems evolve now from a more direct confrontation with an objective yet ambiguous image of the self. Disgust has been replaced by a more dispassionate (if nonetheless ironic and humorous) investigation of the paradoxes and unrealities of the artist's life.

* * *

The problems encountered in compiling this bibliography have been those which anyone would come up against in the process of dealing with the work of an established poet. Poets, particularly in the early stages of their careers, tend to publish in magazines which are frequently obscure and often short-lived. This type of material rarely shows up in periodical indexes, and sometimes it is not available in even the largest library collections. In Cohen's case, the problem of obscure publications is increased, because many of his books do not contain acknowledgements of previous publication. When they do appear (as in *The Spice-Box of Earth*) they are not complete. This leaves the bibliographer the task of searching through every likely little magazine, a tiring and ineffective manner of proceeding. Without unlimited funds it also leaves one dependent on a limited number of libraries, which, however large, cannot be expected to own copies of every Canadian literary magazine published in the last thirty years. With Cohen this difficulty is mitigated by the fact that, after the early 1960s, he seems to have submitted very little work for magazine publication.

Cohen's high profile as both poet and singer creates a second major problem for the bibliographer. Is one to include every squib and article ever published in the press, given the fact that many of them are of the gossip-page variety? On the one hand, such inclusiveness would clog a work which one presumes will be of use primarily to scholars and librarians; the latter are unlikely to be interested in the attention Cohen has received at the hands of *Seventeen* or *People*. On the other hand, this aspect of Cohen's public career is not wholly irrelevant to his work as a poet and novelist; it would be manifestly to distort "the Cohen phenomenon" if one were to ignore all the writing about him except for the articles which have been published in the academic and literary press. In any case, the bibliographer has to choose. He may be accused of lacking comprehensiveness (the worst charge in a bibliography court), but perhaps such sifting is the one chance he has to give a personal direction to what is otherwise the most impersonal document outside a volume of mathematical tables.

Where the poet's own work is concerned there is no choice: one has to find everything. If I have made omissions, it is neither by virtue of a lack of time spent thumbing through long rows of the PS section, nor through the fault of any of those who have lent a helping hand. I have been most helpfully received everywhere, but would be quick to point out that any holes in the fabric are no one's fault but my own.

Acknowledgements

My thanks are due to many: the librarians (all nameless) of the University of Toronto, Metropolitan Toronto Central Library, McGill, the National Library, and York University; to Mr. Ronald Finegold of the Jewish Public Library in Montreal, to Ms. Lily Miller of McClelland and Stewart who kindly loaned me a galley proof of *Death of a Lady's Man*, and to Stephen Scobie, who provided me with information on the elusive Manuel Cadafaz de Matos book.

Part I

Works by Leonard Cohen

A Books (Poetry and Novels) and Manuscripts

Poetry

A1 *Let Us Compare Mythologies.* McGill Poetry Series, No. 1. Toronto: Contact, 1956. 79 pp.
>   With drawings by Freda Guttman.
>   Toronto: McClelland and Stewart, 1966. 76 pp.

A2 *The Spice-Box of Earth.* Toronto: McClelland and Stewart, 1961. 99 pp.
>   With drawings by Frank Newfeld.
>   New York: Viking, 1965. 88 pp.
>   Toronto: McClelland and Stewart, 1965. 88 pp.
>   New York: Bantam, 1968. 83 pp.
>   *Lauluja.* Trans. Jarkko Laine. Helsinki: Otava, 1974. 79 pp.

A3 *Flowers for Hitler.* Toronto: McClelland and Stewart, 1964. 128 pp.
>   London: Jonathan Cape, 1973. 154 pp.

A4 *Parasites of Heaven.* Toronto: McClelland and Stewart, 1966. 80 pp.

A5 *Selected Poems 1956-1968.* New York: Viking, 1968. 245 pp.
>   Toronto: McClelland and Stewart, 1968. 245 pp.
>   London: Jonathan Cape, 1969. 245 pp.
>   *Poems 1956-1968.* London: Jonathan Cape, 1969. 94 pp.

An abridged version, including fifty-eight poems.
Blumen fur Hitler: Gedichte und Lieder 1965-1970. Trans. Anna von Gramer-Klett and Anja Hauptmann. Frankfurt am Main: Marz-Verlag, 1971. 229 pp.
>   Selections, in English, of poems and songs, with German translations on facing pages.
Gedichten. Trans. Remco Campert. Amsterdam: Bezige Bij [1971]. 60 pp.
Poetry of Leonard Cohen. Trans. Ruth Oren, Zvia Ginor Ben-Yosef, and Zviv Ekroni. Tel Aviv: Traklin, 1971. 43 pp.
Dikter Fran Ett Rum. Trans. Staffan Soderblom and Goran Tunstrum. Stockholm: Pan/Norstedt [1972]. 150 pp.
Poèmes et Chansons. Adaptés par Anne Rives et al. Paris: Union générale d'éditions, 1972. 299 pp.
>   Selections in English, of poems and songs, with French translations on facing pages.
Like a Bird on the Wire: Selected Poems. Introd. and trans. Yosi Gamzu. Tel Aviv: Reshafim Publishing House, 1973. 84 pp.
>   Includes illustrations by David Mashilin.
Poémas Escogidos. Trans. Jorge Ferrer-Vidal. Barcelona: Plaza and Janés, 1974. 188 pp.

A6 *The Energy of Slaves.* London: Jonathan Cape, 1972. 127 pp.
>   Toronto: McClelland and Stewart, 1972. 127 pp.
>   New York: Viking, 1973. 127 pp.
L'Energie des Esclaves. Trans. Dashiell Hedayat. Paris: Union générale d'éditions, 1974. 255 pp.
>   English text with French translations on facing pages.
Puckelryggens sanger. Trans. Staffan Soderblom. Stockholm: Pan-Norstedt, 1974. 129 pp.
Rakkauden orjat. Trans. Jarkko Laine. Helsinki: Otava, 1975. 128 pp.

A7 *Death of a Lady's Man.* Toronto: McClelland and Stewart, 1978. 216 pp.

Harmondsworth: Penguin, 1979. 216 pp.
New York: Viking, 1979. 216 pp.

Novels

A8   *The Favourite Game*. London: Secker and Warburg, 1963. 223 pp.
New York: Viking, 1963. 244 pp.
New York: Avon, 1965. 192 pp.
Alsklingsleken. Trans. Olov Jonason. Stockholm: Pan/Norstedts, 1970. 277 pp.
Introd. R. J. Smith. New Canadian Library, No. 73. Toronto: McClelland and Stewart, 1970. 223 pp.
London: Jonathan Cape, 1970. 244 pp.
The Favourite Game. Trans. Michel Doury. Paris: Christian Bourgois Editeur, 1971. 342 pp.
The Favourite Game. Trans. Michel Doury. Paris: Union générale d'éditions, 1971. 314 pp.
New York: Bantam, 1971. 248 pp.
Yndlingslegen. Trans. Arne Herlov Petersen. Copenhagen: Lindhardt and Ringhof [1971]. 187 pp.
Das Lieblingsspiel. Trans. Elisabeth Hannover-Druck. Frankfurt am Main: Marz-Verlag, 1972. 301 pp.
Yndlingsleken. Trans. Kaj Skagen. Oslo: Tiden [1972]. 210 pp.
El juego favorito. Trans. Blanca Tesa. Barcelona: Fundamentos, 1974. 264 pp.
Il gioco favorito. Trans. Anna Caiavatti and Francesca Valente. Milan: Casa di Longanesci, 1975. 283 pp.

A9   *Beautiful Losers*. New York: Viking, 1966. 243 pp.
Toronto: McClelland and Stewart, 1966. 243 pp.
New York: Bantam, 1967. 307 pp.
London: Jonathan Cape, 1970. 243 pp.
Nageki No Kabe. Trans. Osawa Masayoshi. Tokyo: Shûeisha [1970]. 322 pp.
Schone Verlierer. Trans. Elisabeth Hannover-Druck. Frankfurt am Main: Marz-Verlag, 1970. 279 pp.
Glorieuse Verliezers. Trans. John Vandenbergh. Amsterdam: Bezige Bij [1971]. 279 pp.

Skona Forlorare. Trans. Erik Sandin. Stockholm: Pan/Norstedt [1971]. 210 pp.
Belli e Perdenti. Trans. Bruno Oddera. Milan: Rizzoli Editore, 1972. 256 pp.
Dejlige Tabere. Trans. Arne Herlov Petersen. Copenhagen: Lindhardt and Ringhof [1972]. 202 pp.
Les Perdants Magnifiques. Trans. Michel Doury. Paris: Christian Bourgois Editeur, 1972. 323 pp.
Skjonne Tapere. Trans. Kaj Skagen. Oslo: Tiden [1972]. 261 pp.
Les perdants magnifiques. Trans. Michel Doury. Paris: Union générale d'éditions, 1973. 317 pp.
Los hermosos vencidos. Trans. Javier Sainz and Susan Hendry. Madrid: Fundamentos, 1975. 266 pp.

Manuscripts

A10   Thomas Fisher Rare Book Library
University of Toronto
Toronto, Ontario

Cohen's papers are contained in Manuscript Collection 122. The collection is comprised of 13 boxes of correspondence, working drafts, typescripts, clippings, memorabilia, and related items. Included are the drafts of *Let Us Compare Mythologies*, *The Spice-Box of Earth*, *The Favourite Game*, and *Flowers for Hitler*, as well as an unpublished novel entitled "The Ballet of Lepers," 3 plays written in collaboration with Irving Layton, and many unpublished poems and prose pieces. The material dates from mid-1950 to 1968. One box is restricted.

B6   "The Sparrows." *CIV/n*, No. 7 (1954), p. 14. Rpt. in *McGill Daily*, 44, No. 38 (7 Dec. 1954), 1. *LUCM*; *SP*.

B7   "To Be Mentioned at Funerals." *Forge* (1954), p. 51.

B8   "Les Vieux." *CIV/n*, No. 5 (1954), pp. 11-12. *LUCM*.

B9   "For Wilf and His House." *Forge* (Spring 1955), p. 26. Rpt. "Pour Wilf et les siens." Trans. Roch Carrier. In *Ellipse*, No. 2 (Winter 1970), pp. 40-43. *LUCM*; *SP*.

B10   "The Fly." *Forge* (March 1956), p. 43. *LUCM*; *SP*.

B11   "Had We Nothing to Prove." *Forge* (March 1956), p. 43. *LUCM*.

B12   " 'Perfumed pillows of night.' " *The Phoenix*, 1, No. 1 (April 1957), n. pag.
     The Phoenix was a literary magazine edited by Cohen during his stay in New York after graduating from McGill in 1956.

B13   "Poem for Marc Chagall." *The Phoenix*, 1, No. 1 (April 1957), n. pag. Rpt. in *The Tamarack Review*, No. 6 (Winter 1958), pp. 62-63. Rpt. "Du royaume de ciel." Trans. Richard Giguère and Joseph Bonenfant. In *Ellipse*, No. 2 (Winter 1970), pp. 42-45. *SBE* ("Out of the Land of Heaven"); *SP*.

B14   "Song." *The Phoenix*, 1, No. 1 (April 1957), n. pag. *SBE* ("Go by Brooks"); *SP*.

B15   " 'Whatever cities are brought down.' " *The Phoenix*, 1, No. 1 (April 1957), n. pag. *SBE* ("You All in White"); *SP*.

B16   " 'What shadows the pendulum sun.' " *The Phoenix*, 1, No. 1 (April 1957), n. pag.

B17   " 'You tell me that silence.' " *The Phoenix*, 1, No. 1

B   Contributions to Periodicals and Books (Poetry, Selected Anthology Contributions, Short Stories, Drama), Miscellaneous, and Audio Recordings

Note: When an item is reprinted in one of Cohen's books, this fact is noted in the entry through one of the following abbreviations:

Let Us Compare Mythologies .... LUCM
The Spice-Box of Earth .... SBE
Flowers for Hitler .... FH
Parasites of Heaven .... PH
Selected Poems 1956-1968 .... SP
The Energy of Slaves .... ES
Death of a Lady's Man .... DLM

Poetry

B1   "An Halloween Poem to Delight My Younger Friends." *CIV/n*, No. 4 (1953), p. 8. *LUCM* ("Halloween Poem").

B2   "Poème en Prose." *CIV/n*, No. 4 (1953), p. 13.

B3   "Folk Song." *CIV/n*, No. 5 (1954), p. 11. *LUCM*.

B4   "Just the Worst Time." *Forge* (1954), p. 52. *LUCM*.

B5   "Satan in Westmount." *CIV/n*, No. 5 (1954), p. 11. *LUCM*.

(April 1957), n. pag. Rpt. "Gift." In *The Tamarack Review*, No. 6 (Winter 1958), p. 63. *SBE*; *SP*.

B18   "Brighter than Our Sun." *Prism* [Sir George Williams College] (1958), p. 12. *SBE*.

B19   "A Cloud of Grasshoppers." *Prism* [Sir George Williams College] (1958), p. 24. Rpt. "Credo." Trans. Monique Grandmangin. In *Ellipse*, No. 2 (Winter 1970), pp. 50-53. *SBE*; *SP*.

B20   "The Cuckold's Song." In *Pan-ic: A Selection of Contemporary Canadian Poems*. Ed. Irving Layton. New York: n.p., 1958, n. pag. Rpt. "La chanson du cocu." Trans. Camille Cusson. In *Ellipse*, No. 1 (Fall 1969), pp. 78-81. *SBE*; *SP*.
    Published as Number Two of "Pan, 4 Issues of Poetry."

B21   "Master and Slave." In *Pan-ic: A Selection of Contemporary Canadian Poems*. Ed. Irving Layton. New York: n.p., 1958, n. pag. *SBE* ("Alone the Master and Slave Embrace").
    Published as Number Two of "Pan, 4 Issues of Poetry."

B22   "Bait." *The Tamarack Review*, No. 6 (Winter 1958), p. 64.

B23   "Before the Story." *The Tamarack Review*, No. 6 (Winter 1958), pp. 61-62. Rpt. in *Congress Bulletin* [Montreal: Canadian Jewish Congress], Oct. 1959, p. 3. *SBE*.

B24   "It Swings, Jocko." In *The McGill Chapbook*. Ed. Leslie L. Kaye. Toronto: Ryerson, 1959, n. pag. *SBE*; *SP*.

B25   "Now of Sleeping." In *The McGill Chapbook*. Ed. Leslie L. Kaye. Toronto: Ryerson, 1959, n. pag. *SBE*; *SP*.

B26   "Song to Make Me Still." In *The McGill Chapbook*. Ed. Leslie L. Kaye. Toronto: Ryerson, 1959, n. pag. *SBE*.

B27   "Dead Song." *Queen's Quarterly*, 66, No. 2 (Summer 1959), 303. *SBE*; *SP*.

B28   "The Flowers That I Left in the Ground." *Queen's Quarterly*, 66, No. 2 (Summer 1959), 302-03. *SBE*; *SP*.

B29   "An Orchard of Shore Trees." *Queen's Quarterly*, 66, No. 2 (Summer 1959), 305-06. *SBE*.

B30   "Twelve O'Clock Chant." *Queen's Quarterly*, 66, No. 2 (Summer 1959), 303-04. *SBE*.

B31   "As the Mist Leaves No Scar." *Congress Bulletin* [Montreal: Canadian Jewish Congress], Oct. 1959, p. 3. *SBE*; *SP*.

B32   "Isaiah." *Congress Bulletin* [Montreal: Canadian Jewish Congress], Oct. 1959, p. 3. *SBE* (revised); *SP*.

B33   "Messiah." *Congress Bulletin* [Montreal: Canadian Jewish Congress], Oct. 1959, p. 3.

B34   "A Kite Is a Victim." *Saturday Review*, 24 Oct. 1959, p. 54. *SBE*; *SP*.

B35   "Beneath My Hands." *Moment*, No. 1 (1960), pp. 14-15. *SBE*; *SP*.

B36   "It Is Late Afternoon." *Moment*, No. 1 (1960), p. 14. *SBE*.

B37   "Owning Everything." *Moment*, No. 1 (1960), p. 15. *SBE*; *SP*.

B38   "There Are Some Men." *Moment*, No. 1 (1960), p. 16. *SBE*; *SP*.

B39 "To a Teacher." *Moment*, No. 1 (1960), p. 16. *SBE*; *SP*.

B40 "Action." In *Poetry 62*. Ed. Eli Mandel and Jean-Guy Pilon. Toronto: Ryerson, 1961, p. 92. *PH*.

B41 "The First Vision." In *Poetry 62*. Ed. Eli Mandel and Jean-Guy Pilon. Toronto: Ryerson, 1961, p. 94.

B42 "For Marianne." In *Poetry 62*. Ed. Eli Mandel and Jean-Guy Pilon. Toronto: Ryerson, 1961, pp. 91-92. *FH*; *SP*.

B43 "My Mentors." In *Poetry 62*. Ed. Eli Mandel and Jean-Guy Pilon. Toronto: Ryerson, 1961, p. 91. *FH*; *SP*.

B44 "On the Sickness of My Love." In *Poetry 62*. Ed. Eli Mandel and Jean-Guy Pilon. Toronto: Ryerson, 1961, p. 93. *FH*; *SP*.

B45 "Prayer for Messiah." *Shaar Hashomayim Bulletin* [Montreal], March-April 1961, p. 7. *LUCM*; *SP*.

B46 "Another Cherry Brandy." *Evidence*, No. 3 (Fall 1961), p. 15.

B47 "Promise." *Evidence*, No. 3 (Fall 1961), p. 14. *FH*.

B48 "Song" ['I remember you, pretty frock']. *Exchange*, 1, No. 1 (Nov. 1961), 24.

B49 "Song" ['I almost went to bed']. *Maclean's*, 20 Oct. 1962, p. 33. *SBE*; *SP*.

B49a "All There Is To Know About Adolph Eichmann." *Catapult*, No. 1 (Winter-Spring 1964), p. [8]. *FH*; *SP*.

B49b "The Compleat Physician." *Catapult*, No. 2 (Summer 1964), p. [1].

B49c "For My Old Layton." *Catapult*, No. 2 (Summer 1964), p. [8]. *FH*; *SP*.

B50 "'Snow is falling.'" *Intercourse*, No. 2 (Spring 1966), p. 4. *PH*; *SP*.

B51 "Poem" ['This is for you']. *Mademoiselle*, Jan. 1967, p. 44. *SP* ("This Is for You").

B52 "Le génie." Trans. Camille Cusson. *Ellipse*, No. 1 (Fall 1969), pp. 74-77. *SBE* ("The Genius"); *SP*.

B53 "Autre nuit à l'observatoire." Trans. Michel Euvrard. *Ellipse*, No. 2 (Winter 1970), pp. 38-39. *FH* ("Another Night with Telescope"); *SP*.

B54 "Célébration." Trans. Monique Grandmangin. *Ellipse*, No. 2 (Winter 1970), pp. 54-55. *SBE* ("Celebration"); *SP*.

B55 "Complainte." Trans. Paul Allard. *Ellipse*, No. 2 (Winter 1970), pp. 44-47. *LUCM* ("Song"); *SP*.

B56 "Extraits du journal de mon grand-père." Trans. Jacques Baron-Rousseau. *Ellipse*, No. 2 (Winter 1970), pp. 58-69. *SBE* ("Lines from My Grandfather's Journal"); *SP*.

B57 "Letter." Trans. Camille Cusson. *Ellipse*, No. 2 (Winter 1970), pp. 56-57. *LUCM*; *SP*.

B58 "Sous mes doigts." Trans. Richard Giguère and Joseph Bonenfant. *Ellipse*, No. 2 (Winter 1970), pp. 46-49. *SBE* ("Beneath My Hands"); *SP*.

B59 "Across the Street." *Exile*, 5, Nos. 1 and 2 (1977), 54-55. *DLM*.

B60 "Another Room." *Exile*, 5, Nos. 1 and 2 (1977), 10-13. *DLM*.

B61 "Daily Commerce." *Exile*, 5, Nos. 1 and 2 (1977), 56-57. *DLM*.

B62 "Death to This Book." *Exile*, 5, Nos. 1 and 2 (1977), 8-9. *DLM*.

B63 "The Dream." *Exile*, 5, Nos. 1 and 2 (1977), 34-35. *DLM*.

B64 "The House." *Exile*, 5, Nos. 1 and 2 (1977), 16-17. *DLM*.

B65 "I Bury My Girl Friend." *Exile*, 5, Nos. 1 and 2 (1977), 26-27. *DLM*.

B66 "I Like the Way You Opposed Me." *Exile*, 5, Nos. 1 and 2 (1977), 38-39. *DLM*.

B67 "I Think I Like It Raw." *Exile*, 5, Nos. 1 and 2 (1977), 46-47. *DLM*.

B68 "It's Probably Spring." *Exile*, 5, Nos. 1 and 2 (1977), 20-21. Rpt. in *CV/II*, 3, No. 3 (Jan. 1978), 45. *DLM*.

B69 "It Would Be Cruel." *Exile*, 5, Nos. 1 and 2 (1977), 14-15. *DLM*.

B70 "Kefi." *Exile*, 5, Nos. 1 and 2 (1977), 24-25. *DLM*.

B71 "The Kwikanice Café." *Exile*, 5, Nos. 1 and 2 (1977), 36-37. *DLM*.

B72 "Letter from the Government-in-Exile." *Exile*, 5, Nos. 1 and 2 (1977), 5-7. *DLM*.

B73 "The Lover after All." *Exile*, 5, Nos. 1 and 2 (1977), 22-23. *DLM*.

B74 "My Life in Art." *Exile*, 5, Nos. 1 and 2 (1977), 58-60. *DLM*.

B75 "The Plan." *Exile*, 5, Nos. 1 and 2 (1977), 44-45. *DLM*.

B76 "The Promise." *Exile*, 5, Nos. 1 and 2 (1977), 28-29. *DLM*.

B77 "The Radio." *Exile*, 5, Nos. 1 and 2 (1977), 40-41. *DLM*.

B78 "This Marriage." *Exile*, 5, Nos. 1 and 2 (1977), 18-19. *DLM*.

B79 "Traditional Training and Service." *Exile*, 5, Nos. 1 and 2 (1977), 48-51. *DLM*.

B80 "The Unclean Start." *Exile*, 5, Nos. 1 and 2 (1977), 30-33. *DLM*.

B81 "The Visit." *Exile*, 5, Nos. 1 and 2 (1977), 42-43. *DLM*.

B82 "Which Is So Beautiful." *Exile*, 5, Nos. 1 and 2 (1977), 52-53. *DLM*.

B83 "I Knelt Beside a Stream." *CV/II*, 3, No. 3 (Jan. 1978), 45. Rpt. (with italic "commentary") in *Toronto Life*, Feb. 1978, p. 50. *DLM*.

B84 "The Night I Joined." *CV/II*, 3, No. 3 (Jan. 1978), 45. *DLM*.

B85 "The Absence of Monica." *Toronto Life*, Feb. 1978, p. 51. *DLM*.

B86 "Death of a Ladies' [sic] Man." *Toronto Life*, Feb. 1978, 50-51. *DLM*.

B87 "The Beetle." *Toronto Life*, May 1978, p. [68]. *DLM*.

Selected Anthology Contributions

B88 "As the Mist Leaves No Scar," "The Cuckold's Song," "Dead Song," "For Anne," "Go by Brooks," "If It Were Spring," "Inquiry into the Nature of Cruelty," "Last

Dance at the Four Penny," "Lines from My Grandfather's Journal," "On the Sickness of My Love," "Sing to Fish, Embrace the Beast," "Story," "You All in White." In *Poetry of Mid-Century 1940-60*. Ed. Milton Wilson. Toronto: McClelland and Stewart, 1964, pp. 184-95.

B89   "For E. J. P.," "I Have Not Lingered in European Monasteries," "The Sleeping Beauty," "Song," "You Have the Lovers." In *Canadian Anthology*. Ed. Carl F. Klinck and Reginald E. Watters. Toronto: Gage, 1966, pp. 485-88.

B90   "The Genius," "The Only Tourist in Havana Turns His Thoughts Homeward," "Out of the Land of Heaven." In *Modern Canadian Verse in English and French*. Ed. A. J. M. Smith. Toronto: Oxford Univ. Press, 1967, pp. 756-59.

B91   "Another Night with Telescope," "Credo," "What I'm Doing Here." In *The Penguin Book of Canadian Verse*. 2nd rev. ed. Ed. Ralph Gustafson. Harmondsworth: Penguin, 1967, pp. 275-77.

B92   "The Bus," "Disguises," "Elegy," "The Genius," "The Music Crept by Us," "Now of Sleeping," "Story," "Style," "Suzanne Takes You Down," "You Have the Lovers." In *20th-Century Poetry and Poetics*. Ed. Gary Geddes. Toronto: Oxford Univ. Press, 1969, pp. 326-37.

B93   "As the Mist Leaves No Scar," "For Anne," "For E. J. P.," "I Met a Woman Long Ago," "Lovers," "The Only Tourist in Havana Turns His Thoughts Homeward," "Out of the Land of Heaven," "Suzanne Takes You Down," "What I'm Doing Here." In *Five More Canadian Poets*. Ed. Eli Mandel. Toronto: Holt, Rinehart and Winston, 1970, pp. 75-84.

B94   "Gift," "God Is Alive," "I Have Not Lingered in

European Monasteries," "The Only Tourist in Havana Turns His Thoughts Homeward." In *The Oxford Anthology of Canadian Literature*. Ed. Robert Weaver and William Toye. Toronto: Oxford Univ. Press, 1973, pp. 71-75.

B95   "Claim Me, Blood, If You Have a Story," "For E. J. P.," "Letter," "Lovers," "One of the Nights I Didn't Kill Myself," "A Person Who Eats Meat," "The Reason I Write," "There Are No Traitors among Women," "This Is the Poem We Have Been Waiting For," "What I'm Doing Here," "You All in White," "You Have the Lovers," "You Know Where I Have Been." In *Canadian Poetry: The Modern Era*. Ed. John Newlove. Toronto: McClelland and Stewart, 1977, pp. 63-74.

Short Stories

B96   "Luggage Fire Sale." *Partisan Review*, 36, No. 1 (Winter 1961), 91-99. Rpt. in *Parallel*, 1, No. 2 (May-June 1966), 40-44.

B97   "Barbers and Lovers." *Ingluvin*, No. 2 (Jan.-March 1961), pp. 10-19.

B98   "Trade." *The Tamarack Review*, No. 20 (Summer 1961), pp. 59-65.

B99   "Tamara." *Cavalier Magazine*, Sept. [1962?], pp. 18, 58-61. *FG* (excerpt).

Drama

B100   "A Man Was Killed." *Canadian Theatre Review*, No. 14 (Spring 1977), pp. 53-68.
     A collaborative work written with Irving Layton originally in 1959. Preceded by commentary from Layton.

Miscellaneous

B101 Owen, Don, dir. *Ladies and Gentlemen ... Mr. Leonard Cohen.* National Film Board of Canada, 1965. 41 minutes, b&w.

A film written by Donald Brittain and Don Owen, directed by Don Owen. The most telling image in this fascinating film is that of Cohen, sitting in his bathtub (in a scene that was not used in the main body of the film, but is shown as Cohen watches the movie after its completion); he takes a pen and writes "Caveat Lector" on the tile wall. One would be hard put to image better the ambiguous relation between truth and con both in the film and in the Cohen phenomenon as a whole.

B102 *Angel.* National Film Board of Canada, 1966. 7 minutes, b&w.

A film by Cohen's friend, sculptor Derek May, with music by the poet played by the Stormy Clovers.

B103 *Poen.* National Film Board of Canada, 1967. 5 minutes, b&w.

A collaged film made by Tom Daly and based on Cohen's reading of a passage from *Beautiful Losers.*

B104 *Songs of Leonard Cohen.* New York: Amsco Music Publishing Company, 1969.

Arrangements of songs from B114 and B115, edited by Harvey Vinson. Reprints William Kloman's article on Cohen from the *New York Times* (C17).

B105 *Leonard Cohen.* Paris: Editions Musicales Pathé-Marconi, 1972.

Includes two articles, a biography, photographs, and songs with French versions.

B106 *Songs of Love and Hate.* New York: Amsco Publishing Company, 1972.

Arrangements for voice and guitar of the songs from the album of the same name (B114). Reprints Jack Hafferkamp's "Ladies and Gents, Leonard Cohen" from *Rolling Stone.*

B107 *Leonard Cohen Folk Guitar.* New York: Charles Hansen Educational Music and Books, n.d. [1973].

Arrangements of Cohen's songs for guitar by Jerry Snyder.

B108 *La Complainte du partisan.* Paris: Editions Musicales Pathé-Marconi, 1974.

"Anthologie 'spéciale guitare.'" Includes an interview, biography, photographs, songs, and French versions of the latter.

B109 *New Skin for the Old Ceremony.* New York: Amsco Music Publishing Company, 1975.

Arrangements for guitar and voice of the songs from the album of the same name (B116). Includes review articles reprinted from *Crawdaddy* (D144), *Rolling Stone* (D142), etc.

Audio Recordings

B110 *Six Montreal Poets.* Folkways, FL 9805, 1957. 2s. l.p., 33 1/3.

Readings by Cohen, A. J. M. Smith, Irving Layton, Louis Dudek, F. R. Scott, and A. M. Klein. Cohen reads eight poems from *Let Us Compare Mythologies.*

B111 *Canadian Poets 1.* CBC Publications, 1966. 4s., l.p., 33 1/3.

Readings by Cohen, Phyllis Webb, Earle Birney, John Newlove, Al Purdy, Irving Layton, George Bowering, and Gwendolyn MacEwen. Cohen reads seven poems from *The Spice-Box of Earth* and *Flowers for Hitler.*

B112 *Songs of Leonard Cohen.* Columbia, CL 2733 [1968]. 2s., l.p., 33 1/3.

Contents: "Suzanne," "Master Song," "Winter Lady," "The Stranger Song," "Sisters of Mercy," "So Long, Marianne," "Hey, That's No Way to Say Goodbye," "Stories of the Street," "Teachers," "One of Us Cannot Be Wrong."

B113 *Songs from a Room*. Columbia, CS 9767 [1969]. 2s., l.p., 33 1/3.

Contents: "Bird on the Wire," "Story of Isaac," "A Bunch of Lonesome Heroes," "The Partisan," "Seems So Long Ago, Nancy," "The Old Revolution," "The Butcher," "You Know Who I Am," "Lady Midnight," "Tonight Will Be Fine."

B114 *Songs of Love and Hate*. Columbia, C 30103 [1971]. 2s., l.p., 33 1/3.

Contents: "Avalanche," "Last Year's Man," "Dress Rehearsal Rag," "Diamonds in the Mine," "Love Calls You By Your Name," "Famous Blue Raincoat," "Sing Another Song, Boys," "Joan of Arc."

B115 *Live Songs*. Columbia, KC 31724 [1973]. 2s., l.p., 33 1/3.

Contents: "Minute Prologue," "Passing Thru," "You Know Who I Am," "Bird on the Wire," "Nancy," "Improvisation," "Story of Isaac," "Please Don't Pass Me By," "Tonight Will Be Fine," "Queen Victoria."

B116 *New Skin for the Old Ceremony*. Columbia, KC 33167, 1974. 2s., l.p., 33 1/3. (Also CBS 69087.)

Contents: "Is This What You Wanted," "Chelsea Hotel #2," "Lover Lover Lover," "Field Commander Cohen," "Why Don't You Try," "There Is a War," "A Singer Must Die," "I Tried to Leave You," "Who by Fire," "Take This Longing," "Leaving Greensleeves."

B117 *The Best of Leonard Cohen*. Columbia, ES 90334, 1975. 2s., l.p., 33 1/3.

Contents: "Suzanne," "Sisters of Mercy," "So Long, Marianne," "Lady Midnight," "The Partisan," "Bird on the Wire," "Hey, That's No Way to Say Goodbye," "Famous Blue Raincoat," "Last Year's Man," "Chelsea Hotel #2," "Who by Fire," "Take This Longing."

B118 *Death of a Ladies' Man*. Columbia, 90436, 1977. 2s., l.p., 33 1/3.

Contents: "True Love Leaves No Traces," "Iodine," "Paperthin Hotel," "Memories," "I Left a Woman Waiting," "Don't Go Home with Your Hard-on," "Fingerprints," "Death of a Ladies' Man."

Part II

Works on Leonard Cohen

C Books, Articles and Sections of Books, Theses and Dissertations, Interviews, and Awards and Honours

Books

C1 Ondaatje, Michael. *Leonard Cohen*. Canadian Writers, No. 5. New Canadian Library. Toronto: McClelland and Stewart, 1970. 64 pp.

A fine study of Cohen's work up to the "New Poems" included in *Selected Poems 1956-1968*. Ondaatje nicely distinguishes the mixture of egocentrism and sainthood that fuels Cohen's writing virtually from the start. The book, though brief, manages somehow to seem leisurely in its treatment of Cohen's books, and the analysis of *Beautiful Losers* is in particular highly valuable and revealing. A short bibliography is included.

C2 Vassal, Jacques. *Leonard Cohen*. Collection Rock & Folk. Paris: Editions Albin Michel, 1974. 189 pp.

This book contains songs (with French translations on facing pages), a biographical section, photographs, and a critical essay on Cohen's work.

C3 Matos, Manuel Cadafaz de. *Leonard Cohen: Redescoberta da Vida e uma Alegoria a Eros*. Lisbon: E (co) logiar a Terra, 1975. 286 pp.

Matos investigates the relationship in Cohen's work of love and a renewed life. Through Eros, says Cohen, rather than through religion, lies the path of the resurrection of the spiritual life of man.

C4 Gnarowski, Michael, ed. *Leonard Cohen: The Artist and His Critics*. Critical Views on Canadian Writers. Toronto: McGraw-Hill Ryerson, 1976. 169 pp. (Hereafter abbreviated as *LC*.)

A collection of twenty-four critical articles on Cohen published between 1956 and 1974, this book is an important source of Cohen criticism. The articles in this book are annotated individually throughout Section C of this bibliography.

Contributors include: Douglas Barbour (C50, D100), Lawrence M. Bensky (D61), George Bowering (D86), David Bromige (D13), Frank Davey (C30), Sandra Djwa (C12), Allan Donaldson (D4), Dennis Duffy (D68), Richard Goldstein (C15), Michael Harris (C84), Ed Kleiman (D36), Susan Lumsden (C85), Patricia A. Morley (C42), Desmond Pacey (C13), Juan Rodriguez (C27), Stephen Scobie (C34), Burr Snider, John Wain (D56), Milton Wilson (D5, D45), George Woodcock (C33).

C5 Scobie, Stephen. *Leonard Cohen*. Vancouver: Douglas and McIntyre, 1978. 192 pp.

This monograph provides a basically thematic approach to all of Cohen's work, including the songs but excluding the final published version of *Death of a Lady's Man*. Within the limits of this kind of criticism, Scobie's book is well-written, informative, and contains few points of interpretation or methodology that one would hasten to take issue with. There is no index, but the bibliography is extensive and useful.

Articles and Sections of Books

C6 Purdy, A.W. "Leonard Cohen." *Moment*, No. 1 (1960), p. 13.

This is a brief introduction to the five poems

which follow. Purdy remonstrates with Cohen for his stated lack of a political stance. Nevertheless he thinks the poems are "brilliant virtuoso pieces."

C7   Pacey, Desmond. *Creative Writing in Canada*. 2nd. ed. Toronto: Ryerson, 1961, pp. 247-48.

Cohen is "easily the most promising" in a group of young poets that includes Al Purdy, Peter Miller, George Ellenbogan, and Phyllis Webb. Pacey makes the rather surprising comment (given the nature of Cohen's work at the time) that "the most hopeful feature of his poetry is its straight-forwardness."

C8   Beattie, Munro. "Poetry: 1950-1960." In *Literary History of Canada: Canadian Literature in English*. Gen. ed. and introd. Carl F. Klinck. Toronto: Univ. of Toronto Press, 1965, pp. 814-16. 2nd. ed. Toronto: Univ. of Toronto Press, 1976, Vol. III, 242-43, 312.

Beattie comments on the Jewish Montreal influence on Cohen's work. The poet is spoken of as one "who has not entirely organized his talent." The third volume of the second edition contains brief comments by William H. New (on the two novels) and George Woodcock (on the poetry).

C9   Purdy, A. W. "Leonard Cohen: A Personal Look." *Canadian Literature*, No. 23 (Winter 1965), pp. 7-16.

An interesting essay in which Purdy pays homage to Cohen's great craft and the fine quality of the love poems. Admiration is qualified only by Purdy's feeling that Cohen "must simply be living in another time dimension than my own," for the poems are nostalgic and dream-like. The article concludes with a review of *Flowers for Hitler*, which Purdy finds unsatisfying, too much a book of "playful exercises."

C10   Ruddy, Jon. "Is the World (or Anybody) Ready for Leonard Cohen?" *Maclean's*, 1 Oct. 1966, pp. 18-19, 33-34.

This article embodies an interview, and much typical Cohenesque talk is heard. Biographical material and photographs are included.

C11   Sutherland, Ronald. "Twin Solitudes." *Canadian Literature*, No. 31 (Winter 1967), pp. 5-24. Rpt. in *Second Image: Comparative Studies in Québec/Canadian Literature*. Don Mills: new press, 1971, pp. 1-27.

Beautiful Losers is part of the "Search for Vital Truth," in company with Godbout (*"Beautiful Losers* could almost be a sequel to Godbout's *La couteau sur la table"*) and Aquin.

C12   Djwa, Sandra. "Leonard Cohen: Black Romantic." *Canadian Literature*, No. 34 (Autumn 1967), pp. 32-42. Rpt. in *Poets and Critics: Essays from* Canadian Literature *1966-1974*. Ed. George Woodcock. Toronto: Oxford Univ. Press, 1974, pp. 179-90. Rpt. trans. Jacques Baron-Rousseau. In *Ellipse*, No. 2 (Winter 1970), pp. 70-82. *LC*.

This essay sees Cohen as the inheritor of a tradition of "black Romanticism" that stretches from Baudelaire to Genet. The author finds this body of literature too removed from the ordinary to be fully convincing, particularly in its substitution of a "hierarchy of art" for the values of human experience.

C13   Pacey, Desmond. "The Phenomenon of Leonard Cohen." *Canadian Literature*, No. 34 (Autumn 1967), pp. 5-23. Rpt. in *Essays in Canadian Criticism 1938-1968*. Toronto: Ryerson, 1969, pp. 241-67. *LC*.

The approach of this interesting essay is basically thematic. Pacey observes in *Beautiful Losers* ("the most intricate, erudite, and fascinating Canadian novel ever written") the close relation between sex and religion, and the frequent links which Cohen forges between polar opposites. The novel's technique is basically symbolist, "weaving recurrent themes, symbols, and images."

C14   Arn, Robert. "Obscenity and Pornography." *The*

Cambridge Review, 2 Dec. 1967, pp. 60-63.

Musings prompted by the trial in England on charges of obscenity of Hubert Selby's *Last Exit to Brooklyn*. Terry Southern and Cohen find obscene language an antidote for the "deception of rational discourse."

C15 Goldstein, Richard. "Beautiful Creep." *The Village Voice*, 28 Dec. 1967, pp. 18, 20, 27. *LC*.

A rather pointless piece of journalism that includes such details as that Cohen "pisses in quick panting spurts."

C16 Fiedler, Leslie A. *The Return of the Vanishing American*. New York: Stein and Day, 1968, pp. 155-57, 164-67, 175-77.

Fiedler has long been an admirer of Cohen (he was one of the readers of *Beautiful Losers* when it was originally submitted to Viking). This book contains scattered commentary on *Beautiful Losers*.

C17 Kloman, William. "'I've Been on the Outlaw Scene Since 15.'" *New York Times*, 28 Jan. 1968, pp. D21-22.

A slick article that, for example, quotes the description of a saint from *Beautiful Losers* and comments: "A saint, then, is literally someone who is groovy. *With* it."

C18 Brown, Sharon. "King of the Now People." *Saturday Night*, Feb. 1968, p. 41.

Cohen is very popular with the "in-group," and only Dylan can measure up to his brilliance.

C19 Boyers, Robert. "Attitudes toward Sex in American 'High Culture.'" *Annals of the American Academy of Political and Social Science*, No. 376 (March 1968), pp. 36-52.

This study explores the idea that sex is the key to what is most authentic in life, as it can be found in Mailer, Kesey, Barth, and Cohen (*Beautiful Losers*).

Sex for Cohen is a means of self-transcendence, it makes man receptive to the "possibility of harmony among things."

C20 New, William H. "A Wellspring of Magma: Modern Canadian Writing." *Twentieth Century Literature*, 14, No. 3 (Oct. 1968), 123-32.

This article includes brief comments on Cohen, in particular how one finds a new kind of logic in his work, an approach akin to the work of Marie-Claire Blais and Réjean Ducharme.

C21 Haite, Barbara, and Carolyn Riley, eds. *Contemporary Authors*. Detroit: Gale, 1969, pp. 21-22, 113-14.

A brief biography and description of Cohen's work, drawing largely on sources such as D75 and D88.

C22 Moritz, Charles, ed. *Current Biography Yearbook 1969*. New York: Wilson, 1969, pp. 98-100.

General and biographical material, some of which is inaccurate (*Let Us Compare Mythologies*, for example, is given as published by McClelland and Stewart).

C23 Murphy, Karen, and Ronald Gross. "'All You Need Is Love. Love Is All You Need.' So Writes a Rock Poet. But Is That Poetry?" *New York Times Magazine*, 13 April 1969, pp. 36-38, 40, 42, 45, 48, 50.

This article contains a few remarks on Cohen as a rock-poet, and reprints the recorded version of "Suzanne" (p. 50).

C24 Batten, Jack. "Leonard Cohen: The Poet as Hero 1." *Saturday Night*, June 1969, pp. 23-26.

A general article on Cohen's songs, his fame, and his pop sainthood.

C25 Owen, Don. "Leonard Cohen: The Poet as Hero 3." *Saturday Night*, June 1969, pp. 31-32.

Personal reminiscences by the maker of *Ladies and Gentlemen ... Mr. Leonard Cohen* (B101).

C26   Mothner, Ira. "Leonard Cohen: Songs Sacred and Profane." *Look*, 10 June 1969, pp. 92-96.

A mostly biographical article, with photographs by Michael A. Vaccaro.

C27   Rodriguez, Juan. "Poet's Progress — To Sainthood and Back." *Montreal Star*, 21 June 1969, pp. 3-4. *LC*.

A retrosepctive look at Cohen's books and songs on the occasion of the recent release of *Songs from a Room*.

C28   Dudek, Louis. "Poetry in English." *Canadian Literature*, No. 41 (Summer 1969), pp. 111-20. Rpt. in *The Sixties: Canadian Writers and Writing of the Decade*. Ed. George Woodcock. Vancouver: Univ. of British Columbia Publications Centre, 1969, pp. 111-20. Rpt. "Poetry of the Sixties." In *Selected Essays and Criticism*. Ottawa: Tecumseh, 1978, pp. 269-81.

The dissatisfaction of Dudek (see D16) here finds full flower. In his look at the poetry of English Canada in the 1960s, Dudek excoriates Cohen mercilessly. He is "Canada's Messianic hippie," and his career as a singer is the "Quod Erat Demonstrandum of absurdity." Cohen "has wasted his talents in wilful excess; he is a sad and tragic figure, not the triumphant success one would imagine."

C29   New, W. H. "The Novel in English." *Canadian Literature*, No. 41 (Summer 1969), pp. 121-25. Rpt. in *The Sixties: Canadian Writers and Writing of the Decade*. Ed. George Woodcock. Vancouver: Univ. of British Columbia Publications Centre, 1969, pp. 121-25.

New's retrospective includes a brief look at *Beautiful Losers*.

C30   Davey, Frank. "Leonard Cohen and Bob Dylan: Poetry and the Popular Song." *Alphabet*, No. 17 (Dec. 1969), pp. 12-29. *LC*.

Both Cohen and Dylan have elevated the pop song to a work of art; their songs "project a self rather than a mirror image of the culture." Cohen presents a world of desperation whose salvation is to be found through love.

C31   Fiedler, Leslie A. "Cross the Border, Close the Gap." *Playboy*, Dec. 1969, pp. 151, 230, 252-54, 256-58. Rpt. in *The Collected Essays of Leslie Fiedler*. New York: Stein and Day, 1971, Vol. II, pp. 461-85.

Beautiful Losers fits into a developing tradition of the pop or anti-novel that uses such frames as the western, science-fiction, and pornography.

C32   Jones, D. G. *Butterfly on Rock: A Study of Themes and Images in Canadian Literature*. Toronto: Univ. of Toronto Press, 1970, pp. 77-82 et passim.

As well as commentary scattered throughout the text, there is a section on *Beautiful Losers* in the chapter "The Dictatorship of Mind." Jones sees the novel as a cry for irrationality and freedom in a world dominated by the masculine logos. Cohen seeks "a larger and more mysterious order ... in which [mind] must speak through the flesh or with the flesh, and not against it."

C33   Woodcock, George. "The Song of the Sirens." In *Odysseus Ever Returning*. Toronto: McClelland and Stewart, 1970, pp. 93-110. *LC*.

Woodcock sees Cohen as basically a conservative poet working in derivative and structured forms. With the exception of *Flowers for Hitler* ("Cohen's only real attempt to emerge from his romantic inner self and face the actual modern world") the poet's writing is solipsistic and passionless. Woodcock's unhappiness with Cohen's work is a long-standing one, but he seems to have no sense of the ironies of the poet's career, ironies of which Cohen is himself aware, and which come (in *The Energy of Slaves* and *Death of a Lady's Man*) to play an important part in the work itself.

C34 Scobie, Stephen. "Magic, Not Magicians: 'Beautiful Losers' and 'Story of O.'" *Canadian Literature*, No. 45 (Summer 1970), pp. 56-60. *LC*.

Beautiful Losers deals with "the deliberate attempt to destroy one's own individuality" through sex as an answer to the predicament of life.

C35 Harrison, Dick. "The American Adam and the Canadian Christ." *Twentieth Century Literature*, 16, No. 3 (July 1970), 161-67.

While American fiction often contains a figure representing Adam, Canadian novels are dominated by a redemptive figure who approximates Christ. This idea is applied somewhat superficially to *Beautiful Losers*.

C36 Mandel, Eli. "Modern Canadian Poetry." *Twentieth Century Literature*, 16, No. 3 (July 1970), 175-83.

Modernism coalesces around the "longing for history . . . for out of that longing emerge finally both the hallucinated terror and the diminished self of contemporary art." Cohen enters this discussion somewhat peripherally, but *Beautiful Losers* is called "the most striking manifestation of the return of the primitive as hallucination."

C37 Bem, Jeanne. "Avec Leonard Cohen poète canadien: "Magic Is Alive." *Les Langues Modernes*, 65, Nos. 5-6 (1971), 514-21.

Basically a descriptive article. Cohen develops "une poétique des rapports," i.e., he is always speaking to someone, a "you," and a "them," as in "The Master Song," for example.

C38 Fiedler, Leslie A. "Some Notes on the Jewish Novel in English or Looking Backward from Exile." In *The Collected Essays of Leslie Fiedler*. New York: Stein and

Day, 1971, Vol. I, pp. 156-63.

Unlike Richler, Cohen is a post-modernist working in a world where the distinctions between high and low art, between mass culture and *belles-lettres* have fallen away. Cohen has discovered a language "not gross and elegant by turns, but gross and elegant at once."

C39 Talbot, Norman. "The Stranger Songs: Pop Lyrics of the 60's." *Poetry Australia*, No. 38 (1971), pp. 52-60.

Many popular songs, Cohen's preeminent among them, have lyrics which are superior to much of the poetry published today.

C40 Morley, Patricia A. *The Immoral Moralists: Hugh MacLennan and Leonard Cohen*. Toronto: Clarke, Irwin, 1972. 144 pp.

Despite the equal billing given the two novelists in the title, this book contains much more commentary on MacLennan than on Cohen (five chapters against two). In fact, Cohen seems almost like a guest invited at the last minute to make a foursome at some game. The criticism of *The Favourite Game* and *Beautiful Losers* (one chapter on each) is nevertheless eminently competent and dispels any suspicions that the book's title may have raised in a prospective reader.

Morley sees Cohen as an iconoclast, but a moralist all the same. The messages of *Beautiful Losers* in particular are quasi-religious admonitions for us to return to the world of the body. The excesses of his style (parody, scatology, pornography, hyperbole) are an attempt to break down puritanical resistance, the first step in the reintegration process. Cohen's fiction, then, "poses the artist in his traditional role as teacher, prophet, seer . . . ."

C41 de Venster, Dagmar. "Leonard Cohen's Women." In *Mother Was Not a Person*. Ed. Margret Andersen. Montreal: Content and Black Rose, 1972, pp. 96-97.

This short piece takes Cohen to task for his

portrayal of women. "Do you have an orifice and a pair of breasts? These are the essential if not sole requirements for a female character in a Leonard Cohen novel." Unimaginative as it may be, this article states a point of view very close to that of George Woodcock in C33.

C42 Morley, Patricia A. "'The Knowledge of Stranger-hood': 'The Monuments Were *Made* of Worms.'" *Journal of Canadian Fiction*, 1, No. 3 (Summer 1972), 56-60. *LC*.

The Favourite Game deals with two themes: the distance of the artist from other people, and the fact of decay in human life. This essay was delivered at a conference at Bishop's University on March 28, 1972, and subsequently revised somewhat and incorporated into C40.

C43 Buitenhuis, Peter. "Two Solitudes Revisited: Hugh MacLennan and Leonard Cohen." *The Literary Half-Yearly*, 13, No. 2 (July 1972), 19-32.

Both novelists are interested in history, but where MacLennan writes it, Cohen deals with it. The comparison made here is a rather odd one, which in the end fails to convince. The essay trails off into moralisms about violence, the Jews, and the blacks.

C44 Cavanagh, David. "Magic in Leonard Cohen's The Favourite Game and Beautiful Loser's" [sic]. *Alive*, No. 28 (1973), pp. 19-22.

Magic in *The Favourite Game* is the ability to make things happen through the power of will; this creates a distance between people. In *Beautiful Losers*, by contrast, F. admonishes the narrator to be magic, to be part of the process rather than outside it.

C45 D[avey]., F[rank]. "Leonard Cohen." *Supplement to the Oxford Companion to Canadian History and Literature*. Ed. William Toye. Toronto: Oxford Univ. Press, 1973, p. 45.

Outlines Cohen's career and publications, with general remarks on his work.

C46 Wetherell, Nancy B. "Leonard Cohen: Poems Set to Music." *English Journal*, 62, No. 4 (April 1973), 551-55.

An article on using Cohen in the high school English class.

C47 Macri, F. M. "*Beautiful Losers* and the Canadian Experience." *Journal of Commonwealth Literature*, 8, No. 1 (June 1973), 88-96.

A somewhat turgid essay that uses *Beautiful Losers* to demonstrate a view of Canadian literature as embodying a radical split in consciousness. The four main characters are schematized to represent two opposing poles, and the novel is seen as an attempt to reintegrate these opposites (flesh/spirit etc.).

C48 Davey, Frank. "Leonard Cohen." In *From There to Here: A Guide to English-Canadian Literature Since 1960*. Our Nature — Our Voices. Vol. II. Erin, Ont.: Porcépic, 1974, pp. 68-73.

Davey sees Cohen as basically a late romantic, content to write traditionally structured verse that more or less ignores most of the developments in North American poetry since 1945. Only *Beautiful Losers* and *The Energy of Slaves* are at all experimental, and Davey's lack of generosity regarding the former is odd in light of his stated bias for writing that embodies a Heraclitean world view. A bibliography is included.

C49 Hutcheon, Linda. "Beautiful Losers: All the Polarities." *Canadian Literature*, No. 59 (Winter 1974), pp. 42-56. Rpt. in *The Canadian Novel in the Twentieth Century: Essays from* Canadian Literature. New Canadian Library, No. 115. Ed. George Woodcock. Toronto: McClelland and Stewart, 1975, pp. 298-311.

A strangely unfocussed essay that attempts to

explore a cluster of dichotomies in *Beautiful Losers*, and finds them ultimately unresolved.

C50   Barbour, Douglas. " 'Down With History': Some Notes towards an Understanding of *Beautiful Losers*." *Open Letter*, 2nd ser., No. 8 (Summer 1974), 48-60. *LC*.

F. attacks history as a limit and a structure; it must be broken out of in order to live in the present, "on the edge." Cohen shows the gradual disintegration of reason and time as the narrator learns to reside in a world of process.

C51   Scobie, Stephen. "Scenes from the Lives of the Saints: A Hagiology of Canadian Literature." *Lakehead University Review*, 7, No. 1 (Summer 1974), 3-20.

This fine study demonstrates how there have been a few figures in our literature who have wanted to break down the walls of the garrison and let the wilderness in. These characters Scobie calls saints, and they are connected with sex, madness, and death. It is such a state of sainthood that the narrator in *Beautiful Losers* attains, through F.'s "classroom of hysteria."

C52   Lavigne, Yves. "Leonard Cohen: At the Mercy of Time." *Canadian Review*, 2, No. 2 (July-Aug. 1975), 36-37.

A lacklustre piece that finds *The Energy of Slaves* a disappointment, and includes such sentences as: "[Cohen] believes that inhibitions inhibit creativity, thinking, and experience."

C53   Almansi, G. "An Erotic Writer: The 'Minestrone' Novels of Leonard Cohen." *London Magazine*, NS, 15, No. 3 (Aug.-Sept. 1975), 20-39.

The term "minestrone novel" is proposed for such books as those of Cohen and Henry Miller. Because there has been no tradition of serious erotic writing, these novelists "are tempted to throw everything on the page, pell-mell, hoping that the miracle of artistic creation, the poetic catalysis, will take place, *motu proprio*, within the cauldron holding the *minestrone* ingredients."

C54   Macdonald, Ruth. "Leonard Cohen, A Bibliography, 1956-1973." *Bulletin of Bibliography*, 31, No. 3 (July-Sept. 1974), 107-10.

This unannotated bibliography lists all of Cohen's work (excluding separately published poems) and most of the writing about him up to 1973. A few inaccuracies have crept into the text, but generally this is a most useful summary list, and one to which the present writer owes a debt of gratitude.

C55   Jones, D. G. "In Search of America." *Boundary 2*, 3, No. 1 (Fall 1974), 227-46.

One page or so of this essay is devoted to a discussion of *Beautiful Losers* in terms of the Manichaean dualism of mind and matter that Jones sees operative in Western culture. Cohen underlines our "sado-masochistic contempt for the flesh," at the same time affirming both the spirit and the physical world.

C56   Monkman, Leslie. "*Beautiful Losers*: Mohawk Myth and Jesuit Legend." *Journal of Canadian Fiction*, 3, No. 3 (1974), 57-59.

Explores Cohen's use of Edoward Lecompti's *Une Vierge Iroquoise Catherine Tekakwitha: Le lis des bords de la Mohawk et du St-Laurent*, particularly in relation to the myth of Oscotarich.

C57   Garebian, Keith. "Desire As Art: Leonard Cohen's *The Favourite Game*." *Le Chien d'Or/The Golden Dog*, No. 4 (Nov. 1974), pp. 29-34.

This paper (which smacks somewhat of the graduate school essay) attempts to show how Cohen deals with the artist "self-consciously [creating] his own myth." Garebian does not really come to grips with the complex relations between art and life, truth and falseness in *The Favourite Game*.

C58   Slonim, Leon. "Exoticism in Modern Canadian Poetry." *Essays on Canadian Writing*, No. 1 (Winter 1974), pp. 21-26.

Within the general drabness ("in the widest sense of the word") of Canadian poetry there is a minor tradition of the exotic, to which Cohen's early work made a contribution.

C59   Houle, Ghislaine, and Jacques Lafontaine. *Ecrivains Québécois de Nouvelle Culture*. Montréal: Ministère des Affaires Culturelles du Gouvernment du Québec, 1975, pp. 21-32.

An unannotated bibliography of works by and about Cohen, based in large part on C54.

C60   Northey, Margot. "Toward the Mystical Grotesque: *Beautiful Losers*." In *The Haunted Wilderness: The Gothic and Grotesque in Canadian Fiction*. Toronto: Univ. of Toronto Press, 1976, pp. 101-07.

Cohen's efforts in *Beautiful Losers* to lead us "out of the bondage of our dualistic, rationalistic attitudes" fail, in part because he does not come to grips with the problem of evil. What remains is merely grotesqueries of "sado-masochistic extremism."

C61   Lee, Dennis. *Savage Fields: An Essay in Literature and Cosmology*. Toronto: House of Anansi, 1977, pp. 63-125.

This book contains what is undoubtedly the most thought-provoking commentary on *Beautiful Losers* published so far. Lee begins by outlining the basic conflict between earth and world that he sees as pervading modern existence, and then proceeds to demonstrate how this cosmological and ontological structure operates in two Canadian works, Michael Ondaatje's *The Collected Works of Billy the Kid* and *Beautiful Losers*.

Regardless of whether or not one is willing to accept Lee's cosmology (based in large part on the philosophy of Heidegger and the political criticism of George Grant), his interpretation of Cohen's novel is extremely perceptive. He sees Catherine Tekakwitha as instancing a fall from "carnal participation in unified being," in this case a fall that has since more or less defined the course of Canadian history. F., in this view, becomes a psychopomp who attempts to lead the narrator out of "the domination of History" into a new and integrated planet (this is the meaning of F.'s advice to "go down on a saint"). F.'s attempt and failure to accomplish this soteriological mission thus constitutes the greater part of the novel. Lee sees Book 3 as an effort to show the narrator in an enlightened state, but he finds the coda unconvincing and cheap, "a copout." The novel, he feels, does not present a way out; rather it affirms the endless "nervegrinding oscillation" between the fallen world (Lee's "savage field") and a state of cosmic integration (the "Isis continuum").

C62   Mandel, Eli. "Cohen's Life As a Slave." In *Another Time*. Erin, Ont.: Porcépic, 1977, pp. 124-36.

A fine and stimulating essay that places Cohen in a post-modern tradition that most critics are unwilling to grant him. Mandel probes the relation in Cohen's work between art and the audience, and he sees *The Energy of Slaves* as a logical progression in Cohen's oeuvre. The book "remains valuable because it elucidates with the precision we used to call poetry the failure of contemporary poetry."

C63   Moss, John. "Forgive Us Our Saints: The Sacred and the Mundane in *Beautiful Losers*." In *Sex and Violence in the Canadian Novel: The Ancestral Present*. Toronto: McClelland and Stewart, 1977, pp. 169-84.

Essentially an attack on the novel as an artificial, not a lived, experience. Moss blasts Cohen for his romanticism, his obscenity, his humdrum philosophy (the novel is said to lead into "the private reality of a self-interested prophet, not to the possession of a new terrain for his community of readers — whatever the intent may be"). Only Catherine Tekakwitha is a real and moving figure. Like Dennis Lee (C61) Moss thinks Book 3 a failure: "only the ideas as artifact remain."

C64 Grant, Judith Skelton. "Leonard Cohen's Poems-Songs." *Studies in Canadian Literature*, 2, No. 1 (Winter 1977), 102-07.

The few revisions that Cohen has made have been felicitous ones, and it is a pity that he revises so little. Cohen, says Grant, is guilty of "mere laziness."

C65 Rodriguez, Juan. "A Sitting with Leonard Cohen: Ladies' Man Is Home, Not Dead." *The Gazette* [Montreal], 7 Jan. 1978, p. 35.

An article mostly about the recording of *Death of a Ladies' Man*. Cohen talks about working with Phil Spector and then a little about living in Québec and about his work.

C66 Amiel, Barbara. "Leonard Cohen Says That to All the Girls." *Maclean's*, 18 Sept. 1978, pp. 55-58.

An article rather too typical of the sort of journalism that Cohen has attracted and, in some cases no doubt, encouraged. Cohen's relationships with women are catalogued in order to demonstrate that the title of his forthcoming book (*Death of a Lady's Man*) is not to be taken without a grain of salt.

C67 French, William. "Monastery Is Vital to Lady's Man." *The Globe and Mail*, 24 Oct. 1978, p. 21.

An article written after a brief meeting with Cohen. Mention is made of Stephen Scobie's recently published critical book on Cohen, and included is a poem from a notebook.

C68 Petrowski, Nathalie. "Leonard Cohen: Portrait Robot d'un Poète Perdu." *Le Devoir*, 4 Nov. 1978, p. 21.

Cohen talks (in French) about *Death of a Lady's Man*, and in particular about the theme of marriage ("Le thème du livre c'est le mariage").

Theses and Dissertations

C69 Lyons, Roberta. "Jewish Poets from Montreal: Concepts of History in the Poetry of A. M. Klein, Irving Layton, and Leonard Cohen." M.A. Thesis Carleton 1966.

This study attempts to determine how the experience of growing up in the Montreal Jewish community created in the writing of these three poets a strong and distinctive sense of history. Chapter ii contains an outline of Cohen's life and career as a writer, and Chapter v is devoted entirely to an examination of his use and concept of history.

C70 Djwa, Sandra Ann. "Metaphor, World View and the Continuity of Canadian Poetry: A Study of the Major English Canadian Poets with a Computer Concordance to Metaphor." Diss. British Columbia 1968.

The continuity of Canadian poetry is broken down into four hypothesized stages, the last of which is characterized by an inquiry into the evil of human nature. It is into this group (the "contemporary Black Romantics") that Cohen falls, and his works are examined, along with those of Margaret Avison, "in relationship to a world view which stresses the fallen world and the primary metaphors of sun-destructive and sun-creative."

C71 Elson, Nicholas William. "Love in the Writings of Leonard Cohen." M.A. Thesis New Brunswick 1969.

This paper examines Cohen's attitudes toward love, how they reflect the age, and what they have to say to it. Love is seen to offer a kind of balance to the chaos of existence, and in this sense it functions as a substitute for religious belief.

C72 Kerwin, Elizabeth Anne. "Themes of Leonard Cohen." B.A. Thesis Acadia 1969.

A brief analysis of the interrelated themes of love, sex, religion, and history in Cohen's work as a whole.

C73 Knelsen, Richard John. "Flesh and Spirit in the Writings of Leonard Cohen." M.A. Thesis Manitoba 1969.

Cohen's search for a fulfilment of both the spirit and the flesh can be shown to parallel the same concerns as those of Hasidism. The sainthood which he seeks is an effort to find a meaning for life inside the confines of the everyday.

C74 Allan, Roy. "The Worlds of Leonard Cohen: A Study of His Poetry." M.A. Thesis Simon Fraser 1970.

One of Cohen's major themes is the "creation of interior escape worlds." This thesis outlines the development of the idea of escape through love and art as it is manifested in Cohen's poetry, up to and including the new work published in *Selected Poems 1956-1968*.

C75 Clifford, Jean Marie. "The Theme of Suffering in the Novels of Jack Kerouac, Leonard Cohen, and William Burroughs." M.A. Thesis British Columbia 1970.

In a consideration of the theme of suffering in the work of these three novelists, Clifford examines *The Favourite Game* and *Beautiful Losers* from the point of view of their rejection of the "old ritual patterns in which suffering once took its form": religion and history. It is through suffering that Cohen sees the way to a sense of the magical life.

C76 Jantzen, Dorothy Helen. "The Poetry of Leonard Cohen: His Perfect Body." M.A. Thesis York 1971.

An important concern in Cohen's poetry is that of art and the artist. With each successive book, Cohen's sense of the role of the artist changes, and this change is mirrored in the techniques and voices which he adopts.

C77 Wilson, Paula Marie. "In Search of Magic: A Study of the Creative Process in the Novels of Leonard Cohen." M.A. Thesis Queen's 1972.

In both of his novels, Cohen shows how history must be subsumed in a "present" that is a constant renewal of vision. This vision and the process that produces it form the subject of this thesis.

C78 Johnson, Lewis David. "Bird on the Wire: The Theme of Freedom in the Works of Leonard Cohen." M.A. Thesis Dalhousie 1974.

This thesis deals with the theme of the quest for freedom through a chronological examination of Cohen's work. Cohen feels that the artist must be free of all bonds (including those of romantic love), and must seek a "mystical transcendence of corporeal existence."

C79 Kanary, Reynolds. "Leonard Cohen: Sexuality and the Anal Vision in 'Beautiful Losers.'" M.A. Thesis Ottawa 1974.

In *Beautiful Losers* Cohen contrasts sex and anality as forces of life and fear of death respectively. F.'s concept of the erotogenic body can be shown to be similar to Freud's understanding of the infantile experience of pleasure, a pansexuality that is lost as a child grows up.

C80 Malus, Avrum. "The Face of Holiness in the Writing of Leonard Cohen." Diss. Montréal 1975.

An examination of certain figures (teachers, messiahs, priests, heroes, and saints) that appear in Cohen's work. Cohen's sense of a saint is of someone who transcends his separateness in a vision usually achieved through an excess of sexual experience.

C81 Stearns, Linda J. Fong. "The Saint Figure in Leonard Cohen and Robertson Davies." M.A. Thesis Calgary 1975.

Cohen in *Beautiful Losers*, and Davies in *Fifth Business*, reinterpret the saint figure as someone who lives on the borders of madness and death. Through an emptying of the personality the main characters come to experience a form of divine love.

Interviews

C82 Ballantyne, Michael. "Poet-Novelist Reflects on the Quebec Scene." *Montreal Star*, 26 Oct. 1963, pp. 2-3.

An article based on an interview about Cohen's life and writings, with particular reference to *The Favourite Game*.

C83 Djwa, Sandra. "After the Wipe-out, a Renewal." *The Ubyssey* [Univ. of British Columbia], 3 Feb. 1967, p. 8.

A fine interview. Cohen expatiates on his ideas, and to a lesser extent talks about his work, *Beautiful Losers* and *Flowers for Hitler* in particular. He is articulate, and says many interesting things concerning his intuition of where art and the world have come to.

C84 Harris, Michael. "An Interview with Leonard Cohen." *Duel*, 1, No. 1 (Winter 1969), 90-114. Rpt. "Leonard Cohen: The Poet As Hero 2." In *Saturday Night*, June 1969, pp. 26-31. *LC*.

The only extensive interview with Cohen. The poet obviously liked the interviewer, and he talks about his life and work with a surprising degree of honesty — i.e., with less con than usual.

C85 Lumsden, Susan. "Leonard Cohen Wants the 'Unconditional Leadership of the World.'" *Weekend Magazine*, 12 Sept. 1970, pp. 22-25. *LC*.

Based on an interview in Paris. This article contains a lot of silly things, and some interesting quotations from Cohen. Like most of the journalism about Cohen, however, this piece overreaches itself: "So women and God have left the deepest traces on Leonard Cohen."

C86 Saltzman, Paul. "Famous Last Words from Leonard Cohen: The Poet's Final Interview He Hopes." *Maclean's*, June 1972, pp. 6-7, 77-80.

A rather typically slick piece of writing, the last part of which embodies an interview.

C87 Kapica, Jack. "The Trials of Leonard Cohen." *The Gazette* [Montreal], 25 Aug. 1973, p. 37.

A story based on an interview undertaken after the publication of *The Energy of Slaves*, and following Cohen's statement that he was abandoning pop music. Includes a nice cartoon (by Aislin).

C88 "Leonard Cohen." *Beetle*, 5, No. 1 (Aug. 1973), n. pag.

An uninformative interview that portrays Cohen as evasive as usual.

C89 MacSkimming, Roy. "'New' Leonard Cohen Opens Up His Thoughts." *Toronto Star*, 22 Jan. 1975, p. E16.

Cohen, in Toronto on a concert tour, talks about his life and about a book he is working on entitled "The Woman Being Born." Of *The Energy of Slaves*, he says: "I wanted to clean out the anarchy of language and thought that's all around us, so I could get back into my own baroque from a clean position."

C90 Holden, Stephen. "A Haunting by Spector." *Rolling Stone*, 26 Jan. 1978, p. 17.

An interview on the occasion of the release of B118. Cohen tells about the difficulties of working with Phil Spector, and calls the disc "an experiment that failed" due to Spector's monomaniacal need to control all aspects of the production.

C91 Williams, Stephen. "The Confessions of Leonard Cohen." *Toronto Life*, Feb. 1978, pp. 48-49, 59-62.

An interview that combines the usual mixture of confession, thinly disguised braggadocio, and outright con. Says Cohen, "there's nobody in Canada who can judge my work." He goes on to declare that "some decades embrace your work, some decades repudiate it. Shakespeare was eclipsed for 200 years. Donne was eclipsed. Keats. It all goes up and down. The next century probably belongs to Raymond Souster."

C92   Hille, Edward. "Itinerant Cohen Digs Roots." *Canadian Jewish News*, 14 July 1978, p. 4.
       Cohen, recently returned to Montreal, talks about *Death of a Lady's Man*, about his plans, and about poetry in general ("I don't think anyone should try to be a poet; this is a verdict, not a vocation").

C93   Godfrey, Stephen. "A New Artistic Twist for Pied Piper Poet." *The Globe and Mail*, 1 March 1980, Sec. Entertainment, p. 1.
       An account of Cohen's discussion with the press about his current lifestyle. The piece was occasioned by Cohen's appearance "to talk about a new portfolio featuring seven of his poems and seven lithographs by the Italian artist Gigino Falconi."

Awards and Honours

C94   Literary Award, McGill University, Montreal, Quebec (1956).

C95   Canada Council Arts Grant (1960-61).

C96   CBC Competition for New Canadian Writers Under 30 for *Opium for Hitler* [earlier title of *Flowers for Hitler*] (1962).

C97   Quebec Literary Award for *Flowers for Hitler* (1964).

C98   Governor-General's Award for *Selected Poems* (1968). Declined.

C99   D. Litt., Dalhousie University, Halifax, Nova Scotia (1971).

D   Selected Book and Record Reviews

Selected Book Reviews

Let Us Compare Mythologies

D1   House, Vernal. "Quarry in the Myrtle Marshes." *The Globe and Mail*, 16 June 1956, p. 8.
      A brief non-committal review. "His themes . . . are personal problems, resolved dispassionately."

D2   Avison, Margaret. "Poetry Chronicle." *The Tamarack Review*, No. 1 (Autumn 1956), pp. 78-79.
      A very favourable review, which speaks of Cohen as "a new poet of stature."

D3   Pacey, Desmond. "A Group of Seven." *Queen's Quarterly*, 63, No. 3 (Autumn 1956), 438-39. Rpt. in *Essays in Canadian Criticism 1938-1968*. Toronto: Ryerson, 1969, pp. 114-15.
      Pacey praises Cohen's ear for music, and points to his opposing themes of lyricism and violence. The book he calls "a brilliant beginning of what we hope may be a long and distinguished poetic career."

D4   Donaldson, Allan. Rev. of *Let Us Compare Mythologies*. *The Fiddlehead*, No. 30 (Nov. 1956), pp. 30-31.
      Cohen is honest and imaginative, but uses images of sex and violence to excess.

D5   Wilson, Milton. "Turning New Leaves." *The Canadian*

Forum, March 1957, pp. 282-84. *LC.*

Thinks the book a promising one, and praises Cohen's attempt to turn experience into a myth that won't be "academic nostalgia or archetypal primitivism."

D6   Frye, Northrop. "Letters in Canada: 1956." *University of Toronto Quarterly*, 26, No. 3 (April 1957), 308-09. Rpt. in *The Bush Garden: Essays on the Canadian Imagination.* Toronto: House of Anansi, 1971, pp. 66-68.

Cohen's most outstanding quality is "a gift for macabre ballad reminding one of Auden, but thoroughly original." *Let Us Compare Mythologies* has "the normal characteristics of a good first volume."

D7   Lochhead, D. G. Rev. of *Let Us Compare Mythologies. Dalhousie Review*, 36, No. 4 (Winter 1957), 425, 427.

Cohen is self-conscious in his handling of his Jewishness and love, but he has the "energy capable of writing the long poem about a Canada without flags."

The Spice-Box of Earth

D8   Eakins, Rosemary. "Cohen's Poems Show New Grace and Skill." *Montreal Star*, 3 June 1961, p. 8.

A generally favourable review that faults Cohen only for his lack of a unifying vision.

D9   Weaver, Robert. "Leonard Cohen's 'Spice-Box' Presents Sombre Vision." *Toronto Daily Star*, 10 June 1961, p. 29.

A laudatory review that basically lists Cohen's themes and speaks of him as "probably the best young poet in English Canada right now."

D10   Bedingfield, Dolores. "Montrealer's Love Poems Win Praise." *The Globe and Mail*, 17 June 1961, p. 9.

The love poems are excellent, but Cohen's propensity for a "prophetic" voice makes for a lack of clarity and for wordiness.

D11   Edinborough, Arnold. Rev. of *The Spice-Box of Earth. The Canadian Reader*, 2, No. 9 (July 1961), 5-6.

Cohen has taken over from Layton as Canada's major poet.

D12   Mandel, E. W. "Turning New Leaves." *The Canadian Forum*, Sept. 1961, pp. 140-41.

A fine review that emphasizes Cohen's wit and playfulness. The reviewer finds the book diverse, but unified, and sees "the wedding of heaven and earth" as the central metaphor.

D13   Bromige, David. "The Lean and the Luscious." *Canadian Literature*, No. 10 (Autumn 1961), pp. 87-88. *LC.*

The spare quality of such poems as "For Anne" is effective, but too often Cohen is guilty of a flabby romantic diction.

D14   Hornyansky, Michael. "Festive Bards." *The Tamarack Review*, No. 21 (Autumn 1961), pp. 80-81.

Cohen's Jewish poems work well, but frequently his imagery is overwrought and unfocussed.

D15   Edinborough, Arnold. "Elegant Forms." *Saturday Night*, 14 Oct. 1961, p. 45.

Cohen's poems are fresh and his imagery brilliant. Edinborough again calls him the "best young poet in Canada."

D16   Dudek, Louis. "Three Major Canadian Poets — Three Major Forms of Archaism." *Delta*, No. 16 (Nov. 1961), pp. 23-25. Rpt. in *Selected Essays and Criticism.* Ottawa: Tecumseh, 1978, pp. 153-56.

Here can be found the beginnings of Dudek's great disappointment with Cohen's developing career (he had published the poet's first book). Dudek finds *The Spice-Box of Earth* a less exuberant book than *Let Us Compare Mythologies*, though better written. "The sacred-oil and sewage-water mixture runs right through the poems."

D17 Vizinczey, Stephen. "Leonard Cohen." *Exchange*, 1, No. 1 (Nov. 1961), 71-72.

The Jewish poems betray a provincialism, but for the most part Cohen's great courage and imagination serve to transform into poetry the most important realities of our time: "the effects of the technological age on man's inner world."

D18 Wilson, Milton. "Letters in Canada: 1961." *University of Toronto Quarterly*, 31, No. 4 (July 1962), 432-37.

An important review that has a curious surface ambiguity. The themes of love and horror in the poems are related ("For this poet, scratch a lover and you find a Bluebeard"); any attempt to evaluate Cohen must deal with the "high ferment of his style and the religious opportunism of his stance."

The Favourite Game

D19 Bedingfield, Dolores. "Hero of Montreal Novel Rebels against Society." *The Globe and Mail*, 7 Sept. 1963, p. 17.

The novel is a very uneven, and though interesting, it "all seems a pose."

D20 Poore, Charles. "Young Bohemians — Canadian Style." *New York Times*, 12 Sept. 1963, p. 35.

A somewhat ambiguous review, that nevertheless calls the book a "churningly avant-garde novel." *The Favourite Game* will be popular on campus.

D21 Cobb, David. "Not Penny Dreadful This One Costs $4." *Toronto Daily Star*, 13 Sept. 1963, p. 21.

Calls it a pretty dreadful book, whose central character is a "prosaic bore."

D22 Gold, Arthur. "New Fiction." *Book Week*, 15 Sept. 1963, p. 26.

The triviality of the novel stems from a lack of vitality in Breavman.

D23 Kervin, Ray. "Leonard Cohen Tries His Hand at a Novel." *The Gazette* [Montreal], 21 Sept. 1963, p. 47.

A favourable review that fits the book into the coming-of-age theme and does not apologize for the obscenities.

D24 Parton, Lorne. "The Written Word." *Vancouver Province*, 23 Sept. 1963, p. 17.

A very favourable review that speaks admiringly of the magic of Cohen's language and his portrayal of youth.

D25 Pollock, Venetia. "New Fiction." *Punch*, 2 Oct. 1963, pp. 505-06.

Cohen is perhaps not yet experienced enough to "fill out a whole novel," but the book is recommended for its "spark and spike."

D26 Fulford, Robert. "On Books: A Rich Vein of Satire in This Fall's Canadian Novels." *Maclean's*, 5 Oct. 1963, pp. 79-80.

Both the style and the substance of the novel are bad; it could easily have been half as long or twice as long, without affecting the book.

D27 Stern, Daniel. "Picaros in Montreal." *Saturday Review*, 5 Oct. 1963, p. 42.

Finds the novel interesting and enjoyable.

D28 Cohen, Peter. "Journey into Life." *The Spectator*, 25 Oct. 1963, p. 538.

"Breavman, the hero of Mr. Cohen's book, is 'that sort of person / Who wanders about announcing his sex / As if he had just discovered it.' His favourite game is supposed to be making love, but in a burst of purely gratuitous self-analysis he declares to one of his lady-loves that he prefers self-abuse to fair women, and opines that this is because he is a 'creative person.' To prove this last assertion Mr. Cohen has inserted in the text a number of poems purportedly by Breavman but really by Mr. Cohen. If I were Breavman I should feel insulted, but I am not Breavman, and I am grateful."

D29 Gibson, Graeme. "Two Troubled Young Men." *Saturday Night*, Nov. 1963, pp. 40-41.

Compares the sex-ethos of *The Favourite Game* to that of *Playboy* magazine, and complains of a lack of form and selection.

D30 Henault, Gilles. " 'The Favourite Game,' ou le jeu de l'amour et du hasard." *La Presse*, 7 dec. 1963, Sec. Entertainment, p. 7.

A very favourable review. He speaks of the book as a "roman de poète cinéaste," and compares Breavman's quest to that of Rimbaud, "cherchant à 'posséder la verité dans une âme et un corps.' "

D31 Irwin, Joan. "A Zest for Life." *The Tamarack Review*, No. 30 (Winter 1964), p. 95.

Praises Breavman's zest for life and the intensity of the novel.

D32 Robertson, George. "Love and Loss." *Canadian Literature*, No. 19 (Winter 1964), pp. 69-70.

The reviewer likes the book, but finds it somewhat sentimental. Its failures are due to its being too autobiographical.

D33 Adam, Ian. "The Human Centre." *Edge*, No. 2 (Spring 1964), pp. 127-28.

Calls it a fine first novel that effectively uses the poet's technique. Its compassion and convincingness falter only when Breavman approaches too closely to the author himself.

D34 Percy, H. R. "Two Looks at Love." *Canadian Author & Bookman*, 39 (Spring 1964), 12.

By comparison with June Franklyn's *Catch Me If You Can* (the other "look at love" in question here), Cohen's novel is very successful.

D35 Watt, F. W. "Letters in Canada: 1963." *University of Toronto Quarterly*, 33, No. 4 (July 1964), 343-44.

The novel is lyrical, but it "suffers from a confusion of intentions."

D36 Kleiman, Ed. "Blossom Show." *Alphabet*, No. 9 (Nov. 1964), p. 78. *LC.*

Cohen has a great gift for comic situations and illuminating metaphors. The book's weakness resides in its repetition of similar situations throughout its length.

D37 "First Installment." *Times Literary Supplement*, 18 Sept. 1970, p. 1027.

The reviewer finds the book better than any of Cohen's subsequent work (the verse he terms "poetry for people who do not know much about poetry and have no intention of learning more"). Despite this, he thinks the novel suffers from being calculated and mechanical, and too "tuned to media exploitation."

Flowers for Hitler

D38 Dudek, Louis. "Peripatetic Poets Show Their Wares." *Montreal Star*, 31 Oct. 1964, p. 8.

Dudek sees the book as manifesting nothing but Cohen's "neurotic affiliations." Despite its fantasy and wit, it is unilluminating. See also Irving Layton's letter to the editor in reply, "Unflattering Review Elicits Equally Uncomplimentary Reply," November 4, 1964, page fourteen.

D39 "Nation's Poets Show Vitality." *Toronto Daily Star*, 5 Dec. 1964, p. 22.

Flowers for Hitler is a "prickly, ambitious book" in a style to which Cohen's readers will take some time adjusting.

D40 Watt, F. W. "Barnstorming Poets Create in Solitude." *Globe Magazine*, 19 Dec. 1964, p. 20.

The book is gay, and Cohen celebrates with "a wonderful lyric grace" all those things for which the flowers of the title stand.

D41   Arnold, A. J. "Leonard Cohen — Disturbing Contrasts." *Congress Bulletin* [Canadian Jewish Congress], 19, No. 1 (Jan. 1965), 3. Rpt. in *Canadian Jewish Outlook*, 3, No. 7 (Aug. 1965), 10-11.

A comparative review of *Flowers for Hitler* and *The Spice-Box of Earth*. The former is a far poorer book, in part because of Cohen's cynicism.

D42   Rev. of *Flowers for Hitler. Canadian Poetry*, 28, No. 2 (Feb. 1965), 38.

All the myths of *The Spice-Box of Earth* have withered or been left behind, and no poetry remains.

D43   Howith, Harry. "Three Poets." *Canadian Author & Bookman*, 40, No. 3 (Spring 1965), 12-13.

The poems are original and the imagery is hauntingly effective.

D44   Pacey, Desmond. "Three Books of Canadian Verse." *The Fiddlehead*, No. 64 (Spring 1965), pp. 71-75.

It is those poems which continue in the lyric mode of *The Spice-Box of Earth* that stand out. There are too many poems that should never have been published, and the horrors often are artificial and contrived.

D45   Wilson, Milton. "Letters in Canada: 1964." *University of Toronto Quarterly*, 34, No. 4 (July 1965), 352-54. *LC.*

A perceptive review that sees Cohen's histrionics as an important aspect of his search for spiritual stability, for the poet is fully aware of the ironies of such a quest. Cohen is "potentially the most important writer that Canadian poetry has produced since 1950."

D46   McCarthy, Brian. "Poetry Chronicle." *The Tamarack Review*, No. 36 (Summer 1965), p. 73.

With the exception of "The New Step" most of the work in *Flowers for Hitler* is "vacant posturing"; Cohen is too disengaged from his inner self.

D47   Marshall, Tom. Rev. of *Flowers for Hitler. Quarry*, No. 14 (1965), p. 54.

The book is uneven, and Cohen seems to be in a state of transition; he is searching for a tougher and more colloquial style.

D48   Jones, B. W. Rev. of *Flowers for Hitler. Queen's Quarterly*, 72, No. 4 (Winter 1965-66), 695-96.

The poems gain from an overall thematic cohesiveness — "the celebration of a dark self-knowledge."

D49   Gnarowski, Michael. "Canadian Poetry Today." *Culture*, 27, No. 1 (March 1966), 76-77.

This book evidences a failing of the poet's powers, and an attempt to revive them by taking on emotional and violent subjects. More than half of the poems are failures.

Beautiful Losers

D50   Rev. of *Beautiful Losers. Kirkus Reviews*, 1 March 1966, p. 267.

A mixed review that speaks of "[playing] Russian roulette with a phallic pistol," and calls the novel a "*via dolorosa* of psychosexual decadence." It nevertheless admits that Cohen manages to fuse the sexual and the spiritual to achieve "some sort of transubstantiation."

D51   Clarke, Austin. "Love Is Not All a Bed of Sex." *Toronto Telegram*, 23 April 1966, p. 21.

The characterization of *Beautiful Losers* is paper-thin, and the book abounds with unrelieved and unredeemed sex.

D52   Legate, David M. "Exercise in Introspection." *Mon-*

treal Star, 23 April 1966, p. 6.

A review in the form of question and answer. He finds *Beautiful Losers* distasteful, and after quoting D. H. Lawrence ("You can recognize pornography by the insult it offers, invariably, to sex and the human spirit"), the reviewer comments: "Beautiful Losers fits."

D53 West, Paul. "The Gooseflesh You Love to Touch." *Book Week*, 24 April 1966, pp. 5, 12.

A very favourable review that calls the book a great advance in Cohen's art. The sex is "not so much Krafft-Ebbing as Krafft-Flowing," and it adds up to a "sardonic mosaic of guiltiness."

D54 Fulford, Robert. "Leonard Cohen's Nightmare Novel." *Toronto Daily Star*, 26 April 1966, p. 27.

As well as being too derivative and in general a failure, *Beautiful Losers* is "the most revolting book ever written in Canada." It is nonetheless a very interesting novel. See also the author's "The Protectoress of Canada." *Toronto Daily Star*, April 29, 1966, page twenty-five, on Catherine Tekakwitha and F.

D55 Fremont-Smith, Eliot. "Howl." *New York Times*, 27 April 1966, p. 45.

Beautiful Losers is about the fact that coherence and intensity in human experience are, after a certain point in one's life, basically antithetical. The novel fails in its attempt to deny this idea.

D56 Wain, John. "Making It New." *New York Review of Books*, 28 April 1966, pp. 17-19. *LC.*

A receptive review that laments Cohen's use of the modern techniques of narration and free-association, but praises his bravery in dealing with the loneliness of man in a world "where the very idea of contact has vanished."

D57 Hill, Harriet. "Exhibitionism and Sex." *The Gazette*

[Montreal], 30 April 1966, p. 25.

Despite its power and erudition, *Beautiful Losers* only amounts to "an ode to nothingness."

D58 Waddington, Miriam. "Bankrupt Ideas and Chaotic Style." *Globe Magazine*, 30 April 1966, p. 17.

Only the passages which deal with Catherine Tekakwitha are coherent. Otherwise, Cohen offers only "verbal masturbation, rhetorical excess, and, instead of a miracle, a death wish."

D59 Edinborough, Arnold. "New Canadian Fiction." *Saturday Night*, May 1966, pp. 45-49.

The novel is a failure, an "unsuccessful hymn to Onan."

D60 "Nosepicking Contests." *Time*, 6 May 1966, pp. 83-84.

A tiringly typical *Time* review that consigns *Beautiful Losers*, Farina's *Been Down So Long It Looks Like Up To Me*, and Pynchon's *The Crying of Lot 49* all to the flames. Cohen's novel is called "a sluggish, stream-of-concupiscence exposition of what Sartre called nausea."

D61 Bensky, Lawrence M. "What Happened to Tekakwitha." *New York Times Book Review*, 8 May 1966, pp. 30-31. *LC.*

"What he's done is more of a pastiche of the bodily functions than a created 'story.' If only he and his messy gang would stop jabbering about cosmic issues and leave us to our enjoyment of the rest!"

D62 Watmough, David. "Maverick Style in New Novel." *Vancouver Sun*, 13 May 1966, Sec. Leisure, p. 20B.

A fine and articulate review that calls the novel "one of the most impressive artistic statements ever to come out of Canada." Despite its violence, *Beautiful Losers* is also gentle and melancholy.

D63 Bannerman, James. "Is Lavatory Scribbling Necessary." *Maclean's*, 14 May 1966, p. 46.

A negative review. "Such relentless insistence in terms of the genitals" makes for a boring and unsavory book.

D64 Kattan, Naïm. "'Les Beaux Perdants' et les provocations de Leonard Cohen." *Le Devoir*, 14 May 1966, p. 14.

The central theme is Canada, and Cohen treats sex as the final refuge from an enervated and hollow culture.

D65 Rosenthal, Raymond. "The Lost Treasure." *The New Leader*, 23 May 1966, pp. 21-22.

A basically favourable review that takes Cohen to task for limiting his characters by his extravagant style. Cohen "writes almost as gorgeously as D'Annunzio."

D66 Lamb, Sidney. "'Libalobaglobawoganummynummy' or The Lusts That Bleat or Low.' Sidney Lamb Reviews Leonard Cohen." *The Montrealer*, June 1966, pp. 35-36.

Finds the novel incoherent, too Romantic, and often badly written. The review, however, fails to measure up to its high-faluting title.

D67 Woodcock, George. Rev. of *Beautiful Losers*. *Commentator*, 10, No. 6 (June 1966), pp. 25-26.

Beautiful Losers is repetitious and boring, despite the fact that at times it comes as close to poetry as prose can. In his treatment of his material, Cohen fails where a novelist like Genêt has been successful.

D68 Duffy, Dennis. "Beautiful Beginners." *The Tamarack Review*, No. 40 (Summer 1966), pp. 75-79. *LC*.

Though the novel could easily have been shorter, it deserves praise for its Lawrencian investigation of "the corruption of love and its replacement by masochism and mechanism."

D69 Feldman, Burton. Rev. of *Beautiful Losers*. *Denver Quarterly*, 1, No. 2 (Summer 1966), 116-17.

Though Cohen has "wit and language to burn," *Beautiful Losers* is basically "fun"; as a revolutionary book it is hopeless and superficial.

D70 Gose, E. B. "Of Beauty and Unmeaning." *Canadian Literature*, No. 29 (Summer 1966), pp. 61-63.

A favourable and well-argued evaluation of the novel. He sees it as an affirmation of "something in or behind the pain and chaos of experience."

D71 Mills, John. Rev. of *Beautiful Losers*. *West Coast Review*, 1, No. 2 (Fall 1966), 58-60.

A mixed review that finds the novel comic, rhetorical (in a positive sense), moral ("Fuck, Cohen seems to tell us, and you'll be a loser. What could be more moral than that?"), but dull at times, and "marred by the preciousness one finds in the author's poetry."

D72 Bowering, George. "Canadian Novel Chronicle." *Edge*, No. 6 (Spring 1967), pp. 114-19.

Beautiful Losers is uneven, but brilliant in parts. *The Favourite Game* is a better-wrought novel.

D73 bissett, bill. "!!!!!" *Alphabet*, No. 13 (June 1967), pp. 94-95.

"i give th book of Cohens a good review, a great review, easily million stars."

D74 Mathews, Robin. "Coming of Age in Canada." *The Journal of Commonwealth Literature*, No. 3 (July 1967), pp. 111-13.

Mathews rather predictably berates Cohen for his Americanism, his use of a form and subject that is continental and not Canadian. *Beautiful Losers* presents the "ultimate North American thing: man out of history in a chaos of stimuli seeking meaning in random, undiscriminated sensation as the criterion of human value."

D75 Purdy, Alfred. Rev. of *Beautiful Losers*. *The Canadian Forum*, July 1967, p. 91.

The theme of salvation through degradation is an important one, but Cohen sacrifices his characters to the message and smothers them with his wild language.

D76 Stedmond, J. M. "Letters in Canada: 1966." *University of Toronto Quarterly*, 36, No. 4 (July 1967), 379-80.

The novel is at best an unrelated congeries of fragments, at worst a failure, and possibly a hoax.

D77 Halio, Jay L. "Second Skins." *The Southern Review*, NS, 4, No. 1 (Jan. 1968), 240-41.

Cohen is an extremist whose excesses detract from an otherwise beautiful and powerful novel. He "dissipates his very real gifts . . . on grounds that whatever is, is good."

D78 Jordon, Clive. "Savage Saviour." *New Statesman*, 3 April 1970, p. 482.

Cohen is talented but the book's form is inconsistent. *Beautiful Losers* is about extremes, and F. can be seen as "a Nietzschean tribute to the Canadian dream."

D79 "Automotively Erotic." *Times Literary Supplement*, 23 April 1970, p. 445.

Beautiful Losers is "an abstraction of all searches for a lost innocence." Though Cohen is talented, his writing is too undisciplined and rhetorical.

D80 Baker, Roger. "Arresting Images." *Books and Bookmen*, June 1970, p. 47.

A favourable review that mistakenly refers to the book as Cohen's first novel. *Beautiful Losers* possesses economy and precision, and it "genuinely extends the scope of the novel."

Parasites of Heaven

D81 Colombo, John Robert. "Cohen: The Operative I." *Globe Magazine*, 10 Dec. 1966, p. 22.

The book is charming, but limited in its success. Cohen's too evident intensity must be taken *cum grano salis*.

D82 Pearson, Alan. "Leonard Cohen's New Work." *Montreal Star*, 10 Dec. 1966, p. 8.

This book fails to show any development beyond *Flowers for Hitler*. Though few of the poems work as a whole, there are many outstanding lines.

D83 Smith, Robert A. Rev. of *Parasites of Heaven*. *Quarry*, 16, No. 2 (Jan. 1967), 44.

Parasites of Heaven is more a notebook than an achieved volume of poetry.

D84 Francis, Wynne. "Five Poets." *The Tamarack Review*, No. 43 (Spring 1967), pp. 84-86.

Cohen's poetry of love and religion are related in that the lover often functions as a surrogate for God. This book by Cohen ("the sweetest singer in our midst") continues his spiritual search.

D85 Ó Broin, Padraig. Rev. of *Parasites of Heaven*. *Canadian Author & Bookman*, 42, No. 3 (Spring 1967), 19-20.

Despite the few good poems in *Parasites of Heaven*, Cohen appears to have abandoned any desire to communicate.

D86 Bowering, George. "Inside Leonard Cohen." *Canadian Literature*, No. 33 (Summer 1967), pp. 71-72. *LC*.

A fine review that discovers in *Parasites of Heaven* both Cohen's greatest strengths and most obvious failings. Cohen is, says Bowering, "ultimate lyric man. That means that he shows any range of his discoveries, mundane to metaphysical, through his consciousness of singular self." Like Frye ten years earlier (D6), Bowering finds the poet at his best when he uses some variation on the ballad form.

D87 MacCallum, Hugh. "Letters in Canada: 1966." *University of Toronto Quarterly*, 36, No. 4 (July 1967), 361-62.

That *Parasites of Heaven* was written over a period of ten years or so is evident from the lack of unity in the book. Central to Cohen's poetry is what is called here "verbal gesture"; everything else remains in soft focus.

D88 Sparshott, Francis. "Turning New Leaves (1)." *The Canadian Forum*, July 1967, pp. 85-86.

An interesting review that probes the ambiguities of the book's title and finds it in the end to possess only a "weakly charming evocativeness." Like D87, this review faults Cohen for a softness that will not stand up to the slightest demand for particularized emotion or tough intelligence.

D89 Kattan, Naïm. "Les écrits canadiens-anglais." *Liberté*, 9, No. 1 (jan.-fev. 1969), 60-63.

Parasites of Heaven confirms both the good and the bad elements of Cohen's work. He is nevertheless "parmi les plus brillants de sa génération."

Selected Poems 1956-1968

D90 Rev. of *Selected poems 1956-1968*. *Kirkus Reviews*, 15 May 1968, p. 566.

It is to be noted that the book is reviewed in the juvenile section of *Kirkus*. Cohen's talent is genuine, but the book is very uneven. It will have much appeal to the young.

D91 Dobbs, Kildare. "Leonard Cohen, Pop Poet Hero." *Toronto Daily Star*, 27 June 1968, p. 29.

Dobbs comments rather darkly that it is Cohen's exploitation of sex and violence that makes his work poetry. He suggests that one "send a copy each to members of the Royal Commission on Women."

D92 Gellatby, Peter. Rev. of *Selected Poems 1956-1968*. *Library Journal*, 93 (July 1968), 2663-64.

A very favourable review that notes Cohen's struggles with the boogey of Romanticism, but nevertheless finds him very contemporary, and a poet "for all seasons and all readers."

D93 Pearson, Alan. "A Creative Drive That's Ready to Accelerate." *Montreal Star*, 13 July 1968, p. 7.

This reviewer finds the collection too narcissistic, but admits that it contains many fine poems.

D94 Callaghan, Barry. "Leonard Cohen: Heavy, Heavy, Heavy Hangs His Sense of Evil." *Toronto Telegram*, 27 July 1968, p. 49.

The evil and despair in Cohen's work is Swinburnian: it amounts to no more than a superficial posturing.

D95 Waddington, Miriam. "A Showman in His Images' Grip." *Globe Magazine*, 27 July 1968, p. 13.

A mixed review that finds Cohen "a true poet," but faults him for excesses of language and for empty posturing. The selections from *The Spice-Box of Earth* and *Flowers for Hitler* are the most effective.

D96 Walsh, Chad. "Poets, Out of Their Shells." *Book World* [Washington Post], 28 July 1968, p. 4.

Comments rather oddly that Cohen shows "a keen love of normality in the midst of every abnormality." The poems are sensuous and lyrical in the manner of Theodore Roethke, "with a dash of the Song of Solomon."

D97 Kattan, Naïm. "Leonard Cohen, Poète et Troubadour,

Nouvelle Idole Chevelue." *Le Devoir*, 24 Aug. 1968, p. 9.

This article reviews Cohen's progress as a poet, noting how his themes have changed, and how this is evident in *Selected Poems 1956-1968*. Though not literally stated, the sense one has is of a favourable review.

D98 "Black Romanticism." *Time*, 13 Sept. 1968, pp. 92, 96, 98.

Cohen is burdened by the past and seeking regeneration. His most authentic voice is found in "anxiety and bitterness."

D99 Robinson, Edgar. Rev. of *Selected Poems 1956-1968*. *New: American and Canadian Poetry*, No. 8 (Dec. 1968), pp. 45-46.

Cohen is a natural, but glib poet. The persona of the poems is his greatest creation of all, a "holy fool, eunuch-stud, laughing-crying man."

D100 Barbour, Douglas. "Canadian Books." *The Dalhousie Review*, 48, No. 4 (Winter 1968-69), 566-71. *LC*.

Cohen's vision has remained constant over the years, but his language has failed him in the books that succeeded *The Spice-Box of Earth*.

D101 MacCallum, Hugh. "Letters in Canada: 1968." *University of Toronto Quarterly*, 38, No. 4 (July 1969), 340.

A favourable review which praises Cohen's presentation of contemporary experience and his style. "Such writing leads one to feel that perhaps facility of style alone matters."

The Energy of Slaves

D102 Rev. of *The Energy of Slaves*. *Kirkus Reviews*, 1 Nov. 1972, p. 1273.

Cohen's rage and disgust cannot be taken seriously, because he is too much of a success. This short review takes the book at face value, and rejects it as Cohenesque con.

D103 Shain, Merle. "Hurry Marita. Hear the Gathering Volleys of Foreboding." *The Globe and Mail*, 11 Nov. 1972, p. 33.

The Energy of Slaves is a great disappointment, its contents being "masturbations more than poems."

D104 Jackson, Marni. "Leonard Cohen: He's Bored, Bitter and out of Love." *Toronto Daily Star*, 25 Nov. 1972, p. 64.

A negative review. Cohen "sounds like a bored spectator to his own state of mind."

D105 Smith, Beverly. "By Self Possessed." *Books in Canada*, Nov.-Dec. 1972, pp. 52-53.

A generally favourable review that sees *The Energy of Slaves* as continuing the themes of slavery and the master-slave relationship from earlier books. Cohen is adept at juxtaposing ordinary language with unusual ideas.

D106 Bagchee, Shyamal. Rev. of *The Energy of Slaves*. *Quill & Quire*, Dec. 1972, p. 8.

The Energy of Slaves is a very uneven book, but it is fascinating to see Cohen, the Romantic poet, repeatedly complaining that he cannot write poetry anymore.

D107 Rockett, W. H. "Leonard Cohen and the Killer Instinct." *Saturday Night*, Dec. 1972, pp. 52, 54, 56.

The book has little variety, but more continuity than Cohen's previous books. From being victim, Cohen has made the transition to being killer. "With Atwood he remains in a class of excellence apart from all other contemporaries."

D108 Estok, Michael. "All in the Family: The Metaphysics of Domesticity." *The Dalhousie Review*, 52, No. 4

(Winter 1972-73), 655-58.

Reading *The Energy of Slaves* we are spectators watching a poet "losing a war with his own craft." Cohen is deliberately sabotaging his work.

D109 Almon, Bert. Rev. of *The Energy of Slaves*. *New: American and Canadian Poetry*, No. 20 (Jan. 1973), pp. 57-60.

The book is a "new road" for Cohen, but one on which he has a long way to go. The poems in *The Energy of Slaves* are too casual; they lack "style, idea, everything."

D110 Macfadden, Patrick. "Has Cohen Become His Admirers." *The Last Post*, Jan. 1973, pp. 45-46.

The Energy of Slaves should not have been published. Cohen, who has gone "from *poète maudit* to a kind of male Rod McKuen" (one supposes that the reviewer believes Rod McKuen to be a woman in disguise), has totally lost his gift for lyric.

D111 "Along the Fingertip Trail." *Times Literary Supplement*, 5 Jan. 1973, p. 10.

A very negative review that complains of Cohen's lack of vision, his prosiness, the uncompelling nature of the poems. The rather inane comment is made that "teenyboppers of all ages will have the book on their shelves between the Bhagavad Gita and the unopened copy of the *Cantos*."

D112 Bedient, Calvin. "A Soft Confusion, a Hard Clarity." *New York Times Book Review*, 18 Feb. 1973, p. 26.

The poems in *The Energy of Slaves* are rhetorical and abstract, and they fail because of Cohen's insistence on talking "rather naggingly" about himself.

D113 Johnson, Rick. Rev. of *The Energy of Slaves*. *Quarry*, 22, No. 2 (Spring 1973), 66-68.

An excellent review that calls the book "important and valuable," but judges it as scribbling. Cohen is

unable to distance himself enough from his present situation. Nevertheless, *The Energy of Slaves* is symptomatic of the state of literature in our time.

D114 Hoffman, Avron. Rev. of *The Energy of Slaves*. *British Columbia Library Quarterly*, 36, No. 4 (April 1973), 74-75.

The book is mostly a put-on, and not worth bothering with. "At times he thinks he's King Phallus and all the world full of salivating clitori, and why can't they get together so he doesn't have to be male chauvinistic."

D115 Healy, James W. "Bookmarks." *Prairie Schooner*, 47, No. 2 (Summer 1973), 185.

The Energy of Slaves is a terrible disappointment. Cohen has sacrificed his lyricism to politics, and the poems suffer greatly thereby.

D116 Hornyansky, Michael. "Letters in Canada: 1972." *University of Toronto Quarterly*, 42, No. 4 (Summer 1973), 368.

A brief review that sees *The Energy of Slaves* as a decline from the poet's previous accomplishments, and finds the book too self-deprecating to be witty.

D117 Scobie, Stephen. Rev. of *The Energy of Slaves*. *The Humanities Association Review*, 24, No. 3 (Summer 1973), 240-43.

A very perceptive review that penetrates beyond the anti-poetic surface of the poems and sees Cohen using the book to commit "suicide on his own image as a poet." In this he fails, because the anti-poet is only another role of the poet. Cohen's voice is unique and tough, and he speaks in the voice which "may be the voice of our time."

D118 Levenson, Christopher. Rev. of *The Energy of Slaves*. *Queen's Quarterly*, 80, No. 3 (Autumn 1973), 469-71.

Cohen is mostly cynical and sardonic, and *The*

Energy of Slaves is a great decline from *Selected Poems 1956-1968*.

D119 Lehman, David. "Politics." *Poetry*, 123, No. 3 (Dec. 1973), 177-78.

The tension in Cohen's work is between poetry and the elements of songwriting, and the result is superficial. Taking lines from five different poems, the reviewer makes up "the model Cohen statement":

> I don't want you to know who I am
> I don't want a purpose
>   in your life
> Keep me out of politics
> I dream of torturing you
> I'm going to burn down your house
> and fuck you in the ass

D120 Morley, Patricia. "Solitary Adventure, or Shared Pain?" *The Lakehead University Review*, 6, No. 2 (Fall-Winter 1973), 262-65.

A favourable review that points out the many-sidedness of the metaphor of the slave. The poems are less egotistical than some of Cohen's earlier work; they read like "shock treatment for his own pain and darkness."

D121 Wayman, Tom. "Cohen's Women." *Canadian Literature*, No. 60 (Spring 1974), pp. 89-93.

The Energy of Slaves is a "collection of tedious male supremacy, vagueness, sententiousness and mental self-titillation." Cohen's attitude to women makes the poems dull and predictable.

Death of a Lady's Man

D122 Geddes, Gary. "Death of a Lady's Man." *The Globe and Mail*, 30 Sept. 1978, p. 27.

This new book re-establishes Cohen's reputation as a poet. The form of work-and-commentary allows him to accomodate both the lyrical and the satirical impulses, and the result is "a sort of Prufrockian excursion into the collective mind of the '60s and '70s."

D123 Purdy, Al. "Cohen Has Lost That Special Magic." *Toronto Star*, 30 Sept. 1978, p. D7.

Though this book continues Cohen's dialogue with himself about his ladies, the magic touch is gone. "The suitcase beside the bed now belongs to a wandering troubador with tonsillitis, and the Sleeping Beauty has insomnia." Cohen now appears to believe the myth he has created about himself.

D124 Ajzenstat, Sam. "The Ploy's the Thing." *Books in Canada*, Oct. 1978, pp. 10-11.

The theme of this complex and successful book is Cohen's poetic failure. The poet meditates, Hamlet-like, on his art and life, and the result is inspired and moving. The text is considerably improved over the earlier one that was withdrawn just prior to publication.

D125 Sivyer, E. "Leonard's Back in the Ring." *The Varsity*, 99, No. 20 (25 Oct. 1978), 4.

An interesting review, despite certain pretentious intrusions ("All at once it became stylish at cocktail parties to recite that one 'always *had* liked Cohen'"). *Death of a Lady's Man* is a comic work, with the voice of the editor-critic combining with that of the artist in a complicated and interesting fashion. The resultant ironies permit Cohen "to accept his public image as Hero Manque [sic] with comic aplomb."

D126 Mandel, Eli. "Leonard Cohen's Brilliant Con Game." *Saturday Night*, Nov. 1978, pp. 51-53.

Mandel is obviously attracted by the book, and speaks enthusiastically of its lyric beauty, its irony, and its zany combination of "Pop culture, apocalyptic yearning, religiosity, and a kind of insane contemporary sociology." The notebook form places the book, in his opinion, in the post-modern tradition of "the poem in process and the forged documentary." Nevertheless, *Death of a Lady's Man* is, finally, "slack at the centre." Cohen is generally content to depend on the virtuosity of his voice, but as a substitute for true poetic structure this approach is not successful.

D127   Marshall, Tom. "Self-Indulgent Cohen." *The Canadian Forum*, Feb. 1979, pp. 33-34.

Although it contains some interesting bits, the book as a whole is tiresome and self-indulgent. It is a development from Cohen's earlier work in that the subject is marriage, but typically it deals with little "other than a now very familiar public personality."

D128   Virgo, Sean. Rev. of *Death of a Lady's Man. Quill & Quire*, 8 Sept. 1978, p. 11.

Death of a Lady's Man is an interesting book, but it presents Cohen the man, not the poet at his best. Though "a sincere *cri de coeur*," the book is too self-regarding, and the best passages are lost in a tangle of surrealism.

D129   Precosky, Don. Rev. of *Death of a Lady's Man. Canadian Book Review Annual* (Toronto: Peter Martin, 1978), p. 104.

Death of a Lady's Man is a failure. There are half a dozen fine pieces, but the "greater part is disjointed, dull and self-indulgent."

D130   Dempster, Barry. "Three New Books of Poetry." *University of Toronto Review*, No. 3 (Spring 1979), pp. 22-23.

Cohen's book is reviewed along with books by Purdy and Atwood. Dempster thinks the book a mixture of the very good and the deplorable. Cohen's egocentricity prevents it from achieving any coherence.

D131   Oliver, Michael Brian. "Not Much Nourished by Modern Love." *The Fiddlehead*, No. 121 (Spring 1979), pp. 143-46.

This rave review calls Cohen "the most significant Canadian writer to have ever lived." In *Death of a Lady's Man*, he has tried to rid himself of despair and alienation, but his only partial success results from an uncertainty as how best to free himself. Cohen's lyricism is beyond reproach.

D132   Scobie, Stephen. Rev. of *Death of a Lady's Man. Quarry*, 28, No. 2 (Spring 1979), 73-76.

Scobie claims several times that "this is not a review." Yes and no. It begins with a poem, and then goes on, attempting to avoid the "Fallacy of Imitative Form," to review the book, in a manner of speaking: "for the average reader the whole book is a set of highly specific references to a reality one step removed."

D133   McNally, Paul. Rev. of *Death of a Lady's Man. Queen's Quarterly*, 86 (Summer 1979), 343-45.

This argumentative review faults Cohen for his familiar vices — self-indulgence and self-pity — but comes out grudgingly in favour of the book. Cohen is a Byron *manqué*, but "we will doubtless continue to pay attention to his hobbling."

D134   Whiteman, Bruce. "The Tygers of Wrath and the Horses of Instruction." *Essays on Canadian Writing*, No. 16 (Fall-Winter 1979-80), pp. 243-47.

Death of a Lady's Man embodies structurally some of the multiple levels of meaning which Cohen had hitherto expressed in imagery or tone. This gives the book a post-modernist tone. It is, nevertheless, badly edited and too long, for Cohen's surrealism becomes tiring in its self-indulgence.

Selected Record Reviews

Canadian Poets 1

D135 "Platters of Poets." *Books in Canada*, April-May-June 1973, pp. 10-11.

Finds the recording an interesting and enjoyable one. Cohen has "a sleepy, priest-like voice."

Songs of Leonard Cohen

D136 Beker, Marilyn. "Leonard Cohen: Poet-Minstrel." *The Globe and Mail*, 25 Jan. 1968, p. 13.

Cohen's songs are almost too private to be shared. They are beautiful, but depressing.

D137 Rev. of *Songs of Leonard Cohen. Maclean's*, Feb. 1968, p. 72.

This brief review finds Cohen's lyrics excellent, but states that his technique as a singer is negligible.

Songs of Love and Hate

D138 Goddard, Peter, "Leonard Cohen's Album — The Poet Still Speaks." *Toronto Telegram*, 13 April 1971, p. 47.

Cohen deals with states of mind that "can't be described by words." He is a surgeon of the emotions.

D139 Schmidt, Arthur. Rev. of *Songs of Love and Hate. Rolling Stone*, 2 Sept. 1971, p. 43.

The disc lacks style, and Cohen has returned to the "trash" that filled his first album. "Cohen mostly sets music to verses."

Live Songs

D140 Clark, David. Rev. of *Live Songs. Records and Recording*, 16, No. 10 (July 1973), 81-82.

"Note: do not check the speed, there is nothing wrong with your gramophone, it is just Leonard sounding even more than usual as though he has dropped a couple of jars of *quaaludes*."

D141 "Leonard Cohen Needs Us and We Still Need Him." *Toronto Daily Star*, 14 July 1973, p. 67.

A favourable review. Cohen appeals to both the mind and the body.

D142 Valdez, Carlotta. Rev. of *Live Songs. Rolling Stone*, 19 July 1973, pp. 55-56.

Cohen is better live than in the studio.

D143 "The Voice of Canadian Poetry." *Quill & Quire*, Aug. 1973, p. 10.

Cohen writes songs that are poems in their own right.

D144 Wallenstein, Barry. Rev. of *Live Songs. Crawdaddy*, Aug. 1973, p. 69.

Cohen is a better poet in his songs than in his poetry. The album is mixed, but well worthwhile.

D145 Samotie, Bill. Rev. of *Live Songs. Sound*, 4, No. 5 (Sept. 1973), 66-67.

The album is mediocre, more of the same.

D146 Swan, Susan. "Wholly Moses." *Books in Canada*, Oct. 1973, pp. 11-12.

The message in *Live Songs* and Layton's *Layton* is "identical — embrace the joy and pain, the good and evil with all the passion in your soul."

D147 Coppage, Noel. Rev. of *Live Songs. Stereo Review*, Nov. 1973, p. 80.

A poor album that is not at all helped by being recorded live. The music is too contrived, and Cohen is far too melancholy.

D148 Jahn, Mike. Rev of *Live Songs. High Fidelity and Musical America*, Jan. 1974, p. 110.

A very favourable review.

New Skin for the Old Ceremony

D149 W., M. Rev. of *New Skin for the Old Ceremony*. *Melody Maker*, 28 Sept. 1974, p. 58.

An interesting review that comments on the tension in Cohen's work between "a deeply religious conviction of things and a well-attested carnality." There is no great song on the album to give it focus.

D150 Sloman, Larry. Rev. of *New Skin for the Old Ceremony*. *Crawdaddy*, Feb. 1975, p. 83.

Calls the album "a monumental [one]." Cohen's work is truly important and "shines like a gem."

D151 Nelson, Paul. "Lovers and Other Strangers." *Rolling Stone*, 27 Feb. 1975, p. 50.

The album is not one of Cohen's best, but its lyricism and optimism help to give it strength.

D152 Stuewe, Paul. Rev. of *New Skin for the Old Ceremony*. *Beetle*, 6, No. 4 (March 1975), n. pag.

This album repeats what Cohen has already done, and his songs, while "bittersweet friends in a lonely space," are merely that and no more.

D153 Coppage, Noel. Rev. of *New Skin for the Old Ceremony*. *Stereo Review*, April 1975, p. 75.

A negative review that finds the album a mere rehash of old material.

D154 DeVan, Fred. Rev. of *New Skin for the Old Ceremony*. *Audio*, Aug. 1975, p. 73.

This reviewer was unable to make it through a hearing of the whole album.

D155 Tudor, Dean. "The Record Track." *Ontario Library Review*, 59, No. 4 (Dec. 1975), 259.

The album is "out-takes and leftovers that were found in the can." Cohen "quit making records a long time ago."

The Best of Leonard Cohen

D156 "Short Takes." *Melody Maker*, 6 Dec. 1975, p. 37.

"The title seems rather far-fetched." Most of Cohen's songs are merely depressing.

D157 Tearson, Michael. Rev. of *The Best of Leonard Cohen*. *Audio*, June 1976, p. 81.

A fine retrospective of Cohen's work.

D158 Tudor, Dean. "The Record Track." *Ontario Library Review*, 60, No. 3 (Sept. 1976), 188.

Most of Cohen's songs sound monotonous after a single sitting.

Death of a Ladies' Man

D159 Waxman, Ken. "Rebirth of a Ladies' Man." *Saturday Night*, March 1978, pp. 61-62.

Cohen's music now measures up to the high quality of his lyrics. The record has benefited greatly from Phil Spector's production.

D160 Tudor, Dean. "The Record Track." *Ontario Library Review*, 62, No. 3 (Sept. 1978), 223.

Cohen's lyrics are good, but the production by Phil Spector is "empty."

Index to Critics Listed in the Bibliography

Archibald Lampman
An Annotated Bibliography

George Wicken

Introduction

Born on November 17, 1861, in Morpeth, a village in western Ontario, Archibald Lampman was the son of the village's Anglican minister. Raised in a home with a fine library, and educated in the best schools of the new province of Ontario, Lampman eventually entered Trinity College at the University of Toronto. There, he contributed poems and essays to the college newspaper, the *Rouge et Noir*, and for a time, was the paper's editor. English, French, German, Greek, Latin, and Hebrew were among the subjects studied by Lampman at Trinity, and he graduated in 1882 with second-class honours in Classics. A brief stint as a school teacher in Orangeville, Ontario, was followed by a job in the Post Office Department in Ottawa which he retained until his death.

Lampman was a prolific contributor of poetry to Canadian, American, and British periodicals, and his work was read widely during his lifetime. His first volume of poetry, *Among the Millet, and Other Poems* (1888), was praised by William Dean Howells, and his second book, *Lyrics of Earth* (1895), also received favourable critical notices. With William Wilfred Campbell and Duncan Campbell Scott, Lampman collaborated on "At the Mermaid Inn," a column in *The Globe* [Toronto]. Lampman belonged to several organizations, among them the Royal Society of Canada, the Ottawa Literary and Scientific Society, and the Fabian Society of Ottawa. He often delivered addresses to these groups. In the midst of his busy life as a man of letters, Lampman died of a long-standing heart problem on February 10, 1899. A life of thirty-seven years, and a literary career of less than twenty, came to an abrupt halt.

A key figure in the life of Lampman, Duncan Campbell Scott is also a key figure in Lampman's bibliography. Scott was a good friend of Lampman's: they worked with Campbell on "At the Mermaid Inn," exchanged ideas on poetry and philosophy, and took fishing trips together in Quebec. Scott sought patronage for Lampman and, after Lampman's death, became his literary executor. He edited and oversaw the publishing of *The Poems of Archibald Lampman*. The book's major purpose was to raise money for Lampman's widow and children. Scott even shared the funeral expenses when Mrs. Lampman died in 1910. By publishing Lampman's collected works and various selected editions of his poetry, Scott kept Lampman's work before the public. A number of articles, written about Lampman by Scott, also served to keep Lampman's work fresh in the mind of the public. It is unlikely that Lampman's poetry would have been as widely read in the twentieth century, nor would it have received as much critical attention, had it not been for Duncan Campbell Scott. Stan Dragland has stated that we owe Scott a debt for his "noble record of activity on behalf of Archibald Lampman." For his selfless dedication to Lampman and his family, and for keeping Lampman's work and name before us, Scott does, indeed, deserve our thanks. As an editor, however, Scott cannot be excused for his radical, yet silent, editing of Archibald Lampman's poetry.

Although Lampman had proof-read *Among the Millet, and Other Poems*, *Lyrics of Earth*, and the unpublished "Alcyone," Scott disregarded his friend's creative judgement in editing *The Poems of Archibald Lampman* in 1900 (reprinted in 1974). Spelling, punctuation, and capitalization were changed. A stanza was omitted from one poem, and the verse structure of "The City of the End of Things" was altered. The previously unpublished poems which Scott included in the collection were given similar treatment; some even had their titles changed. From these altered poems, Scott selected several for inclusion in *Lyrics of Earth: Sonnets and Ballads* (1925) and *Selected Poems of Archibald Lampman* (1947). Both books contain sections entitled "Lyrics of Earth," yet the poems in these sections are not all drawn from Lampman's *Lyrics of Earth*. Instead, the sections include poems from various stages in Lampman's career. Moreover, the "Lyrics of Earth" sections are different in the 1925 and 1947 books. *At the Long Sault and Other New Poems* (1943, and reprinted in 1974) consists of poems which Scott and E. K. Brown drew from Lampman's manuscript books. All of Scott's editing, in all the aforementioned books, is silent. Bruce Nesbitt has stressed the necessity of returning to the Lampman manuscripts. It is to be hoped that scholars will heed Nesbitt's advice, and that new, collated editions of Lampman's poems will be forthcoming. Only when we see what Lampman, himself, wrote can a just assessment of his work begin.

Criticism of Archibald Lampman's work has been dominated by three general areas of concern. The first area of critical inquiry explores the degree to which Lampman is a poet of nature. Ancestral and biographical approaches to Lampman's poetry constitute the second dominant strain of Lampman criticism, and a third channel of analysis has examined literary and philosophical influences on Lampman's work.

The first area of critical concern—the degree to which Lampman is a poet of nature—begins in 1890 with articles praising him for his skill as a descriptive nature poet. "I venture to assert that there is no living poet in either hemisphere who can present such pictures of natural scenery and natural phenomena as Lampman." In every decade since 1890, Lampman has been lauded for his achievement in writing of the world of nature. A smaller number of critics have de-emphasized Lampman's commitment to nature, and argued that Lampman had a highly developed social conscience. Irving Layton has admitted that Lampman's "Epitaph on a Rich Man" and "Liberty" hit him "like two mortar blasts," when he first read them. Louis Dudek and F. W. Watt have similarly discussed the social criticism inherent in Lampman's work. More recently, critics have looked upon Lampman's nature poetry as something other than merely descriptive. Barrie Davies has examined the manner in which Lampman tries "to bring to society the organic values of the natural world." John Ower has explored nature as "aesthetic symbol" in Lampman's poetry, and Eli Mandel has shown how Lampman strives "to get past nature" in his poetry.

Seeking connections between Lampman's poetry and his ancestry or biography is the second dominant avenue of

inquiry into Lampman's poetry. Attributing qualities in Lampman's verse to inherited qualities in Lampman, himself, was a short-lived, but nevertheless major, preoccupation with a number of Lampman's early critics. Lilly E. F. Barry, for one, was convinced that Lampman's "contemplative disposition" was "a tendency inherited from his Teutonic forefathers." A very strong debate has raged over whether or not Lampman was happy in Ottawa, or in his job at the Post Office. Suggestions that Lampman was dissatisfied with his lot began as early as 1890, found their most maudlin expression in Lampman's mother's 1899 claim that living in a country unsympathetic to art had hastened her son's death, and occasionally find their way into Lampman criticism today. However, Duncan Campbell Scott, Claude Bissell, and Desmond Pacey have been very articulate and persuasive in denying that Lampman's creative growth was stunted by life in Ottawa, or a job in the Post Office. Other biographical approaches to Lampman's poetry have centred on a connection between the death of Lampman's infant son in 1894, and a troubled tone in much of the poetry written by Lampman around that time. Ralph Gustafson, in a 1947 article, argued that a crisis other than the boy's death appears to pervade much of Lampman's poetry. In recent years, Bruce Nesbitt and Margaret Coulby Whitridge have proven Gustafson correct, through their exploration of the relationship between Lampman and Katherine (Kate) Waddell.

Literary and philosophical influences on Lampman's work form the third general area of inquiry with which Lampman's critics have been concerned. Most often, Lampman's poetry is said to be influenced by Keats. Wordsworth and Arnold are also cited on more than one occasion. Burns, Whitman, Tom Moore, Leconte de Lisle and the Parnassians, Thomson, and Poe have also been said to have exerted an influence on Lampman's work. Few recent critics have examined poetic influence on Lampman. Rather, they have broadened the term "influence" to include the historical sources of Lampman's "At the Long Sault: May, 1660" and the influence of religion and social pressures on Lampman's work. The connections between Lampman's essays and his poetry, which is to say the influence of one facet of Lampman's work on another, have also received attention of late. Both Barrie Davies and D. M. R. Bentley have been instrumental in illuminating this previously obscured relationship.

Perhaps the most remarkable fact to emerge from this Lampman bibliography is the consistent and continuing presence of Archibald Lampman as an influence on Canadian writing. There are few characteristics common to the poetry of Duncan Campbell Scott, William Wilfred Campbell, Raymond Knister, Nathaniel Benson, Leo Kennedy, Ralph Gustafson, Irving Layton, Louis Dudek, Eli Mandel, Raymond Souster, and Doug Jones, yet each of these poets has written a critical article, a poem, or both about Archibald Lampman. Whether these poets deal with Lampman favourably or unfavourably, whether they seek to emulate him or to eschew all that he stands for, to some extent they consciously define their aesthetics in relationship to those of Archibald Lampman. With Lampman, Canadian poetry begins; in relation to Lampman, each generation of poets determines our poetry's course.

* * *

In the case of Archibald Lampman, the standard bibliographies of Canadian literature contain a great deal of information about secondary sources on the poet's work. While these bibliographies also list Lampman's own books, under primary works, no references are given for the many poems Lampman published in the newspapers and magazines of the late nineteenth century. References for a few of these poems were found in the bibliographies of nineteenth-century American periodicals but the single best source of information proved to be Carl Y. Connor's 1929 work, *Archibald Lampman: Canadian Poet of Nature*. In an appendix to his biography of Lampman, Connor lists dozens of poems by Lampman and their date and place of publication in periodicals. Tracking down the references Connor provided was the bibliographer's first task, and all but one of Connor's references were found to be correct. On the hunch that Lampman may have published other poems in the magazines and newspapers Connor lists, the annual index of each periodical was checked for the span of Lampman's writing career and for about five years after his death. The hunch proved profitable, for additional poems were found as a result of this line of investigation.

University and public libraries in Metropolitan Toronto hold many of the periodicals for which Lampman wrote or in which he was written about. In some cases, however, microfilm or photocopies of poems and articles were requested from libraries throughout North America. Every poem, article, and review listed in this bibliography was read by the bibliographer to ensure its actual existence, to synthesize its content, and to verify its date, page number, volume number, and so forth. In the case of the poems, the titles, wording, line arrangement, and verse arrangement were checked against the poems as they exist in published volumes of Lampman's poetry. Changes were duly noted in the annotations. It was found that poems by Lampman often appeared in the same issue of periodicals which published articles about the poet. A few previously unlisted poems and articles were found by looking through issues known to contain at least one item by or about Archibald Lampman. The poet's death on February 10, 1899, and the unveiling of a memorial cairn on September 13, 1930, provided specific dates around which newspapers and magazines might be likely to publish material on Lampman. Several articles about Lampman were, indeed, found to date from those periods.

Reading Lampman's poems in their original place of publication is a markedly different experience from reading the poems in Lampman's books. In the newspapers of the last century, Lampman's work is often found amid advertisements for elixirs and corsets. Even in the handsomely produced magazines, where prints complementary to specific poems sometimes accompany Lampman's work, the poems are never more than a page away from accounts of unusual new contraptions or gossip about the privileged and titled. The juxtaposition of art and popular culture in the late nineteenth century is nowhere better illustrated than in the periodicals in which Lampman made his first appearance as a poet. It is hoped that readers of this bibliography will be led back to those journals to see for themselves the manner in which art seeks a place among the more ephemeral concerns of the age. A bibliography may give shape to a writer's canon, but a writer's era has a symmetry that only its artifacts can reveal.

Acknowledgments

I would like to express my thanks to the following people for their co-operation in the preparation of this bibliography: Mary Hudecki and Gary MacDonald of the Scott Library, York University; Henri Pilon, Archivist, Trinity College, University of Toronto; the staff of the John P. Robarts Research Library and the Thomas Fisher Rare Book Library, University of Toronto; and the staff of the Metropolitan Toronto Library.

Part I

Works by Archibald Lampman

A   Books (Poetry and Prose) and Manuscripts

Poetry

A1   *Among the Millet, and Other Poems.* Ottawa: Durie, 1888. 151 pp.

A2   *Lyrics of Earth.* Boston: Copeland and Day, 1895. 56 pp.
Ed. D. M. R. Bentley. Ottawa: Tecumseh, 1978. 64 pp.
     The 1978 edition restores the poems to Lampman's intended order.

A3   *Alcyone.* Ottawa: Ogilvy, 1899. 110 pp.

A4   *The Poems of Archibald Lampman.* Ed. Duncan Campbell Scott. Toronto: Morang, 1900. 473 pp.
Holiday Edition. 2 vols. Toronto: Morang, 1901. 473 pp.
Toronto: Morang, 1905. 473 pp.
Toronto: Univ. of Toronto Press, 1974. 473 pp.
     Scott took a number of editorial liberties in preparing this volume. He made changes within poems, and assigned poems different names in cases where two poems bore the same name. However, the changes Scott made are not specified anywhere in the book.

A5   *Lyrics of Earth: Sonnets and Ballads.* Ed. Duncan Campbell Scott. Toronto: Musson, 1925. 276 pp.

A6   *At the Long Sault and Other New Poems*. Ed. Duncan Campbell Scott and E. K. Brown. Toronto: Ryerson, 1943. 45 pp.
Toronto: Univ. of Toronto Press, 1974. 45 pp.

A7   *Selected Poems of Archibald Lampman*. Ed. Duncan Campbell Scott. Toronto: Ryerson, 1947. 176 pp.

A8   *The City of the End of Things*. Ed. Michael Gnarowski. Montreal: Golden Dog, 1972. N. pag.

A9   *The Poems of Archibald Lampman (Including At the Long Sault)*. Introd. Margaret Coulby Whitridge. Toronto: Univ. of Toronto Press, 1974. 518 pp.

This volume combines the works listed in A4 and A6.

A10   *Lampman's Kate, Late Love Poems of Archibald Lampman, 1887-1897*. Ed. Margaret Coulby Whitridge. Ottawa: Borealis, 1975. 52 pp.

A11   *Lampman's Sonnets, 1884-1899*. Ed. Margaret Coulby Whitridge. Ottawa: Borealis, 1976. 194 pp.

A12   *Comfort of the Fields. The Best-Known Poems*. Ed. Raymond Souster. Sutton West, Ont.: Paget, 1979. 125 pp.

Prose

A13   *Hans Fingerhut's Frog Lesson, A Fairy Tale*. Ottawa: Golden Dog, 1973. N. pag.

A14   *Archibald Lampman: Selected Prose*. Ed. Barrie Davies. Ottawa: Tecumseh, 1975. 127 pp.

This volume contains a wide range of Lampman's prose works, from fairy tales to literary criticism. The eleven chapters include: "At the Mermaid Inn," "Descriptive Fragments of Canoe Trips," "The Fairy Fountain," "Friendship" (B149), "Hans Fingerhut's Frog Lesson" (B156), "Happiness" (B157), "The Modern School of Poetry in England," "Poetic Interpretation," "The Revolt of Islam" (B148), "Untitled Essay on Socialism" (B161), and some letters written by Lampman to E. W. Thomson.

Manuscripts

A15   University of Toronto Library
Toronto, Ontario

The Thomas Fisher Rare Book Library holds the following Lampman material: a bound manuscript volume of 92 poems inscribed "Christmas 1889," a manuscript copy of "October," a partial manuscript of "The Child's Music Lesson," 3 letters written by Duncan Campbell Scott to Archibald Lampman, 2 letters by Lampman to Scott, and 3 letters written by Lampman to J. E. Wetherell. Lampman was an 1882 graduate of Trinity College, and the College retains the "Minutes of Trinity Literary Institute, 1879-1882." Lampman was a member of the Institute and, for a time, its secretary. Some of the "Minutes" are in his handwriting. The College also has copies of its newspaper, the *Rouge et Noir*, and its successor, the *Trinity University Review*. Lampman published poetry and prose in these papers. Christmas cards and letters from Lampman to the Reverend Charles H. Shortt, microfilm copies of letters from Lampman to Mrs. May McKeggie and from Miss Annie Lampman to Mrs. May McKeggie are also held by the College.

A16   Public Archives of Canada
Ottawa, Ontario

Lampman material in the Public Archives includes 22 manuscript workbooks containing over 400 draft poems dating from 1883-99, a bound volume of poems dating from 1894-99, holograph poems, and

Christmas cards issued jointly by Lampman and Duncan Campbell Scott. The Archives also contain 112 letters from Lampman to E. W. Thomson, 26 letters from E. W. Thomson to Lampman, 1 letter from Lampman to Duncan Campbell Scott, and 2 letters from Scott to Lampman. Lampman's prose works held by the Archives include an unfinished novel; "The Fairy Fountain"; "Hans Fingerhut's Frog Lesson"; 6 notes on fishing trips, etc.; Lampman's essay on "Happiness"; an untitled essay on socialism; and 9 critical essays. The 9 essays are "Armadis of Gaul," "George F. Cameron," "Keats," "The Modern School of Poetry in England," "Poetic Interpretation," "The Poetry of Byron," "The Poets," "Style," and "Two Canadian Poets: A Lecture." Poems by Lampman's father, the Reverend Archibald Lampman who sometimes wrote under the name of "Crowquill," are also held by the Public Archives. Some works by Duncan Campbell Scott, Bliss Carman, and Charles G. D. Roberts are included, as well, in the Archives' Lampman collection.

A17   Library of Parliament
        Ottawa, Ontario

Four bound manuscript volumes of poems are held by the Library of Parliament: "Alcyone," "David and Abigail," "Miscellaneous Poems," and "The Story of an Affinity."

A18   Library
        Simon Fraser University
        Burnaby, British Columbia

An untitled volume of poems; *Alcyone*, with a note by Duncan Campbell Scott; poems written by Lampman for members of his family; and a fragment of "Love and Death" constitute the University's holdings of Lampman's poems. The University also retains a copy of Lampman's prose work "The

Character and Poetry of Keats," and letters from Lampman to various members of his family. Also in the Simon Fraser collection are letters to Lampman from several friends and writers (Bliss Carman, Charles G. D. Roberts, William Wilfred Campbell, J. E. Collins, Gilbert Parker, and others); correspondence by various members of Lampman's family; Lampman's sketchbook, family photographs, and certificates.

A19   Library
        Queen's University
        Kingston, Ontario

Letters by Lampman to Horace Scudder, Boston; to Copeland and Day, Boston; and to Bliss Carman are held by the University. Queen's also retains part of the printer's copy of *Lyrics of Earth*.

A20   Library
        University of New Brunswick
        Fredericton, New Brunswick

Included in the "Rufus Hathaway Collection" are manuscript copies of "By the Sea" and "To the Warbling Vireo"; 3 letters about Lampman: 1 from Bliss Carman to Duncan Campbell Scott and 2 from Duncan Campbell Scott to Edward Doak Mead (the editor of the *New England Magazine*); and a letter from Rufus Hathaway to Lampman's son.

A21   Library
        McGill University
        Montreal, Quebec

The university holds 2 poems by Lampman: "Ballad of Summer's Rest" and "Winter," 15 letters from Lampman to W. D. Lighthall, and a portrait of Lampman by A. D. Patterson.

A22   Library

Women's Canadian Historical Society
Toronto, Ontario

Lampman's poem "The Passing of Spring" is held by the Society.

A23 Metropolitan Toronto Library
Toronto, Ontario

The "Melvin Hammond Papers" contain the texts of 2 letters written by Charles G. D. Roberts to Archibald Lampman.

A24 Ottawa Public Library
Ottawa, Ontario

A 1 page memorandum from Lampman to W. A. Code is held by this library.

A25 Archives of Ontario
Toronto, Ontario

In the papers of Sir Alexander Campbell (Postmaster General of Canada) are 4 letters from his son, Archibald Campbell, requesting employment in the civil service for his friend, Archibald Lampman.

B Contributions to Periodicals and Books: Poetry, Essays and Short Stories, Letters, and Selected Anthology Contributions

Note: When an item is reprinted in one of Lampman's books, this fact is noted in the entry through one of the following abbreviations:

Among the Millet, and Other Poems . . . . *AM*
Lyrics of Earth . . . . *LE*
Alcyone . . . . *A*
The Poems of Archibald Lampman . . . . *PAL*
Lyrics of Earth: Sonnets and Ballads . . . . *LSB*
At the Long Sault and Other New Poems . . . . . *ALS*
Selected Poems of Archibald Lampman . . . . *SPL*
The City of the End of Things . . . . *CET*
Lampman's Kate, Late Love Poems of Archibald
    Lampman, 1887-1897 . . . . *LK*
Lampman's Sonnets, 1884-1899 . . . . *LS*
Comfort of the Fields . . . . *CF*
Hans Fingerhut's Frog Lesson, A Fairy Tale . . . . *HF*
Archibald Lampman: Selected Prose . . . . *ALP*

Poetry

B1 "The Last Sortie." *Rouge et Noir*, 3, No. 4 (Nov. 1882), 4.

B2 "Derelict." *Rouge et Noir*, 4, No. 1 (Dec. 1882), 5.

B3 "A Monition." *The Week*, 6 Dec. 1883, p. 6. *AM* (revised—"The Coming of Winter"); *PAL*.

B4 "Three Flower Petals." *The Week*, 17 Jan. 1884, p. 102. *AM*; *PAL*; *LSB*; *SPL*.

B5 "A Fantasy." *The Week*, 7 Feb. 1884, p. 155.

B6 "Spring on the River." *Rouge et Noir*, 5, No. 5 (May 1884), 5. *AM*; *PAL*; *LSB*; *SPL*.

B7 "The King's Sabbath." *The Week*, 18 Dec. 1884, p. 39. *AM*; *PAL*; *LSB*; *SPL*; *LS*.

B8 "A January Sunset." *The Current*, 17 Jan. 1885, p. 35. Rpt. in *Rouge et Noir*, 6, No. 1 (March 1885), 11. *LS*.

B9 "Bird Voices." *Century*, 30, No. 1 (May 1885), 163. Rpt. in *Rouge et Noir*, 6, No. 3 (May 1885), 9. *AM*; *PAL*.

B10 "The Hepalica." *Rouge et Noir*, 6, No. 3 (May 1885), 5.

B11 "An August Warning." *Rouge et Noir*, 6, No. 4 (June 1885), 3.

B12 "The Weaver." *The Week*, 16 July 1885, p. 522. *AM*; *PAL*.

B13 "Ballade of Summer's Sleep." *The Week*, 12 Nov. 1885, p. 794. *AM*; *PAL*.

B14 "An October Sunset." *Rouge et Noir*, 6, No. 6 (Dec. 1885), 8. *AM*; *PAL*.

B15 "Winter's Nap." *Rouge et Noir*, 6, No. 6 (Dec. 1885), 11.

B16 "The Three Pilgrims." *Rouge et Noir*, 7, No. 4 (July 1886), 5-6. *AM* (revised); *PAL*.

B17 "The Organist." *The Week*, 8 July 1886, p. 514. Rpt. (excerpt). In *Review of Reviews*, 2, No. 8 (Aug. 1890), 140. *AM*; *PAL*.

B18 "The Little Handmaiden." *The Week*, 11 Aug. 1887, p. 593. *AM*; *PAL*.

B19 "The Loons." *Scribner's*, 2, No. 3 (Sept. 1887), 291. *AM*; *PAL*; *LSB*; *SPL*; *LS*.

B20 "Abu Midjan." *The Week*, 29 Sept. 1887, p. 710. *AM*; *PAL*.

B21 "An Old Lesson from the Fields." *Scribner's*, 2, No. 5 (Nov. 1887), 627. Rpt. in *Rouge et Noir*, 8, No. 8 (Nov. 1887), 6. *AM*; *PAL*; *LSB*; *SPL*; *LS*; *CF*.

B22 "The Railway Station." *The Week*, 22 Dec. 1887, p. 55. *AM*; *PAL*; *LSB*; *SPL*; *LS*; *CF*.

B23 "New Year's Eve." *The Week*, 29 Dec. 1887, p. 69. *AM*; *PAL*; *LS*.
    The poem begins "Once on the year's last eve in my mind's might" and should not be confused with a different poem of the same name in *At the Long Sault and Other New Poems*.

B24 "Winter." *The Week*, 5 Jan. 1888, p. 90. *AM*; *PAL*; *LSB*; *SPL*.

B25 "Gentlemen." *Trinity University Review*, 1, No. 2 (Feb. 1888), 3. *LS*.

B26 "Hope and Fear." *Trinity University Review*, 1, No. 2 (Feb. 1888), 7.

B27 "A God-Speed to the Snow." *Trinity University Review*, 1, No. 4 (April 1888), 3. Rpt. "God-Speed to the Snow." In *Youth's Companion*, 31 March 1892, p. 164. *LE*; *PAL*.

In Lampman's books, both the word "A" and the hyphen are omitted from the title and the poem is called "Godspeed to the Snow."

B28 "Despondency." *Scribner's*, 3, No. 6 (June 1888), 732. *AM*; *PAL*; *LSB*; *SPL*; *LS*; *CF*.

B29 "Midsummer Night." *Scribner's*, 4, No. 2 (Aug. 1888), 173. Rpt. in *Living Age*, 26 June 1897, p. 842. *AM*; *PAL*; *LSB*; *SPL*; *LS*.

B30 "Winter Evening." *Scribner's*, 4, No. 6 (Dec. 1888), 748. *A*; *PAL*; *LSB*; *SPL*; *LS*; *CF*.

The poem is illustrated by J. H. Twachtman in *Scribner's*.

B31 "April Night." *Scribner's*, 5, No. 4 (April 1889), 442. *A*; *PAL*; *SPL*; *LS*; *CF*.

B32 "Drought." *Scribner's*, 6, No. 3 (Sept. 1889), 362. *PAL*; *LSB*; *SPL*; *CF*.

B33 "Evening." *Scribner's*, 6, No. 6 (Dec. 1889), 692. Rpt. in *Canadian Nature*, 14, No. 1 (Jan.-Feb. 1952), 27. *A*; *PAL*; *LSB*; *SPL*; *LS*; *CF*.

In *Scribner's*, the poem is illustrated by A. Lemaire.

B34 "Knowledge." *Trinity University Review*, 2, No. 10 (Dec. 1889), 154. *AM*; *PAL*; *LSB*; *SPL*; *LS*.

B35 "Among the Orchards." *The Week*, 27 Dec. 1889, p. 55. *A*; *PAL*; *LSB*; *SPL*; *LS*; *CF*.

B36 "The Moon-Path." *Scribner's*, 7, No. 2 (Feb. 1890), 219. *LE*; *PAL*; *LSB*; *SPL*.

B37 "The Sun Cup." *Harper's*, 80 (Feb. 1890), 435. *LE*; *PAL*; *LSB*; *SPL*.

B38 "Dead Cities." *Scribner's*, 7, No. 5 (May 1890), 624. *PAL*; *LSB*; *SPL*; *LS*.

Only the first sonnet is printed in *Scribner's*. Revisions were made before the poem was published in Lampman's books.

B39 "A Morning Summons." *Trinity University Review*, 3, No. 5 (May 1890), 97. *PAL*; *LSB*; *SPL*; *LS*.

B40 "River-Dawn." *Independent*, 22 May 1890, p. 1. *PAL* ("A Dawn on the Lièvre"); *LSB*; *SPL*; *LS*; *CF*.

B41 "To the Cricket." *Scribner's*, 8, No. 1 (July 1890), 80. *A*; *PAL*; *LSB*; *SPL*; *LS*; *CF*.

B42 "Across the Pea-Fields." *Independent*, 14 Aug. 1890, p. 1. *PAL*; *LSB*; *SPL*; *LS*; *CF*.

B43 "An Invocation." *New England Magazine*, 3, No. 1 (Sept. 1890), 41. *PAL*; *LSB*; *SPL*; *LS*.

B44 "In November." *Harper's*, 81 (Nov. 1890), 936. *LSB*; *SPL*; *CF*.

This poem, which begins "With loitering step and quiet eye, / Beneath the low November sky," has been published in *Harper's*, *Lyrics of Earth: Sonnets and Ballads*, *Selected Poems of Archibald Lampman*, and *Comfort of the Fields*. A different poem, beginning "The hills and leafless forests slowly yield / To the thick-driving snow," but also bearing the title "In November," appears in *Among the Millet, and Other Poems*, *The Poems of Archibald Lampman*, and *Comfort of the Fields*. This latter poem appears under the title "Late November" in *Lyrics of Earth: Sonnets and Ballads* and *Selected Poems of Archibald Lampman*, and under both titles in *Lampman's Sonnets, 1884-1899*.

B45 "Life and Nature." *Scribner's*, 8, No. 5 (Nov. 1890),

556. Rpt. in *Current Literature*, 21 (March 1897), 246-47. *LE*; *PAL*; *LSB*; *SPL*.

B46 "Golden Rod." *Trinity University Review*, 3, No. 12 (Dec. 1890), 194. Rpt. "Goldenrod." In *Youth's Companion*, 28 July 1892, p. 380. *PAL*; *LSB*; *SPL*; *LS*.

B47 "The March of Winter." *Harper's*, 82 (Jan. 1891), 228. Rpt. in *Canadian Nature*, 11, No. 2 (March-April 1949), 64. *PAL*; *LSB*; *SPL*; *LS*; *CF*.

B48 "Snowbirds." *Atlantic Monthly*, Jan. 1891, p. 44. Rpt. in *Current Literature*, 21 (March 1897), 247. *LE*; *PAL*; *LSB*; *SPL*; *CF*.

B49 "In March." *Independent*, 5 March 1891, p. 1. *A*; *PAL*; *SPL*; *LS*; *CF*.

B50 "Winter Break." *Independent*, 5 March 1891, p. 1. *A* ("Winter-Break"); *PAL*; *LSB*; *SPL*; *LS*; *CF*.

B51 "Night." *Scribner's*, 9, No. 4 (April 1891), 515. *PAL*; *LSB*; *SPL*; *LS*.

B52 "The Meadow." *Independent*, 9 April 1891, p. 1. *LE*; *PAL*; *LSB*; *SPL*; *CF*.

B53 "In Absence." *Scribner's*, 10, No. 2 (Aug. 1891), 194. *PAL*; *LSB*; *SPL*; *LS*.

B54 "A Sunset on the Lower St. Lawrence." *Independent*, 1 Oct. 1891, p. 1. *PAL* ("A Sunset at Les Eboulements"); *LSB*; *SPL*; *LS*; *CF*.

B55 "The Voices of Earth." *Scribner's*, 10, No. 4 (Oct. 1891), 417. Rpt. in *Book Buyer*, 18, No. 3 (April 1899), 189. *A*; *PAL*; *LSB*; *SPL*; *LS*.

B56 "A Midnight Landscape." *Cosmopolitan*, 12, No. 1 (Nov. 1891), 104. *PAL*; *LSB*; *SPL*; *LS*.

B57 "Music." *Century*, Nov. 1891, p. 132. *LS*.
This poem, beginning "Oh, take the lute this brooding hour for me" is a different poem from the one which appears as "Music" in *Among the Millet, and Other Poems*, *The Poems of Archibald Lampman*, *Lyrics of Earth: Sonnets and Ballads*, and *Selected Poems of Archibald Lampman*.

B58 "A Reassurance." *Youth's Companion*, 5 Nov. 1891, p. 572. *LE* (revised—"A Re-Assurance"); *PAL*; *LSB*; *SPL*.

B59 "Sunset." *Independent*, 3 Dec. 1891, p. 1. Rpt. in *Current Literature*, 21 (March 1897), 247. *LE*; *PAL*; *LSB*; *SPL*.

B60 "The Sweetness of Life." *Youth's Companion*, 3 Dec. 1891, p. 630. *LE*; *PAL*; *LSB*.

B61 "A March Day." *Cosmopolitan*, 12. No. 3 (Jan. 1892), 312. *PAL*; *LSB*; *SPL*; *LS*; *CF*.

B62 "Comfort of the Fields." *Scribner's*, 11, No. 2 (Feb. 1892), 255-56. *LE*; *PAL*; *LSB*; *SPL*; *CF*.

B63 "With the Night." *Atlantic Monthly*, Feb. 1892, p. 153. *LE*; *PAL*; *LSB*; *SPL*.

B64 "The Better Day." *The Week*, 13 May 1892, p. 374. *A*; *PAL*; *LSB*; *SPL*.

B65 "Sleep." *The Globe* [Toronto], 28 May 1892, p. 9. Rpt. in *Harper's*, June 1892, p. 49. *LS*.
The poem appears as part of the "At the Mermaid Inn" column in *The Globe*. Beginning "Behold I lay in prison like St. Paul," the poem should not be confused with a different poem, also called "Sleep," which

appears in *Among the Millet, and Other Poems* and *The Poems of Archibald Lampman.*

B66 "The Return of the Year." *Scribner's*, 11, No. 6 (June 1892), 675. *LE*; *PAL*; *LSB*; *SPL*.

B67 "Falling Asleep." *The Globe* [Toronto], 4 June 1892, p. 8. *PAL*; *LSB*; *SPL*; *LS*; *CF*.

The poem appears as part of the "At the Mermaid Inn" column in *The Globe.*

B68 "Reality." *The Globe* [Toronto], 4 June 1892, p. 9. *LS*.

The poem appears as part of the "At the Mermaid Inn" column in *The Globe.*

B69 "The Poet's Possession." *Youth's Companion*, 9 June 1892, p. 296. *LE*; *PAL*; *LSB*; *SPL*; *CF*.

B70 "The City." *The Week*, 1 July 1892, p. 486. *LSB*; *SPL*; *CF*.

Beginning "Canst thou not rest o city," this poem appears in *The Week*, *Lyrics of Earth: Sonnets and Ballads*, *Selected Poems of Archibald Lampman*, and *Comfort of the Fields*. A different poem, also called "The City," appears in *Among the Millet, and Other Poems*, *The Poems of Archibald Lampman*, and *Lampman's Sonnets, 1884-1899.* Both poems are printed in *Lyrics of Earth: Sonnets and Ballads*, *Selected Poems of Archibald Lampman*, and *Comfort of the Fields.*

B71 "By the Sea." *Youth's Companion*, 11 Aug. 1892, p. 404. *PAL*; *LSB*; *SPL*; *LS*; *CF*.

B72 "At the Ferry." *Independent*, 25 Aug. 1892, p. 1. *LE*; *PAL*; *LSB*; *SPL*.

B73 "An Autumn Landscape." *Harper's*, 85 (Oct. 1892), 762. Rpt. in *The Globe* [Toronto], 15 Oct. 1892, p. 9. *LE*; *PAL*; *LSB*; *SPL*.

The poem appears as part of the "At the Mermaid Inn" column in *The Globe.*

B74 "Amor Vitae." *The Globe* [Toronto], 29 Oct. 1892, p. 8. *A*; *PAL*; *LSB*; *SPL*.

The poem appears as part of the "At the Mermaid Inn" column and is untitled in *The Globe.*

B75 "The Cup of Life." *The Globe* [Toronto], 29 Oct. 1892, p. 8. Rpt. in *The Week*, 30 Nov. 1894, p. 10. *PAL*; *LSB*; *SPL*; *LS*; *CF*.

The poem appears as part of the "At the Mermaid Inn" column in *The Globe.*

B76 "Vision." *The Globe* [Toronto], 19 Nov. 1892, p. 8. *LE* ("Winter-Store"); *PAL*.

The poem appears as part of the "At the Mermaid Inn" column, but does not appear in its entirety, in *The Globe.*

B77 "Nature Love." *Youth's Companion*, 1 Dec. 1892, p. 636. *PAL* ("On the Companionship with Nature"); *LSB*; *SPL*; *LS*.

B78 "Beside the Stream." *Youth's Companion*, 15 Dec. 1892, p. 664. *LE* ("By an Autumn Stream"); *PAL*; *LSB*; *SPL*; *CF*.

B79 "After Mist in Winter." *Cosmopolitan*, 14, No. 4 (Feb. 1893), 398. *PAL* ("After Mist"); *LSB*; *SPL*; *LS*; *CF*.

B80 "Cloud-Break." *Independent*, 2 March 1893, p. 1. *LE*; *PAL*; *LSB*; *SPL*.

B81 "April on the Hills." *Youth's Companion*, 13 April 1893, p. 190. Rpt. "April in the Hills." In *Current Literature*, 21 (March 1897), 246. *LE*; *PAL*; *LSB*; *SPL*; *CF*.

In *Current Literature* and Lampman's books the poem has some changes in the third and fourth stanzas, and includes a fifth stanza not present in the *Youth's Companion* version of the poem.

B82 "Before the Robin." *Independent*, 13 April 1893, p. 9. *PAL*; *LSB*; *SPL*; *LS*; *CF*.

B83 "Good Speech." *Youth's Companion*, 25 May 1893, p. 264. *A*; *PAL*; *LSB*.

B84 "June." *Cosmopolitan*, 15, No. 2 (June 1893), 173-75. *LE*; *PAL*; *LSB*; *SPL*.
An illustration by Hamilton Gibson accompanies the poem in *Cosmopolitan*.

B85 "To the Warbling Vireo." *Youth's Companion*, 22 June 1893, p. 320. *PAL*; *LSB*; *SPL*; *LS*.

B86 "The Angel of the House." *Youth's Companion*, 20 July 1893, p. 366. *PAL* ("The Spirit of the House"); *LSB*; *SPL*; *LS*.

B87 "September." *Harper's*, 87 (Sept. 1893), 506-07. *LE*; *PAL*; *LSB*; *SPL*; *CF*.

B88 "Storm Voices." *Century*, Sept. 1893, p. 655. *PAL*; *LSB*; *SPL*; *LS*.

B89 "The Autumn Waste." *Century*, Oct. 1893, p. 938. *A*; *PAL*; *LSB*; *LS*.

B90 "After the Shower." *Youth's Companion*, 12 Oct. 1893, p. 496. *PAL*; *LSB*; *SPL*; *LS*; *CF*.

B91 "Indian Summer." *Scribner's*, 14, No. 5 (Nov. 1893), 548. Rpt. in *Canadian Magazine*, 22, No. 1 (Nov. 1903), 83. *A*; *PAL*; *LSB*; *LS*.

B92 "The City of the End of Things." *Atlantic Monthly*, March 1894, pp. 350-52. Rpt. trans. Jacques Gariépy. In *Delta*, 25 (Nov. 1965), 5-6. *A*; *PAL*; *LSB*; *SPL*; *CET*; *CF*.

B93 "To Chicago." *Arena*, 9 (April 1894), 632. *LS*.

B94 "Successors of Pan." *Independent*, 5 April 1894, p. 1. *LE* ("Favorites of Pan"); *PAL*; *LSB*; *SPL*.
The *Independent* version of the poem includes a stanza, between the usual fifth and sixth stanzas of the poem as it appears in Lampman's books. The extra stanza reads: "The wastes and moonlit solitudes, / And paths of heaven beyond regard or ken, / And gladness of the hills, and earth cool woods, / And the thronged life of men."

B95 "To My Daughter." *Youth's Companion*, 17 May 1894, p. 232. *A*; *PAL*; *LSB*; *SPL*.

B96 "The Wind's Word." *Independent*, 26 July 1894, p. 1. *PAL*; *LSB*; *SPL*.

B97 "Avarice." *The Week*, 30 Nov. 1894, p. 10. *PAL*; *LSB*; *SPL*; *LS*.

B98 "Beauty." *The Week*, 30 Nov. 1894, p. 10. *PAL*; *LSB*; *SPL*; *LS*.

B99 "The Modern Politician." *The Week*, 30 Nov. 1894, p. 10. *PAL*; *LSB*; *SPL*; *LS*; *CF*.

B100 "Salvation." *The Week*, 30 Nov. 1894, p. 10. *PAL*; *LSB*; *SPL*; *LS*.

B101 "Stoic and Hedonist." *The Week*, 30 Nov. 1894, p. 10. *PAL*; *LSB*; *SPL*; *LS*.

B102 "To a Millionaire." *The Week*, 30 Nov. 1894, p. 10. *PAL*; *LSB*; *SPL*; *LS*; *CF*.

B103 "To an Ultra Protestant." *The Week*, 30 Nov. 1894, p. 10. *PAL*; *LSB*; *SPL*; *LS*.

B104 "To Chaucer." *The Week*, 30 Nov. 1894, p. 10. *PAL*; *LSB*; *SPL*; *LS*.

B105 "Virtue." *The Week*, 30 Nov. 1894, p. 10. *PAL*; *LSB*; *SPL*; *LS*.

B106 "The Woodcutter's Hut." *Scribner's*, 16, No. 6 (Dec. 1894), 741-45. *A*; *PAL*; *LSB*.
Illustrations by Frank French accompany the poem in *Scribner's*.

B107 "Alcyone." *Atlantic Monthly*, Jan. 1895, pp. 29-30. *A*; *PAL*; *LSB*; *SPL*.

B108 "Inter Vias." *The Chap-Book*, 15 Jan. 1895, pp. 207-08. *A*; *PAL*; *LSB*; *SPL*.

B109 "Personality." *Cosmopolitan*, 18, No. 6 (April 1895), 751. *A*; *PAL*; *LSB*; *SPL*; *CF*.

B110 "Distance." *Youth's Companion*, 4 April 1895, p. 166. *LE*; *PAL*; *LSB*; *SPL*.

B111 "May." *Youth's Companion*, 2 May 1895, p. 220. *PAL*; *LSB*; *SPL*; *LS*; *CF*.

B112 "When the Bobolink Comes." *Youth's Companion*, 16 May 1895, p. 242. *PAL* ("Nesting Time"); *LSB*; *LS*; *CF*.

B113 "The Passing of the Spirit." *Century*, July 1895, p. 454. *PAL*; *LSB*; *SPL*; *LS*.

B114 "The Cloud-Fleet." *Youth's Companion*, 25 July 1895, p. 358.

B115 "The Mystery of a Year." *Youth's Companion*, 31 Oct. 1895, p. 518. *A*; *PAL*.

B116 "The Ruin of the Year." *Scribner's*, 18, No. 5 (Nov. 1895), 570. *PAL*; *LSB*; *SPL*; *LS*.

B117 "Wind and World." *The Chap-Book*, 1 Nov. 1895, p. 475.

B118 "Paternity." *Youth's Companion*, 14 Nov. 1895, p. 584. *PAL*; *LSB*; *SPL*.

B119 "War." *Cosmopolitan*, 20, No. 5 (March 1896), 481-82. *A*; *PAL*; *LSB*; *SPL*.
A Pierre Fritel painting is the illustration accompanying the poem in *Cosmopolitan*.

B120 "In a Copy of Miss Wetherald's 'House of the Trees.'" *The Week*, 6 March 1896, p. 351.

B121 "The Song of Pan." *Harper's*, 93 (Aug. 1896), 419. *A*; *PAL*; *LSB*; *SPL*.

B122 "Chione." *Canadian Magazine*, 7, No. 6 (Oct. 1896), 496-98. *A*; *PAL*; *LSB*.

B123 "Night and Sleep." *Youth's Companion*, 22 Oct. 1896, p. 530. *PAL* (revised—"A Summer Evening"); *LSB*; *SPL*; *LS*; *CF*.

B124 "Earth: The Stoic." *The Week*, 6 Nov. 1896, p. 1192. *PAL* ("Earth—The Stoic"); *LSB*; *SPL*; *LS*.

B125 "The Bird and the Hour." *Current Literature*, 21 (March 1897), 247. *LE*; *PAL*; *LSB*; *SPL*.
Lampman submitted this poem to the *Youth's Companion* in 1893 under the title "The Hermit Thrush Poem." The magazine, however, rejected it.

B126 "Snow." *Current Literature*, 21 (March 1897), 247. *LE*; *PAL*; *LSB*; *SPL*; *CF*.

B127 "A May Song." *Scribner's*, 21, No. 5 (May 1897), 651.

B128 "White Pansies." *Scribner's*, 22, No. 1 (July 1897), 36. *A*; *PAL*; *LSB*; *SPL*.

B129 "King Oswald's Feast." *Youth's Companion*, 22 July 1897, p. 346. *PAL*; *LSB*.

B130 "We Too Shall Sleep." *Scribner's*, 22, No. 4 (Oct. 1897), 436. *A*; *PAL*.

B131 "Temagami." *Blackwood's Magazine*, 163 (March 1898), 397. Rpt. in *Living Age*, 13 Aug. 1898, p. 410. *PAL*; *LSB*; *SPL*; *LS*; *CF*.

B132 "An Invitation to the Woods." *Youth's Companion*, 23 June 1898, p. 304.

B133 "Yarrow." *Youth's Companion*, 28 July 1898, p. 356. *PAL*; *LSB*; *SPL*.

B134 "Uplifting." *Harper's*, 97 (Sept. 1898), 539. *PAL*; *LSB*; *SPL*; *LS*.

B135 "The Passing of Autumn." *Scribner's*, 24, No. 5 (Nov. 1898), 634. *PAL*; *LSB*.

B136 "To the Robin." *Youth's Companion*, 9 Feb. 1899, p. 68. *LS* ("The Robin").

B137 "Outlook." *Ottawa Evening Journal*, 11 Feb. 1899, p. 4. Rpt. "The Outlook." In *Living Age*, 14 March 1903, p. 704. *AM*; *PAL*; *LSB*; *SPL*; *LS*.

This sonnet appears in the *Ottawa Evening Journal* as part of a tribute to Lampman on the day after his death. The final four lines of the sonnet appear on the eastern face of the Lampman Memorial Cairn, unveiled at Morpeth, Ontario on September 13, 1930.

B138 "Among the Millet." *The Globe* [Toronto], 18 Feb. 1899, p. 1. Rpt. in *Living Age*, 31 Jan. 1903, p. 320. *AM*; *PAL*; *LSB*; *SPL*; *CF*.

The poem is printed in *The Globe* as part of Lampman's obituary.

B139 "The Largest Life." *Atlantic Monthly*, March 1899, pp. 416-17. Rpt. in *Current Literature*, 27 (Feb. 1900), 128. *PAL*; *LSB*; *SPL*; *LS*; *CF*.

B140 "The Winter Stars." *Scribner's*, 25, No. 3 (March 1899), 314. *PAL*; *LSB*; *SPL*; *LS*; *CF*.

B141 "The Violinist." *Independent*, 9 March 1899, p. 678. *PAL*.

B142 "Hepaticas." *Youth's Companion*, 6 April 1899, p. 174. *PAL*; *LSB*; *SPL*; *CF*.

B143 "The Vase of Ibn Mokbil." *Independent*, 31 Aug. 1899, pp. 2344-45. *PAL*; *LSB*; *SPL*.

B144 "Settler's Tale." *Canadian Magazine*, 42, No. 2 (Dec. 1913), 113-16.

B145 "New Year's Eve." *Canadian Magazine*, 42, No. 3 (Jan. 1914), 282. *ALS*.

The poem begins "Yonder through the darkness surging" and appears only in the *Canadian Magazine* and *At the Long Sault and Other New Poems*. A different poem, also bearing the title "New Year's Eve," appears in *Among the Millet, and Other Poems*, *The Poems of Archibald Lampman*, and *Lampman's Sonnets, 1884-1899*.

B146 "Unrest." *Lippincott's*, 94 (Sept. 1914), 341. *AM*; *PAL*; *LSB*; *SPL*.

B147 "Winter Uplands." *Canadian Nature*, 11, No. 2 (March-April 1949), 64. *PAL*; *LSB*; *SPL*; *LS*; *CF*.

Written on January 30, 1899, this is believed to be the final poem written by Lampman before his death on February 10, 1899.

Essays and Short Stories

B148 "The Revolt of Islam." *Rouge et Noir*, 1, No. 4 (Dec. 1880), 4-6. *ALP*.

B149 "Friendship." *Rouge et Noir*, 2, No. 1 (Feb. 1881), 6-7. *ALP*.

B150 "College Days among Ourselves." *Rouge et Noir*, 3, No. 1 (Feb. 1882), 7-8.

B151 "College Days among Ourselves." *Rouge et Noir*, 3, No. 2 (March 1882), 6-7.

B152 "German Patriotic Poetry." *Rouge et Noir*, 3, No. 2 (March 1882), 4-6.

B153 "College Days among Ourselves." *Rouge et Noir*, 3, No. 4 (Nov. 1882), 4-5.

B154 "College Days among Ourselves." *Rouge et Noir*, 4, No. 2 (Feb. 1883), 5-6.

B155 "Gambetta." *Rouge et Noir*, 4, No. 5 (July 1883), 5-10.

B156 "Hans Fingerhut's Frog Lesson." *Rouge et Noir*, 7, No. 1 (Feb. 1886), 9-12. *HF*; *ALP*.

B157 "Happiness." *Harper's*, 93 (July 1896), 309-12. Rpt. in *Archibald Lampman's Letters to Edward William Thomson (1890-1898)*. Ed. Arthur S. Bourinot. Ottawa: Bourinot, 1956, pp. 48-52. Rpt. in *Canadian Poetry Magazine*, 30, No. 2 (Feb. 1967), 40-43. *ALP*.

B158 "Two Canadian Poets: A Lecture." *University of Toronto Quarterly*, 13, No. 4 (July 1944), 406-23. Rpt. in *Masks of Poetry: Canadian Critics on Canadian Verse*. Ed. A. J. M. Smith. New Canadian Library, No. 3. Toronto: McClelland and Stewart, 1962, pp. 26-44. Rpt. in *Canadian Literature; The Beginnings to the 20th Century*. Ed. Catherine M. McLay. Toronto: McClelland and Stewart, 1974, pp. 302-08.

B159 "The Character and Poetry of Keats." *University of Toronto Quarterly*, 15, No. 4 (July 1946), 356-72.

B160 *At the Mermaid Inn, Conducted by A. Lampman, W. W. Campbell, and Duncan C. Scott.* Ed. Arthur S.

Bourinot. Ottawa: Bourinot, 1958. 96 pp.

B161 "A Lampman Manuscript." *Journal of Canadian Fiction*, 1, No. 2 (Spring 1972), 55-58.
This essay, which is taken from Volume IV, pages 2500-13 of Lampman's manuscript papers, and dates from about 1890, outlines the poet's views on socialism.

B162 "The Poetry of Byron." *Queen's Quarterly*, 83, No. 4 (Winter 1976), 623-32.

B163 *At the Mermaid Inn: Wilfred Campbell, Archibald Lampman, Duncan Campbell Scott in* The Globe *1892-3*. Introd. Barrie Davies. Literature of Canada. Poetry and Prose in Reprint, No. 21. Toronto: Univ. of Toronto Press, 1979. 353 pp.
A transcription of the entire run of the "At the Mermaid Inn" column. See also B160.

Letters

B164 *Archibald Lampman's Letters to Edward William Thomson (1890-1898)*. Ed. Arthur S. Bourinot. Ottawa: Bourinot, 1956. 74 pp.
The companion volume is *The Letters of Edward William Thomson to Archibald Lampman (1891-1897)*. Ed. Arthur S. Bourinot. Ottawa: Bourinot, 1957. 49 pp.

B165 *Some Letters of Duncan Campbell Scott, Archibald Lampman, and Others.* Ed. Arthur S. Bourinot. Ottawa: Bourinot, 1959. 63 pp.

Selected Anthology Contributions

B166 "April," "Clouds," "The Frogs," "Heat," "Midsummer Night," "An Old Lesson from the Fields." In *Songs of the Great Dominion: Voices from the Forests and Waters, the Settlements and Cities of Canada*. Ed.

William Douw Lighthall. 1889; rpt. Toronto: Coles, 1971, pp. 369-70, 377, 387, 421-23, 425, 426-28.

B167 "Among the Millet," "The Frogs," "Heat," "Knowledge," "The Largest Life," "Midsummer Night," "A Prayer," "September," "Snowbirds," "The Truth." In *The Oxford Book of Canadian Verse*. Ed. Wilfred Campbell. Toronto: Oxford Univ. Press, 1913, pp. 197-210.

B168 "After Rain," "April in the Hills," "April Night," "Heat," "In March," "A January Morning," "The Largest Life," "Morning on the Lièvre," "The Railway Station," "The Truth," "War," "Winter Evening." In *Canadian Poets*. Ed. John W. Garvin. Toronto: McClelland, Goodchild and Stewart, 1916, pp. 61-74.

B169 "The City of the End of Things," "Heat," "In November" (beginning "With loitering step and quiet eye" and not to be confused with a different poem by the same name), "Midnight," "Solitude," "The Song Sparrow," "A Sunset at Les Eboulements," "Winter Evening," "The Woodcutter's Hut." In *The Book of Canadian Poetry: A Critical and Historical Anthology*. Ed. A. J. M. Smith. 1943; rpt. Toronto: Gage, 1957, pp. 175-85.

B170 "Among the Orchards," "Heat," "Life and Nature," "Midnight," "Personality," "Refuge," "September," "Snow," "Solitude," "A Summer Evening," "Winter Evening," "Winter-Solitude." In *The Penguin Book of Canadian Verse*. Ed. Ralph Gustafson. 1958; rpt. Harmondsworth, Eng.: Penguin, 1969, pp. 73-83.

B171 "After Rain," "Alcyone," "Among the Timothy," "April," "April in the Hills," "At the Long Sault: May, 1660," "The Autumn Waste," "The City of the End of Things," "The Clearer Self," "Death," "Freedom," "The Frogs," "Heat," "In November" (beginning "The hills and leafless forests slowly yield" and not to be confused with a different poem by the same name), "In October," "The King's Sabbath," "The Largest Life," "Midnight," "The Modern Politician," "On the Companionship with Nature," "Personality," "The Railway Station," "Salvation," "The Sun Cup," "To a Millionaire," "To the Prophetic Soul," "Uplifting," "Voices of Earth," "Winter Evening." In *Poets of the Confederation*. Ed. Malcolm Ross. New Canadian Library, No. 1. Toronto: McClelland and Stewart, 1960, pp. 55-84.

B172 "After Rain," "After Snow," "April," "The City of the End of Things," "The Frogs," "Heat," "In the Wilds," "June," "The Lake in the Forest," "The Largest Life," "The Modern Politician," "Morning on the Lièvre," "The Railway Station," "September," "The Woodcutter's Hut." In *100 Poems of Nineteenth Century Canada*. Ed. Douglas Lochhead and Raymond Souster. Toronto: Macmillan, 1974, pp. 127-54.

Part II

Works on Archibald Lampman

C Books, Articles and Sections of Books, Theses and Dissertations, Miscellaneous, and Honour

Books

C1 Guthrie, Norman Gregor. *The Poetry of Archibald Lampman*. Toronto: Musson, 1927. 58 pp.

More of an appreciation of Lampman's poetry than a critical study, this first book devoted solely to Lampman's work examines several facets of his poetry. The influence of other poets on Lampman's work, his use of the city as "a sort of symbol of inhumanity to man," and his devotion to "the higher plane" of writing are examined in Guthrie's study. Lampman is seen primarily as a nature poet, and faulted for placing "too slight a value on the human relationships of life." Guthrie concurs with most critics that it was in the sonnet form that Lampman's best poetry was written.

C2 Connor, Carl Y. *Archibald Lampman: Canadian Poet of Nature*. 1929; rpt. Ottawa: Borealis, 1977. 210 pp.

A fine biography of Lampman, this book also offers a wealth of information about Lampman's social and intellectual milieu. Tracing Lampman's life from boyhood, through his college years and teaching days, to his career as a civil servant and poet, Connor's account is marked by an abundance of detail. Although Connor's analysis of Lampman's poetry is not extensive, the book's chief value is in its clear-sighted exploration of Lampman's life and times. Connor is

one of the first critics to refuse to paint Lampman as a martyr: "Fate did not deal more harshly with him than with other men, but he was more sensitive than most men, and perhaps more conscious than most, of the goal of perfection toward which he must strive. It is that steadfast devotion to the ideal which was his finest characteristic."

C3 Fox, William Sherwood, E. A. Cruikshank, J. H. Cameron, Arthur Stringer, Nathaniel A. Benson, and Duncan Campbell Scott. *Addresses Delivered at the Dedication of the Archibald Lampman Memorial Cairn at Morpeth, Ontario*. London, Ont.: Western Ontario Branch of the Canadian Authors' Association, 1930. 16 pp.

The texts of the six addresses given at the unveiling of the Lampman cairn are contained in this book. They include the Chairman's address by William Sherwood Fox; "The National Importance of Memorials" by Brigadier-General E. A. Cruikshank; "The Place of the Canadian Poet in National Education" by J. H. Cameron; "The Poet in Everyday Life" by Arthur Stringer; Nathaniel A. Benson's sonnet, "The Lampman Cairn at Morpeth"; and "Archibald Lampman," a recollection of the poet's life by his friend, Duncan Campbell Scott.

C4 Gnarowski, Michael, ed. *Archibald Lampman*. Critical Views on Canadian Writers, No. 3. Toronto: Ryerson, 1970. 224 pp. (Hereafter abbreviated as *AL*.)

Contributors include: "Fidelis" (D4), Lilly E. F. Barry (C8), Arthur Stringer (C11), A. W. Crawford (C13), John Marshall (C28), Louis Untermeyer (C31), Lawrence J. Burpee (C30), Bernard Muddiman (C35), G. H. Unwin (C36), Raymond Knister (C47), Leo Kennedy (C59), W. E. Collin (C60), Ralph Gustafson (C69), Duncan Campbell Scott (C83), John Sutherland (C74), Desmond Pacey (C75), Louis Dudek (C80), F. W. Watt (C82).

A collection of eighteen critical articles on

Lampman published between 1889 and 1958, this book is the single best source of Lampman criticism up to 1958. Arranged chronologically, the articles reveal varying attitudes towards Lampman's nature poetry, his acts of withdrawing from the city, his social awareness, and the influence of his family and lineage on his work. Often, Lampman is used to illustrate fashionable concerns or prejudices of the critics. The articles in this book are annotated individually throughout Section C of this bibliography.

C5   McMullen, Lorraine, ed. *The Lampman Symposium*. Re-Appraisals: Canadian Writers. Ottawa: Univ. of Ottawa Press, 1976. 138 pp.

This collection of addresses given at the University of Ottawa's symposium on Lampman in May of 1975 deals with a wide variety of topics of concern to Lampman scholars. In "Life and Nature: Some re-appraisals of Archibald Lampman," Ralph Gustafson strives to "cashier this portrait of a morbid poet bedraggled by routine; this portrait of a despondent socialist." Margaret Coulby Whitridge, in "Love and Hate in Lampman's Poetry," identifies love and rejection as "the guiding forces which tempered the poet's life." Michael Gnarowski deals with "Lampman's critical reception and its bearing...upon his history as a published writer" in "Lampman and His Critics." Carl F. Klinck, in "The Frogs: An Exercise in Reading Lampman," finds that "the frogs do not speak wisdom; they *breath* of it" and "yield symbolic traces, not statements, to the questing heart." Calling Lampman the "last remarkable exponent" of the sonnet in Canada, Louis Dudek discusses the decline of the sonnet in "Lampman and the Death of the Sonnet." Louis K. MacKendrick also discusses Lampman's sonnets in "Sweet Patience and Her Guest, Reality: The Sonnets of Archibald Lampman." MacKendrick derives his title from a passage in Lampman's "To the Warbling Vireo." Dick Harrison, in "'So Deathly Silent:' the Resolution of Pain and Fear in the Poetry of Lampman and D. C. Scott," points out that both mankind and nature are sources of pain and fear in Lampman's poetry. Barrie Davies also examines Lampman's responses to mankind and nature in "The Forms of Nature: Some of the Philosophical and Aesthetic Bases of Lampman's Poetry." Davies finds that "nature for Lampman was both a source of positive, organic values and an implicit criticism of...society." Bruce Nesbitt charts Lampman's publishing history in "The New Lampman" and argues that Lampman "both defined and accomplished the break between what has been called colonial romanticism on the one hand, and a variety of close-focussed poetic imagism on the other." Also included in this collection are four assessments of Lampman's achievement by Sandra Djwa, D. G. Jones, Robin Mathews, and James Steele, and a guide to the Lampman manuscripts prepared by Margaret Coulby Whitridge.

Articles and Sections of Books

C6   "Item." *Rouge et Noir*, 4, No. 2 (Feb. 1883), 9.

This brief item in the Trinity College newspaper notes that Lampman, an 1882 graduate of Trinity, has been appointed to a position in the post office. Remarking upon Lampman's "real ability," the newspaper expresses hope for his future.

C7   Harte, W. Blackburn. "Some Canadian Writers of Today." *New England Magazine*, 3, No. 1 (Sept. 1890), 21-40. Rpt. (excerpt). In *The Search for English-Canadian Literature: An Anthology of Critical Articles from the Nineteenth and Early Twentieth Centuries*. Ed. Carl Ballstadt. Literature of Canada. Poetry and Prose in Reprint, No. 16. Toronto: Univ. of Toronto Press, 1975, pp. 199-202.

Harte's article, accompanied by photographs and sketches of Canadian writers, provides American readers of 1890 with a good survey of literary achievements north of the border. Harte considers

Lampman to be Canada's best poet: "I venture to assert that there is no living poet in either hemisphere who can present such pictures of natural scenery and natural phenomena as Lampman. In England since Wordsworth there has been no poet to equal him in painting the common life of the country."

C8   Barry, Lilly E. F. "Prominent Canadians-XXXV: Archibald Lampman." *The Week*, 10 April 1891, pp. 298-300. *AL*.

Barry provides a biography of Lampman in this article and suggests that his "contemplative disposition" is a "tendency inherited from his Teutonic forefathers...." Elements of Canadian philistinism and the Puritan work ethic surface at points in this study. For example, it is noted that Lampman is not neglecting his postal duties to write poetry. "Yet it is by no means to be feared that the interests of the Department suffer at the hands of Mr. Lampman, for he is a thoroughly conscientious worker at any task." Lampman's poetry is praised as "a continuous revelation of beauty, peace, order and undisguised beneficence." However, "his fondness for the same class of subjects, the same moods and grooves of thought" is considered a shortcoming. "We would like to see more of the exuberance of youth, with its extremes of joy and pain, its laughter and its tears."

C9   [Chamberlin, Joseph Edgar.] "The Listener." *Boston Evening Transcript*, 12 Aug. 1891, p. 4.

"Mr. Archibald Lampman is a Canadian," the newspaper admits, but it is "a great mistake to speak of him as a 'Canadian poet,'" for "if he has expressed Canada in his verse, he is also an American poet." Noting that Lampman is engaged in "a very prosaic employment" at the Ottawa Post Office, the newspaper makes the following suggestion: "Boston has proved a sort of Mecca for American literary people. It would be a matter for congratulation, certainly for Boston, and perhaps for Mr. Lampman, if he could be persuaded to take up his residence here too." Lampman's work is compared to that of Burns, Whitman, and Tom Moore, and the article concludes with the comment that "Lampman expresses vague inward moods by outward impressions very delicately, and nebulous feelings without any nebulous verse...."

C10   "Encourage Merit." *The Empire* [Toronto], 2 Jan. 1892, p. 6.

Noting that Lampman will soon be invited to a chair of literature in an American university, *The Empire* strongly attacks the provincial government for allowing talented Canadians to be lured to the United States. Lampman declined the offer.

C11   Stringer, Arthur. "A Glance at Lampman." *Canadian Magazine*, 2, No. 6 (April 1894), 545-48. *AL*.

Stringer begins his article by warning against the excesses of literary nationalism. Proceeding to a discussion of Lampman, Stringer finds him "the true nature poet." Lampman "has an artist's eye for color, and the quiet thoughtfulness of a student for scenery ...."

C12   Miller, Joseph Dana. "The Singers of Canada." *Munsey's Magazine*, 13, No. 2 (May 1895), 128-36.

Miller finds Lampman's work to be particularly fine: "Lampman's knowledge of nature is something more than intellectual — it is affinitive. It is impossible not to feel that the passionate love of the country, of outdoor life, of the pastoral panorama, the brown bees, the birds, the brooks, the oxen, the grass, the sky, are not merely the furnishings of Lampman's verse, but the utterance of a close and genuine sympathy."

C13   Crawford, A. W. "Archibald Lampman." *Acta Victoriana*, 17 (Dec. 1895), 77-81. *AL*.

One of the first critics to use the term "the Ottawa School," Crawford identifies Lampman as "one of the foremost poets of this school...." Lampman's poetry is "brilliant by reason of its polish, rather than by reason of the inward fire which brightens and gives form to the whole structure." The "essentially ethical and religious" quality of Lampman's work is commended: he has "that supreme regard for everything good and true which characterized Keats."

C14   Waldron, Gordon. "Canadian Poetry." *Canadian Magazine*, 8, No. 2 (Dec. 1896), 101-08. Rpt. (excerpt). In *The Search for English-Canadian Literature: An Anthology of Critical Articles from the Nineteenth and Early Twentieth Centuries*. Ed. Carl Ballstadt. Literature of Canada. Poetry and Prose in Reprint, No. 16. Toronto: Univ. of Toronto Press, 1975, pp. 179-82.

Waldron attempts to dislodge the Confederation poets from their position of prominence and popularity in late nineteenth-century Canada. Noting that many Canadian poets show early promise, but then stop writing, Waldron speculates on the reasons for "this lack of sustained enthusiasm." Lampman "has a habit of broadly suggesting scenes which is very effective, and of going on to treat them in a way that is very tiresome." However, though his "range of ideas is not very wide, there is an earnest tone in his poetry which, in itself, wins our sympathy, and makes us hope that he will do more than any of the writers mentioned."

C15   "American Poets of To-day: Archibald Lampman." *Current Literature*, 21 (March 1897), 246.

This brief introduction to six of Lampman's poems (listed in Section B of this bibliography) gives a summary of Lampman's life and career.

C16   [Whiteside, Ernestine R.] "Canadian Poetry and Poets. II." *McMaster University Monthly*, 8 (Nov. 1898), 68-74.

Calling Lampman essentially a nature poet who excels in his sonnets, Whiteside points out that "the ruling characteristic through all Lampman's poetry is his passion for beauty.... If Lampman were to be criticized, it would be for his indulgent surrender to mere external beauty. This being 'content to watch and dream,' leaves him weak to pierce into the heart of things, or even fully to analyze and express his own feelings."

C17   "Decease of Fellows—the Historian Kingsford and the Poet Lampman." *Royal Society of Canada Proceedings and Transactions*, 2nd. ser., No. 5, Proceedings (1899), xxiv-xxxi.

Obituary.

C18   "Canadian Poet Dead. Archibald Lampman Passed Away from an Attack of Pneumonia." *Ottawa Citizen*, 10 Feb. 1899, p. 1.

This article provides details of Lampman's final illness, and his death at his residence, 187 Bay Street, Ottawa, at 1:00 a.m. on Thursday, February 10, 1899.

C19   "Death of Mr. A. Lampman. Canada's Leading Poet Passes Away." *Ottawa Evening Journal*, 10 Feb. 1899, p. 3.

A summary of Lampman's life and career as a poet, this article notes that "he was formerly a member of the Fabian Society of Ottawa, and was one of the leading Socialists of the city. One of the last views Mr. Lampman expressed with reference to Canadian nationality and the purpose of a national life was that 'Canada has an opportunity of giving the world an object lesson in the adoption of socialism as a form of government, which would not only make us a nation, but give us a unique place in the world's history. But,' he remarked with a shrewdness which characterized him, 'there is probably no country under heaven in which it would be more difficult to convince the people of the desirability of such a form of government.'"

C20   [Ross, P. D.] "Archibald Lampman." *Ottawa Evening*

Journal, 11 Feb. 1899, p. 4. Rpt. in *Ottawa Evening Journal*, 12 April 1930, p. 8.

Ross's tribute to Lampman is, in large part, an attack on Canadian philistinism and a lament for Lampman's plight in a country unsympathetic to the artist. "One can hardly help believing that a man of such essentially refined and artistic feeling as Archibald Lampman's poems and tastes showed him to be would have been better nourished intellectually, and personally far happier had fate placed him in another and artistically richer atmosphere." Ross's article prompted an immediate response from Lampman's mother who agreed entirely with Ross's point of view. (See C49.)

C21   Richardson, Augusta Doan. "The Late Archibald Lampman. Deceased February 10th, 1899." *The Globe* [Toronto], 18 Feb. 1899, p. 1.

An obituary accompanied by photographs of Lampman and his birthplace in Morpeth, Ontario.

C22   "Item." *Book Buyer*, 18, No. 3 (April 1899), 188-89.

Notes Lampman's recent death, and gives a short biography.

C23   Scott, Duncan Campbell. "Memoir." In *The Poems of Archibald Lampman*. Ed. Duncan Campbell Scott. 1900, pp. xi-xxv. Rpt. Toronto: Univ. of Toronto Press, 1974, pp. xi-xxv. Rpt. in *Selected Poems of Archibald Lampman*. Ed. Duncan Campbell Scott. Toronto: Ryerson, 1947, pp. xiii-xxvii.

A memoir containing several anecdotes about Lampman's youth.

C24   Burpee, Lawrence J. "Archibald Lampman. A Canadian Poet." *North American Notes and Queries*, 1, No. 3 (Aug. 1900), 84-92.

A prelude to Burpee's 1909 study of Lampman in *A Little Book of Canadian Essays* (see C30). The "very keynote" of Lampman's poetry "is the comfort, the consolation, the peace which Nature has in store for hearts weary of the stress and sordidness of these latter days." Burpee also discusses Lampman's ancestry, biography, and the influence of Arnold, Keats, and Wordsworth on his work.

C25   Wendell, Winifred Lee. "Modern School of Canadian Writers." *Bookman* [New York], 11 (Aug. 1900), 515-26.

Assessing the work of several Canadian writers, Wendell finds that Lampman "has given us poetry of such unusual strength and originality that his untimely death . . . has undoubtedly robbed the world of much which would have helped us not a little in our knowledge of the beauty and use of life."

C26   Burpee, Lawrence J. "Archibald Lampman. A Canadian Poet." *North American Notes and Queries*, 1, No. 4 (Sept. 1900), 105-17.

The second part of Burpee's prelude to his book entitled *A Little Book of Canadian Essays* (see C30).

C27   Scott, Duncan Campbell. "A Decade of Canadian Poetry." *Canadian Magazine*, 17, No. 2 (June 1901), 153-58. Rpt. (excerpt). In *The Search for English-Canadian Literature: An Anthology of Critical Articles from the Nineteenth and Early Twentieth Centuries*. Ed. Carl Ballstadt. Poetry and Prose in Reprint, No. 16. Toronto: Univ. of Toronto Press, 1975, pp. 187-90.

In the portion of the article devoted to Lampman, Scott responds to the often expressed criticism that Lampman concerned himself too much with nature, while neglecting human issues in his poetry. "There are but few of Lampman's poems that do not lead from nature by a very short path to human life. The first impulse of his genius was the interpretation of nature, no doubt, but the desire to deal with human emotion, with the spring of human action, with the great hopes and desires of the human soul, was implicit in his mind. From the earliest of his writings to the latest this secondary quality demands attention, will be heard, keeps gaining strength and importance." In fact, Scott stresses, Lampman "had begun to observe a more just balance between the divisions of his genius" in the year or two before he died. Such poems as "The Cup of Life," "The Land of Pallas," and "The Largest Life" are indicative of Lampman's concern with human themes in his work.

C28   Marshall, John. "Archibald Lampman." *Queen's Quarterly*, 9, No. 1 (July 1901), 63-79. *AL.*

Lampman's work bears the brunt of Marshall's attack on the derivativeness of Canadian poetry. He is attacked for "his lack of originality, his narrow range of thought and feeling and the almost entire absence of any evidence of progress towards clearer and more consistent views of life and art." Noting that Lampman preferred to be judged by his sonnets, Marshall adds: "Like all distinct art forms, the sonnet is great support to a weak writer." Marshall rearranges lines in "Stoic and Hedonist" yet still finds it wanting: "But I cannot be expected to furnish rhyme and structure as well as criticism."

C29   "A Poet's Birthplace." *Canadian Magazine*, 28, No. 2 (Dec. 1906), 201.

Accompanied by a photograph of the parsonage in Morpeth, Ontario, where Lampman was born, this article laments that the house has been torn down in order to build a new parsonage.

C30   Burpee, Lawrence J. "Archibald Lampman." In *A Little Book of Canadian Essays*. Toronto: Musson, 1909, pp. 30-42. *AL.*

Burpee parallels some of the qualities in Lampman's poetry with qualities which Lampman, himself, embodied. Lampman is also given credit for recognizing the poetic potential in Canadian subject matter: "...he could find beauty and helpfulness in the storm and stress of our northern winter, as well as in the haunting charm of a Canadian mid-summer's day."

C31   Untermeyer, Louis. "Archibald Lampman and the Sonnet." *Poet Lore*, 20, No. 6 (Nov.-Dec. 1909), 432-37. *AL.*

Lampman's "dream and flower philosophy" is well suited to the sonnet form. Untermeyer believes that "the sonnet with all its restrictions and limitations" is "the most ravishing of all the classical forms. And it is in the sonnet that Lampman is at the very height of his genius." Lampman's "Among the Orchards" is a masterpiece; no sonnet in the English language excels it.

C32   Logan, J. D. "Literary Group of '61." *Canadian Magazine*, 37, No. 6 (Oct. 1911), 555-63.

Logan's intention in this article is to deal first with the "historical position of the primary group of Canadian authors"; secondly with "the quality of their writings as literature"; and thirdly with the "significance and potency of the social ideas inspiring, or openly expressed in, them." In the segment of his article devoted to Lampman, Logan argues that "Lampman's attitude to nature is not the attitude of an impressionistic portrait painter, but of one for whom physical loveliness is supremely a spiritual revealment." Lampman's "Sapphics" is examined in great detail, and the article concludes on a very optimistic note: "Canadians are notably in the eyes of the nations a sane and happy people and they are so because they keep their souls always clear and valiant, having, as Lampman and Roberts and the rest of the literary group of '61, a sure vision of the greatness of their fate and the means to it."

C33   Marquis, T. G. "English-Canadian Literature." In *Canada and Its Provinces*. Ed. Adam Shortt and Arthur G. Doughty. 1913; rpt. Toronto: Glasgow, Brook, 1914, XII, pp. 566-89.

Marquis stresses that Lampman "ranks high as a

nature poet." He "lived close to the heart of nature, and nature revealed herself to him and gave him the power to reveal her to others with a natural magic." Although "he stands by himself" as an interpreter of nature, Lampman's work, according to Marquis, "has not the splendid sensuousness of Carman's verse, nor has he handled as many and varied themes as Roberts; he lacks, too, the moral profundity of William Wilfred Campbell in that poet's inspired moments...."

C34 Munday, Don. "Soul-Standards of Archibald Lampman." *Westminster Hall Magazine and Farthest West Review*, 6, No. 3 (Oct. 1914), 15-17.

"Like many a poet," Munday writes of Lampman, "it was in descriptions of the beauties of Nature that he developed his powers of expression before seeking other fields."

C35 Muddiman, Bernard. "Archibald Lampman." *Queen's Quarterly*, 22, No. 3 (Jan.-Feb.-March 1915), 233-43. *AL*.

Muddiman attributes certain characteristics of Lampman's poetry to the poet's ancestry. The "meticulous minuteness of detail in much of his verse" and "its calm nonchalence and unruffled flow of thought" are said to derive from his German and Dutch descent. Although Lampman's talent for creating a mood of "solemn melancholy" is acknowledged, Muddiman faults Lampman for his numerous retreats to the country. The excursions are not part of a "philosophy of energy or aggression."

C36 Unwin, G. H. "The Poetry of Archibald Lampman." *University Magazine* [Montreal], 16 (Feb. 1917), 55-73. *AL*.

At a time when the poetry of Robert Service is being made into a silent movie, Unwin is pleased to note that "a considerable proportion of readers... do not confine their attentions to the vaudeville school of poets." Unwin offers a detailed comparison of the work of Lampman and Charles G. D. Roberts and concludes that "while Roberts gives us beautiful impressions of Nature, Lampman interprets her."

C37 Macdonald, Elizabeth Roberts. "A Little Talk about Lampman." *Canadian Magazine*, 52, No. 6 (April 1919), 1012-16.

Macdonald recalls her sadness upon learning of Lampman's death from her brother (Theodore Goodridge Roberts), gives a brief biography of Lampman, and quotes a number of lines from his poems. "It is Lampman's nature-poems, and his strangely haunting songs," Macdonald declares, "that constitute to my mind his greatest and most individual contribution to literature."

C38 Voorhis, Ernest. "The Ancestry of Archibald Lampman, Poet." *Royal Society of Canada Proceedings and Transactions*, 3rd ser., No. 15, Sec. 2 (1921), 103-21.

As Archibald Lampman's brother-in-law, Reverend Ernest Voorhis had access to unpublished family records in the preparation of this paper, read at the May 1921 meeting of the Royal Society of Canada. Voorhis traces Lampman's father's family back to eighteenth-century Hanover under George II. He is able to trace Lampman's mother's family, the Gesner family, to a village in sixteenth-century Switzerland, near the German border.

C39 Scott, Duncan Campbell. "Poetry and Progress." *Canadian Magazine*, 60, No. 3 (Jan. 1923), 187-95.

Deploring the provincialism of late nineteenth-century Canada, and pointing to the "dull environment" in which Lampman wrote, Scott notes that "we still feel that lack of national consciousness, but perhaps it is a trifle less evident now." As proof of this claim, Scott notes that the recently deceased Marjorie Pickthall attracted a following in Canada without first receiving praise from critics elsewhere. Lampman, on the other hand, could not attract an audience in Canada until an American critic (William Dean Howells) lauded his work.

C40 MacMechan, Archibald. *Headwaters of Canadian Literature*. 1924; rpt. New Canadian Library, No. 107. Toronto: McClelland and Stewart, 1974, pp. 109-17.

MacMechan sees Lampman as a distinctly Canadian poet. "Like most Canadians, he knows the delight of life in the open; he had camped out; he had canoed; he had noted the inexhaustible beauty of the early summer morning, incense-breathing, far from the stain of civilisation."

C41 Macdonald, Adrian. "Archibald Lampman." In *Canadian Portraits*. Toronto: Ryerson, 1925, pp. 220-30.

Macdonald provides a biography of Lampman before proceeding to critical matters. He feels that Lampman's "diction is too frequently marred by a certain affectation to meet the more austere requirements of good taste. He is so much in love with being a poet that he cannot resist a phrase, however weak, if it seems poetic...." Macdonald, however, points out that "when a poet sings of our own land he touches us very closely," and "it is here that Lampman excels."

C42 Scott, Duncan Campbell. "Introduction." In *Lyrics of Earth: Sonnets and Ballads*. By Archibald Lampman. Ed. Duncan Campbell Scott. Toronto: Musson, 1925, pp. 3-47.

In addition to discussing Lampman's early life and offering a lengthy account of his ancestry Scott attempts to dispel any suggestion that Lampman was a lonely man. "Lampman never worked in loneliness or without appreciation. He might feel that his spirit was parched by routine, but he never felt that other desolating consciousness that no one heeded or comprehended him." Although "his letters show a constant stress of strong feeling,... the happiness he had in living manifested itself indirectly." Scott concludes that "the true heart of this poet lies in his

marvellous interpretations of nature and the breadth and serenity of his outlook through nature upon human life and destiny."

C43 "Lampman, Archibald." *The Dictionary of Canadian Biography*. Toronto: Macmillan, 1926. Rpt. in *The Encyclopedia of Canada*. 1936; rpt. Toronto: Murray, 1948.

This very brief entry, identical in the two reference works, gives a biography of Lampman and notes that "he has been described as 'the Canadian Keats';... he is perhaps the most outstanding exponent of the Canadian school of nature poets."

C44 Scott, Duncan Campbell. "Who's Who in Canadian Literature: Archibald Lampman." *Canadian Bookman*, 8, No. 4 (April 1926), 107-09.

Summarizing Lampman's work, Scott calls him a master of the sonnet, and states that there is "nothing feigned" in Lampman's poetry. "It is inspired by true feeling and first hand observation.... His task was to capture the essential in the object and not to obscure it with conventions.... He desired to transfigure life and to strengthen and glorify the universal yearning for order and beauty and peace. The hope was high, but the task was accomplished."

C45 Stevenson, O. J. "The Song of the Spirit." In *A People's Best*. Toronto: Musson, 1927, pp. 127-33.

After providing a biography of Lampman, Stevenson argues that Lampman's nature poetry is not merely descriptive. "He is the interpreter of Nature, the critic of life, the moralist and teacher." Natural scenes "are described not for their own sake, but as part of his own spiritual experience. The poet is himself inseparable from the scene."

C46 Swift, S. C. "Lampman and Leconte de Lisle." *Canadian Bookman*, 9, No. 9 (Sept. 1927), 261-64.

Swift speculates that Lampman was conversant

with the Parnassians of France, whose "chief and greatest poet" was Leconte de Lisle. "The principal character of the Parnassian School—faultlessness of form—was exactly the quality which would attract Lampman, who, in that respect, was a very good Parnassian himself." Swift offers a detailed comparison of "Midi" by Leconte de Lisle, and "Heat" by Lampman, and concludes that "Heat" is the "direct and legitimate offspring" of "Midi."

C47 Knister, Raymond. "The Poetry of Archibald Lampman." *Dalhousie Review*, 7 (Oct. 1927), 348-61. *AL*.

"The combination of racial tendencies, Celtic temperament and Saxon endurance...made Lampman what he was, and gave him an unusual balance of qualities." Knister, like many critics before him, points to the influence of Keats on Lampman's poetry. Unlike previous critics, however, Knister recognizes the pressure of provincialism on Lampman's writing. "It is obvious...that the audience to which he is addressing himself exerts a pressure of influence upon the artist, and that his work is really an adjustment made so that he can be understood, even when it is essentially self-expression. Hence came the peculiarities of much of the literary work of Lampman's time." In his late poetry, "a sense of character, if not psychological subtlety" appeared, and "he probably would have developed" this aspect of his work had he lived longer. "The Cup of Life" with its "explicit doubt and misgiving before life" exemplifies this psychological concern in Lampman's work. Lampman's best work was in the sonnet: "the discipline of the form was one which, sympathetic to him, he did not allow to become too rigid."

C48 Burton, Jean. "Archibald Lampman's Poetry of Release." *Willison's Monthly*, April 1928, pp. 425-27.

Entirely a biographical reading of Lampman's poetry. Burton claims that "his nostalgic melancholy, the oppressed languor of so much of his work, came...

from definite frustrations in his personal experience ...." Burton cites Lampman's uncongenial occupation and ill health as contributing to his frustration and maintains that "his poetry was...a means to an end, a search for release...."

C49 Ross, P. D. "Retrospects XLIX. Archibald Lampman." *Ottawa Evening Journal*, 12 April 1930, p. 8.

Noting that a monument to Lampman will be built in Morpeth, Ross states: "But Archibald Lampman belongs most of all to Ottawa. Here he lived his short manhood; here he wrote." Ross reprints his tribute to Lampman published in February 1899 (see C20) and reveals that he received a letter from Lampman's mother, written the day after the tribute appeared. Written at 222 Daly Avenue, Ottawa, and dated February 12, 1899, the letter reads: "Dear Mr. Ross—Accept a deeply grieved mother's heartfelt thanks for your tribute to my dear son's memory. I had not thought anyone but myself so fully understood the blockade of adverse circumstances surrounding his life, and which I know too well has helped him to a premature grave. Yours ever sincerely and gratefully, S. Gesner Lampman."

C50 Elson, John Melbourne. "The Lampman Memorial." *Canadian Bookman*, 12, No. 5 (May 1930), 105-06.

A note on the efforts of the Canadian Authors' Association in organizing the ceremony to honour Lampman.

C51 "The Lampman Memorial. Unveiling the Cairn at Morpeth." *The Authors' Bulletin*, 8, No. 1 (Sept. 1930), 42-43.

Account of the memorial ceremonies at Morpeth.

C52 "Lampman's Memory Honored. Impressive Ceremonies at the Dedication of a Commemorative Cairn in Trinity Churchyard at Morpeth." *Canadian Bookman*, 12, No. 9 (Sept. 1930), 175-76.

An account of the ceremonies and speeches at the dedication of the Lampman cairn.

C53   "Archibald Lampman Lives." *The Free Press* [London, Ont.], 15 Sept. 1930, p. 6.

The newspaper's lead editorial asserts that "the unveiling of the cairn erected to the memory of Archibald Lampman will become, we venture to predict, an event of historical significance."

C54   Hammond, M. O. "Archibald Lampman Is Honored as Poet and Great Canadian." *The Globe* [Toronto], 15 Sept. 1930, pp. 1-2.

An account of the dedication of the Lampman Memorial Cairn at Morpeth, Hammond's article lists many of those present at the ceremony.

C55   "Lampman Cairn Unveiled in Kent." *The Free Press* [London, Ont.], 15 Sept. 1930, p. 11.

Account of the ceremonies at Morpeth, marking the unveiling of the Lampman cairn.

C56   "A Memorial to Archibald Lampman." *The Farmer's Advocate* [London, Ont.], 25 Sept. 1930, p. 1404.

This account of the ceremonies at the dedication of the Lampman cairn at Morpeth notes that "the present generation reveres" Lampman's memory "and feels that he made a real contribution to the little library of Canadian literature."

C57   Benson, Nathaniel A. "The Lampman Cairn at Morpeth." *Saturday Night*, 27 Sept. 1930, p. 8.

Benson's account includes a description of the cairn itself: "a strong, dignified monument of vari-colored stone, chaste and austere and enduring...." Benson also includes some human interest anecdotes.

C58   "A Memorial to Lampman: Cairn at Morpeth, On-tario." *Commonweal*, 8 Oct. 1930, p. 566.

The writer believes that "many will surely pause

at Morpeth churchyard to wonder during a moment at this strange lad who may have dreamed that a lyric was more enduring than bronze."

C59   Kennedy, Leo. "Canadian Writers of the Past V: Archibald Lampman." *The Canadian Forum*, May 1933, pp. 301-03. *AL.*

"Archibald Lampman... has been too long and too loudly publicized as John Keats' little Canadian brother, with literary kinship to Wordsworth on the tedious side.... Like the late Bliss Carman, his name and work have been seized upon by patriotic women's groups, hot for national cultural advancement at any cost." Kennedy, a spokesman for Modernism in Canadian poetry, sets Lampman's work up as an example of the kind of poetry the Moderns are seeking to overthrow. "His devotion to the rag-tags of the poet's dictionary—the methinks, lo's, o'ers, begones, yesternights and yestereves—is dispiriting and try-ing." Kennedy and his contemporaries "are impatient of reading into the face of nature the conservative policies of an Anglican omnipotence. We have detected, as the Lampman's do not appear to have done, that all is not right with the world; we suspect that God is not in his Heaven." Lampman's "second-hand poetic inheritance... does not stand the harsh light of our day...we are over prone to greet the versified manifestations of both inheritance and outlook with a Bronx cheer."

C60   Collin, W. E. "Archibald Lampman." *University of Toronto Quarterly*, 4, No. 1 (Oct. 1934), 103-20. *AL.* Rpt. (revised—"Natural Landscape"). In *The White Savannahs*. 1936; rpt. Toronto: Univ. of Toronto Press, 1975, pp. 3-40.

Collin finds that Lampman "produces the effect of opiate slowness by lines of leaden monosyllables ... or by languid words...." Collin feels that "The City of the End of Things" was influenced by Thomson's "The City of Dreadful Night." Collin explores the provincialism of Ottawa and its effect on Lampman's work, as well as the different literary standards which distinguish the late nineteenth century from the 1930s.

C61 Stringer, Arthur. "Wild Poets I've Known: Archibald Lampman." *Saturday Night*, 24 May 1941, p. 29.

Stringer's recollection of events forty-three years earlier, when he was a young man working for the *Montreal Herald*, provides the basis of this article. W. H. Drummond invited Stringer to his home one evening to meet the visiting Archibald Lampman. "The carelessly dressed figure before me," Stringer recalls, "looked frail. But from it I harvested an impression of some stubborn inner strength that would mock and defy the fragility of the flesh."

C62 Klinck, Carl F. "In Canada's Capital." In *Wilfred Campbell: A Study in Late Provincial Victorianism*. 1942; rpt. Ottawa: Tecumseh, 1977, pp. 72-116.

"In the thoroughly political environment of Ottawa," Lampman and his fellow-poets "struggled to keep politics out of literature. Nature and books were their inspiration, meditation and congenial companions their sources of strength."

C63 Brown, E. K. "Introduction." In *At the Long Sault and Other New Poems*. Toronto: Ryerson, 1943, pp. xi-xxix. Rpt. in *On Canadian Poetry*. Toronto: McGraw-Hill Ryerson, 1943, pp. 72-116. Rpt. in *On Canadian Poetry*. Ottawa: Tecumseh, 1973, pp. 88-118.

"In Canada, Lampman is the nearest approach to a national classic in verse.... In his later years, Lampman's conception of life was much more comprehensive than his readers and interpreters have generally supposed." Had Lampman lived, Brown believes that his "development likely would have tended towards the drama of life and away from the picture of nature." Considering "At the Long Sault" to be Lampman's greatest work, Brown notes that Lampman had a great theme, and an issue of epic significance, yet he chose

"to concentrate tightly upon the climactic action," rather than write a long narrative poem.

C64 Scott, Duncan Campbell. "Foreword." *At the Long Sault and Other New Poems*. By Archibald Lampman. Ed. Duncan Campbell Scott and E. K. Brown. Toronto: Ryerson, 1943, pp. vii-x.

Scott maintains that *At the Long Sault and Other New Poems*, drawn from poems in recently acquired notebooks of Lampman's, is "a gathering together, in a liberal spirit, of all that is left of the poet's work." It should be compared, he believes, with *The Poems of Archibald Lampman* (1900), in that it is inclusive, rather than selective. In editing *At the Long Sault and Other New Poems*, Scott made a few minor changes in some of the poems: "slight rearrangement here and there," and corrections in punctuation.

C65 Scott, Duncan Campbell. "Archibald Lampman." *Educational Record* [Quebec], 59, No. 4 (Oct.-Dec. 1943), 221-28. Rpt. in *Leading Canadian Poets*. Ed. W. P. Percival. Toronto: Ryerson, 1948, pp. 98-106.

In addition to providing a biography of Lampman, Scott argues that Lampman's contact with the Quebec landscape, rather than that of Ontario, had the most significant effect on his poetry.

C66 Creighton, Donald Grant. *Dominion of the North*. 1944; rpt. Toronto: Macmillan, 1967, pp. 369-71.

Lampman and his contemporaries "made Canadians aware of Canadian nature through the tradition of nineteenth-century Romanticism."

C67 Brown, E. K. "Prefatory Note. 'Two Canadian Poets: A Lecture.' [By Archibald Lampman.]" *University of Toronto Quarterly*, 13, No. 4 (July 1944), 406.

Because Lampman wrote the accompanying piece as a lecture, "doubtless he depended upon his voice to bring out the importance and relevance of the material." The lecture "contains notable ideas about the nation and the national literature, expresses a many-sided judgment of Sir Charles G. D. Roberts, which will surprise those who have thought of the poets born in the sixties as a group of like-minded men, and closes with an enthusiastic tribute to George Frederick Cameron, whose fame has been under a long eclipse."

C68 Brown, E. K. "Prefatory Note. 'The Character and Poetry of Keats.' [By Archibald Lampman.]" *University of Toronto Quarterly*, 15, No. 4 (July 1946), 356-57.

Brown argues that "Keats was the strongest literary influence on Lampman, except, perhaps, in the last years of his life.... For the man, whose life in several respects was significantly like his own, he felt an intimate sympathy and a reverent respect." Brown believes that the accompanying essay started on the scale of a somewhat larger work and that Lampman made his quotations and comments briefer as he drew towards a close. "The passages on 'Endymion' and on the odes are studied with happy and suggestive phrases such as only a kindred spirit could find. They enrich the treasury of Keats-criticism."

C69 Gustafson, Ralph. "Among the Millet." *Northern Review*, 1, No. 5 (Feb.-March 1947), 26-34. *AL*.

Gustafson believes that Lampman's poetry reveals a crisis in his life other than the 1894 death of his young son. (Subsequent research has proven Gustafson right, for there is considerable evidence to suggest that Lampman was involved with Kate Waddell, while remaining married to Maud Playter.) "From such sensitive unrest derives much of the essential appeal of Lampman's poetry. It has given his best sonnets their valid profundity." Regarding Lampman's attacks on Ottawa and its inhabitants, Gustafson feels that "the suspicion cannot be avoided that Lampman protested too much and in too general terms. The conclusion is forced upon one that Lampman was shifting respon-

sibility from himself, that his protests were compensation for a lack that lay elsewhere than wholly in his environment." Lampman would not have been happy in literary London, for he could not face "life" in Ottawa. There are indications, Gustafson notes, "that Lampman partook willingly of puritan provincialism" and points to the pinning down of the pages of his notebook which contained love sonnets as proof of this claim. Lampman's disapproval of "brawny passages" in some of Charles G. D. Roberts' work and his temperance beliefs exemplified in "Abu Midjan" are further indications of his puritanism. 'Lampman's inability to fulfil the worldly role he thought he should assume led him to postulations that the world was well lost." By rationalizing his incapacity into a virtue, Lampman could justify his forays into nature. This article elicited a response from Duncan Campbell Scott. (See C83.)

C70 Brown, E. K. "Archibald Lampman 1861-1899: What We Lost." *Saturday Night*, 8 Feb. 1949, p. 15.

"To this day no one has captured as Lampman did the beauty of the Canadian landscape, the march of the seasons in their astonishing extremes, the passing of day and night, land and water, storm and stillness, the fields at the city's edge and the untrodden wilds."

C71 Bourinot, Arthur S. "Archibald Lampman and What Some Writers Have Said of Him." *Canadian Author and Bookman*, 26, No. 2 (Summer 1950), 20-22. Rpt. in *Five Canadian Poets*. Ed. Arthur S. Bourinot. 1954; rpt. Ottawa: Bourinot, 1968, pp. 8-11.

Lampman's critics "have overstressed the difficulties of the poet's life and underestimated the joy and happiness."

C72 Bissell, Claude T. "Literary Taste in Central Canada during the Late Nineteenth Century." *The Canadian Historical Review*, 31, No. 2 (Sept. 1950), 237-51. Rpt. in *Twentieth Century Essays on Confederation Litera-*

ture, Ed. Lorraine McMullen. Ottawa: Tecumseh, 1976, pp. 24-40.

In assessing the role of the writer in nineteenth-century Canada, Bissell terms the literary establishment of the day "the family compact of intellectuals and men of letters...." The career of Lampman "gives us a pattern of the normal development. It is founded on a family tradition that stresses devotion to things British, to the Church, and to classical literature. It is subsequently toughened by exposure to the world of politics and education, and by immersion in journalism." It is "abundantly clear," according to Bissell, "that Lampman was no pale recluse but an active participator and an acknowledged leader in the intellectual and cultural life of Central Canada." In his poetry, "the cultivated taste of the age finds its most eloquent apology."

C73   Phelps, Arthur. "Archibald Lampman." *Canadian Writers*. 1951; rpt. Freeport, N.Y.: Books for Libraries, 1972, pp. 51-59.

Phelps sees Lampman as a minor poet. "He did not even leave behind him a single poem or group of poems whose vitality of spirit or unflawed craftsmanship might guarantee an incidental immortality."

C74   Sutherland, John. "Edgar Allan Poe in Canada." *Northern Review*, 4, No. 3 (Feb.-March 1951), 22-37. *AL*.

Sutherland's examination of Poe's influence on Lampman is one of a series of articles in the *Northern Review* dealing with the relationship between the Canadian writer and his literary influences. Lampman mistrusted art, Sutherland maintains. "He regarded poetry as an escape into dream, a kind of opiate, but he never ceased to feel that the desire to escape was slightly corrupt. Hence...he always felt obliged to relate the hazy reaches of the dream to a large moral truth, no matter how incongruous it might seem. What was, in effect, a split between the imagination and reality grew steadily wider." Sutherland compares Poe's "The City in the Sea" with Lampman's "The City of the End of Things" by offering a line by line analysis of how Lampman's poem echoes Poe's. Proceeding to the thematic similarities between the two works, Sutherland writes that both poems "involve a contrast between death or madness and a state of paradisal bliss." The two poems "develop this contrast in an identical manner: they begin with images of death, then evoke memories of a blissful happiness, and end with a prophecy of utter destruction."

C75   Pacey, Desmond. "A Reading of Lampman's 'Heat.'" *Culture*, 14 (Sept. 1953), 292-97. *AL*.

Pacey's sensitive *explication de texte* of "Heat" is one of the most important works of Lampman criticism. Beginning with an examination of the poem's rhythm, Pacey points out that the first seven lines of each stanza are written in iambic tetrameter, while the last line of each stanza is in iambic trimeter. Thus, a sense of inconclusiveness is developed through the rhythm, urging us on to the next stanza. This effect is in keeping with Lampman's intention of "projecting a linked sequence of emotional impressions." Pacey sees the poem as being "constructed on the principle of balanced opposites." Recalling Vaughan's glimpse of eternity as a ring of pure and endless light, and noting the dominant image of the wheel in "Heat," Pacey sees the opposites in Lampman's poem as spokes of the wheel: "they have their place in an endless cycle which gives them meaning and a final unity."

C76   Brown, E. K. "Lampman, Archibald." *Chambers's Encyclopedia*. 1955; rpt. London: International Learning Systems, 1969.

Brown gives a biography of Lampman and notes that "Lampman's rendering of nature in Ontario and the valley of the Gatineau is at once faithful and poetically suggestive."

C77   Beattie, Munro. "Archibald Lampman." In *Our Living Tradition*. Ser. 1. Ed. Claude T. Bissell. Toronto: Univ. of Toronto Press, 1957, pp. 63-88.

Beattie believes that "...the theory that Ottawa drudgery suffocated Lampman and robbed us of masterpieces he was never permitted to create is best refuted by his decision to remain at his civil service job in Ottawa." For example, Lampman turned down an opportunity to teach at Cornell University. Beattie points to Lampman's "unremitting fastidiousness as a craftsman" and calls him one of the four finest Canadian poets.

C78   Pierce, Lorne. "Lampman, Archibald." *Encyclopedia Canadiana*. 1957; rpt. Toronto: Grolier, 1977.

Lampman "had a genius for marshalling details of minute artistic unity of mood and manner. 'The spirit's birthright of immortal youth' was his, but in time confinement in a dull and mediocre world galled him. He was something of a socialist, and advocated the complete independence of Canada." Pierce believes that "there is little metrical invention in his art, and much of his work is lacking in depth and range," but Lampman was a supreme nature poet.

C79   Colgate, William. "Archibald Lampman: A Dedication and a Note." *The Canadian Forum*, March 1957, pp. 279-80.

Colgate came across an 1886 romance by Edmund Collins entitled *Annette, the Métis Spy; A Heroine of the N. W. Rebellion*, whose dedication read: "To my friend / Archibald Lampman / Whose beautiful and unaffected genius / men will some day be / delighted to honor / with / unvarying and unextinguishable love / I dedicate / This volume / The Author." Collins was a Toronto journalist and friend of Lampman's.

C80   Dudek, Louis. "The Significance of Lampman." *Culture*, 18 (Sept. 1957), 277-90. Rpt. in *Selected Essays and Criticism*. Ottawa: Tecumseh, 1978, pp. 65-78. *AL*.

"At the personal level," Lampman "reveals the temperament of the typical melancholic, undergoing alternate phases of depression and sudden relief. This provides a pattern of central experience for his poetry.... But raised to a philosophical plane, it reveals a questioning and troubled view of nature and man, a dissatisfaction with the complacencies of the popular romantic formula and moves toward new positions of doubt and mental struggle." Dudek sees the subtle expression of social criticism in Lampman's pessimism, and believes that Lampman's struggle with the problems of fundamental emotion and belief mark him as a forerunner of the significant poetry of the twentieth century. There is a marked dearth of references to God in Lampman's poetry. Most often God appears as "Energy" or "the energy divine," Dudek notes. "As a socialist, that is, a rationalist in his approach to society, Lampman might be expected to extend his critical thought to his religious ideas; and this is precisely what we find." However much Lampman "tries to be the romantic seer, the truth forces through; the formula of nature as the great comforter, as entire harmony, and the duty of the poet to achieve joy, in order to justify himself, all these fade before the conviction he gives of his inner unrest, melancholy, and pervading pessimism." His "poems dealing with the city, with social questions, and with ideas, although not Lampman's preferred subjects, since he would rather eschew them, are his most significant work."

C81   Pacey, Desmond. "Archibald Lampman." In *Ten Canadian Poets: A Group of Biographical and Critical Essays*. Toronto: Ryerson, 1958, pp. 114-40.

Lampman is usually "represented as a poet who was deprived of intellectual stimulation and intelligent appreciation, and who therefore sought refuge in the detailed but superficial description of natural landscape." The contention of Pacey's essay is "that this is an incomplete and unfair conception of both Lampman and his Canadian environment, and that his personality and his poetry were more complex than is commonly recognized."

C82 Watt, F. W. "The Masks of Archibald Lampman." *University of Toronto Quarterly*, 27, No. 2 (Jan. 1958), 169-84. *AL*.

Watt examines Lampman's concern with social issues. Lampman's life in Ottawa "was not at all one of quiet fruitfulness, but on the contrary one of unrest, dissatisfaction often to the point of despair, and unresolved tension and conflict within himself and with the society in which he lived." Distressed by "the excessive pieties of Victorian Canada," Lampman sought a release from social pressures in the countryside around Ottawa. However, for Lampman, escape created tension. The "grim Idiot at the gate" in "The City of the End of Things" is Lampman's figuring of the creative spirit of the artist in the sterile condition to which the nightmare of rampant industrial urbanism might one day reduce it." In contrast, "The Land of Pallas" presents "an egalitarian, communistic, peaceful, unchanging land of brotherly love."

C83 Scott, Duncan Campbell. "Copy of a Letter ... to Ralph Gustafson, 17 July 1945 [about Archibald Lampman]." *The Fiddlehead*, No. 41 (Summer 1959), pp. 12-14. *AL*.

Scott answers some of the charges levelled against Lampman by Ralph Gustafson in his *Northern Review* article (see C69). Scott insists that Lampman was not unhappy in the post office and never wanted to be a man of affairs, as Gustafson had claimed. Hence, he felt no sense of failure or conflict over his role as poet. "He was interested in both life and nature" writes Scott, in response to Gustafson's claim that Lampman escaped into nature because he could not face life. To Gustafson's charge that Lampman's anti-city poetry arose from his dislike of Ottawa, Scott stresses that "The City of the End of Things" had "no possible source in Ottawa past or present."

C84 Begley, Lucille. "Harmonies canadiennes: Pamphile le May, Archibald Lampman." *Lectures*, 6 (juin 1960), 296-97.

In this article, written in French, Begley points out that in spite of great differences in language and culture, Pamphile le May and Archibald Lampman were both disciples of the Romantic school of poetry. The former was an admirer of Lamartine and Victor Hugo, and the latter, of Keats and Matthew Arnold. Begley proceeds to point out the resemblance between the work of le May and Lampman, noting in particular, the likeness between le May's "La Terre" and Lampman's "Earth — The Stoic."

C85 Beattie, Munro. "Lampman, Archibald." *Encyclopedia Britannica*. 1961; rpt. Toronto: Britannica, 1970.

After providing a biography of Lampman, Beattie points out that the poet derived the material for his poems "from his contemplation of Ottawa and its environs, and the Gatineau countryside of Quebec.... A few short poems severely criticizing contemporary abuses of power and wealth show him to have been of radical tendencies in politics and economics, but do not create the kind of conviction communicated by his poems of description and reflection."

C86 Burnett, Ian. "Archibald Lampman, Our Most Gifted 19th Century Poet." *Ottawa Journal*, 18 Nov. 1961, p. 39.

Appearing the day after the centenary of Lampman's birth, this article offers a review of Lampman's life and career. For the person interested in tracking down the sites of Lampman's various homes in Ottawa, this article provides a wealth of information.

C87 Coblentz, Stanton A. "Archibald Lampman: Canadian Poet of Nature." *Arizona Quarterly*, 17, No. 4 (Winter 1961), 344-51.

Coblentz examines "Late November," "A Forest Path in Winter," and "Among the Timothy" in the context of nature poetry, before proceeding to discuss poems of Lampman's which are not concerned with nature, notably "The City of the End of Things." Of the latter poem, Coblentz states that "to us of the atomic age, with the menace of hydrogen doom overhanging us like a storm cloud, Lampman's dire foresight should have an immediacy it could not possess for the smug nineteenth century."

C88 Daniells, Roy. "Lampman and Roberts." In *Literary History of Canada: Canadian Literature in English*. Gen. ed. and introd. Carl F. Klinck. 1965; Toronto: Univ. of Toronto Press, 1976, Vol. I, 405-21.

"The heart of Lampman's poetic achievement consists of a small group of nature poems.... Lampman makes to the Ontario landscape a characteristic response, to which we must apply the word of his own choice—dream." "...But it is notable that Lampman refuses to give specific content to his dream or to allow his dreaming to lead him towards philosophic or theological concepts or to make of his dreams any incitement or prelude to action. It follows that as we move outward from this dream,...we move into spheres which are less and less relevant to his vision. It is nature, and...only nature, that induces in him the trance of insight into the life of things." Daniells also discusses the tension of opposites in Lampman's poetry and, before proceeding to a discussion of Charles G. D. Roberts, notes that Roberts is of less significance as a poet, but more of an influence on Canadian writing than Lampman.

C89 Story, Norah. "Lampman, Archibald." In *The Oxford Companion to Canadian History and Literature*. Toronto: Oxford Univ. Press, 1967.

Story notes that Lampman was "repelled by urban materialism and the growing mechanization of life and felt lost when the bulwarks of traditional belief fell before the Darwinian concept of evolution and higher criticism of the Bible. For the most part, Lampman did not grapple with the problems of his age...."

C90 Nesbitt, Bruce. "Matthew Arnold in Canada: A Dialogue Begun?" *Culture*, 28 (mars 1967), 53-54.

In this article, Nesbitt speculates as to whether Louis Fréchette and Lampman may have been friends. In their lost letters there may exist an early attempt to establish a literary dialogue between French and English Canadians.

C91 Greig, Peter. "A Check List of Lampman Manuscript Material in the Douglas Library Archives." *Douglas Library Notes*, 15, No. 3 (Winter 1967), 8-16; *Douglas Library Notes*, 16, No. 1 (Autumn 1967), 12-27.

The first instalment is devoted to Lampman's letters to Bliss Carman, while the second deals with Lampman's correspondence with the publishers Scudder, Copeland and Day.

C92 Jones, D. G. "The Problem of Job." In *Butterfly on Rock: A Study of Themes and Images in Canadian Literature*. 1970; rpt. Toronto: Univ. of Toronto Press, 1976, pp. 83-110.

Jones argues that the Confederation poets "are conventionally regarded as the poets of nature. They were clearly influenced by the nineteenth-century Romantics. But they also reflect an authentic desire to get out of a garrison culture that was becoming increasingly oppressive.... Dissatisfied with the established culture, they clearly look to nature in the hope of discovering a larger and more vital conception of life." However, in abandoning the garrison, they are "forced to reconcile themselves to the various threats against which the walls were initially built.... Lampman's attempt to escape from boredom and sterility led him to a search for the vital in nature and in language. The cultural confusion of the time is reflected in the mixed diction of his poetry." For example, he attempts to replace conventional expressions with more technical sounding words. "When Lampman maintains that the growth of the soul consists in each creature's following his own bent, he diametrically opposes the central impulse of his culture, which would change or transform life to make it fit some ideal pattern—which would impose an order upon life. Thus, though he may not be fully aware of it, he becomes a spokesman for the God of Job, who recommends all his creatures as equally good."

C93 Ower, John. "Portraits of the Landscape as Poet: Canadian Nature as Aesthetic Symbol in Three Confederation Writers." *Journal of Canadian Studies*, 6 (Feb. 1971), 27-32. Rpt. in *Twentieth Century Essays on Confederation Literature*. Ed. Lorraine McMullen. Ottawa: Tecumseh, 1976, pp. 140-51.

Ower's article examines the way in which Lampman, Campbell, and Roberts "tackle the job of mastering their native environment in a particularly direct and sophisticated manner by projecting upon the Canadian landscape complex and subtle discussions of their aesthetic concerns." A third of the article is devoted to a discussion of Lampman's "Heat." Lampman perceives an analogy between the human psyche and nature, allowing him "to project his mental processes upon external nature, and also to evolve a contrapuntal symbolism which is simultaneously psychological and metaphysical...."

C94 Davies, Barrie. "Lampman: Radical Poet of Nature." *The English Quarterly*, 4, No. 1 (Spring 1971), 33-43.

"...Lampman is very much a poet of the city. Lampman did not escape into nature; he was an exile there. He constantly strove to bring to society the organic values of the natural world.... Thus Lampman, using the basic image of the city, directed his poetry against anything which debased, diminished, and degraded the human spirit."

C95 Haines, Victor Yelverton. "Archibald Lampman: This

or That." *Revue de l'Université d'Ottawa*, 41 (July-Sept. 1971), 455-71.

The final stanza of Lampman's "Heat" begins: "And yet to me not this or that / Is always sharp or always sweet"; and Haines argues that these lines "are the poem's fulcrum where meditation can pry up the central themes common to a great deal of Lampman's poetry. In this particular poem itself they subsume three or four colloquial meanings over which they are positioned with intricate ambiguity. A careful look at each of these meanings by way of explication that drills right into the verse not only clarifies the structure of this well-known Canadian poem but broadens to an enlightening view of all Lampman's nature poetry."

C96 Nesbitt, Bruce. "A Gift of Love: Lampman and Life." *Canadian Literature*, No. 50 (Autumn 1971), pp. 35-40. Rpt. in *Colony and Confederation: Early Canadian Poets and Their Background*. Ed. George Woodcock. Vancouver: Univ. of British Columbia Press, 1974, pp. 142-47.

Lampman's "inability to resolve his personal conflicts," particularly his love for Katherine Waddell, led to the writing of poetry of social protest. "There exists positive documentary evidence...to indicate that at this time his vaguely humanistic sentiments were being sharply focussed into poems of social protest. Lampman's letters to Edward William Thomson describe his 'spiritual revolution'; the manuscript he presented to Katherine reveals some of the results of this disturbance."

C97 Gnarowski, Michael. "A Note on the Text." *The City of the End of Things*. By Archibald Lampman. Montreal: Golden Dog, 1972, n. pag.

In editing Lampman's poem, Gnarowski notes, he relied on three manuscript versions of "The City of the End of Things." These are a poem in the Public Archives of Canada, dated June 1892, entitled "The

City of the End of Things or the Issue of Things that Are"; a poem in the University of Toronto Library, dated August 1892, entitled "The Nameless City"; and a manuscript copy in the Library of Parliament. Gnarowski also points out that he has restored the poem to its original arrangement of five verses of eight, twenty, sixteen, twenty, and twenty-four lines respectively.

C98   Thomas, Clara. "Archibald Lampman." In *Our Nature — Our Voices: A Guidebook to English-Canadian Literature*. Vol. I. Toronto: new press, 1972, pp. 55-57.

This summary of Lampman's life and work points out that "he was distressed by all the doubts and fears that tormented sensitive men of the nineteenth century." Lampman confronted those doubts and fears in "The City of the End of Things," though most of his poetry is concerned not with man and society but with nature. A "close-woven and continuing aesthetic" can be discerned in all of Lampman's writing.

C99   Davies, Barrie. "A Lampman Manuscript." *Journal of Canadian Fiction*, 1, No. 2 (Spring 1972), 55-56.

In addition to providing bibliographic information about Lampman's accompanying essay on socialism, Davies places the ideas expressed in the essay into the context of Lampman's entire body of work. "Throughout his work Lampman is concerned with the consequences of the massing of people in cities, the breakdown of tradition, communal patterns, and the acquisitive and competitive stresses promoted by the principles of laisser-faire [sic]. Thus for the human bonds which linked man to man, or 'friendship,' Lampman saw the century as substituting economic ones. Thus industrial society was not a society in any meaningful sense but a collection of individuals motivated by self-interest."

C100   Davies, E. Barrie. "Answering Harmonies." *The Humanities Association Bulletin*, 23 (Spring 1972), 57-68.

"Lampman consciously thought of poetry as a symbol-making art and assigned this as the chief function of the creative imagination....Thus the world viewed through the imagination was organically constructed and the cosmos a unity of sympathetic parts arranged in a pattern or a harmony." Davies examines two image patterns connected with man's origins and subsequent history, as they are expressed in Lampman's poetry. The first derives from the myth of Paradise or the Golden Age, producing images of birth, dawn, spring light, gold, the garden, great stature, movement, music, dancing, and eternity. The second originates in moral and psychological concepts both ancient and modern. The concept of man as a compound of the divine and the bestial is central here. Thus, "a major portion of Lampman's poetry deals with the fallen world of man, a world of warring contraries fragmented, disharmonious, without unity." Nature "is only the concrete manifestation of a spiritual integer of which the sun is Lampman's most suitable symbol...." The sun is the "source and centre of energy permeating and irradiating matter, manifesting the ubiquitous unity inherent in multiplicity."

C101   Davies, Barrie. "Lampman and Religion." *Canadian Literature*, No. 56 (Spring 1973), pp. 40-60. Rpt. in *Colony and Confederation: Early Canadian Poets and Their Background*. Ed. George Woodcock. Vancouver: Univ. of British Columbia Press, 1974, pp. 103-23.

Davies deals with Lampman's religious experience in three stages: his rejection of institutional religion, his perplexity and doubt; and the nature of his religious beliefs. Regarding the first stage, Davies cites a letter written to E. W. Thomson on November 2, 1897, in which Lampman admits "It always depresses me to go to church." Lampman's perplexity and doubt are illuminated by applying to Lampman's poetry the theories expressed in J. Hillis Miller's *The Disappearance of God*. Romantic poets attempt to re-establish communication between the divine and the human in their poetry. "To Chaucer" and many of Lampman's poems on the seasons explore this "possibility of re-entry into a divine harmony...." Lampman's religious beliefs emerge "through rather than in nature." Lampman became acquainted with transcendentalism through his friendship with William Wilfred Campbell.

C102   Davies, Barrie. "Makeshift Truce: Lampman and the Position of the Writer in Nineteenth-Century Canada." *The Dalhousie Review*, 53 (Spring 1973), 121-42.

The conflict between art and society is explored in Davies' article: "art affirms identity and is the means to selfhood, wholeness, and unity; society and the times demand self-deception, compromise, and eventual dehumanization." Implicit in Lampman's nature poetry is a struggle between commitment to art, and a society that cannot appreciate such a commitment. Although it is distressing, alienation from society is necessary if the poet's artistic vision is to remain uninhibited by the forces of society. Hence, the numerous escapes from the city in Lampman's poems are not acts of voluntary and deliberate self-exile. Rather, they are a kind of exorcism, or coming to terms with the environment. The "domination of material ends and self-interest is a blight to sensitivity and unworldliness." Therefore the "artist accepts as a blessing his alienation from a society that needs regeneration."

C103   Djwa, Sandra. "Lampman's Fleeting Vision." *Canadian Literature*, No. 56 (Spring 1973), pp. 22-39. Rpt. in *Colony and Confederation: Early Canadian Poets and Their Background*. Ed. George Woodcock. Vancouver: Univ. of British Columbia Press, 1974, pp. 124-41.

"Lampman's varied poetic stances are related to his exploration of an abyss which he perceives gaping between the benevolent nature which he would like to affirm and the often unpleasant 'reality' of everyday life." The rift is bridged through the metaphor of the "dream," and Djwa points to the final lines of Lampman's "A Vision of Twilight" in developing her argument. Djwa believes that "Lampman's use of the same adverb to describe both states (and the fact that both are perceived through a poem which is itself a 'vision') points up his transitory sense of both states and may be taken to support the view that he often sees the 'visionary' and the so-called 'real' world from the essentially passive state of the observer in the dream." In Lampman's poetry, "the dream, coupled with the stoic stance, becomes a way of circumventing the pain of everyday reality." However it is not always possible to maintain the dream and keep reality at bay. Lampman accepted "the Wordsworthian belief that it is possible to be 'laid asleep in body' and so 'see into the life of things' at the very moment when changing social structures, the Darwinistic imperative, and above all the loss of a settled faith, made it impossible to assert man's spiritual transcendence in nature." When Lampman "was no longer psychologically able to participate in the comfort of nature's dream," a "great press of new realities" appeared in his poetry.

C104   Whitridge, Margaret Coulby. "Introduction." In *The Poems of Archibald Lampman (Including At the Long Sault)*. Ed. Margaret Coulby Whitridge. Toronto: Univ. of Toronto Press, 1974, pp. vii-xxix.

Whitridge discusses the channels of communication among members of the Confederation group of poets and stresses that "sincere praise and interested criticism from his fellow poets provided a continuing stimulus for Lampman, who was locked by illness and insecurity into a life which seemed to him both narrow and provincial." She argues that Lampman "struck the first authentic note of fear in Canadian literature, a fear stripped bare of Victorian dream-garden mysticism and expressed in poems about politicians and money lenders, towering impersonal city buildings and solitary, homeless figures prowling the city streets...."

C105 Davies, Barrie. "Introduction." In *Archibald Lampman: Selected Prose*. Ed. Barrie Davies. Ottawa: Tecumseh, 1975, pp. 1-9.

In addition to providing bibliographic information about the prose pieces included in *Archibald Lampman: Selected Prose*, Davies stresses that Lampman's prose frequently incorporates "many of the preoccupations and metaphors which characterize his poetry." Davies goes on to comment specifically on each of the selections in the book, their relationship to Lampman's poetry, and the manner in which they illuminate Lampman's philosophical, social, and literary concerns.

C106 Nesbitt, Bruce. "Lampmania: Alcyone and the Search for Merope." In *Editing Canadian Texts*. Ed. Francess G. Halpenny. Toronto: Hakkert, 1975, pp. 33-48.

Lampman scholars must return to the poet's manuscripts in order to determine his intentions in writing his poetry. Nesbitt reveals that Duncan Campbell Scott made substantial changes in Lampman's poems in the process of preparing the 1900 volume, *The Poems of Archibald Lampman*. He altered punctuation and capitalization, substituted words at will, and even excised an entire stanza from one of Lampman's poems. Criticism of Lampman has been based on these published, and therefore altered, versions of Lampman's poems. Future criticism must be based on Lampman's manuscripts if an accurate assessment of Lampman's work is to be achieved.

C107 Whitridge, Margaret Coulby. "Introduction." In *Lampman's Kate, Late Love Poems of Archibald Lampman, 1887-1897*. Ed. Margaret Coulby Whitridge. Ottawa: Borealis, 1975, pp. 11-23.

Whitridge argues for a biographical reading of the poems she has included in the volume. Lampman and Maud Playter were married on September 3, 1887. Within a few months, according to Whitridge, Lampman was trying to convince himself that he could remain faithful to Maud, and this struggle is illustrated in "The Faithful Lover." Six months later, "Silence!" explores Lampman's growing frustration in his marriage. Whitridge gives 1889 as the year in which Lampman fell in love with Katherine (Kate) Waddell, his co-worker at the post office. In the mid-1890s, Lampman left his wife and took rooms in Ottawa. At the same time, Kate left her family home. Her name is missing from the *Ottawa City Directory* for this two-year period only, yet records show that she continued to work at the post office. Lampman declined offers to teach in the United States during this same period. Whitridge is convinced that Lampman and Kate were living together. However, Lampman's friends and relatives always denied any relationship between Lampman and Kate. Several letters, presumably concerning Kate, are missing from Lampman's correspondence, and some appear to have been removed neatly with scissors.

C108 Morley, William F. E. "Archibald Lampman's 'Alcyone.'" *Canadian Notes & Queries*, No. 15 (July 1975), p. 3.

Morley accounts for four of the twelve copies of *Alcyone* printed in 1899 and asks the whereabouts of the other eight. Morley received three responses to his query (see C117, C121, and C124).

C109 Wortham, Thomas. "Archibald Lampman and William Dean Howells." *Canadian Notes & Queries*, No. 16 (Dec. 1975), p. 2.

At the request of his brother-in-law, Achille Fréchette, William Dean Howells wrote a letter on February 14, 1899, on the death of Lampman. The letter appears to be an official statement and Wortham asks if it was printed.

C110 Whitridge, Margaret Coulby. "Introduction." *Lampman's Sonnets, 1884-1899*. Ed. Margaret Coulby Whitridge. Ottawa: Borealis, 1976, pp. x-xxiv.

Defining a sonnet as "the complete expression of a single idea," Whitridge justifies including poems from twelve to sixteen lines in length in the collection. The introduction also includes biographical data about Lampman.

C111 Dragland, Stan. "Duncan Campbell Scott as Literary Executor for Archibald Lampman: A Labour of Love." *Studies in Canadian Literature*, 1, No. 2 (Summer 1976), 143-57.

Dragland credits Scott with "spreading the word" about Lampman through his work as Lampman's literary executor, and by writing a number of articles about Lampman. On a personal level, Scott was an outstanding friend to Lampman and his family.

C112 McGill, Jean. "Medals and Medallions of R. Tait McKenzie." *Canadian Collector*, 11, No. 4 (July-Aug. 1976), 21-23.

This account of the work of R. Tait McKenzie, Canadian doctor, physical educator, and sculptor, notes that upon the death of his "cherished friend" Archibald Lampman, McKenzie struck a medallion in honour of Lampman.

C113 Bentley, D. M. R. "Archibald Lampman (1861-1899) — A Checklist." *Essays on Canadian Writing*, No. 5 (Fall 1976), pp. 36-49.

Bentley's checklist is divided into seven sections, covering: public collections of Lampman material in Canada; poetry; miscellaneous prose; selected reviews of Lampman's poetry; obituaries and related material; studies, including theses dealing with Lampman; and miscellaneous material.

C114 Bentley, D. M. R. "The Same Unnamed Delight: Lampman's Essay on 'Happiness' and 'Lyrics of Earth.'" *Essays on Canadian Writing*, No. 5 (Fall 1976), pp. 25-35.

In this article, Bentley analyzes Lampman's "Happiness" and shows how one of the essay's major themes — the causality and attainment of happiness — is also a major concern in several of the twenty-nine poems in *Lyrics of Earth*. *Lyrics of Earth*, though dated 1895, was issued in 1896, the same year that "Happiness" was written. "In Lampman's view, 'true happiness' comes ... to those who, by electing to follow or cultivate their individual 'genius' or 'gift,' are led to an optimistic understanding of the universe." To substantiate his insights "Lampman offers a parable concerning a fisherman's search from lake to lake for a 'grey trout,' which is to say, for happiness. Although the fish is never found, the delights of nature which the fisherman experiences in the course of his search, when 'remembered afterward with luxurious joy' become a source of the happiness which had earlier eluded him." Bentley argues that "at a metaphorical level the arrangement of the poems in *Lyrics of Earth* may correspond to the quest outlined in the 'parable ....'" The poet, like the fisherman, begins the volume by seeking happiness itself, proceeds through a joyful experiencing of nature, and ends by discovering, in the memory of his past experience in nature, the source of lasting happiness.

C115 Bentley, D. M. R. "Prefatory Note. 'The Poetry of Byron.' By Archibald Lampman." *Queen's Quarterly*, 83, No. 4 (Winter 1976), 623.

In addition to providing bibliographic information about Lampman's accompanying essay on Byron, Bentley points out that Lampman's assessment of the value of Byron's work "reveals much about the criteria by which," in Lampman's view, "poetry is to be judged. When Lampman says that 'poetry ... which ranges itself on the side of passion against eternal law is a disturbing influence to human progress and is therefore of no real value to us' he is making a statement that is implicit in many of his other literary essays and which may well be important to a full understanding of his own intentions in poetry."

C116 Bentley, D. M. R. "'Archibald Lampman as I Knew Him at Trinity University,' by Archdeacon G. B. Sage (with a Prefatory Note by D. M. R. Bentley)." *Canadian Notes & Queries*, No. 18 (Dec. 1976), pp. 7-8.

Sage, who attended university with Lampman, delivered the "Invocation" at the dedication of the Lampman Memorial Cairn in 1930. The "Invocation," recalling the college age Lampman, is printed in full in this note.

C117 Lamb, W. Kaye, and Peter E. Greig. "Archibald Lampman's 'Alcyone.'" *Canadian Notes & Queries*, No. 18 (Dec. 1976), p. 3.

In response to William F. E. Morley's query about the whereabouts of copies of *Alcyone* (see C108), Lamb suggests that there may be a copy in the National Library. Greig, however, points out that there is no reference to *Alcyone* in the catalogues of the National Library or the Public Archives of Canada.

C118 Mandel, Eli. "The City in Canadian Poetry." In *Another Time*. Erin, Ont.: Porcépic, 1977, pp. 114-23.

Examining the work of such poets as Archibald Lampman, James Reaney, A. M. Klein, Wilfred Watson, Irving Layton, and Dennis Lee, Mandel finds that a two-fold problem faces these writers: "... first, whether it is possible to put together ... nature and imagination; and second, if it is not possible, how to get past nature itself. For both parts of the question the city seems to be a crucial image." Regarding Lampman's "The City of the End of Things," Mandel notes that such motifs as "the blazing furnace, the three who walk there accompanied by a shadowy fourth," and the city built to music, belong to the magic cities of legend and poem, such as Troy and Camelot, and the fiery furnace of the Bible. "The poem, by means of parody, evokes the horror of a *mindless* world. In other words, Lampman sees the real opposition not between the nature and machine, but between nature and imagination. The machine he is writing about is nature itself.... The fire that burns in so many poems on Canadian cities ... may be seen to be the fire of the poet's own creativity burning away the dead husk of the city or the machinery of the natural world. The answer to the question 'how to get past nature?' is: by means of imagination. The furnace or forge symbolizes creative energy, and in that forge new images are hammered into being."

C119 Davies, Barrie. "Lampman Could Tell His Frog from His Toad: A Note on Art versus Nature." *Studies in Canadian Literature*, 2, No. 1 (Winter 1977), 129-30.

Duncan Campbell Scott had claimed that the frogs in Lampman's poetry were really toads, and Stan Dragland concurred with Scott in his article on Scott and Lampman (see C111). In response, Davies stresses that the "value of Lampman's poetry does not lie finally in a 'realistic' presentation of the natural scenery, though it is usually accurate enough to satisfy most and mislead others.... It is precisely because frogs are conventionally unromantic that they are available to the poetry ... of Lampman. He is fascinated by their alienness of shape, their physical unobtrusiveness ... and with their insignificance or unimportance to contemporary civilization.... Lampman identified himself with the frogs, and at one level they represent the poet; at another, the ideal sought by the poet."

C120 Boll, David. "Letters of Archibald Lampman." *Canadian Notes & Queries*, No. 19 (June 1977), p. 5.

Boll seeks letters of Lampman's which have not been catalogued or otherwise recorded.

C121 Smith, W. J. "Archibald Lampman's 'Alcyone.'" *Canadian Notes & Queries*, No. 19 (June 1977), p. 7.

In response to William F. E. Morley's query about the whereabouts of copies of *Alcyone* (see C108), Smith points out that there are copies of the volume in the Public Archives of Canada, and in the Simon Fraser University collection of Lampman material.

C122 Kennedy, Margaret. "Lampman and the Canadian Thermopylae: 'At the Long Sault: May, 1660.'" *Canadian Poetry*, No. 1 (Fall-Winter 1977), pp. 54-59.

Kennedy presents a strong argument that Francis Parkman's *The Old Régime in Canada* (1874) was the major, and perhaps the only, source for Lampman's "At the Long Sault: May, 1660." While drawing on Parkman's work, Lampman "freely omitted whatever he found unsuitable and judiciously added what he felt was necessary for the unity and effectiveness of his poem."

C123 Talman, James J. "Archibald Lampman As I Knew Him." *Canadian Notes & Queries*, No. 20 (Dec. 1977), p. 10.

In response to D. M. R. Bentley's article (see C116), Talman provides further information about Sage.

C124 Townsend, Patricia L. "Archibald Lampman's 'Alcyone.'" *Canadian Notes & Queries*, No. 20 (Dec. 1977), pp. 4-5.

In response to William F. E. Morley's query about the whereabouts of copies of *Alcyone* (see C108), Townsend notes that there is a copy of the volume at Acadia University.

C125 Bentley, D. M. R. "Archibald Lampman on Poets and Poetry." *Essays on Canadian Writing*, No. 9 (Winter 1977-78), pp. 12-25.

Bentley examines the central ideas of Lampman's literary criticism, both published and unpublished, in order "to approach a little closer, not only ... Lampman the thinker, but also ... Lampman the poet." In "The Revolt of Islam" (1880), Lampman sees "nineteenth-century society exerting a corrupting influence on man who ... was 'originally pure and good.' The poet can retain or recover his innocence by entering into communion with nature ...." Lampman's "The Modern School of Poetry in England" (1885), articulates a "quasi-religious conception of poetry as a 'transfiguration'" and argues, as does the undated essay, "The Poetry of Byron," that "poetry which deals with uncongenial aspects of life ... cannot be good art." In "Two Canadian Poets" (1891), Lampman "theorizes about the sort of poetry which a Canadian society might produce ...." Lampman discusses Keats's work in "The Character and Poetry of Keats" (1893), and amplifies his conception of Keats's work in his undated essay on "Poetic Interpretation." Bentley concludes that "the most important single fact for a full understanding and appreciation of Lampman's literary criticism is that it is part of a much larger philosophy ... which is basically and radically realistic, progressive, melioristic, and moralistic. For Lampman, poetry is the servant of spiritual and moral elevation and progress."

C126 Bentley, D. M. R. "Introduction." In *Lyrics of Earth*. By Archibald Lampman. Ed. D. M. R. Bentley. Ottawa: Tecumseh, 1978, pp. 1-20.

After providing a biography of Lampman and tracing the poet's critical reception, Bentley examines the troubled pre-publication history of *Lyrics of Earth*. In this edition of the book, Bentley has restored the poems to Lampman's intended order. "Not only is this true to the original intentions of the poet but it also restores the poems to their correct 'sequence ....'" The poems follow a seasonal pattern which "has a counterpart in the movement of the sun in the course of the day" and "a further counterpart in man's progress from birth ... towards death ...."

C127 Woodcock, George. "Archibald Lampman." In *Faces*

from History. Edmonton: Hurtig, 1978, pp. 192-93. Rpt. (excerpt) "Despairing Critic of Cities." In *Toronto Star*, 2 Oct. 1978, p. A10.

Woodcock discusses Lampman's life and work and points out that his "position among Canadian poets has risen in recent years, largely because his misgivings about the society of his time arouse sympathetic echoes in modern minds."

C128   Davies, Barrie. "Introduction." In *At the Mermaid Inn: Wilfred Campbell, Archibald Lampman, Duncan Campbell Scott in The Globe 1892-3*. Ed. Barrie Davies. Toronto: Univ. of Toronto Press, 1979, pp. vii-xxi.

Davies sees the "At the Mermaid Inn" column as "a work of great importance and fascination because it is a complex record of three writers' involvement in the special problems not only of their time and place, but perhaps ours; for tendencies and reactions initiated in the nineteenth century have persisted with an increasing sense of anxiety and crisis into our own time."

C129   Souster, Raymond. "Archibald Lampman: A Debt Repaid." *Comfort of the Fields. The Best-Known Poems*. Ed. Raymond Souster. Sutton West, Ont.: Paget, 1979, pp. xi-xviii.

Upon reading Lampman's "Morning on the Lièvre" at the age of twelve, Souster recalls that he "came away from it with the crazy thought dancing through [his] head that what [he] wanted almost as much as becoming a no-hit baseball pitcher was to make [his] own poems." Souster surveys Lampman's work and credits him with being "the one true classical poet we have produced in this country."

C130   Doyle, James. "Canadian Poetry and American Magazines, 1885-1905." *Canadian Poetry*, No. 5 (Fall-Winter 1979), pp. 73-82.

In the 1880s and 1890s, Lampman and his fellow Confederation poets "looked southward to the periodicals of Boston and New York for editorial and critical acceptance, and this orientation had an important influence on the kind of poetry they wrote, as well as on their conception of Canadian literature as a whole." American exposure was valuable promotion for Canadian poets. "But the more ambitious and venturesome poets, particularly Lampman and Campbell, began to recognize ... that the relative narrowness of American editorial receptivity and critical praise could impose stringent limitations on Canadian poetry, and reduce ... perceptions of Canada to a string of romantic and pastoral clichés."

C131   Mezei, Kathy. "Lampman among the Timothy." *Canadian Poetry*, No. 5 (Fall-Winter 1979), pp. 57-72.

Mezei traces the development of a "sense of locality" in Lampman's poetry by discussing "first the landscapes and places that inspired him and, second, the moments in our history that he seized upon." Her "main concern, however, is with the forms that he initiated to convey these places and moments and with the language and images that he chose to evoke the sense and spirit of place and to transform history into myth."

C132   Steele, Charles R. "The Isolate 'I' (Eye): Lampman's Persona." *Essays on Canadian Writing*, No. 16 (Fall-Winter 1979-80), pp. 62-69.

Steele discusses Lampman's "persistent use of the first person pronoun." It "functions most obviously and fundamentally as a force of structural coherence" but it serves as more than "a unifying technique" in Lampman's poetry. "Lampman's insistent 'I' always remains ultimately discrete and independent, and finally alone," providing glimpses of his alienation from nature.

C133   Wicken, George. "Prelude to Poetry: Lampman and the *Rouge et Noir*." *Canadian Poetry*, No. 6 (Spring-Summer 1980), pp. 50-60.

The article examines Lampman's six prose contributions to the Trinity College student journal, the *Rouge et Noir*, and points "to a major issue which the essays reveal: Lampman's struggle to define the poet's relationship to his society." The "college essays tend to manifest both an attraction and a repulsion for what might be termed the world of affairs. Lampman wishes to be an artist, and that requires separation from others; yet he needs the kinship of other human beings, and that requires participation in the world of affairs." In the final essay, "Hans Fingerhut's Frog Lesson," Lampman employs allegory to establish "the ideal definition of the relationship between the artist and other men to which he may have addressed himself before undertaking a career as a man of letters."

Theses and Dissertations

C134 Brennan, Ursula. "The Prosody of Archibald Lampman." M.A. Thesis Queen's 1931.

Brennan examines Lampman's poetic craftsmanship. Technical, rather than thematic, concerns of Lampman's poetry are examined in this thesis.

C135 Klinck, Carl F. "Wilfred Campbell: A Study in Late Provincial Victorianism." Diss. Columbia 1943.

Klinck examines the Ottawa milieu which included Lampman, Campbell, and Duncan Campbell Scott. The literary concerns of the three men, and their collaboration on "At the Mermaid Inn," a column in *The Globe*, are discussed by Klinck in considerable detail. The dissertation was published by the Ryerson Press (see C62).

C136 Purcell, Mary Aileen. "The Nature Poetry of Lampman." M.A. Thesis Montréal 1953.

Since the first appearance of his poetry in the 1880s, Lampman has been considered a fine nature poet. Purcell, however, is the first person to undertake a thesis devoted solely to Lampman's nature poetry.

C137 Sylvia, Sister Mary. "Archibald Lampman: Lyrist." M.A. Thesis Montréal 1955.

Lampman's extensive work with the lyric is the central concern of this thesis which stresses a technical, as well as a thematic, approach to Lampman's poetry.

C138 Watt, F. W. "Radicalism in English Canadian Literature Since Confederation." Diss. Toronto 1958.

Watt recognizes Lampman as one of the first Canadian writers to articulate a social consciousness in his work. Lampman's poems about politics, the effects of industrialization on mankind, and his allegorical presentation of an egalitarian, communistic society in his work are indicative of his questioning of the status quo in late nineteenth-century Canada. Lampman is one of the founders of a radical tradition in Canadian writing.

C139 Bedwell, William Thomas. "Archibald Lampman and the Origins of Canadian Nature Poetry." M.A. Thesis Manitoba 1961.

Bedwell examines Lampman's poetry, not only on its own terms, but as part of a tradition of writing nature poetry in Canada.

C140 Rogers, Amos Robert. "American Recognition of Canadian Authors Writing in English 1890-1960." 2 vols. Diss. Michigan 1964.

Volume II, Appendix IX, pages 670-813 of this dissertation lists book reviews of Canadian works in American periodicals from 1890-1960. Some of these reviews, particularly in the 1890s, concern Lampman's poetry, and are indicative of American critical response to Lampman's work.

C141 Nesbitt, Bruce. "Lampman and O'Dowd: A Comparative Study of Poetic Attitudes in Canada and Australia in the Late Nineteenth Century." M.A. Thesis Queen's 1965.

Australia and Canada share certain historical similarities, each having grown from a British colony into nationhood. Nesbitt, in this thesis, examines one late nineteenth-century poet from each country (Canada's Lampman and Australia's O'Dowd), as a means of probing the similarities and differences in literary and cultural attitudes in the two countries.

C142 Anderson, Elmer Lloyd. "Polarities and Neutrality in Archibald Lampman." M.A. Thesis Montréal 1966.

Examines those poems in which a tension of opposites is present, as well as those poems pervaded by a sense of neutrality.

C143 Davies, Edward Barrie. "The Alien Mind: A Study of the Poetry of Archibald Lampman." Diss. New Brunswick 1970.

Davies relies on both published and unpublished works by Lampman. "Lampman is not merely a superficial landscape poet, good at bits of local colour," Davies contends. Davies examines the meaning of nature for Lampman, and considers the implications of Lampman's concept of nature in his poetry. "He is a landscape poet in a special sense because nature has positive organic values for mankind and is ultimately an imaginative order which can allow man to exercise a totality of response and therefore return to him a firmer sense of humanity. The poet, however, alienated from contemporary man and a society tarnished by progressive materialism, is sustained in his exile by an identity through nature with a sense of universal harmony." The poetry of Lampman, Davies points out, "is characterized by an intense questing for real being, for a unified sensibility which fuses intelligence, moral purpose, instinct and imagination." Often, this quest takes place "in a context of hostility and menace … because contemporary society is inimical to the values of the imaginative life." The poet's salvation, however, "is eventually achieved through the exercise of that Divine faculty which holds all contraries in

synthesis and makes nature a diagram of mind and spirit."

C144 Whitridge, Margaret Evelyn. "Annotated Checklist of Lampman Manuscripts and Materials in Known Repositories in Canada." Diss. Ottawa 1970.

Whitridge identifies the chief repositories of Lampman materials as the University of Toronto; the Public Archives of Canada and the Parliamentary Library in Ottawa; and the Simon Fraser University Library. Smaller collections of Lampman material are held at Queen's University, the Women's Canadian Historical Society, McGill University, Ottawa Public Library, and the University of New Brunswick. Letters to Lampman are retained by the Toronto Public Library. There is also an abundance of Lampman material in private hands.

C145 Campbell, Brian R. "Motion in the Poems of Archibald Lampman." M.A. Thesis Alberta 1971.

A number of Lampman's poems involve movement: either of the poet or of the poet's eye. Campbell examines how the process of motion is used by Lampman to develop particular effects in his poetry.

C146 Jobin, Madeline Graddon. "Archibald Lampman: Canadian Nature Poet." M.A. Thesis McGill 1971.

Lampman's poems concerned with nature, rather than those where he develops social themes, are the main focus of Jobin's thesis.

C147 Miller, Judith Helen. "Towards a Canadian Aesthetic: Descriptive Colour in the Landscape Poetry of Duncan Campbell Scott, Archibald Lampman, and William Wilfred Campbell." M.A. Thesis Waterloo 1971.

Lampman, Scott, and Campbell do not use colour in a solely realistic context in their poetry. Rather, colour serves as a means of developing the themes and moods which each poet undertakes to convey in his work. Miller examines the similarities and differences in the presentation of colour in the work of the three late nineteenth-century poets.

C148 Tisdall, Douglas Michael. "The Not Unsimilar Face: A Comparative Study of the Influence of Culture, Religion, and Locale in French-Canadian and English-Canadian Poetry." Diss. Toronto 1971.

Very little attention has been paid to the relationship between French Canadian and English Canadian poetry of the nineteenth century. In this dissertation, which examines works from both the nineteenth and twentieth centuries, Tisdall probes the connections between art and society in Canada's two founding cultures. Lampman is among the nineteenth-century, English Canadian poets studied in Tisdall's dissertation.

C149 Edwards, P. Bruce. "Landscape as a State of Soul in the Poetry of Archibald Lampman and Duncan Campbell Scott." M.A. Thesis Western Ontario 1975.

The manner in which Lampman's philosophical and artistic concerns are manifested in his use of landscape is probed in Edwards' thesis. Nature is not seen as an external force in Lampman's poetry, but rather, as a projection of the poet's soul upon his environment.

C150 Mezei, Kathy. "A Magic Space Wherein the Mind Can Dwell: Place and Space in the Poetry of Archibald Lampman, Emile Nelligan, and Duncan Campbell Scott." Diss. Queen's 1977.

Mezei examines the manner in which tone, form, and diction are used to evoke a sense of place in the poetry of Lampman, Nelligan, and Scott. Lampman's "At the Long Sault: May, 1660" is discussed in considerable detail.

Miscellaneous

C151 Scott, Duncan Campbell. "Written in a Copy of Archibald Lampman's Poems." *The Week*, 4 Oct. 1889, p. 698.

Reading Lampman's poetry inspired Scott to write this poem.

C152 Holmes, C. M. "Among the Millet—By Lampman." *The Week*, 10 April 1891, p. 298.

Upon reading Lampman's first book of poetry, Holmes, a resident of Picton, Ontario, wrote this sonnet.

C153 Campbell, William Wilfred. "Bereavement of the Fields." *Atlantic Monthly*, June 1899, pp. 837-38. Rpt. in *Beyond the Hills of Dream*. Toronto: Morang, 1900, pp. 9-12. Rpt. in *The Collected Poems of Wilfred Campbell*. Toronto: Ryerson, 1905, pp. 176-79. Rpt. in *The Poetical Works of Wilfred Campbell*. London: Hodder, 1923, pp. 84-86.

Campbell's lengthy memorial poem, in honour of his friend Lampman, derives its title and subject matter from Lampman's own "Comfort of the Fields." Campbell wrote his poem very shortly after Lampman's death.

C154 Bernard, Lally. "In Memory of Archibald Lampman." *Canadian Magazine*, 18, No. 4 (Feb. 1902), 375.

A black-bordered memorial poem to Lampman, the poem appeared on the third anniversary of Lampman's death.

C155 Benson, Nathaniel A. "The Lampman Cairn at Morpeth." In *The Wanderer and Other Poems*. Toronto: Ryerson, 1930, p. 30. Rpt. in Fox, William Sherwood, E. A. Cruikshank, J. H. Cameron, Arthur Stringer, Nathaniel A. Benson, and Duncan Campbell Scott. *Addresses Delivered at the Dedication of the Archibald Lampman Memorial Cairn at Morpeth, Ontario*. London, Ont.: Western Ontario Branch of the Canadian Authors' Association, 1930, p. 13.

This sonnet was written in 1928, when the

erection of a memorial to Lampman was first proposed. Benson recited the poem at the dedication of the cairn on September 13, 1930.

C156 Harden, Verna Loveday. "In Memoriam: Archibald Lampman." *Canadian Poetry Magazine*, 12, No. 3 (March 1949), 5.

Harden's memorial poem to Lampman marks the fiftieth anniversary of the poet's death.

C157 Bourinot, Arthur S. "Duncan Campbell Scott — Archibald Lampman." *Canadian Author & Bookman*, 26, No. 2 (Summer 1950), 22. Rpt. in *Archibald Lampman's Letters to Edward William Thomson (1890-1898)*. Ed. Arthur S. Bourinot. Ottawa: Bourinot, 1956, n. pag.

Bourinot's sonnet is a tribute to Scott and Lampman.

C158 Bairstow, David, dir. *Morning on the Lièvre*. National Film Board of Canada, 1961.

This handsomely produced 16 mm. colour film of Lampman's "Morning on the Lièvre" features two paddlers in a canoe gliding along the Lièvre on an autumn's morning. Photographer Grant Crabtree captures the river's changing moods as the paddlers move through sun, mist, and shadow. Poet George Whalley reads Lampman's poem against a background of music composed by Eldon Rathburn. The film was released in the United States in 1964 by Encyclopedia Britannica Films. A French version of the film, under the title *Matin sur la Lièvre*, was released by the National Film Board of Canada in 1962.

C159 Bissell, Keith. *A Summer Evening [for] S.S.A. and Piano*. Waterloo, Ont.: Waterloo Music, 1967. N. pag.

Lampman's "A Summer Evening" provides the words for Bissell's score.

C160 Jones, D. G. "Kate, these flowers . . . [The Lampman Poems]." In *Under the Thunder the Flowers Light up the Earth*. Toronto: Coach House, 1977, pp. 74-87.

Jones adopts the *persona* of a present-day Lampman in these poems addressed to Kate (Katherine Waddell, Lampman's close friend). Jones's poems take the form of a bouquet of flowers to Kate: the first letter of each line of each poem contributes to the spelling out of the names of flowers. Red rose, wild primrose, water hyacinth, and pale snowdrops are among the flowers whose names are contained cryptically in the poems. The volume in which these poems are printed, *Under the Thunder the Flowers Light up the Earth*, won the Governor-General's Award for Poetry.

Honour

C161 Memorial Cairn dedicated and addresses delivered at Morpeth, Ont. (13 Sept. 1930).

The Western Ontario Branch of the Canadian Authors' Association promoted the building of a memorial cairn to Lampman in the town where he was born. The money was raised through subscription, and an impressive ceremony was held at the unveiling on September 13, 1930. A time capsule, containing Lampman material, was placed inside the cairn. On the north and east sides of the cairn are bronze tablets bearing inscriptions. One reads: "In Morpeth was born / the Poet / Archibald Lampman / Buried in Beechwood Cemetery, Ottawa / 1861-1899 / Erected MCMXXX." The other tablet contains a quotation from Lampman's poem "Outlook": "Yet, patience — there shall come / Many great voices from life's outer sea, / Hours of strange triumph, and when few men heed, / Murmurs and glimpses of eternity." The addresses given at the ceremony were later published. (See C3.)

In this generally favourable review, Howland states that "though there is nothing exactly demonstrating true genius in this volume, there is much in it of truth, simplicity, vivacity, and of something that fairly deserves the name of passion...."

D3   "Books of the Month." *Atlantic Monthly*, March 1889, p. 430.

This brief, but favourable, review reads in its entirety: "There is a frequent loving touch of friendliness with nature in these verses, and a restraint of moralizing which makes the poetry genuine even where it is not noticeably strong. It is not impossible that this writer may yet push into the recesses of poetry."

D4   Fidelis [Agnes Maule Machar]. "Some Recent Canadian Poems." *The Week*, 22 March 1889, pp. 251-52. *AL* (excerpt).

Although generally favourable, the review points to "a certain unsatisfactoriness" in some of the poems. Praising Lampman's "imaginative power, delicacy of perception and...high degree of general artistic excellence," Machar finds the lack of a strong human or subjective interest in certain poems to be a drawback.

D5   Howells, William D. "Editor's Study." *Harper's*, April 1889, pp. 821-23.

This very favourable review by the highly respected Howells was of great importance in establishing Lampman's reputation as a poet. The volume, Howells says, "is mainly descriptive; but descriptive after a new fashion, most delicately pictorial and subtly thoughtful, with a high courage for the unhackneyed features and aspects of the great world around us.... We only hint the riches of this poet's book," Howells says. "It is no part of our business to guess his future;

D   Selected Book Reviews

Note: *Among the Millet, and Other Poems* (1888) and *Lyrics of Earth* (1895) were the only books of Lampman's poetry published and reviewed during his lifetime. *Alcyone* (1899) was published in a limited run of twelve copies, shortly after Lampman's death, but the volume was not reviewed. *At the Long Sault and Other New Poems* (1943), also published posthumously, was reviewed.

Among the Millet, and Other Poems

D1   Seranus [S. Frances Riley Harrison]. "'Among the Millet, and Other Poems.'" *The Week*, 28 Dec. 1888, p. 59.

This favourable review admits that it "would be a rare privilege in any country to be called upon to notice so delightful a collection of verses as appears between the warm tinted covers of this latest Ottawa publication, but the privilege is one particularly rare and precious in Canada where works are too often vaunted to the skies on account of mere surface Canadianism." Although Lampman is faulted for not writing of "the ring and the rush" and "the impetuosity...of youth," he is praised for his skilful use of the sonnet form.

D2   Howland, O. A. "A Canadian Poet." *London Spectator*,

but if he shall do no more than he has already done, we believe that his fame can only await the knowledge of work very uncommon in any time."

D6   Adam, G. Mercer. "Two Recent Volumes of Canadian Verse." *Trinity University Review*, 2, No. 10 (Dec. 1889), 153-54.

"If anything good ever came out of Ottawa it is this volume of Mr. Lampman's," Adam asserts in this very favourable review. Lampman is viewed as a philosophical poet. "He has imagination, insight, and sustained powers of reflection. With pathos and delicacy of feeling, he has the gifts that accompany these qualities — geniality and humour."

Lyrics of Earth

D7   "Recent Poetry." *The Nation*, 4 June 1896, p. 439.

This very favourable review notes "the remarkable vigor and freshness with which the younger Canadian poets write of nature, and the manner in which they show also a feeling for the human side; their landscape almost always skilfully including something of that kindlier tie." To illustrate this point, the reviewer points to the introduction of the words "Haytime, and harvest," in the second stanza of "June" as a means of bringing "the human aspect" into "the realm of wild nature."

D8   "Comment on New Books." *Atlantic Monthly*, Sept. 1896, pp. 425-26.

Partially favourable, this review nevertheless expresses disappointment that nature, rather than man, is the main concern of Lampman's book.

D9   "Poetry and Verse." *The Critic*, 16 Jan. 1897, pp. 39-40.

In this very favourable review, Lampman's work is commended for being "refined and clear, rich with imagery and melodious.... There is a freshness, a simplicity, a naturalness about Mr. Lampman's work which gives to it a distinction nowadays quite unusual."

At the Long Sault and Other New Poems

D10   Creighton, Alan. "'At the Long Sault.'" *The Canadian Forum*, Jan. 1944, p. 238.

Partially favourable, this review calls the book "a small but valuable addition to our poetic literature.... The title poem is exceptionally fine in its creation of a distinctly Canadian atmosphere that interpenetrates the description of the event itself...." However in many ways, Lampman's work is "beautiful but passé, like the paintings of Cornelius Kreighoff."

D11   L[ayton]., I[rving]. P. "'At the Long Sault and Other New Poems.' By Archibald Lampman." *First Statement*, 2, No. 5 (March 1944), 16-17.

In this favourable review, Layton chides Canadians for failing to recognize "that they have in Lampman a poet of national importance." Layton praises "At the Long Sault" and is particularly enthusiastic about two other poems in the volume. "To this reviewer... the two poems 'Epitaph on a Rich Man' and 'Liberty' came like two mortar blasts. For these poems reveal an unexpected social awareness in Lampman. They indicate clearly enough that Lampman, an underpaid civil servant, was not only interested in observing Nature but also the shenanigans on Parliament Hill."

D12   R., H. M. "'At the Long Sault.' By Archibald Lampman." *Canadian Poetry Magazine*, March 1944, pp. 34-35.

Basically an unfavourable review, the reviewer believes that "there is not a nature poem in this latest selection that matches the interpretative perfection of such poems as 'Late November,' 'Heat,' and 'The Frogs.'" Regarding the poems "that manifest Lampman's concern with social problems and with love," the reviewer "feels again . . . that little of intrinsic value has been added to the Lampman store treasured by Canadians."

Index to Critics Listed in the Bibliography

E. J. Pratt
An Annotated Bibliography

Lila and Raymond Laakso with
Moira Allen and Marjorie Linden

Introduction

_____

From boyhood E. J. Pratt's bias was toward the common man. Brought up a Methodist minister's son in Newfoundland, Pratt early questioned the justice, mercy, and benevolence of a God who allowed the "endless tragedy" of poverty, violence, and death among the native Newfoundlander. Although apprenticed and educated as a minister, receiving his ordination in 1913 and completing his Ph.D. in 1917, Pratt did not become a full-time preacher, electing instead to teach psychology (1913-20) and eventually English at Victoria University in Toronto (1920-53). Pratt's literary career began in 1917 with the privately printed poem *Rachel*. He went on to play an important role in the development of Canadian poetry as poet, lecturer, and editor of the *Canadian Poetry Magazine*.

A battle of the critics has been waged almost from the beginning of Pratt's literary career, with each critic claiming him for beliefs ranging from Vincent Sharman's Pratt as atheist to John Sutherland's Pratt as total Christian. Religion has been central to all his work: the poems have been the public expression of a continuing inner battle and the driving force of his development. Such diverse elements as the memory of his father, orthodox church tradition, theological training, religious research at university, his Newfoundland experiences, his interest in the sciences (especially evolution), and his faith in the potential of man have all played a role in this struggle. It produced changes in Pratt's outlook, and in turn was reflected in his poetry. His philosophy evolved from a God-centred to a man-centred universe and he created a "New theology" (C110), a man-centred religion.

In *The Witches' Brew*, Pratt whimsically turned his former universe "back-side up" and accomplished his "full and free emancipation" (C27). If *The Witches' Brew* was Pratt's

manifesto of independence, "The Truant" is "a distillation of . . . [his] . . . view of life" (D89), or a "kind of new testament for the poet" (C123). Pratt uses "The Truant" to express his "liberal-democratic defiance of the mechanistic and the inhumane in man, and a reassertion of the creative role of man and of man alone, an 'unrepentant humanism'" (C52). The Christian interpretation that God is evolving "through us and our developing consciousness" (C123) can also be extracted from the poem. Pratt tried to reconcile science and religion, "the old teleology of received religion and the Darwinian world without design, ultimately insisting that design resides within the organism, within the blood and nerve cells of man" (C108). In "The Truant" Genus Homo, in referring to the "All High," states: "Before we came / You had no name" and it is clear from this that man makes his own gods. Pratt "makes man the measure of all things. . . . The myth [of Pratt] is based on the divinity of man. . . . All gods, . . . all godliness, dwell in the human breast. All things begin and end in man" (C53).

Pratt also became one of the foremost interpreters of the relationship of man and machine (C29) and his work has been described as "the poetry of science and the machine age" (C48). In much of his work, he shows the potential for good in the products of science as well as the power for evil, ever present but tenuously controlled. Pratt believed in man, man's science, and the ultimate aim of controlling the universe through understanding and self-knowledge.

The economic and political development of Canada at the end of the nineteenth and the beginning of the twentieth century was the impetus for a nationalism that was reflected in contemporary poetry as an overwhelming pride in Canada. The turn of the century saw Canadian poets seeking beauty in the romantic and the exotic. The most popular group (Bliss Carman, Charles G. D. Roberts, Archibald Lampman, Duncan Campbell Scott, William Wilfred Campbell), described the beauty and majesty of Canada's natural landscape.

In the twenties, when Pratt began to publish, Romanticism, rhetoric, and mechanically rigid nineteenth-century poetic forms were being discarded. The poet used imagistic and free verse techniques to capture everyday life. Steeped in the Newfoundland oral tradition which included pulpit oratory, hymn, folk-song, ballad, recitation, and everyday speech, Pratt readily and naturally developed a story-telling form, the narrative epic. He saw poetry "as a kind of rhetorical friendly persuasion, the winning over of an audience" (C90). Bringing together these various elements in his poetry, Pratt became the first Canadian creative writer to truly express "the spirit that forged the nation" (C8).

Sutherland (C2, C34), in trying to transform Pratt into Canada's T. S. Eliot, argued for a Christian, complex, subtle, mythopoeic Pratt, whose poetry rose out of his subconscious, full of symbols. A. J. M. Smith, Louis Dudek, and Desmond Pacey, influenced by Sutherland, attempted to interpret Pratt as a Modernist. Earle Birney (C52) finds Pratt's philosophy to be the opposite of the Modern movement in Great Britain and the United States. Pratt believed in the ultimate triumph of our age through struggle, while Eliot preached the decline of our age. Pratt remained faithful to objective dramatic narrative and epic, while the Modernists withdrew and narrowed their introspective lyrical craft, afraid to look at the frightening, hopeless chaos they imagined. Unlike the Modernists, who tried to find religions in their negativeness, Pratt evolved a "positive religion of man." Recently Sandra Djwa (C7) has defined Pratt as a "Transitional Modern." After showing Pratt could write free, imagist-like, and Eliot-like verse, Djwa contends with the problem of why he continued to write in what to the initiated "seemed [an] embarrassingly old-fashioned" form. Pratt himself, however, saw the need to express "the democratic visions, the creative impulses at work on myths and national origins" (B183) and set to work creating such national myths in *Brébeuf and His Brethren* and *Towards the Last Spike*.

Some critics have argued that Pratt accepted the values of his society too readily. Others claimed that he was no ordinary citizen, that he viewed with abhorrence the tragic lives of the Newfoundland outporters, and that he, a former minister and the son of a minister, was driven to change the centre of his religious convictions. Moreover World War I caused him much anguish which developed into the pessimism expressed in *The Great Feud*. Yet the survival of the ape mother provides a note of optimism. In the period before World War II he attempted to warn against war, dared to hope for peace, and scrutinized and criticized world political leaders through his *Fable of the Goats*. World War II was to him a struggle of the "democratic vision" against the "slave vision" (C52), and in "Still Life" Pratt condemned the poets who spurned the battlefield as an unpoetic theme.

Pratt's belief in man, his positive view of the function of the poet, and the form which he adopted for the expression of these beliefs, helped make him Canada's national poet. In his vision of the twentieth century, the nuclear age, and man's responsibility to his fellow man, Pratt has been called "the most clear-sighted of our modern poets" (C6). As Northrop Frye has observed, Pratt "took his place at the centre of society where the great myths are formed, the new myths where the hero is man the worker...and where the poet...is shaping also a human reality which is greater than the whole objective world...because it includes the infinity of human desire" (C90).

* * *

Although E. J. Pratt has been an important literary figure in Canada from the 1920s, no bibliographical work had been published about him until "E. J. Pratt: A Preliminary Checklist" by Lila Laakso appeared in the August 1977 issue of *Canadian Library Journal* and in *The E. J. Pratt Symposium*, edited by Glenn Clever and published by the University of Ottawa in 1977. The main purpose of the present revision is to provide a complete listing of Pratt's work and to present an up-to-date, annotated bibliography of all the critical works about him.

It was evident in compiling this bibliography that standard periodical indexes could not be relied upon since they do not cover many of the Canadian journals, or the smaller ones. The *Canadian Periodical Index* did not exist in the early 1900s, and it was necessary to check individual titles. *Acta Victoriana* and *The Rebel* are unindexed Canadian publications which contain early Pratt works. A similar problem was encountered with anthologies. Because of the lack of adequate indexes, individual titles needed checking.

Throughout his literary career, Pratt was a popular public figure. His numerous radio appearances have been recorded; the tapes are available at the CBC Archives, Toronto, and additional material may be found at the Public Archives, Ottawa. A selection of the numerous newspaper reviews has been made. Similarly, only a selection from the many anthologies in which his work has appeared is presented.

Included in the bibliography are broadsides and sheet music as well as the distinctive Pratt family Christmas cards, illustrated by Claire Pratt and containing Pratt poems. Claire Pratt materially assisted with the description of these cards and her interest is much appreciated.

Mrs. Viola Pratt was extremely helpful in drawing our attention to relatively unknown Pratt writings including unsigned introductions, prefaces, and articles. Her Scrapbook (now in Victoria University Library, Toronto) provided invaluable assistance for identifying early newspaper reviews.

Acknowledgements

We wish gratefully to acknowledge the interest and assistance of Mrs. Viola Pratt, Miss Claire Pratt, and Dr. Robert C. Brandeis.

Part I

Works by E. J. Pratt

A   Books (Poetry, Philosophy), Broadsides, and Manuscripts

Poetry

A1   *Rachel: A Sea Story of Newfoundland in Verse*. New York: Privately printed, 1917. 15 pp.

A2   *Newfoundland Verse*. Toronto: Ryerson, 1923. 140 pp.
        Decorations by Fredk. H. Varley.

A3   *The Witches' Brew*. London: Selwyn and Blount, 1925. 32 pp.
        Toronto: Macmillan, 1926. 31 pp.
        Decorations by John Austen.

A4   *Titans*. London: Macmillan, 1926. 67 pp.

A5   *The Iron Door: An Ode*. Toronto: Macmillan, 1927. 30 pp.
        Decorations by Thoreau Macdonald. First limited edition of 1000 copies, of which 100 are numbered and signed by the author.

A6   *The Roosevelt and the Antinoe*. New York: Macmillan, 1930. 44 pp.
        First limited edition of 100 copies, numbered and signed by the author.

A7 *Verses of the Sea.* Introd. Charles G. D. Roberts. St. Martin's Classics. Toronto: Macmillan, 1930. xv, 97 pp.
 Notes by the author.

A8 *Many Moods.* Toronto: Macmillan, 1932. vi, 53 pp.

A9 *The Titanic.* Toronto: Macmillan, 1935. 42 pp.

A10 *The Fable of the Goats and Other Poems.* Toronto: Macmillan, 1937. 47 pp.
 Governor-General's Award.

A11 *Brébeuf and His Brethren.* Toronto: Macmillan, 1940. 65 pp.
Toronto: Macmillan, 1940. 66 pp.
 Second limited edition, slightly revised, with new epilogue. Limited to 500 copies.
Brébeuf and His Brethren: The North American Martyrs. Detroit: Basilian, 1942. 66 pp.
Toronto: Macmillan, 1966. 80 pp.
 Governor-General's Award.

A12 *Dunkirk.* Toronto: Macmillan, 1941. 13 pp.
 First limited edition of 300 copies. Printed especially for Messrs. Johnston, Everson, and Charlesworth, Christmas, 1941. With Christmas greetings from J. G. Johnston, R. G. Everson, and J. L. Charlesworth.

A13 *Still Life and Other Verse.* Toronto: Macmillan, 1943. 40 pp.

A14 *Collected Poems.* Toronto: Macmillan, 1944. 314 pp. Introd. William Rose Bénet. New York: Knopf, 1945. xv, 269 pp.

A15 *They Are Returning.* Toronto: Macmillan, 1945. 15 pp.

A16 *Behind the Log.* Toronto: Macmillan, 1947. xiv, 47 pp. Drawings by Grant Macdonald.

A17 *Ten Selected Poems.* St. Martin's Classics. Toronto: Macmillan, 1947. ix, 149 pp.
 With notes by the author.

A18 *Towards the Last Spike: A Verse Panorama of the Struggle to Build the First Canadian Transcontinental from the Time of the Proposed Terms of Union with British Columbia (1870) to the Hammering of the Last Spike in the Eagle Pass (1885).* Toronto: Macmillan, 1952. 53 pp.
 Governor-General's Award.

A19 *The Collected Poems of E. J. Pratt.* Ed. and introd. Northrop Frye. 2nd ed. Toronto: Macmillan, 1958. xxviii, 395 pp.

A20 *Here the Tides Flow.* Introd. D. G. Pitt. Toronto: Macmillan, 1962. xiv, 169 pp.
 With notes and questions by D. G. Pitt.

A21 *Selected Poems of E. J. Pratt.* Ed. and introd. Peter Buitenhuis. Toronto: Macmillan, 1968. xxx, 221 pp.
 Bibliography and notes by Peter Buitenhuis.

Philosophy

A22 *Studies in Pauline Eschatology, and Its Background.* Diss. Toronto 1917.
Toronto: William Briggs, 1917. 203 pp.

Broadsides

A23 "The Line of Ascent: A Tribute to the British Stock." N.p.: n.p., n.d. Broadside.
 "Written on the occasion of the visit of a delegation of the Publisher's Branch of the Board of Trade [Toronto] to Britain, October 1945."

A24 "A Victory Message and Pledge of Friendship from the Canadian People to the USSR." N.p.: n.p. [1945?]. Broadside.

A25 "Snowfall on a Battlefield." N.p.: n.p., n.d. Broadside.

A26 "The Deed." N.p.: n.p., n.d. Broadside.

A27 "In Memoriam." N.p.: n.p., n.d. Broadside.

A28 "Newfoundland Calling." London: Macmillan, 1949. Broadside.

A29 "A Club's Inventory of Hades." N.p.: n.p. [1958?]. Broadside.
     Privately printed on the occasion of the fiftieth anniversary of the Toronto Arts and Letters Club.

A30 "Sea-Gulls." N.p.: n.p. [1959?]. Broadside.

A31 "Inventory of Hades." N.p. [1959]. Broadside. Illustrated by Frank Newfeld.

Manuscripts

A32 E. J. Pratt Library
    Victoria University
    Toronto, Ontario

Pratt Manuscript Collection:

This major collection, of the manuscripts of E. J. Pratt, consists of notebooks, working papers, rough drafts of poems, typescripts, lecture notes, addresses, essays, and correspondence. Photographs of and materials relating to Pratt are also included. The following outline of the arrangement of the collection lists only the most prominent items in the boxes; the *Inventory of the E. J. Pratt Collection of Manuscripts* provides a complete listing.

The items in Boxes 1-6 include notebooks, typescripts, printer's proofs.

Box 1:
Rachel. A Sea Story of Newfoundland in Verse — typescripts.
Newfoundland Verse — typescript.
Titans — draft, notes, and an address.
The Witches' Brew — drafts.
The Iron Door: An Ode — draft and commentary.

Box 2:
The Roosevelt and the Antinoe — partial draft, typescripts, and an address.
Many Moods — draft poems.

Box 3:
The Titanic — drafts, notes, and an address.
The Fable of the Goats — drafts and notes.
Brébeuf — draft, notes, typescript.

Box 4:
Dunkirk — drafts, page proofs, and introductory material.
Still Life — draft poems and typescripts.
Collected Poems — proof sheets.

Box 5:
They Are Returning — draft and notes.
Behind the Log — draft, typescripts, proof sheets, and an address.

Box 6:
Towards the Last Spike — drafts, notes, typescripts, and an address.

Box 7:
Holograph and typescript drafts of individual poems, some of which have been collected in earlier editions as

well as those unpublished in book form or those written after *Collected Poems*, second edition, 1958. Including: "Cycles," "Bereft," "The Empty Room," "The Deed," "The Human Doctor," "Carlo," "Blind from Singapore," "The Shell," "The Osprey," "Sea-Variations," and "Newfoundland Calling."
Holograph and typescript comments on individual poems. Including: "Erosion," "The Fog," and "The Way of Cape Race."

Box 8:
Photocopy of typescript of E. J. Pratt's M.A. thesis, University of Toronto, 1912: "The Demonology of the New Testament [Synoptics] in its relation to earlier developments, and to the mind of Christ."
Typescripts of unpublished drama *Clay*.

Box 9:
Notes and drafts for academic lectures on English literature; public lectures, formal and informal speeches, toasts, and introductions.

Box 10:
Notes and drafts for lectures on Shakespeare, courses on American Literature, radio broadcasts, essays, and book reviews.

Box 11:
Correspondence.

Box 12:
Material on Pratt:
Scrapbook on E. J. Pratt 1923-64, compiled by Mrs. Viola Pratt consisting of press cuttings of reviews and articles on Pratt.
Typescripts of interviews, talks, and tributes to E. J. Pratt: programmes, announcements, cards, brochures of dinners, receptions, and autographic sessions.
Typescript of *The Silent Ancestors; the Forebears of*

E. J. Pratt, by Mildred Claire Pratt. Related correspondence.
Audio recordings and tapes.
Formal studio portraits; informal photographs and illustrations.
Woodcuts by Claire Pratt.

Edgar Collection:

Correspondence, E. J. Pratt to Pelham Edgar.

A33   Archives
Queen's University
Kingston, Ontario

Manuscripts of individual poems, notes, other prose, typescripts; correspondence.

A34   Thomas Fisher Rare Book Library
University of Toronto
Toronto, Ontario

W. A. Deacon Papers:
Correspondence between W. A. Deacon and E. J. Pratt.

Birney Collection:
Correspondence between Earle Birney and E. J. Pratt.

A. J. M. Smith Papers:
Correspondence, E. J. Pratt to A. J. M. Smith.

A35   University of Saskatchewan Library
Saskatoon, Saskatchewan

Gustafson Collection:
Correspondence between Ralph Gustafson and E. J. Pratt.

B   Contributions to Periodicals and Books: Poetry, Short Story, Articles, Miscellaneous Works and Contributions, Audio Recordings, and Selected Anthology Contributions

Note: When an item is reprinted in one of Pratt's books, this fact is noted in the entry through one of the following abbreviations:

B1   "A Poem on the May Examinations." *Acta Victoriana*, 32 (April 1909), 561-64.

B2   "The Wind of the West." *Acta Victoriana*, 39 (Oct. 1914), 14.

B3   "The Sea." *Acta Victoriana*, 39 (Dec. 1914), 126. Rpt. in *The Rebel*, 2, No. 3 (Dec. 1917), 88.

B4   "Unseen Allies." *Acta Victoriana*, 39 (March 1915), 331.

B5   "By the Sea." *Acta Victoriana*, 40 (Oct. 1915), 14.

B6   "The Sacrifice of Youth." *Acta Victoriana*, 40 (Dec. 1915), frontispiece.

B7   "Dead on the Field of Honour." *Acta Victoriana*, 40 (June 1916), 373.

B8   "The Seed Must Die. (To the British Dead)." *Acta Victoriana*, 41 (March 1917), 255. *NV*.

B9   "The Greater Sacrifice." *Acta Victoriana*, 41 (June 1917), 320-21.

B10   "For Valor." *Acta Victoriana*, 42 (Oct. 1917), 11-13.

B11   "The Great Mother." *Acta Victoriana*, 42 (Dec. 1917), 135. *NV*; *VOTS*.

B12   "The Largess of 1917." *Acta Victoriana*, 42 (Feb. 1918), 248-49.

B13   "The Angler." *The Rebel*, 2, No. 6 (March 1918), 230.

B14   "The Dear Illusion." *Acta Victoriana*, 42 (March 1918), 312.

B15 "The Wooden Cross." *Acta Victoriana*, 42 (June 1918), 363-64.

B16 "October, 1918." *Acta Victoriana*, 43 (Oct. 1918), 19-20.

B17 "Amerongen." *Acta Victoriana*, 43 (Jan. 1919), 157.

B18 "The Dear Illusion." *The Rebel*, 3, No. 5 (March 1919), 218.

B19 "The Hidden Scar." *Acta Victoriana*, 43 (June 1919), 332. *NV*.

B20 "A Dialogue by a Stream." *The Rebel*, 4, No. 3 (Dec. 1919), 131.

B21 "In Memoriam." *Acta Victoriana*, War Supplement (Dec. 1919), p. 7. *NV*.

B22 "Blow! Winds, and Roar!" *Acta Victoriana*, 44 (Jan. 1920), 170.

B23 "On the Shore." *The Rebel*, 4, No. 6 (March 1920), 232. *NV*; *VOTS*; *CP*; *CP2*.

B24 "Carlo." *The Canadian Forum*, Nov. 1920, p. 55. *NV*; *VOTS*; *CP2*; *HTTF*; *SPOEJP*.

B25 "Anticipations." *The Canadian Forum*, June 1921, p. 271.

B26 "The Flood-Tide." *The Canadian Forum*, June 1921, p. 272. *NV*; *VOTS*; *CP*; *CP2*; *HTTF*.

B27 "In Absentia." *The Canadian Forum*, June 1921, pp. 271-72. *NV*; *VOTS*; *CP*; *CP2*.

B28 "The Pine Tree." *The Canadian Forum*, June 1921, p. 272. *NV*.

B29 "Sea Variations." *Canadian Bookman*, 2 (Jan. 1922), 50-51. *NV*.

B30 "The Ice-Floes." *The Canadian Forum*, April 1922, pp. 591-93. *NV*; *VOTS*; *CP*; *CP2*; *TSP*; *HTTF*.

B31 "The Ground Swell." *Acta Victoriana*, 47 (Jan. 1923), 15. *NV*; *VOTS*; *CP*; *CP2*; *HTTF*.

B32 "The History of John Jones." *The Canadian Forum*, Jan. 1923, p. 110. *NV*; *VOTS*; *CP*; *CP2*.

B33 "In Lantern Light." *The Canadian Forum*, Jan. 1923, p. 111. *NV*; *VOTS*; *CP*; *CP2*; *HTTF*.

B34 "The Shark." *The Canadian Forum*, Jan. 1923, p. 111. *NV*; *VOTS*; *CP*; *CP2*; *HTTF*; *SPOEJP*.

B35 "A Student's Prayer at an Examination." *The Canadian Forum*, Jan. 1923, p. 111.

B36 "Comrades." *Canadian Magazine*, 62 (April 1924), 381. Rpt. in *The Atlantic Advocate*, 52 (May 1962), 24. *MM*; *CP*; *CP2*.

B37 "The Frost Over-Night." *Canadian Bookman*, 6 (April 1924), 87.

B38 "The Lie." *Canadian Bookman*, 6 (April 1924), 88.

B39 "The Alternative." *Canadian Bookman*, 6 (June 1924), 135.

B40 "The Last Survivor." *The Canadian Forum*, June 1924, p. 274.

B41 "The Drag Irons." *The Canadian Forum*, July 1924, p. 301. *MM*; *CP*; *CP2*; *HTTF*; *SPOEJP*.

B42 "Tokens." *The Canadian Forum*, Sept. 1924, p. 365.

B43   "The Ritual." *Canadian Magazine*, 63 (Oct. 1924), 347. Rpt. in *Acta Victoriana*, 50 (Dec. 1925), 52. *VOTS*; *MM*; *CP*; *CP2*; *HTTF*.

B44   "The Dear Illusion." *Dalhousie Review*, 4 (Jan. 1925), 437.

B45   "The Cachalot." *The Canadian Forum*, Nov. 1925, pp. 47-51. *T*; *VOTS*; *CP*; *CP2*; *TSP*; *HTTF*; *SPOEJP*.

B46   "Tatterhead." *Acta Victoriana*, 50 (Jan. 1926), 13-14. Rpt. in *Queen's Quarterly*, 34 (April 1927), 442. Rpt. in *Acadie*, 1, No. 2 (15 April 1930), 13. *MM*; *HTTF*.

B47   "The Sea Cathedral." *Acta Victoriana*, 51 (Dec. 1926), 17. Rpt. in *The Canadian Forum*, May 1927, p. 237. Rpt. in *Acadie*, 1, No. 2 (1 May 1930), 2. *VOTS*; *MM*; *CP*; *CP2*; *HTTF*.

B48   "The Lee-Shore." *The Canadian Forum*, Oct. 1927, p. 406. *VOTS*; *MM*; *CP*; *CP2*; *HTTF*.

B49   "Cherries." *Saturday Night*, 8 Oct. 1927. *MM*; *CP*; *CP2*.

B50   "The Decision." *London Mercury*, 17 (Jan. 1928), 244. *MM*; *CP*; *CP2*.

B51   "Fair-Grounds, Columbus, Ohio." *The Canadian Forum*, June 1930, p. 314.

B52   "Blind." *Acta Victoriana*, 55 (Dec. 1930), 23. Rpt. in *The Canadian Forum*, May 1931, p. 301. *MM*; *CP*; *CP2*.

B53   "Sea-Gulls." *Acta Victoriana*, 55 (Dec. 1930), 23. Rpt. in *London Mercury*, 27 (Dec. 1932), 109. *MM*; *CP*; *CP2*; *HTTF*.

B54   Untitled. *World Friends*, 2, No. 4 (Dec. 1930), back cover.
       "That Night There Came to Bethlehem" (first line).

B55   "To Angelina an Old Nurse." *The Canadian Forum*, Jan. 1931, p. 141. *MM*; *CP*; *CP2*; *TSP*.

B56   "Fugitive." *Canadian Magazine*, 75 (Feb. 1931), 8. *MM*.

B57   "Old Age." *Canadian Magazine*, 75 (March 1931), 16. *MM*; *CP*; *CP2*.

B58   "Doors." *The Canadian Forum*, May 1931, p. 301. *MM*; *HTTF*.

B59   "For Better or Worse." *The Canadian Forum*, May 1931, p. 301.

B60   "At a Sanitarium." *The Canadian Forum*, July 1931, p. 326.

B61   "Erosion." *The Canadian Forum*, July 1931, p. 326. *MM*; *CP*; *CP2*; *HTTF*.

B62   "A Prairie Sunset." *Dalhousie Review*, 11 (July 1931), 217. Rpt. in *Literary Digest*, 110 (19 Sept. 1931), 24. Rpt. in *Canadian National Railway Magazine*, Sept. 1931, p. 24. *MM*; *CP*; *CP2*.

B63   "Time-Worn." *The Canadian Forum*, July 1931, p. 326. *MM*; *CP*; *CP2*; *HTTF*.

B64   "Water." *The Canadian Forum*, July 1931, p. 380.

B65   "The Highway." *Acta Victoriana*, 56 (Oct.-Nov. 1931), 15. Rpt. in *Dalhousie Review*, 11 (Jan. 1932), 472. Rpt. in *The Atlantic Advocate*, 52 (May 1962), 23. *MM*; *CP*; *CP2*; *SPOEJP*.

B66   "Armistice Silence." *Canadian Home Journal*, Nov. 1931, p. 17. *MM*.

B67   "No. 6000." *Canadian National Railway Magazine*, Dec. 1931, p. 9. *MM* ("The 6000"); *CP*; *CP2*; *TSP*; *HTTF*.

B68 "January the First." *World Friends*, Jan. 1932, back cover.

B69 "The Lost Cause." *Queen's Quarterly*, 39 (May 1932), 209. *MM*.

B70 "The Depression Ends." *The Canadian Forum*, Oct. 1932, pp. 10-11. *MM*; *CP*; *CP2*; *SPOEJP*.

B71 "Putting Winter to Bed." *Dalhousie Review*, 12 (Oct. 1932), 340-44. *MM*; *CP2*; *TSP*; *HTTF*.

B72 "A Reverie on a Dog." *University of Toronto Quarterly*, 2 (Oct. 1932), 40-41. *MM*; *CP*.

B73 "Bereft." *The Twentieth Century*, 1, No. 1 (Nov. 1932), 21. Rpt. in *Canadian Magazine*, 79 (Feb. 1933), 22. Rpt. in *Dalhousie Review*, 14 (April 1934), 64. Rpt. in *The Tamarack Review*, No. 41 (Autumn 1966), p. 78.

B74 "The Mirage." *The Twentieth Century*, 1, No. 1 (Nov. 1932), 21. *FOTG*; *CP2*; *SPOEJP*.

B75 "The Way of Cape Race." *London Mercury*, 27 (Dec. 1932), 109. *MM*; *CP*; *CP2*; *HTTF*; *SPOEJP*.

B76 "The Empty Room." *Canadian Magazine*, 79 (June 1933), 8. *FOTG*; *CP*; *CP2*.

B77 "Prayer-Medley." *The Canadian Forum*, Dec. 1933, pp. 92-93. *FOTG*.

B78 "The Text of the Oath." *Acta Victoriana*, 58 (Christmas 1933), 13. *FOTG*.

B79 "Credo Quia non Intellego." *Queen's Quarterly*, 41 (May 1934), 255.

B80 "The Prize-Winner." *Queen's Quarterly*, 42 (Feb. 1935), 109.

B81 "The Weather Glass." *The Canadian Forum*, Nov. 1935, p. 362. *FOTG*; *CP*; *CP2*; *HTTF*.

B82 "The Prize-Cat." *Canadian Poetry Magazine*, 1, No. 2 (April 1936), 23. *FOTG*; *CP*; *CP2*; *SPOEJP*.

B83 "Seen on the Road." *New Frontier*, 1, No. 2 (May 1936), 15. *FOTG*; *CP*; *CP2*.

B84 "Silences." *The Canadian Forum*, May 1936, p. 9. *FOTG*; *CP*; *CP2*; *HTTF*; *SPOEJP*.

B85 "Text of the Oath." *New Frontier*, 1, No. 2 (May 1936), 15. *FOTG*.

B86 "Thanksgiving." *The Missionary Monthly*, Oct. 1936, front cover.

B87 "Dictator (Baritone)." *The Canadian Forum*, Dec. 1936, p. 7. *FOTG* ("The Baritone"); *CP*; *CP2*.

B88 "Mother and Child." *World Friends*, N.S. 8, No. 4 (Dec. 1936), back cover.

B89 "The Twentieth Century Prophet." *The Canadian Forum*, Dec. 1936, p. 7.

B90 "Puck Reports Back." *Canadian Poetry Magazine*, 2, No. 2 (Oct. 1937), 43-49. *FOTG*.

B91 "The Impatient Earth." *Queen's Quarterly*, 45 (Nov. 1938), 542. *SLAOV*; *CP*; *CP2*.

B92 "The Manger under the Star." *World Friends*, N.S. 10, No. 4 (Dec. 1938), front cover.

B93 "The Submarine." *The Canadian Forum*, Dec. 1938, pp. 274-75. *SLAOV*; *CP*; *CP2*; *TSP*.

B94 "Old Harry." *Queen's Quarterly*, 46 (Feb. 1939), 66. *SLAOV*; *CP*; *CP2*; *HTTF*.

B95 "Still Life." *Saturday Night*, 28 Oct. 1939, p. 3. *SLAOV*; *CP*; *CP2*.

B96 "The Radio in the Ivory Tower." *The Canadian Forum*, Dec. 1939, pp. 276-77. *SLAOV*; *CP*; *CP2*.

B97 "The Old Eagle." *Queen's Quarterly*, 46 (Winter 1939), 428-30. *TSP*.

B98 "Fire-Worship." *Saturday Night*, 3 Feb. 1940, p. 1.

B99 "Dunkirk." *Maclean's*, 15 July 1940, p. 20. Rpt. in *Canadian Poetry Magazine*, 5 (Sept. 1940), 26.
   This poem is unrelated to the long narrative poem "Dunkirk."

B100 "Come Away, Death." *Poetry*, 58 (April 1941), 2-4. *SLAOV*; *CP*; *CP2*; *SPOEJP*.

B101 "The Invaded Field." *Poetry*, 58 (April 1941), 1-2. *SLAOV*; *CP*; *CP2*.

B102 "Dunkirk" (excerpts). *Poetry*, 59 (Oct. 1941), 10-15. Rpt. (excerpt) in *New World Illustrated*, 10 Dec. 1941, p. 7. *D*; *CP*; *CP2*; *TSP*; *HTTF*.

B103 "Heydrich." *Saturday Night*, 20 June 1942, p. 14.

B104 "The Truant." *The Canadian Forum*, Dec. 1942, pp. 264-65. Rpt. in *Voices*, No. 113 (Spring 1943), pp. 10-15. *SLAOV*; *CP*; *CP2*; *SPOEJP*.

B105 "The Stoics." *Queen's Quarterly*, 49 (Winter 1942), 344. *SLAOV*; *CP*; *CP2*; *SPOEJP*.

B106 "Father Time." *Saturday Night*, 13 March 1943, p. 12. *SLAOV*, *CP*; *CP2*.

B107 "Autopsy on a Sadist." *Voices*, No. 113 (Spring 1943), p. 15. *SLAOV*; *CP*; *CP2*.

B108 "Niemoeller." *Queen's Quarterly*, 50 (Aug. 1943), 268.

B109 "Fuehrer's Pot-Pourri." *Saturday Night*, 16 Oct. 1943, p. 40. *SLAOV*.

B110 "They Are Returning." *Maclean's*, 15 June 1945, pp. 5-6. *TAR*.

B111 "Behind the Log." *Canadian Poetry Magazine*, 10 (June 1947), 21-37. *CP2*; *BTL*; *SPOEJP*.

B112 "Lake Success." *Outposts*, No. 10 (Summer 1948), pp. 6-7.

B113 "Newfoundland Calling." *Star Weekly*, 31 March 1949. *HTTF*.

B114 "Displaced." *Here and Now*, 1 (June 1949), 77.

B115 "Last Watch." *Canadian Poetry Magazine*, 12 (Summer 1949), 5.

B116 "A November Landscape." *Missionary Monthly*, 24 (Nov. 1949), front cover. *MM*; *CP2*.

B117 "Blind from Singapore (Our Orders Are to Burn the City)." *Northern Review*, 3, No. 2 (Dec.-Jan. 1949-50), 5. Rpt. "Blind from Singapore." In *The Tamarack Review*, No. 41 (Autumn 1966), p. 75.

B118 "A Call." *Northern Review*, 3, No. 2 (Dec.-Jan. 1949-50), 6. *CP2*.

B119 "The Good Earth." *Canadian Poetry Magazine*, 13 (Summer 1950), 4-5. Rpt. in *The Atlantic Advocate*, 52 (May 1962), 23. *CP2*.

B120 "Myth and Fact." *Poetry Commonwealth*, No. 8 (Spring 1951), p. 2. *CP2*.

B121 "Cycles." *Contemporary Verse*, No. 36 (Fall 1951), pp. 8-9. *CP2.*

B122 "The Great Feud: A Dream of a Pleiocene Armageddon." *Northern Review*, 5, Nos. 3 and 4 (Feb.-March and April-May 1952), 3-35. *T; CP; CP2.*

B123 "The Deed." *Canadian Poetry Magazine*, 15 (Summer 1952), 7. *CP2; SPOEJP.*

B124 "The Unromantic Moon." *Poetry*, 82 (June 1953), 143. Rpt. in *Canadian Author & Bookman*, 34 (Spring 1958), 17. *CP2.*

B125 "Come Not the Seasons Here." *The Atlantic Advocate*, 52 (May 1962), 24. *NV; CP; CP2; SPOEJP.*

B126 "The Decision." *The Atlantic Advocate*, 52 (May 1962), 23. *MM; CP; CP2.*

B127 "Erosion." *The Atlantic Advocate*, 52 (May 1962), 23. *MM; CP; CP2; HTTF.*

B128 "The Lament of the Wets." *Douglas Library Notes*, 12, No. 2 (Spring 1963), 3.

B129 "But Mary Kept All These Things, and Pondered Them in Her Heart." *The Tamarack Review*, No. 41 (Autumn 1966), pp. 78-79.

B130 "Displaced." *The Tamarack Review*, No. 41 (Autumn 1966), p. 81.

B131 "The Doctor in the Boat." *The Tamarack Review*, No. 41 (Autumn 1966), pp. 76-77.

B132 "The Head of the Firm." *The Tamarack Review*, No. 41 (Autumn 1966), p. 80.

B133 "To D. H. Lawrence." *The Tamarack Review*, No. 41 (Autumn 1966), p. 77.

B134 "To G. B. S." *The Tamarack Review*, No. 41 (Autumn 1966), p. 74.

Short Story

B135 "'Hooked': A Rocky Mountain Experience." *Acta Victoriana*, 38 (March 1914), 286-91.

Articles

B136 "A Western Experience." *Acta Victoriana*, 34, No. 1 (Oct. 1910), 3-8.

B137 "The Scientific Character of Psychology." *Acta Victoriana*, 37, No. 6 (March 1913), 300-04.

B138 "The University and Social Service." *The Rebel*, 2, No. 6 (March 1918), 266-67.
      Letter.

B139 "Introduction." "The Last Home Letter of Hedley Goodyear." *Acta Victoriana*, 43, No. 1 (Oct. 1918), 60. Rpt. from *Free Press* [St. John's].

B140 "Mental Measurements as Applied to a Toronto School." *Public Health Journal*, No. 12 (1921), pp. 148-55.

B141 "The Application of the Binet-Simon Tests (Stanford Revision) to a Toronto Public School." *Canadian Journal of Mental Hygiene*, 3, No. 1 (April 1921), 95-116.

B142 Rev. of *Memories in Melody*, by A. C. Nash. *The Canadian Forum*, June 1921, p. 280.

B143 Rev. of *Poems*, by A. L. Phelps. *The Canadian Forum*, June 1921, p. 280.

B144 "Golfomania." *Acta Victoriana*, 49, No. 2 (Nov. 1924) 9-13.

B145 Rev. of *A Florentine Celebrity 'Life of Benevenuto Cellini' by Himself. Saturday Night*, Sec. Literary, 12 March 1927, p. 3.

B146 "Introduction." *In Caribou Land*, by P. Florence Miller. Toronto: Ryerson, 1929, p. 5.

B147 "Introduction." *Moby-Dick: Or, the Whale*, by Herman Melville. Toronto: Macmillan, 1929, pp. v-xvii.

B148 Rev. of *Whiteoaks of Jalna*, by Mazo de la Roche. *Acta Victoriana*, 54, No. 2 (Nov. 1929), 21.

B149 "Foreword." In *Our Great Ones: Twelve Caricatures Cut in Linoleum*, by Jack McLaren. Toronto: Ryerson, 1932, n. pag.

B150 "Preface" and "Notes" by Adrian Macdonald [and E. J. Pratt]. In *A Pedlar's Pack: Narrative Poetry for Secondary Schools*. Ed. Adrian Macdonald [and E. J. Pratt]. St. Martin's Classics. Toronto: Macmillan, 1932, pp. v-viii, 211-40.

B151 "Canadian Writers of the Past: Marjorie Pickthall." *The Canadian Forum*, June 1933, pp. 334-35.

B152 "Literature: The Decay of Romance." *Canadian Comment*, 2, No. 7 (July 1933), 24-25.

B153 "Literature: Changing Standpoints." *Canadian Comment*, 2, No. 8 (Aug. 1933), 25.

B154 "Literature: Lord Macaulay." *Canadian Comment*, 2, No. 9 (Sept. 1933), 29.

B155 "Literature: The Nature of Poetry." *Canadian Comment*, 2, No. 10 (Oct. 1933), 26.

B156 "Literature: Francis Bacon." *Canadian Comment*, 2, No. 11 (Nov. 1933), 30.

B157 "Literature: English Meat and Irish Gravy." *Canadian Comment*, 2, No. 12 (Dec. 1933), 8.

B158 "Literature: Twenty Years A-Growing." Rev. of *Twenty Years A-Growing*, by Maurice O'Sullivan. *Canadian Comment*, 3, No. 1 (Jan. 1934), 31.

B159 "Literature: New Notes in Canadian Poetry." *Canadian Comment*, 3, No. 2 (Feb. 1934), 26-27.

B160 "Literature: The Great Diary." *Canadian Comment*, 3, No. 3 (March 1934), 26.

B161 "Literature: With Hook and Worm." *Canadian Comment*, 3, No. 4 (April 1934), 13.

B162 "Literature: The Dickens Vogue." *Canadian Comment*, 3, No. 5 (May 1934), 23.

B163 "Literature: Simplicity in Poetry." *Canadian Comment*, 3, No. 6 (June 1934), 22-23.

B164 "Literature: Charles Lamb." *Canadian Comment*, 3, No. 7 (July 1934), 28-29.

B165 "Literature: A Study in Poetic Development. I. The Earlier Yeats." *Canadian Comment*, 3, No. 8 (Aug. 1934), 20.

B166 "Literature: A Study in Poetic Development. II. The Later Yeats." *Canadian Comment*, 3, No. 9 (Sept. 1934), 21.

B167 "Literature: The Drama of Ideas." *Canadian Comment*, 3, No. 10 (Oct. 1934), 17.

B168 "Literature: The Comic Spirit." *Canadian Comment*, 3, No. 11 (Nov. 1934), 17.

B169 "Literature: The Fourth Column." *Canadian Comment*, 3, No. 12 (Dec. 1934), 21-22.

B170 Rev. of *Halt and Parley*, by G. H. Clarke. *Canadian Comment*, 4, No. 3 (March 1935), 27.

B171 "The Titanic: The Convergence of the Twain." *Canadian Comment*, 4, No. 10 (Oct. 1935), 9-10.

B172 "Foreword." *Canadian Poetry Magazine*, 1, No. 1 (Jan. 1936), 5-7.
Editorial.

B173 "Slang: Why and Why Not." *Canadian Comment*, 5, No. 3 (March 1936), 28-29.

B174 "Comment." *Canadian Poetry Magazine*, 1, No. 2 (April 1936), 5-6.
Editorial.

B175 "Comment." *Canadian Poetry Magazine*, 1, No. 3 (July 1936), 5-6.
Editorial.

B176 "Introduction and Notes." In *Under the Greenwood Tree: Or, The Mellstock Quire: A Rural Painting of the Dutch School*, by Thomas Hardy. St. Martin's Classics. Toronto: Macmillan, 1937, pp. ix-xiii, 275-79.

B177 "Brighter Days Ahead." *Canadian Poetry Magazine*, 1, No. 4 (March 1937), 5-6.
Editorial.

B178 "Entering the Second Year." *Canadian Poetry Magazine*, 2, No. 1 (June 1937), 5-6.
Editorial.

B179 "Canadian Poetry Night." *Canadian Poetry Magazine*, 2, No. 3 (Dec. 1937), 5.
Editorial.

B180 "Foreword." In *Down the Years*, by Samuel Morgan-Powell. Toronto: Macmillan, 1938, pp. v-viii.

B181 "Bookman Profiles: Annie Charlotte Dalton." *Canadian Bookman*, 20 (April-May 1938), 11.

B182 "The Third Year." *Canadian Poetry Magazine*, 3, No. 1 (June 1938), 7-8.
Editorial.

B183 "Canadian Poetry—Past and Present." *University of Toronto Quarterly*, 8 (Oct. 1938), 1-10.

B184 Rev. of *By Stubborn Stars and Other Poems*, by Kenneth Leslie. *Canadian Poetry Magazine*, 3, No. 4 (April 1939), 44-45.

B185 Rev. of *Cross Country*, by Alan Creighton. *Canadian Poetry Magazine*, 4, No. 2 (Oct. 1939), 45-46.

B186 Rev. of *Fancy Free*, by Carol Coates. *Canadian Poetry Magazine*, 4, No. 4 (May 1940), 47.

B187 Rev. of *Postlude to an Era*, by Verna Loveday Harden. *Canadian Poetry Magazine*, 5, No. 1 (Sept. 1940), 45-46.

B188 "Preface and Notes." In *Heroic Tales in Verse*. St. Martin's Classics. Toronto: Macmillan, 1941, pp. v-x, 207-17.

B189 "Canadian Poetry Night." *Canadian Poetry Magazine*, 5, No. 3 (April 1941) [5-6].
Editorial.

B190 Rev. of *Poems*, by Carol Cassidy. *Canadian Poetry Magazine*, 5, No. 3 (April 1941), 53-55.

B191 Rev. of *The Flying Bull and Other Tales*, by Watson Kirkconnell. *Canadian Poetry Magazine*, 5, No. 3 (April 1941), 53-55.

B192 Rev. of *Lords of the Air*, by A. M. Stephen. *Canadian Poetry Magazine*, 5, No. 4 (Aug. 1941), 43-45.

B193 Rev. of *The King Who Loved Old Clothes*, by Arthur Stringer. *Canadian Poetry Magazine*, 5, No. 4 (Aug. 1941), 43-45.

B194 Rev. of *Victoria Poetry Chapbook, 1941-42. Canadian Poetry Magazine*, 5, No. 4 (Aug. 1941), 43-45.

B195 Rev. of *Contemporary Verse: A Canadian Quarterly. Canadian Poetry Magazine*, 6, No. 1 (Dec. 1941), 46.

B196 "Special Editorial Notice." *Canadian Poetry Magazine*, 6, No. 1 (Dec. 1941), 11.

B197 Excerpt from a letter by E. J. Pratt. In *Night Is Ended, Thoughts in Lyric*, by Joseph S. Wallace. Winnipeg: Contemporary Pub., 1942, p. 7.

B198 "Foreword." *Photography, a Craft and Creed*, by Sir Ellsworth Flavelle. Toronto: Ryerson, 1943, [2 pp.].

B199 Rev. of *David and Other Poems*, by Earle Birney. *Canadian Poetry Magazine*, 6, No. 4 (March 1943), 34-35.

B200 "Saint-Denys-Garneau's World of Spiritual Communion." *Canadian Poetry Magazine*, 6, No. 4 (March 1943), 5-6.
　　　Editorial comment to Guy Sylvestre's article on Saint-Denys-Garneau.

B201 Rev. of *Tasting the Earth*, by Mona Gould. *Canadian Poetry Magazine*, 7, No. 1 (Aug. 1943), 35-36.

B202 Source Material and Poetry (from an Address to the Poetry Group, Montreal Branch, C.A.A.). *The Canadian Author & Bookman*, 21, No. 1 (March 1945), 15.

B203 "A Greeting." *Here and Now*, 1, No. 1 (Dec. 1947), 7.

B204 "Foreword." In *Saint Ignace, Canadian Altar of Martyrdom*, by William Sherwood Fox with the collaboration of Wilfrid Jury. Toronto: McClelland and Stewart, 1949, pp. vii-viii.

B205 "Prologue, the Poem 'Newfoundland.'" In *This is Newfoundland*. Ed. Ewart Young. Toronto: Ryerson, 1949, pp. ix-xii.

B206 "Foreword." In *Hidden Springs: A Narrative Poem of Old Upper Canada, and Other Poems*, by Jenny O'Hara Pincock. Waterloo, Ont.: n.p., 1950, pp. vii-viii.

B207 "My First Book." *Canadian Author & Bookman*, 28 (Winter 1952-53), 5-7.

Miscellaneous Works and Contributions

B208 "The Great Appeal and Final Triumph."
　　　Epilogue written for United Church of Canada, Pictorial Pageant held in Massey Hall, Toronto, 1928.

B209 "The Fly-Wheel Lost." In *Open House*. Ed. William Arthur Deacon and Wilfred Reeves. Ottawa: Graphic, 1931, pp. 246-55.

B210 "God of All Children of the Earth." Toronto: Woman's Missionary Society, The United Church of Canada, 1937.
　　　Part of a closing Ritual on inside back cover. Written especially for *One Family*, by Viola Whitney Pratt.

B211 "Memories of Newfoundland." *The Book of Newfoundland*, Vol. II. Ed. J. R. Smallwood. St. John's: Newfoundland Book Publishers, 1937, pp. 158-59. Rpt. in *A Book of Canada*. Ed. William Toye. London: Collins, 1962, pp. 206-07.

B212 "Keep Us Free." Oscar Morawetz, composer. Toronto: Gordon V. Thompson, 1942, 14 pp. Sheet music.

An anthem for mixed voices with piano or orchestral accompaniment. The words by E. J. Pratt.

B213 "Mother and Child." [1950].

Christmas greetings card with commercial illustration.

B214 "Hymns." *Triumph of the Faith. A Pictorial Presentation*, produced by Denzil G. Ridout. 1954.

B215 *Magic in Everything.* ("With Christmas and New Year greetings from The Macmillan Company of Canada Limited, Toronto, in its fiftieth anniversary year.") Toronto: Macmillan, 1955, 6 pp. *CP2; HTTF.*

B216 "Magic in Everything." [1957].

Christmas greetings card with pictorial accompaniment by Claire Pratt.

B217 "Sea-Gulls." [1958].

Christmas greetings card with woodcut accompaniment by Claire Pratt.

B218 "Sea-Gulls." New York: M. Witmark, 1958, 8 pp. Sheet music.

Words by E. J. Pratt. Music by Joseph Roff.

B219 An excerpt from "The Truant." Toronto: Oscar Ross, 1959, 4 pp.

Edition of one thousand copies. "Prepared for the International Competition for Book Designers... Leipzig, 1959."

B220 *Lines on the Occasion of Her Majesty's Visit to Canada, 1959.* Toronto: Canadian Broadcasting Corporation, Information Services, Aug. 1959, 4 pp.

B221 "They Tell Us That the Ocean's Birth" [Sea-Shell]. [1960].

Christmas greetings card with aquatint etching [1954] entitled "Pearl" by Claire Pratt.

B222 "Mother and Child." [1961].

Christmas greetings card with wood engraving entitled "Peace" by Claire Pratt.

B223 "Snowflakes on a Battle-field." [1962].

Christmas greetings card with woodcut by Claire Pratt.

B224 "Grant Us Lord Amidst the Carols." [carol] [1964].

Christmas greetings card with woodcut by Claire Pratt.

B225 "The Osprey." [1967].

Christmas greetings card with woodcut by Claire Pratt.

B226 "The Lost Cause." In *Three Songs of Contemplation.* Scarborough: Berandol Music, 1970, 5 pp. Sheet music.

Words by E. J. Pratt. Music by Patricia Blomfield Holt.

Audio Recordings

B227 *Brébeuf and His Brethren.* Non-commercial CBC recording P.A.T. 430926-1 and 480317-3 CMC397.

With musical arrangement by Healy Willan.

B228 *E. J. Pratt Reading His Own Poems.* Harvard Vocarium Records P-1124-27.

As originally recorded for the poetry room, Harvard College Library, 1949. Contents: v.1: "The Shark," "Sea-Gulls," "The History of John Jones," Selections from "The Cachalot": v.2: Selections from *Brébeuf and His Brethren*: His letter to the Priests in

France. The Passion and Death of Brébeuf and Lalemant.

B229 *Reminiscences of Newfoundland.* Phonodisc. Non-commercial. Recorded at CBC. T-9915 to T-9924.
Delivered at St. John's, Newfoundland, January 27, 1949.

B230 "E. J. Pratt Reading from His Collected Poems." Non-commercial. Audio tape reel-to-reel.
Taped March 1956.

B231 "E. J. Pratt Delivering Lecture on *King Lear*." Non-commercial. Audio tape reel-to-reel.
Recorded December 15, 1960.

Selected Anthology Contributions

B232 "In Memoriam." In *Our Canadian Literature: Representative Prose and Verse.* Ed. Albert D. Watson and Lorne Albert Pierce. Toronto: Ryerson, 1922, pp. 169-70.

B233 "The Convict Holocaust," "The Drag-Irons," "From Java to Geneva," "The Man and the Machine," "The Prize Winners," "Sea-Gulls," "Seen on the Road," "Text of the Oath." In *New Provinces: Poems of Several Authors.* Ed. F. R. Scott. Toronto: Macmillan, 1936, pp. 41-48.

B234 "The Cachalot, I and II," "Come Away Death," "*Dunkirk*: In the Skies," "The Old Eagle," "Silences." In *The Book of Canadian Poetry: A Critical and Historical Anthology.* Ed. A. J. M. Smith. Chicago: Univ. of Chicago Press, 1943, pp. 277-91.

B235 "Autopsy on a Sadist (after Lidice)," "The Decision," "Erosion," "A Feline Silhouette," "Invisible Trumpets Blowing" from *Brébeuf and His Brethren.* In *Canadian*

Poems 1850-1952. Ed. Louis Dudek and Irving Layton. Toronto: Contact, 1952, pp. 47-49.

B236 "Behind the Log," "Brébeuf and His Brethren," "Erosion," "Newfoundland," "The Prize Cat," "Sea-Gulls," "The Titanic." In *Twentieth Century Canadian Poetry.* Ed. Earle Birney. Toronto: Ryerson, 1953, pp. 11-13, 30, 33, 87-88, 115-17, 121, 122-24.

B237 "Burial at Sea," "The Cachalot," "Erosion," "The Ground-Swell," "The Ice-Floes," "Invisible Trumpets Blowing," "The Sea Cathedral." In *Canadian Poetry in English.* Ed. Bliss Carman, Lorne Pierce, and V. B. Rhodenizer. Rev. ed. Toronto: Ryerson, 1954, pp. 218-28.

B238 "Brébeuf and His Brethren," "Come Away Death," "Come Not the Seasons Here," "From Stone to Steel," "The Prize Cat," "The Titanic." In *The Penguin Book of Canadian Verse.* Ed. Ralph Gustafson. Harmondsworth Eng.: Penguin, 1958, pp. 119-25.

B239 "Behind the Log," "The Cachalot," "Towards the Last Spike." In *Modern Canadian Verse: In English and French.* Ed. A. J. M. Smith. Toronto: Oxford Univ. Press, 1967, pp. 1-12.

B240 "The Death of Brébeuf," "The End of the 'Titanic.'" In *The Oxford Anthology of Canadian Literature.* Ed. Robert Weaver and William Toye. Toronto: Oxford Univ. Press, 1973, pp. 392-400.

B241 "The Toll of the Bells," "The Shark," "Sea-Gulls," "The Sea-Cathedral," "From Stone to Steel," "The Prize Cat," "Come Away, Death," "The Truant," "Towards the Last Spike." In *Literature in Canada*, Vol. 2. Ed. Douglas Daymond and Leslie Monkman. Toronto: Gage, 1978, pp. 249-63.

Part II

Works on E. J. Pratt

C   Books, Articles and Sections of Books, Theses and Dissertations, Interviews, Audio Recordings, and Awards and Honours

Books

C1   Wells, Henry Willis, and Carl F. Klinck. *Edwin J. Pratt, the Man and His Poetry.* Canadian Men of Letters. Toronto: Ryerson, 1947. viii, 197 pp.

The book is both a biography of Pratt and a critical appreciation of his poetry. Klinck explores Pratt's background and its influence on his work. The chapter "Writing in Canada" looks into the Canadian literary scene of the time and shows that Pratt did not wish to be a "link between the Victorians and the disciples of T. S. Eliot"; rather his stated aim is "to write of the struggle of man against himself." Klinck analyses Pratt's philosophy, themes, and method: "The scholar and the common man being united in him.... He rarely goes ... into the realm of literary complexities reserved only for the few. His sources are democratic." The biographer observes that Pratt's "poetry is modern and even feminist in that he accepts women as participants in all human affairs, as partners in life, not as children, dolls, idols or foils for masculine sensitivity." Wells examines in essay form Pratt's major narratives in relation to traditional archetypes: "Aeschylean Tragedy" examines *The Titanic,* "Aristophanic Fooling" deals with *The Witches' Brew,* "The Religious Epic" studies *Brébeuf and His Brethren,* and "Epic Valour" concerns *The Roosevelt and the Antinoe.* Poems which use animal imagery, and poems that deal with tools and machines in relation to man are other areas discussed. Wells observes how Pratt, more than most poets, shows men as "workmen" and he "expresses with no slight imagination the great cultural problem of our age: the relation of man, compounded of flesh, blood, nerves, and thoughts, to his cold, impersonal and arrogant machines." In his summation, Wells concludes that Pratt "aspires to a day when man shall be not victim but master of his machines, and when wars abroad and the still deadlier depressions at home may have been conquered by human intelligence."

C2   Sutherland, John. *The Poetry of E. J. Pratt: A New Interpretation.* Toronto: Ryerson, 1956. viii, 109 pp.

Sutherland concerns himself "with the symbolic implications of Pratt's work, and specifically, though not exclusively, with the Christian symbolism it contains." Sutherland claims he was not primarily concerned with Pratt's conscious aim in his poetry, "but with some part of the vast residue of thought and feeling which may come into a poem in the course of composition irrespective of the poet's intention." He also finds that even if Pratt is not an orthodox Christian, still it is possible that Christian revelation is in the poems. From his study, Sutherland finds a religious meaning behind Pratt's poetry: *The Titanic* is an allegory of death and resurrection, "The Cachalot" and Tyrannosaurus Rex in *The Great Feud* symbolize Christ. According to Sutherland, "Pratt is drawn back to a position ultimately very close to the traditional Christian one." "Whatever his beliefs, he shows that deep respect for matter which derives from the Christian dogma of incarnation...." In an age of strife he has lived as though in "the core of the cyclone, and given the most powerful to the phantasms of the war of machines."

C3   Pitt, David G., ed. *E. J. Pratt.* Critical Views on Canadian Writers, 1. Toronto: Ryerson, 1969. xx, 155 pp. (Hereafter abbreviated as *EJP*. Annotations of individual articles and reviews appear with their original publication citation.)

The purpose of the collection is "to provide in convenient and accessible form a representative selection of critical writings on the poetry of E. J. Pratt. Books, reviews, and critical analyses reprinted cover the period beginning with a review of *Newfoundland Verse* written in 1923 to a Pratt lecture delivered at Memorial University of Newfoundland in 1969. The editor provides a bibliography of additional important critical writings excluded from the collection because of lack of space and because they are readily available. In the "Introduction," Pitt summarizes the history of Pratt scholarship, giving some possible reasons for the direction it has taken. "In the long run, 'all the adulation' of the 'Upper Canadian critics' was probably a disservice done to Pratt." He agrees that the poet was "'an outsize personality'" who affected critics' analyses; however, he concludes that "it cannot but be helpful and illuminating to readers and critics of Pratt to have at hand the thoughtful appreciations and considered judgements of those who knew both the spirit and the flesh."

C4   Wilson, Milton Thomas. *E. J. Pratt*. New Canadian Library: Canadian Writers, No. 2. Toronto: McClelland and Stewart, 1969. 64 pp.

In an excellent, if short critical analysis, Wilson examines Pratt's poetry under the headings: "Shorter Poems," "Extravaganzas," "The Sea, the Railway and Brébeuf." There is not a sharp dividing line between Pratt's short lyrics and his long narratives and often the shorter works "read like reshaped chips from the floor of an epic workshop." Pratt wrote about "things in action and in contact." In the lyrics the sense of touch is important: "the fingers, which etch and trace or handle and absorb," the tides are "'great hands'" and the fog, "'silent fingering.'" Wilson finds that in the best of Pratt's last lyrics, death is emphasized. He divides Pratt's narratives into a "four-beat or a five-beat" rhythmic norm. Pratt called the first group "extravaganzas" while Wilson, analyzing *The Witches' Brew*, "would call it a kind of scientific-cum-theological-cum-literary farce." He is critical of Pratt's use of irony and omens in *The Titanic*. In *The Roosevelt and the Antinoe*, the style is "more ornate and more direct than its two successors," but the critic can accept this while "touches of showy over-writing in *Behind the Log* leave me cold." The first lifeboat's journey is selected as "a candidate for the finest sustained passage in all Pratt." *Towards the Last Spike* is criticized because of "the way the poem assumes the story rather than narrates it." *Brébeuf and His Brethren* Wilson concedes is a masterpiece; Pratt has said of the poem that it "'typifies the struggle to obtain dramatic objectivity.'"

C5   Pratt, Mildred Claire. *The Silent Ancestors: The Forebears of E. J. Pratt*. Toronto: McClelland and Stewart, 1971. 239 pp.

The Silent Ancestors is Claire Pratt's quest which covered three continents and five years of work to unravel the background of the Pratt heritage. She found that "my story is meagre, . . . unenlivened by family legend and . . . tall tales." It is the "background of an ordinary family . . . warm and close knit . . . now completely forgotten in the very village in which its members had lived for over a century." The concluding chapter, "The Poetry of E. J. Pratt," gives personal, probing insights into the art of Pratt. There is more in Pratt than the sea and Newfoundland: "forces are inevitably at work forming and composing the sinews of thought." The "element of hugeness" is from his Yorkshire ancestry. His "gentleness and sensitivity" are "predominant qualities among the Pratts" and thus ancestral. "The Great Feud" is described as "the bloodiest and most ludicrous carnage ever staged." Referring to the often evoked symbolism, Claire Pratt states "deeper layers exist . . . but there is . . . no doubt that the ... [poem was] written primarily for pure joy." Other poems are discussed and analyzed in a refreshing way. Pratt worshipped "the group hero, the anonymous man ... whose unsung deeds permeate his verse." Miss Pratt concludes with her father's poem "Silences" which has relevance to "his life and ... his ancestors [but also reveals] the civilized need for ordered, meaningful sound."

C6   Djwa, Sandra. *E. J. Pratt: The Evolutionary Vision.* Montreal: McGill-Queen's Univ. Press; Toronto: Copp Clark, 1974. 160 pp.

This "introductory study," the most complete yet undertaken of Pratt's works, combines what Djwa has perceived as Pratt's central concern: "the conflict between Darwinian Nature and Christian ethics — and demonstrating the centrality of this evolutionary theme in each of the major poems." Djwa has thoroughly researched her project. She used the E. J. Pratt Manuscript Collection at Victoria University and also received help from Mrs. Viola Pratt and Miss Claire Pratt. Pratt's first attempts are "rooted in Victorian evolutionary thought." Still his "sensibility and his developed poetic technique are thoroughly modern in tone." Djwa believes Pratt was "a transitional figure whose poetic development has its roots in both centuries." Each chapter represents "a series of evolutionary parables." "Pratt is greatly distressed by the cruelty of nature; ... [he] opposes it with human and ethical values." He saw that since man is a part of nature, that man has the potential for amoral action within himself. Pratt often "explores the possibility of making some acceptable compromise between science and religion." For Pratt, "human will," courage, and determination, are what establish a moral frame of reference for human action. He is "a modern story teller and myth maker; ... he successfully embodies his ethical concern within the national myth." "In a nuclear age ... Pratt may be the most clear-sighted of our modern poets: long before his contemporaries, he

had perceived the true temper of the century and the responsibility it would place upon individual man."

C7   Clever, Glenn, ed. *The E. J. Pratt Symposium.* Reappraisals: Canadian Writers. Ottawa: Univ. of Ottawa Press, 1977. 172 pp.

The volume includes the program, some of the papers and panel presentations of The Pratt Symposium held at the University of Ottawa, May 1-2, 1976, and a Preliminary Checklist of Publications by and about Pratt. Editor Clever points out that the intention of the Symposium is "to help establish the literary identity of the author." The opening panel was a biographical one from which both Ralph Gustafson's and Carl Klinck's presentations are published. Germaine Warkentin's "The Aesthetics of E. J. Pratt's Shorter Poems" is an argument for Pratt's shorter poems. She concludes that "In Pratt's completeness, the short poems play not merely a significant, but an essential part. They do so . . . by defining and articulating what Pratt could give voice to in no other way." Sandra Djwa's presentation, "The 1920's: E. J. Pratt, Transitional Modern," shows how "Romanticism came late to Canada and it had not run its course when suddenly revived by the new nationalism, it had a new function to perform — the heroic affirmation of the land and its people," a need to which Pratt responded.

In "Language and Man in the Poetry of E. J. Pratt" Peter Stevens presents "the various paradoxes associated with silence and language" as well as the poet as paradoxical and possibly deceitful "spokesman for heroism." The precise role of the sea, the force it embodies, and the development of its function in Pratt's poetry are the problems tackled in Peter Buitenhuis' "E. J. Pratt: Poet of the Sea." Since *Brébeuf and His Brethren* "is largely misinterpreted by the critics," in his contribution, "E. J. Pratt's *Brébeuf and His Brethren* — The Critics and the Sources," Peter Hunt undertakes to show how they have erred. In

"Pratt as War Poet" Glenn Clever finds that Pratt's war poems do not "seriously concern the morality of war." Pratt believes in certain myths — "progress" and "political freedom" — which cause many of his war poems to be "verse propaganda." Following Cogswell, Clever relegates some of Pratt's war poems "to the stoney limbo of that which was not for all time but for an age." Agnes Nyland in "Pratt and History" finds that Pratt "knew our history well and used it accurately...." Using *Brébeuf and His Brethren* as an example Nyland sees in the poem "a profound study of the reaction of a pagan people to the teachings of Christianity, especially those of the Catholic faith ... the trained mind against superstition, the saint against the savage."

In "A True Voice: Pratt as a Lyric Poet" Robert Gibbs poses the question, did Pratt find "for his lyric poems a true voice ... of feeling"? Gibbs concludes that Pratt's "lyrics are far from being simple rationalizations of complex feelings; ... the voice or voices which speak the poems are ... the poet's own. They are true voices, true to a peculiar vision and particular feelings ... that impelled him to express himself in verse." In the concluding essay "Disjecta Membra: The Uncollected Pratt" Louis K. MacKendrick finds that "there is a substantial amount of Pratt's poetic work which remains uncollected but in print." He samples some of these and nominates "several new candidates for inclusion" in a definitive collected poems.

C8   Clever, Glenn. *On E. J. Pratt*. Ottawa: Borealis, 1977. 70 pp.

Clever surveys the "myths on which Pratt's poetry is assumed to rest" and decides that in Pratt "the essential myth is achievement, to moral purpose." In Pratt's age "the times were epic ... [and] human science replaced the church as the teleological representative in man." Of the poetry that resulted, Clever concludes that Pratt is "the first and only Canadian creative writer to express truly the spirit that forged the nation." Pratt's overall tone is "democratic and optimistic" with "willing participation in great deeds — not the mindless collective action cited by Davey." Pratt has been criticized by critics for his poetry's lack of human individuals. His "characters are elemental, cast from a heroic mould ... fixed and unchanging ... representative of historical forces, symbols of stages of civilization" and therefore individualization would "be a defect in a fictional world predicated on heroic achievement." In examining *Brébeuf and His Brethren*, the critic suggests how melodrama results because "rhetoric and plot are inconsistent with the narrative imperatives of the topic." Clever believes that because Pratt "takes sides," shows biases, some of his work, like *Dunkirk* and *Behind the Log*, is "verse propaganda." He concludes with a brief critical reading of *The Iron Door: An Ode*.

Articles and Sections of Books

C9   Pierce, Lorne. "The Poets." In *An Outline of Canadian Literature, French and English*. Montreal: L. Carrier, 1927, pp. 102-03.

A brief but enthusiastic review of the *Newfoundland Verse*, *The Witches' Brew*, and *The Titans*. "Nothing like his later work has appeared in Canada: its sheer exuberance combined with art, is a fine portent."

C10   Benson, Nathaniel A. "Who's Who in Canadian Literature: Edwin J. Pratt." *The Canadian Bookman*, 9 (Nov. 1927), 323-26.

The article begins with a biographical account of Pratt and his statement to Benson: "At heart I shall always be a Newfoundlander...." Of Pratt's first volume of poetry, the critic says "He feels and translates the sorrow of the labouring ships and the fierce exultation of men grappling with a power that is not to be conquered." Benson heaps praise on *The Witches' Brew* which is "ingenious satire upon almost any theme necessary." "The Cachalot," a narrative "of great power and originality, quite unlike any poem in our language" and the allegory "The Great Feud" Benson feels ends "with a superb, almost terrifying bitterness that is overwhelming in its finality." Superlative praise is given Pratt's latest work: *The Iron Door*. "It may be heresy to say so, but here is no native lyricist, or impassioned child of nature singing of vernal rapture, amorous delights and autumnal woe beneath the inevitable maple or in the usual purpurate haze. *The Iron Door* is more than Canadian—it is universal."

C11   Creighton, J. H. "The Poems of Mr. E. J. Pratt." *The New Outlook*, 30 Nov. 1927, n. pag.

An early review article about "the Poems of Mr. E. J. Pratt" written because Pratt is "The most original poet in Canada" and "he has received less than his due of attention from the Canadian public." The article illustrates the level of Pratt criticism and interpretation of the time. "'The Great Feud' is driving at something deeper than appears on the surface and it fails to bring it to view." "The Iron Door" on opening "is a lofty vision of the after-life.... As a statement of faith in God and immortality one feels it will long remain unique in Canadian poetry."

C12   Rhodenizer, Vernon B. "Poets Since Service." In *A Handbook of Canadian Literature*. Ottawa: Graphic, 1930, pp. 240-41.

Brief favourable mention of Pratt's work up to 1930.

C13   Roberts, Charles G. D. "Introduction." In *Verses of the Sea*. By E. J. Pratt. Toronto: Macmillan, 1930, pp. v-xiv.

In order to give an idea of the breadth and range of the author's genius, which would not be obvious in this collection of sea verse, Roberts gives a brief survey of Pratt's poetry. "In *Newfoundland Verse*, by reason of the blunt primitive speech employed and bold hand-

ling of the themes, the effect achieved was distinctly that of originality and strength." *The Witches' Brew* is "a masterpiece of exuberant imagination, riotous humour, and sound, constructive craftsmanship." "The Great Feud" does not come up to the standards of its predecessors. Confusion results from the combination of the scientific basis and the "sheer extravaganza" of imagination.

C14   Benson, Nathaniel A. "Ned Pratt, Poet of the Sea: 'At Heart He Will Always Be a Newfoundlander.'" *The New Outlook*, 5 March 1930, p. 223.

Benson, in an early excellent short critique, reviews Pratt's life and work "in order to understand the peculiar and powerful genius that has at last produced an epic work [*The Roosevelt and the Antinoe*] which is the first truly great narrative poem of the sea, that has been written by a Canadian." Although by 1930 Pratt had lived in Canada for twenty years, "At heart I shall always be a Newfoundlander," he claimed. Benson believes Pratt's love and understanding of Newfoundland, the sea, and his people helped inspire him and which when combined with his unique poetic technique has helped immortalize such sea epics as *The Roosevelt and the Antinoe*. Benson, in an inspired conclusion, finds *The Roosevelt and the Antinoe* "has in it the sombre pathos of his early *Newfoundland Verse*, the hurdling verbal skill of *The Witches' Brew*, the resonant thunder of diction and power of description memorable in *Titans*, and the tragic earnestness of *The Iron Door*."

C15   Graham, Jean. "Among Those Present: XXI—Dr. E. J. Pratt." *Saturday Night*, 14 May 1932, p. 5.

A review article in which the Pratt background is set down, the major works to 1932 are succinctly reviewed, and the most recent work, *The Roosevelt and the Antinoe*, is studied in more detail.

C16   Collin, W. E. "Pleiocene Heroics." In *The White*

Savannahs. Toronto: Macmillan, 1936, pp. 119-44. Rpt. (revised) Literature of Canada. Toronto: Univ. of Toronto Press, 1975. *EJP*.

"From his earliest published verse, from his shorter epic of sealing off Labrador to his last important works, *The Roosevelt and the Antinoe* and *The Titanic*, he has been absorbed in the heroic." Collin describes Pratt's imagination as heroic and young. *The Witches' Brew*, a "chantefable, makes no demands on us, it simply invites us to a rollicking ecumenical stag party" while *The Roosevelt and the Antinoe* depicts the heroic seamen in "a drama of adequate magnitude, purging us of pity and fear which, in the Aristotelian tradition, is the characteristic of tragedy." In *The Titanic*, Pratt emphasizes "the sense of security felt by officers and passengers alike in a ship designed to meet any conceivable emergency." Because it is unable to fulfill that expectation and fate plays a role, Collin shows that *The Titanic* belongs to the Greek order of tragedy in the sense that it is blind, it is epic." Collin analyses Pratt's work using T. S. Eliot's definition of "objective correlative" and draws comparisons with other poets. "Pratt has rejuvenated our poetry; a Canadian Masefield has enriched its vocabulary.... If a newer generation of poets, reared in a tempest, render homage to Pratt . . . it is because of his heroic imagination and his grip on life."

C17   Collin, W. E. "Poetry." In *Canadian Literature Today: A Series of Broadcasts Sponsored by the Canadian Broadcasting Corporation*. Canadian Broadcasting Corporation Publications, No. 6. Toronto: Univ. of Toronto Press, 1938, pp. 28-30.

Pratt is "the great-hearted poet who has always celebrated generous living and heroic fights." Pratt's view of life and his sense of the heroic are expressed in "gigantic pictures." This is illustrated by quotations from "The Fable of the Goats," "a satire on dictatorships.... The satire comes out in the compromise the poet arranges between the two goat leaders."

C18   Wilson, H. Rex. "Idol Gossip: Edwin J. Pratt." *Acta Victoriana*, 67, No. 2 (Nov. 1942), 12-15.

An intimate, humorous, biographical, and anecdotal article briefly covering Pratt's life from early youth to his position of Professor at Victoria College. Included is a listing of Pratt's publications to *Dunkirk*, along with his literary awards.

C19   Brown, E. K. "E. J. Pratt." In *On Canadian Poetry*. Toronto: Ryerson, 1943, pp. 132-52. 2nd ed. Toronto: Ryerson, 1944, pp. 143-64. *EJP*.

Newfoundland Verse, Pratt's first collection of poetry, was the "work of a poet who has not yet come to grips with himself;... it is the work of an experimenter who is continuing to clutch at a tradition although that tradition is actually stifling him." *Titans*, three years later, "is the work of a poet who has defined his personality and determined his form." Pratt has in "The Cachalot" resourcefully changed the tetrameter couplets, using quatrains, not rhyming regularly, and distributing stresses in a manner to counteract over-resonant monotony of the form which "remained a favourite with him." In *Brébeuf and His Brethren*, for the first time, there is a lifelike character in his poetry. Pratt came to believe "that human beings radiate such excitement as he long found only in ice-bergs, whales, prehistoric giants and ocean storms." Still Brébeuf is only a symbol, who certainly belongs in epic poetry but who is not the "epic hero that Homer drew." In *The Fable of the Goats and Other Poems*, Pratt foresaw the war and complained of the inadequacy of "brain in the leaders, whose shortcomings must be made good by the fatal courage of young heroes." Pratt's range was limited in his lyrics because love and passion are an "almost negligible part" of his poetry.

C20   Edgar, Pelham. "E. J. Pratt." *Educational Record* [Quebec], 59 (July-Sept. 1943), 178-80. Rpt. in *Leading Canadian Poets*. Ed. W. P. Percival. Toronto: Ryerson, 1948, pp. 177-83.

Edgar establishes Pratt "not only as a singularly attractive human being but as a genuinely important poet." After brief careers as a dry goods salesman and a producer of patent medicine Pratt continued his education, his first published work being his thesis *Pauline Eschatology.* Pratt's own description of his attempts to get his first long poem *Clay* published and its eventual fiery destruction is given. The publication in 1925 of *The Witches' Brew* established his reputation. His major poems that followed have been "narratives of actual or imagined incident" remarkable for "his concern for accuracy of detail." This is evident in both *The Roosevelt and the Antinoe* and *Brébeuf and His Brethren.* A musical score for the latter has been written by Dr. Healey Willan and there is the possibility of a "musical and dramatic pageant near the site of the martyrdom."

C21   Brown, E. K. "The Originality of E. J. Pratt." In *Canadian Accent.* Ed. Ralph Gustafson. London: Penguin, 1944, pp. 32-44.

A study of Pratt's work "in relation to the tradition of Canadian poetry and as a powerful expression of an original personality." At the time Pratt began to publish, the Canadian literary tradition was mainly regional in nature. Poetry tended to be descriptive landscape poetry with very little originality evident. Pratt's early works were not very successful, even *Newfoundland Verse* is the "work of an experimenter who is continuing to clutch at a tradition although that tradition is actually stifling him." Pratt's originality becomes evident in *Titans.* This starts with his subject matter which "arose from his revolt against the abstract themes suggested to him by his philosophic formation" and expresses itself "in the exaltation that Pratt experiences in the mere existence before his imagination of supreme strength." Humour and metrical skill are also evident in *Titans.* Brown quotes the opening lines of "The Cachalot" to reveal "absolute originality of texture." Canadian literature is weak in its treatment of character and Pratt is no exception. *Brébeuf* is the "closest that Pratt has ever come to animating a character" and even here he is dealing more with a symbol than a flesh and blood human being. Pratt occupies a unique position in the Canadian literary scene. He is "the link between the elder and the younger poets."

C22   Brown, E. K. "To the North: A Wall against Canadian Poetry." *Saturday Review of Literature,* 29 April 1944, pp. 9-11. Rpt. in *Responses and Evaluations: Essays on Canada.* Ed. and introd. David Staines. New Canadian Library, No. 137. Toronto: McClelland and Stewart, 1977, pp. 78-82.

Brown of Cornell University believes that "the wall that prevents Canadian poetry from becoming known in this country still stands high and firm." He shows that the wall is "a new erection" for the best Canadian poets used to appear in nineteenth century American journals; and he gives proof of why the wall should be "blown up." Pratt, who has produced twelve volumes of poetry, is "not even a name in this country." Brown refers to Pratt's narratives, epics, and lyrics, his "bounding, resonant tetrameter . . . grave, slow-moving kind of blank verse perfect for epics." Pratt's poetry "is a bigger thing than Robinson's or Masefield's ever was, [in] that it offers something comparable with what you can get from Jeffers." Comments on other Canadian poets conclude the article.

C23   Bénet, William Rose. "Introduction." In *Collected Poems.* By E. J. Pratt. New York: Knopf, 1945, pp. xi-xv.

Pratt "is an exciting discovery in modern verse; a man of range, of stature, of great accomplishment." His sustained narratives "of great gusto and imaginative power" depict the heroic in man. Bénet relates personal reminiscences of Pratt and observes his "vitality," "exuberance, enthusiasm, generosity, and good-fellowship." He quotes from a letter Pratt had written him: "poetry ought to be, at least in part, the expression of a grand binge, making for healthy physiological releases where the world for a time is seen backside-up and the poet becomes gloriously emancipated from the thralldoms of day-by-day routine."

C24   Sutherland, John. "The Poetry of E. J. Pratt." *First Statement*, 2 (Feb.-March 1945), 27-30.

This article is a rebuttal to one (see C22) written by Professor Brown. Pratt occupies an "isolated position" in Canadian poetry because of his "resolute decision to deal only with symbols of power in the external world.... His work stems ultimately from a depth of experience that is beyond the reach of the conventional poet. . . . And at the same time, being based upon the divorce of poetry from the intellect, it negates all that is most characteristic of modern poetry." By placing the "pictures of strength" in a world farthest from the human, Pratt is able to operate without being "hampered by any statement of creed." The closer Dr. Pratt comes to the human "the more he gives the impression of passing judgement." This explains the weakness of *Dunkirk*: "the forces of good and ... evil are not evenly matched, ... [he has sided with] the forces of good." Pratt's importance decreases "the longer one compares him with those ... writing in other countries.... He is the first of our poets who has shaken himself completely free from literary influences ... [and speaks] ... in a voice that is entirely his own." The critic believes that Pratt's narratives are the best that have come out of Canada.

C25   Wells, H. W. "The Awakening in Canadian Poetry." *New England Quarterly*, 18 (March 1945), 6-11.

Wells in his study of Canadian poetry's awakening finds that "by 1925 or 1930 at least one poet of considerable nature had appeared [in Canada], namely Edwin J. Pratt." Two streams in Canadian poetry can be delineated: one "stressing social content, led by Edwin J. Pratt, and that stressing refinement of form, subjective subtlety, and cosmopolitan outlook...." Pratt, "the oldest as well as the ablest of the leaders of the new era in Canadian poetry" has written poetry of humane and epic spirit. These "narrative poems with epic flavour" depict "man's most strenuous labors and boldest heroism." Against pessimism and despair of the "social aristocracy" he pits the "common man." Beside Pratt "Masefield seems strangely outmoded and outdistanced; ... the school of Eliot ... may well look to its laurels; . . . Pratt belongs not only to Canada; he belongs also to the present and to the future."

C26   MacMurray, W. Brock. "Professor Ned Pratt." In *Great Canadians*. Toronto: Imperial Optical, 1946, Talk No. 38, ser. 3, n. pag.

A brief biographical sketch, which was originally broadcast as a radio talk. Pratt's early life in Newfoundland is described, with a stress on his belief in the "necessity of a thorough education" and his reputation as a "prolific worker." Although he has gained renown as a poet — "his poetry is known from sea to sea in Canada ... and it enjoys a fine reputation in the United States" — he remains "modest," "natural," and "unaffected."

C27   Edgar, Pelham. "The Poetry of E. J. Pratt." *Gants du Ciel*, 11 (printemps 1946), 31-45. Rpt. in his *Across My Path*. Ed. Northrop Frye. Toronto: Ryerson, 1952, pp. 109-17.

Edgar begins by quoting from a letter from Pratt describing his visit to Halifax to gather material for a poem. His preparations and method of work for *The Roosevelt and the Antinoe* and *Brébeuf and His Brethren* show "when facts are vital that he recognizes his responsibility." A "consideration of his verbal and rhythmical technique" reveals that "The impressiveness of his poetic statement is not a matter of mere metrical expertness. It is the expression rather of a genuinely noble nature which had the good fortune to be endowed not only with a riotously rich vocabulary but with the rare ability also to find the discriminating phrase." "*Brébeuf and His Brethren* is generally regarded as Pratt's most solid achievement . . . it is more revelatory of Pratt's quality than the sea narratives with which his name is usually associated." His shorter poems reveal "meditative depth" and "evidence of a keen satiric talent." Although it is too soon (1946) to give a "final evaluation" of his work, Edgar feels that with the publication of *The Witches' Brew* Pratt achieved "full and free emancipation."

C28   Frye, Northrop. "La Tradition Narratif dans la Poésie Canadienne-Anglaise." *Gants du Ciel*, 11 (printemps 1946), 19-30. Rpt. (trans.) "The Narrative Tradition in English-Canadian Poetry." In *Canadian Anthology*. Ed. Carl F. Klinck and Reginald E. Watters. Rev. ed. Toronto: Gage, 1966, pp. 527-28. Rpt. in *The Bush Garden: Essays on the Canadian Imagination*. Toronto: House of Anansi, 1971, pp. 145-55.

Pratt brings Canadian narrative poetry to its highest stage of development with *Brébeuf and His Brethren*. "A narrative tradition begotten in the nineteenth century, and heir to all the philosophical pessimism and moral nihilism of that century, reaches its culmination in *Brébeuf* and is hardly capable of much further development."

C29   Wells, Henry W. "Canada's Best-Known Poet: E. J. Pratt." *College English*, 7 (May 1946), 452-56.

Paralleling developments at this "stage in our culture and civilization" poetry finds "new movements and voices" are taking the place of the prevalent "chief modes." Europe is still our main poetic inspiration but "highly distinguished and refreshing lyricism in Latin America has rightly held considerable attention." The East's verse has become known but "few searchlights have been seriously turned upon the north." Edwin J. Pratt has provided an "unobserved northern light . . . a long-awaited and fresh note in modern verse." He has

been able to be "democratic and distinguished." His frank and masculine approach to life has made him one of the best "interpreters of the relation of man to machine." Pratt's "extraordinary poetry dealing with animals" arises from his closeness to nature and his study of natural science. In his "robust folk humor [Pratt] proves far closer to the people than Robert Frost. . . . Pratt not only belongs to Canada; in a peculiar pregnant sense he belongs both to the present and to the future."

C30   "Biography." *Current Biography*, Oct. 1946, 491-93.

A biographical account giving background, personal, and factual information about Pratt, including the honours he has received to date. The major works are listed with evaluative and descriptive quotes from critics Brown, Bénet, and others. The article indicates that Pratt, who is Canada's "most famous contemporary poet, became more widely known as one of today's greatest writers of verse upon the publication in the United States of his *Collected Poems*."

C31   Wells, H.W. "The Ascendancy of Impersonalism." In *Where Poetry Stands Now*. Toronto: Ryerson, 1948, pp. 35-36.

In a study which examines the personal and impersonal aspects of poetry, Pratt's longer poems are related to the impersonal as "pieces in which a social theme plays a more conspicuous role than any subjective subtleties." Pratt is most successful "in his highly objective poems celebrating human heroism in public places, and written close to the impersonal point of view of the ancient popular ballads."

C32   Phelps, A. L. "E. J. Pratt." In *Canadian Writers*. Toronto: McClelland and Stewart, 1951, pp. 1-9.

The emergence of Pratt's unique style marks a turning point for Canadian poetry. "He loaded his lines with the integrity and authority of personal experience . . . he revelled in his subject matter and out of his subject matter evoked thematic direction and drive." This is exemplified in *The Witches' Brew*. In *Brébeuf and His Brethren* Pratt shows his ability to handle "Canadian material with unabashed vigour and enthusiasm, not because it is Canadian, but because it comes as appropriately as anything else within a poet's compass."

C33   Pacey, Desmond. "The Poetry of the Last Thirty Years." In *Creative Writing in Canada: A Short History of English-Canadian Literature*. Toronto: Ryerson, 1952, pp. 118-24.

In the section devoted to Pratt, Pacey states that Pratt's best work displays "his metrical versatility, his mastery of a clear, colloquial style, his exact response to the concrete sensory world, his deftness in the choice of image and illusion . . . plus the vision of man as an errant but ever-seeking pilgrim on the road from the barbaric cave to the divine temple." Pratt's philosophy of life is "Christian humanism" and the values of "courage, courtesy and compassion" are embodied in his poems—most clearly seen in "The Truant" and "From Stone to Steel." During World War II, Pratt was a spokesman in the fight against Hitler. "Pratt emerged as a solitary poet in Canada, and he has always remained an isolated figure."

C34   Sutherland, John. "E. J. Pratt: A Major Contemporary Poet." *Northern Review*, 5 (1952), 36-64.

Sutherland attacks other critics' interpretations of Pratt as a "heroic poet . . . concerned with strength and with the celebration of strength." Pratt is concerned with power but more with its social and psychological expression than with its manifestation in nature or in human heroism. Sutherland believes "compassion is to be found, not in the act of sacrifice, but in the moment of contemplation and acceptance of all that power in the world may mean." He finds this "is the deepest meaning of Pratt's three major poems—*The Titanic*, *The Cachalot*, and *The Great Feud*—and of the main

body of his work." The rest of the essay investigates each of these poems in great detail to prove this thesis. The "emotional content of *The Titanic* has the ambiguity common to Pratt's work as a whole; it holds these contrasting feelings, of terror and delight, in an ironic balance which is varied with great subtlety but never substantially changed." In *The Great Feud* the ape mother with her young is considered a Christian symbol which when taken in "its widest sense . . . becomes the basis of genuine compassion." This arises with the death of the dinosaur "and it is fully revealed when the creature who is responsible for armageddon returns to her lair and her young." "*The Cachalot* is a psychological drama" where the basic conflict is not between crew and whale, man and nature, but "arises from the psychological nature of power which the whale also symbolizes."

C35   Sandwell, Bernard Keble. "E. J. Pratt, Poet of Martyrdom." *St. Paul's Library Guild Bulletin*, 1, No. 2 (Dec. 1952), 4-5.

Sandwell observes the change of attitude in English literature toward martyrdom which has been made "a manifestation of the working of the spirit of God in contemporary life." Pratt's hero, Brébeuf, is an ordinary human being except for his "capacity for martyrdom." With Brébeuf, the "apex of his work," Pratt has made a major contribution to Canadian missionary history for "like the painter of an exquisite and deeply reverent altar-piece, [he] has lifted the prose narrative to the highest level of art." Sandwell concludes by favourably comparing Pratt to Rabelais and Kipling.

C36   Lecocq, Thelma. "Ned Pratt—Poet." In *Our Sense of Identity: A Book of Canadian Essays*. Ed. Malcolm Ross. Toronto: Ryerson, 1954, pp. 192-200.

Lecocq presents an anecdotal biographical sketch of Pratt which is intended to show him as an ordinary man in spite of his poetic talents. "If he dreams sometimes in iambic pentameter, he dreams also of thick juicy steaks and scoring a hole in one." This article presents a superficial picture of Pratt as a poet and as a person.

C37 Reaney, James. "Towards the Last Spike: The Treatment of a Western Subject." *Northern Review*, 7 (Summer 1955), 18-25. *EJP*.

Reaney examines "The treatments of a western subject," the building of the transcontinental railway by Pratt in *Towards the Last Spike*. He draws conclusions about "the Canadian poet or artist and his Canadian subject matter." *Towards the Last Spike* is a logical progression from Pratt's previous work in which he "examines the theme of civilization against Nature, love against evil.... And this is the theme of *Towards the Last Spike*." The critic believes "All too much of our tradition lies only in the history book, the economics textbook and the museum; Dr. Pratt has been one of our poets who has most successfully performed the difficult job of bringing the materials of our tradition into the world of imagination where these materials can perform the useful work of defining and moulding us imaginatively as a nation." The important juxtaposition of the two theories of Canada, "The East-West and the North-South theory" is investigated. Just like at the end of the poem "the workers finish the last tunnels . . . and emerge into daylight," Reaney believes Pratt's poetry is "the first rays of an imaginative daylight" and that *Towards the Last Spike* might teach us "how to advance even further into that daylight."

C38 King, Carlyle A. "Mind of E. J. Pratt." *The Canadian Forum*, April 1956, pp. 9-10. *EJP*.

Pratt's narrative poems are praised for the "verve and gusto" with which they tell "a crackling good yarn" but less frequently is it observed that "Pratt is also a thoughtful man reflecting on God and man and concerned with the plight of the human spirit and the fate of the human race in our iron times." King believes that in *Brébeuf and His Brethren* and *Towards the Last Spike* Pratt brings out that "the main struggle is with the inner man and not the outer nature; the task is always to conquer the wilderness of the human spirit."

C39 Daniells, Roy. "Literature: Poetry and the Novel." In *The Culture of Contemporary Canada*. Ed. Julian Park. Ithaca: Cornell Univ. Press, 1957, pp. 54-55.

Pratt is described as "the link between older and newer generations of poets." "His constant theme is that of gigantic struggle." The many paradoxes in his work include "a combination of verbal force and liberal mildness," the contrast between the "common touch" and a "hint of remoteness," his Methodist environment at Victoria and the Catholic subject matter of *Brébeuf and His Brethren*, and Pratt's "great reputation and his lack of influence upon the oncoming generation of writers."

C40 Frye, Northrop. "Preface to an Uncollected Anthology." In *Studia Varia*. Ed. E. G. D. Murray. Studia Varia, 1. Toronto: Univ. of Toronto Press, 1957, pp. 21-36. Rpt. in *Contexts of Canadian Criticism: A Collection of Critical Essays*. Ed. Eli W. Mandel. Patterns of Literary Criticism, No. 9. Chicago: Univ. of Chicago Press, 1971, pp. 190-92. Rpt. in *The Bush Garden: Essays on the Canadian Imagination*. Toronto: House of Anansi, 1971, pp. 163-79.

In an imaginary anthology of Canadian literature, Frye would include "The Truant" "because it is the greatest poem in Canadian literature." Canadian poets, when faced with poetic content that does not harmonize with traditional forms, have returned to primitive forms. Pratt has done this with his narratives "Chaucerian beast-fable in the *Pleiocene Armageddon* and *The Fable of the Goats*, saint's legend in *Brébeuf*, heroic rescue in *The Roosevelt and the Antinoe*."

C41 Frye, Northrop. "Introduction." In *The Collected*

Poems of E. J. Pratt. Ed. Northrop Frye. 2nd ed. Toronto: Macmillan, 1958, pp. xiii-xxviii.

Frye's stated purpose is "to encourage the reader to commit himself to the poet." In a brief biographical sketch Frye sets Pratt in a historical framework observing that Pratt's life experiences "can be easily traced in his work," "religious views are never obtrusive, but they organize all his poetry." He "never followed or started any particular 'trend' in poetry.... Out of his self-effacing concern with the poetic object, Pratt developed a flexible, unpretentious speaking style which is amazingly versatile, yet always unmistakably his." Already in *Newfoundland Verse* can be seen "the unifying of the poet with his society, and of that society with nature." Pratt's hero is "beleaguered society," a society usually in a state of crisis. Evolution, a common theme of Pratt's poems, is depicted as both "pain and cruelty" as well as being "an exuberant, unquenchable force of life." Frye points out that Pratt was neither anti-intellectual nor did he look down on his fellow man; his "moral and social values are where those of most sensible people are, and where the heart usually is in the body, a little left of centre." Pratt, an "unofficial laureate," understood and interpreted the Canadian environment. Frye concludes: "And as long as that culture can remember its origin, there will be a central place in its memory for the poet in whom it found its tongue."

C42   Frye, Northrop. "Poetry." In *The Arts in Canada: A Stocktaking at Mid-Century*. Ed. Malcolm Ross. Toronto: Macmillan, 1958, pp. 85-88.

Pratt's poetry finds its roots in the Canadian narrative tradition which dates back to pre-Confederation times. "But in striking contrast to the earlier romantics, Pratt's poetry is intensely social, even gregarious.... In relation to what has gone before him, he has clarified and brought into focus a distinctively Canadian kind of imaginative consciousness." Much of contemporary Canadian poetry belongs to what Frye calls the "academic school." Pratt's influence on this group can be seen — "they read him less for the story than for the mythical or symbolic significance of his characters and themes."

C43   Pacey, Desmond. "E. J. Pratt." In *Ten Canadian Poets: A Group of Biographical and Critical Essays*. Toronto: Ryerson, 1958, pp. 165-93.

"An enthusiastic teacher, a warmhearted friend and a human being who restores one's faith in humanity, Pratt has won many honours but has always carried them lightly." Pacey provides brief biographical information relating it to Pratt's developing philosophy; however, he is primarily concerned with the critical analysis of Pratt's work. "Pratt is a poet of deceptive simplicity" and Pacey believes that we fail to "take his poetry seriously enough." Critics are often confused in their interpretations and Pacey observes that no "one hypothesis will serve to elucidate all his poems." Pacey shows why he has concluded that Pratt's values are "courage, courtesy and compassion" and quotes from a letter from Pratt: "My own profession of faith was expressed in 'The Truant,' a comparatively late poem.... It is an indictment of absolute power without recognition of moral ends." Pratt is a "Christian humanist" who finds courage "in simple men such as sailors, courtesy in the tradition of chivalry ... and compassion in Christ." Pacey "tests" Pratt's philosophy, illuminating his thesis with quotes from the poet's significant works. Throughout the penetrating analysis, we see that Pratt's main concern has been "the relation between reason and instinct" in his view of the world which "embraces the most primitive past and an apocalyptic future."

C44   Rashley, Richard Ernest. "The Thirties Group, the Third Step." In *Poetry in Canada: The First Three Steps*. Toronto: Ryerson, 1958, pp. 11-26.

In this developmental study of Canadian poetry Rashley illustrates Pratt's break away from the "sixties group" of poets represented by Carman, Lampman, and D. C. Scott whose work was characterized by the "introspective study of the individual in relation to nature." Pratt reacted against the "emotional involvement on which, for him, at least, the sixties technique seems to depend." His work is examined as a step-by-step rejection of the style of the sixties group in an effort to find a suitable vehicle of expression for his major theme "that man must accept the knowledge of his own nature and make love or compassion a means of defeating the pre-human forces and developing the human capacities." Pratt did not become a major poet because of "his failure to invent, through all his experimentation, a completely satisfying full-scale image for his theme."

C45   Ross, Mary Lowrey. "Dr. E. J. Pratt: A Poet's Quarter-Century." *Saturday Night*, Feb. 1958, cover, pp. 14-15, 35.

Pratt's seventy-fifth birthday is reported with his background history, a list of his major works and his awards, told in an intimate, friendly manner. The tribute points out an interesting fact: that he was "sometimes a little bewildered by the symbolisms that admirers insist on dredging from the obscurer passages."

C46   "E. J. Pratt." *Canadian Author & Bookman*, 34 (Spring 1958), 16.

A brief biographical note on the occasion of Pratt's seventy-fifth birthday listing some of the special honours awarded him at this time. A "first publication" of Pratt's poem "The Unromantic Moon" showing his "pixilated sense of humour" is on the adjoining page.

C47   McGrath, M. Helen. "Bard from Newfoundland: The Story of Dr. E. J. Pratt." *Atlantic Advocate*, 49 (Nov. 1958), 13-15, 17.

An intimate, biographical sketch, full of memor-able anecdotes from Pratt's life. Many of the experiences of his childhood and youth made such a vivid impression upon the poet that he was able to write powerfully about them in later life. Tragedies such as the Greenland Disaster "sowed the first seeds of a lifetime's preoccupation — man's Promethean struggle with the blind forces of nature — which is the underlying theme of all Pratt's poetry in one form or another." The article is full of anecdotes on various aspects of his life: attendance at the wireless demonstration, work in a draper's shop, work as a teacher and probationary minister, sale of "Universal Lung Healer," celebration at a "gold medal" feast, various financial adventures in western Canada.

C48   Dudek, Louis. "Poet of the Machine Age." *The Tamarack Review*, No. 6 (Winter 1958), pp. 65-80. *EJP.*

Dudek finds that "The interpretaion of the meaning of power in Pratt's poetry is the key to both his motivating emotions and ideas and to his form and style." The "first experiment" in power, *The Witches' Brew*, is followed by Pratt's major narratives in which "the imagination is used with more conscious and serious intent to explore the moral problem of power that he had thus uncovered." "The genesis of the problem in his poetry . . . springs from nineteenth-century geology and evolutionary theory. The war of species, as conceived in Lyell and Darwin. . . ." After documenting his interpretation from the poems, Dudek concludes that ". . . Pratt's concern with a naked power-urge as the substratum of nature, of man, and of the civilized life is only the antithesis of a moral and intellectual struggle. The problem is resolved in an approach to faith, or at least in an admiring consideration of the act of faith as a heroic and incomprehensible necessity." Dudek points out that "Compassion, however, does not provide the ground tone of Pratt's poetry. . . . The personal note is rare in his work." This is taken as part of a style which has allowed "the Canadian poet Pratt, more than any other modern poet ... [to write] the poetry of science and the machine age." Pratt's human response, "derives from an earlier, religious source [and] is a mark of his unremitting humanity; but the age of science and machinery ... could only offer him a truncated science, and it is this scientific sense of reality, and even of poetic energy, that is expressed in his poetry."

C49   Mackinnon, Murdo. "The Man and the Teacher." *The Tamarack Review*, No. 6 (Winter 1958), pp. 71-74.

As a teacher Pratt "was the most systematic" of the English teachers at Victoria College. He had carefully "worked up" his notes over the years and "he always knew where he was going." He taught Shakespeare, modern poetry, and modern drama. Although he gave adequate coverage of "the traditional or recent scholarship ... he spent most time on the text, giving us a poet's interpretation and insight." He was "an inspiring lecturer ... warm-hearted friend and host."

C50   Smith, A. J. M. "The Poet." *The Tamarack Review*, No. 6 (Winter 1958), pp. 66-71.

This criticism was written in honour of Pratt's seventy-fifth birthday. The critic finds that like other major poets, Pratt's work continued to change, develop, and "increase in strength and vitality as he grew older." Pratt has been able to please Canadians with his poetry but above all he has pleased himself. He has felt a "strong sense of responsibility ... that is both aesthetic and if not religious at least moral." "Most critics have recognized that the idea of Power is fundamental in the Poetry of Pratt" but Sutherland more exactly analyzed the "... moral and emotional attitudes that condition the poetry and that rise out of it." Sutherland believed that power "is a fusion of ... the destroying force and the creative force" and he found that Pratt was attempting the "resolution of conflict into harmony." This is illustrated in *The Titanic* in which "two poles of creative and destructive power . . . [the ship and the iceberg] . . . are almost identical symbols."

C51   Sutherland, John. "I See Him As a Diver in His Bell." *The Tamarack Review*, No. 6 (Winter 1958), p. 65. Rpt. in *John Sutherland: Essays, Controversies and Poems*. Ed. Miriam Waddington. New Canadian Library, No. 81. Toronto: McClelland and Stewart, 1972, pp. 195-96.

The poem, "I See Him As a Diver in His Bell," is the first item in this tribute to the poet entitled "A Garland for E. J. Pratt; On His Seventy-fifth Birthday."

C52   Birney, Earle. "E. J. Pratt and His Critics." In *Our Living Tradition*. 2nd ser. Ed. Robert McDougall. Toronto: Univ. of Toronto Press, 1959, pp. 123-47. Rpt. in *Masks of Poetry: Canadian Critics on Canadian Verse*. Ed. A. J. M. Smith. New Canadian Library, No. 3. Toronto: McClelland and Stewart, 1962, pp. 72-95. Rpt. (excerpt) in *Canadian Anthology*. Ed. Carl F. Klinck and Reginald E. Watters. Rev. ed. Toronto: Gage, 1966, pp. 528-34.

Birney traces the American critical reception of Pratt, then the Canadian, and contrasts these with Pratt's own views on poetry. The American critics' reception of Pratt can be divided into three stages: "the early indifference, the belated praise by the unfashionable [W. R. Benet] and the contemporary rejection [Winfield Scott]." W. E. Collin in his *White Savannahs* "set the early pattern of Pratt interpretation at home." Although Pratt "lacked metaphysical wit and prosodic subtlety ... the emphasis was upon his undoubted originality, his epic verve and his realism." He was followed by E. K. Brown, Pelham Edgar, and Northrop Frye. John Sutherland changed radically the direction of Pratt criticism: "This writer argued, in effect, that American neglect of Pratt had arisen out of a failure of home-grown critics to interpret him properly to them." Sutherland set out to prove that Pratt was "complex, subtle, even mythopoeic" and "to raise Pratt to the rank of 'Eliot and Frost' by proving that he was equally Christian." However Birney feels that in spite of "sophisticizings" of critics such as Sutherland and Pacey, it is important to look at the poet himself, to see what he stands for and what he is trying to do. He examines the "aims, themes and values of Pratt." It is Birney's opinion that Pratt "has been undervalued also because his poetry is clear and fundamentally reasoned and ordered in an age which has overvalued the neurotic agonies and their distortion of utterance...." Pratt is writing in the Chaucerian tradition and "the critical task ahead is to establish in detail Pratt's great artistry in this tradition."

C53 Horwood, Harold. "E. J. Pratt and William Blake: An Analysis." *Dalhousie Review*, 39 (Summer 1959), 197-207. *EJP*.

Pratt resembles Blake more "in the deeper and more profound sense..." than any other poet. Both their styles are based on "architectural language." A philosophical parallel of Pratt's *The Great Feud* is Blake's epic *The Four Zoas*. In Blake's poetry "creative imagination is the origin of all things, the only 'real' things being things of the imagination, ... there God himself has his abode." Pratt "castigates orthodox conceptions, and makes man the measure of all things." According to the reviewer both produced a "magnificent failure." Blake's *Jerusalem* was an attempt to construct a truly monumental epic, "with the result that he fell into the trap of didactics and exposition...." "Pratt's *Brébeuf*...failed because the theme, though heroic enough is not amenable to the medium." "The very core of the Blake-Pratt sympathy lies" in their very similar myths. "The myth of both poets is based on the divinity of man." Blake sees "man to be both the source and the product of divinity ... Pratt believes...that not only all gods, but all godliness, dwell in the human breast. All things begin and end in man." "Pratt, like Blake ... achieves a myth in which man is absolutely central, but which at the [same] time does not try to deny the validity of science." "Pratt is part of that soul (the soul required for nationhood) in Canada, where he appeared at the most opportune time and became the first poet of real consequence."

C54 "E. J. Pratt." In *The Canada Council Medal, 1961*. Ottawa: n.p. [1962?], 3 pp.

Text of the citation read at the presentation of the Canada Council medals for 1961. Pratt is praised in glowing terms. "The genius with which he has enriched our land will be a precious possession forever in our national treasurehouse."

C55 Pitt, David G. "Introduction." In *Here the Tides Flow*. By E. J. Pratt. Toronto: Macmillan, 1962, pp. vii-xi.

A biographical sketch, decribing Pratt's New-foundland youth as the perfect "seed-bed for a young poetic imagination." Although Pratt is not a "regional poet," "the kind of environment and the circumstances of life that Pratt knew in the Newfoundland outport led the willing imagination with a directness and precision that went straight to the core of things" — "such things as the unremitting, almost 'primordial struggle' for survival of those he knew, whose lives were forever at the mercy of 'Tide wind and crag.'" Pratt is a poet "of life stripped to its core, to its essential elements, biological, emotional and spiritual."

C56 "E. J. Pratt: Most Beloved Poet." *Newfoundland Quarterly*, 61 (Spring 1962), 39.

The citation which was delivered by Leonard W. Brockington on the occasion of the awarding of the Canada Council Medal to Pratt, February 19, 1962, is published here. Brockington opens by naming "a brilliant and sensitive scholar, a dedicated teacher who has inspired many thousands of Canadian students and a true poet of genius, Dr. E. J. Pratt."

C57 Brockington, Leonard W. "Tribute to a Poet: The Canada Council Medal to E. J. Pratt." *The Atlantic Advocate*, 52 (May 1962), 22-23.

The article is a tribute to Pratt on his receiving a Canada Council Medal, one of the first ten so awarded. The citation was delivered by Dr. L. W. Brockington. Inspirer of thousands of "Canadian students," "true poet of genius," "admired and praised by all who read him," and "beloved by all who know him." The final assessment, "his poems will resist and outlive the rust and ravages of time."

C58 French, William. "The Master Poet: From Medicine Maker to Creator of Epics." *The Globe Magazine*, 4 Aug. 1962, pp. 8-11.

Few new stories, anecdotes, or insights are added to the Pratt legend but French has written a popular review of Pratt's early career in an engrossing, humane manner. An interesting insight is that "Although he has lived in Toronto all that time [almost sixty years], the city does not figure at all in his poetry."

C59 French, William. "The Master Poet: E. J. Pratt's Vigor Has Set Him Apart." *The Globe Magazine*, 11 Aug. 1962, pp. 15-17.

A continuation of *The Globe Magazine* August 4th article on Pratt from *Newfoundland Verse* on. The scandal of *The Witches' Brew* is related. French, in this popular, very readable biography, finds that, agreeing with Frye, Pratt was never what we call an "intellectual." "He is not a poet of verbal jigsaw puzzles, of ambiguities or dense textures or erudite allusions nor has he ever built himself a religio-political Eiffel Tower from which to look down on the human situation."

C60 Story, G. M. "The Newfoundlander Who Is Canada's Greatest Poet." *The Newfoundland Record*, 1 (Sept.-Oct. 1962), 7-8.

A brief survey article of Pratt and his work written upon the publication of *Here the Tides Flow* as it is "an event that should not pass unnoticed, least of all in Ned Pratt's native Island" for the poems illustrate "how central and all-pervasive has been his Newfoundland inheritance." The critic points to the two recurring themes in Pratt's poems: one is what Pratt called " 'the ironic enigma of nature and its relation to the Christian view of the world....' The second recurrent pre-occupation in the poems is even more important and has already been suggested: the pre-occupation with the quality of the human response—futile though it may be—in emergent danger."

C61 Lane, Grace. "E. J. Pratt: The Poet Who Gave Canada a Voice." *The United Church Observer*, 24, No. 16 (Nov. 1962), 10-11.

A warm tribute to Pratt, about to turn eighty, combining a biographical account, a short visit with Dr. and Mrs. Pratt, reminiscences from a number of former students and from Victoria's President, Dr. A. Moore. In her brief visit with the ailing poet, Ms. Lane learns of his concerns about modern literature: "It has no form, and little worthy subject matter, he feels. Much of it is obscure, lacking in constructive thought. 'If literature doesn't communicate, it isn't literature,' he says. 'Poetry is hard to write. There is so much to consider—form, rhythm, content, general overall pattern. You don't choose poetry; poetry chooses you.' " Students of Pratt remember him "with affection and gratitude." Northrop Frye, a former student, says "He had a very profound influence on me, as he did on many.... But he didn't try for it. He wasn't a conscious 'shaper.' He was too warm, convivial, and relaxed to deliberately seek to impose a pattern on anyone." Of Pratt's work, Dr. Frye states that "The essence of him is to be found in all his poetry.... You can't cut a chunk out and say, as you can of so many, this is the essential Pratt."

C62 "A Reminiscent Brew; A Note on the E. J. Pratt

Manuscripts in the Douglas Library.: "The Lament of the Wets.'" *Douglas Library Notes*, 12, No. 2 (Spring 1963), 2-3.

A brief piece on the Pratt manuscripts and autographed books in the Edith and Lorne Pierce Collection of Canadiana. "The Lament of the Wets" is printed here for the first time as a toast to Pratt on the occasion of his eightieth birthday. It is from the original and unpublished version of *The Witches' Brew* (in the Douglas Library) and is described as "more extravagant" and "much longer than the printed text."

C63 Deacon, William Arthur. "Laureate Uncrowned: A Personal Study of E. J. Pratt." *Canadian Author & Bookman*, 38 (Spring 1963), 2, 20.

On Pratt's eightieth birthday Deacon salutes Pratt's "signal contribution to Canadian literature." Reviewing his first book, *Newfoundland Verse*, Deacon predicted "if this man could keep this up, or improve on it, Canada would have not only a new man with a new voice, but a very important writer." The critic noted after several of Pratt's narratives were published that "Canada at last had an epic poet—a poet of power." The Frye-edited *Collected Poems* (1958) is superior to the earlier collection (1944) which deserved Adam's (*New York Times*) praise as the best volume of poetry in North America in 1944.

C64 Deacon, William Arthur. "CPM—The First 27 Years: The Launching." *Canadian Author & Bookman*, 39 (Winter 1963), 2-3.

Deacon describes the launching of the *Canadian Poetry Magazine* and recalls the founding meeting where Pratt "bashfully demurred but did accept" the first editorship. "None of us knew a thing about how to go about launching a magazine" and Deacon briefly describes some of the pitfalls. (Pratt is referred to also in the following sections which trace the life of the magazine: "The early years," "Earle Birney 1946-1948," "Arthur S. Bourinot 1948-1954.")

C65 Cogswell, Fred. "E. J. Pratt's Literary Reputation." *Canadian Literature*, No. 19 (Winter 1964), pp. 6-12.

Pratt is compared by the critic to Bliss Carman, who is generally considered a "minor poet," and who was "over-rated" during his life-time while Pratt is presently touted as "Canada's leading poet" by most critics. Sutherland, Dudek, Frye, and Pacey have shown "their desire to supply in Pratt's poetry what currently seems necessary to be found in great poetry." The "mythopoeic symbols ... the justification of poetry," and the proof of the cleverness of the critic have been "often fortuitously" found in Pratt's poems by "his recent admirers." The poet "successfully adapted the epic narrative to the deeds of modern man." He did this by substituting "the language of scientific description ... for the poetically outworn language of physical description"; and by using a "grammatical syntax and a metrical rhythm that suited the pace of his own age." In his poetry Pratt combines "a sophisticated and masterly poetic technique, a wealth of erudition, and a timeliness ... with an obsessive poetic vision that is almost incredibly primitive." In a hundred years the reviewer believes Pratt's "literary reputation [will have] paralleled that of ... Bliss Carman."

C66 Sharman, Vincent. "Illusion and an Atonement: E. J. Pratt and Christianity." *Canadian Literature*, No. 19 (Winter 1964), pp. 21-32. *EJP*.

Important Canadian criticism (Frye, Pacey, Sutherland) assumed that Pratt's poetry is Christian. A thorough analysis of his poetry shows this to be untrue. Only ten percent of the *Collected Poems* can be construed to be Christian. Only *Brébeuf* of the "long, major poems ... is open to pro-Christian interpretations." Sutherland's wild interpretations and Pacey's misreading are exampled. The critic gives his own fairly detailed analysis using poems to illustrate his views. "In charity and defiance is immortality; there is no Heavenly immortality for men in Pratt...." The critic sees in *The Iron Door*'s ending, that, for the poet, "The door ... will open no more.... The unpitying glare of reason will not permit him the solace of unreasoned belief." In "The Truant" God is defined "as the mechanical force of the universe, the Great Pan-jandrum who is scarcely aware of mankind. Yet it is man who has made this disinterested force into a deity...." *Brébeuf* is carefully analyzed from Sharman's viewpoint. A critical examination of *The Titanic* is used to illustrate "Men's illusions of Nature" and the illusions of "their own capabilities, especially as manifested in their machines." Sharman concludes that from his analysis of Pratt's poetry, "For Pratt, what man must understand is that their salvation lies in themselves, not in Nature, God, systems or in ignorant pride in machines."

C67   West, Paul. "E. J. Pratt's Four-Ton Gulliver." *Canadian Literature*, No. 19 (Winter 1964), pp. 13-20. Rpt. in *A Choice of Critics: Selections from* Canadian Literature. Ed. George Woodcock. Toronto: Oxford Univ. Press, 1966, pp. 101-09.

With the publication of *Titans* Pratt emerged as a poet having shed "inherited and acquired mental clutter." Pratt's preoccupation with spectacle and conflict is relieved by his humour and the "absence of terror" — "his cosmology is weirdly genial." West explains Pratt's "relish for the defeat of human presumption" by a "cosmic disgust at man's grandiose incapacity." "Man is not big enough, not near enough to four tons." "For Pratt, man is doomed but, in accepting doom bravely, can be commensurable with Nature and God." Man expresses his humanity, not in trying to exercise power over nature, or even in allying himself with nature but in accepting his fate, stoically and by "inventing spiritualities of his own: charity, courage, honour, love, congeniality over dinner...." Although West is uneasy with some of Pratt's ideas —

"anti-Methodism has led him too far into cosmic solecisms and anti-philosophy has made him a bit of a simplifier" — he nevertheless regards Pratt as a poet of stature to be compared with Milton and Verga.

C68   Edinborough, Arnold. "This Month." *Saturday Night*, June 1964, p. 7.

Editorial. Quoting from *Brébeuf and His Brethren* and *Towards the Last Spike*, Edinborough shows how no one who reads Pratt's epics could do so "without thrilling to the adventure and heroism of the people who built this country." He used "muscular, tough and inspiring" language to create exciting poetry. "Making familiar the unknown. That is what Pratt did in his poetry ... [and his] poems will live on."

C69   Johnston, G. "Ned Pratt's Funeral." *The Canadian Forum*, June 1964, p. 53.

The piece is a moving and perceptive tribute to Pratt who Johnston claims is part of Canada's story, "and whatever that story is to be, his part in it will be one of the most admirable." Johnston reminisces: "One of the privileged occasions of my life" occurred when Pratt read passages from *Behind the Log* while in the midst of composing the work.

C70   Leslie, Arthur K. "E. J. Pratt One of Canada's Leading Poets." *Atlantic Advocate*, 54 (June 1964), 40-41.

A brief, succinct sketch of Pratt's life and work, with a listing of his honourary awards. The writer reveals how Pratt disliked psychology for it was so full of "ids" and "egos" and "perhaps it is pertinent to note that in his subsequent poetry he, as the poet, rarely intrudes." *The Witches' Brew* evoked differing critical analysis, "some saying the poem supported alcoholism, others that it attacked Methodism, and others seeing it in numerous philosophical references." Pratt's narra-tive works illustrate that his "main concern is with Man's struggle in Nature rather than against Nature."

The article concludes with excerpts from Pratt's work.

C71 Daniells, R. "The Special Quality." *Canadian Literature*, No. 21 (Summer 1964), pp. 10-12.

Pratt's "personal image is no more simple than the image of Pratt the poet whose complexity has been the theme" of many critics. Daniells, probing Pratt's "special quality," suggests it was "the 'plain heroic magnitude of mind' with which he got down to his task of writing." Pratt had a "largeness of mind" which saved him from "pride, pedantry, paranoia, the Messiah-complex, the thirst for recognition, the affectation of 'grand old man,' one upmanship of every description and all the other customary side effects of a talent for writing or occupational diseases of academic life." Daniells concludes his sensitive reminiscence by questioning whether our computer world will nourish such qualities as Pratt possessed, so we "should keep green the greatness and uncontriving simplicity of this good man."

C72 Deacon, William Arthur. "Laureate Takes Leave, E. J. Pratt." *Canadian Author & Bookman*, 39, No. 2 (Summer 1964), 2.

A tribute to Pratt by William Arthur Deacon, a friend since college days. In a biographical, personal sketch, Deacon views Pratt as "a warm human being first; secondly he was Canada's greatest poet so far; lastly he was scholar enough to be a university professor. He broke the barrier between the learned writer and the reader for pleasure."

C73 Frye, Northrop. "The Personal Legend." *Canadian Literature*, No. 21 (Summer 1964), pp. 6-9.

A personal reminiscence full of insight about Pratt who "is the only figure in Canadian literature, so far, who was great enough to establish a personal legend." Frye describes the poet's life at Victoria, his guise of a "duffer . . . in order to stay clear of the enormous complication of committees and similar substitutes for thought and action that are such a bane of university life." His hospitality and love of parties was the "central part of the Pratt personal legend. . . . Friends who could talk, and talk with spirit, content, and something to say" shared these occasions. Frye recollects an evening during the war when he heard "Ned read 'The Truant,' and felt, not simply that I had heard the greatest of all Canadian poems, but that the voice of humanity had spoken once more."

C74 Adams, J. R. G. "Ned Pratt—Canadian." *Canadian Poetry*, 27, No. 4 (Aug. 1964), 77.

J. R. G. Adams' contribution to the *Canadian Poetry* tribute to Pratt is a sonnet "Ned Pratt—Canadian."

C75 Ball, Helen. "E. J. Pratt." *Canadian Poetry*, 27, No. 4 (Aug. 1964), 93.

Helen Ball in a short poem in tribute to the enduring memory of E. J. Pratt ends with, "This man was his poetry, his poetry this man."

C76 Frye, Northrop. "Silence upon the Earth." *Canadian Poetry*, 27, No. 4 (Aug. 1964), 71-73.

"Like other great men, [Pratt] . . . created a legend, and the legend . . . was much simpler than the man." In his tribute, Frye tells several short anecdotes to reveal Pratt's kindness and hospitality to all. His love of parties is especially mentioned. Pratt's favourite poetic theme was courage and Frye goes on to show that this good understanding of it arises from Pratt's possessing courage himself. Frye ends on a personal note, remembering Pratt's contribution to his edification as a student through his friendship and his poetry.

C77 Ó Broin, Padráig. "E. J. Pratt—1883-1964." *Canadian Poetry*, 27, No. 4 (Aug. 1964), 63-64.

In *Canadian Poetry*'s tribute to Pratt in 1964

Padráig Ó Broin states that Pratt has been characterized by the statement "This man was his poetry." O'Broin adds "E. J. Pratt is dead. But his poems remain. And his poetry is that man."

C78 "M U N Receives Collection in Honor of E. J. Pratt." *The Daily News* [St. John's, Nfld.], 18 Aug. 1964. Rpt. in *Canadian Association of College and University Libraries Association Canadienne des Bibliothèques de Collège et d'Université Newsletter*, No. 3 (15 Dec. 1964), pp. 11-12.

An account of the ceremonies at the presentation of Pratt manuscripts and first editions, and portrait of E. J. Pratt presented to Memorial University by Mrs. Viola Pratt and her daughter Claire Pratt. An excerpt of the address given by C. C. Pratt, Mrs. Pratt's moving presentation speech, and the statement by University Librarian, F. Eugene Gattinger, upon receiving the Collection are included. The books, manuscripts, typescripts, and tributes making up the Collection are listed.

C79 Wilson, Edmund. "Reporter at Large: O Canada, an American's Notes on Canadian Culture—1." *New Yorker*, 14 Nov. 1964, pp. 134-38. Rpt. in *O Canada: An American's Notes on Canadian Culture*. New York: Farrar, Straus and Giroux, 1965, pp. 95-97.

Pratt and Nelligan are the two Canadian poets who "should be brought to the attention of the non-Canadian world." Although the length and style of Pratt's verse prevent it from being easily "picked up" from the page, Wilson commends his eloquence, imagery, and grandiose subjects. Pratt's imagination "could only have been stimulated to such imagery by the materials provided by Canada."

C80 Beattie, Munro. "E. J. Pratt." In *Literary History of Canada: Canadian Literature in English*. Gen. ed. and introd. Carl F. Klinck. Toronto: Univ. of Toronto Press, 1965, pp. 742-50. 2nd ed. Toronto: Univ. of Toronto Press, 1976, vol. II, 254-62.

In a long favourable review article the critic chronologically surveys Pratt's work. Although "muffled by the idiom and metrics of the early 1920's," the poems in Pratt's first book *Newfoundland Verse* "expressed a new vision ... [a] break-through in tone and subject-matter ... [it] made us see new faces of Canada, hear new voices. The dominant voice was the sound of the sea." *The Witches' Brew* followed in which the poet "spun his fantastic yarn with untiring vivacity in rapid and witty octosyllabics." *Titans* contained two longish narratives of which the *Cachalot* was "the first of his poems to receive the kind of acclaim that was to make Pratt the most popular of Canadian poets." *The Roosevelt and the Antinoe* is the story of a sea-rescue. The poem illustrates "the marvels of science, [and] the resourcefulness of man." Surpassing all the narratives that preceded it, *The Titanic* "draws upon a deeper source of tension ... from the sharply defined conflict between human values and the blind menace of the sea." *Brébeuf and His Brethren* recounts "the adventures of Brébeuf from his novitiate ... to his terrible death" at the hands of Indians. Pratt's heroes are "always men committed to a course of action: ... the drive of Christian faith [for example] ... to explore and exploit the whole range of human experience." In *Towards the Last Spike* "man's struggles against those inveterate opponents, time and space," are recounted in the building of the transcontinental railway.

C81 Frye, Northrop. "Edwin John Pratt, 1882-1964." Proc. of the Royal Society of Canada, 4th ser., vol. III, 1965. Ottawa: The Royal Society of Canada, 1965, pp. 161-65.

After a lengthy apprenticeship of teaching, theological education, and lecturing in psychology, Pratt was appointed to the Department of English at Victoria College and at thirty-eight years of age began a thirty-two-year career. Numerous books of verse followed with two editions of *Collected Poems*. "Pratt is generally acknowledged to be Canada's greatest poet in English ... an interpreter of the Canadian imagination.... He is concerned with energy, courage, exuberance, unquenchable life.... He is also the only figure in Canadian literature in English, so far, great enough to establish a personal legend." His generosity represented "a genuine enthusiasm for human life and personality, and a sense of the reality of love."

C82 Reaney, James. "The Dragonslayer." In *Great Canadians*. The Canadian Centennial Library. Selected by The Rt. Hon. Vincent Massey, et al. Toronto: McClelland and Stewart, 1965, pp. 91-94.

Reaney claims Pratt's story-telling ability comes from his Newfoundland background. "His poems are a sort of Newfoundland, a very welcome addition to the less witty, less narrative remainder of Canada." He examines briefly two aspects of Pratt's poetry, its sound and the use of monsters. The sound of Pratt's poetry is distinctive and results from his love of words: "long hard words and short fat easy ones." Many of Pratt's poems contain monsters as if he "heeded the advice that if you want to tell a good story put a dragon into it" but they illustrate his theme "that if we can defeat the terror within ourselves, we will find that we have defeated the monster that caused the terror." Pratt's poetry spans from Newfoundland to British Columbia and tells us "more about ourselves than we ourselves know."

C83 Frye, Northrop. "A Poet and a Legend." *Varsity Graduate*, 11, No. 6 (Summer 1965), 65-69. Rpt. in *Vic Report*, 7, No. 3 (Summer 1979), 6-7.

In an astute and sensitive tribute to Pratt on the occasion of the opening of the E. J. Pratt Room of Contemporary Poetry at Victoria College, Frye tells of the man and the mask. He describes Pratt's early Newfoundland period, explains how his life at Victoria was a "dramatic reversal" of it. Pratt caricaturized himself in order "to concentrate on the primary work of teaching and writing." Frye concludes that "Ned Pratt is the only figure in Canadian literature, so far, great enough to establish a personal legend. And the legend was unique, because it had the poet behind it."

C84 Livesay, Dorothy. "Polished Lens: Poetic Techniques of Pratt and Klein." *Canadian Literature*, No. 25 (Summer 1965), pp. 33-42.

In this study of the poetic techniques of Pratt and Klein, Livesay's aim is "not an analysis of technique for its own sake, but of technique for the sake of enlightenment." In Canada, Pratt was the first poet to turn from nature to the "human condition" using language that was "fresh, muscular, contemporary and often boisterously amusing." Drawing upon examples from the works of both poets, Livesay compares their evolving techniques in their three "phases" discussing: theme, tone, metre, rhyme, stress, vocabulary, rhythm, imagery. Some of Pratt's shortcomings are examined: dependence on the prepositional phrase, tendency to "use nouns to his disadvantage," lack of adjectives and adverbs, lack of "touch, taste, hearing, scent," and colour. Livesay concludes that "Pratt remained a story-teller to the end, an 'old artificer' collecting artifacts and arranging them cunningly without committing his deeper self ... [while Klein] probed inwards to the human soul, revealing its possibilities for creative joy as well as its predilections for darkness, madness."

C85 McGivern, J. S., Father. *Brébeuf and His Brethren. Martyr's Shrine Message*, 30, No. 4 (Winter 1966), 9-13.

The writer wants to "enjoy the beauty and rhythm, the strength and even weakness, the joy and the tragedy" in *Brébeuf*. Excerpts from the poem are interspersed with commentary on Pratt's research. The critic urges his readers to "be enthralled, be appalled by the dangers, inspired by suffering and encouraged by the spirit of the early missionaries of Huronia." "The story is in itself one of greatness, scarce surpassed if at all, in the entire annals of Canada and here in *Brébeuf and His Brethren* you know its finest telling."

C86   Story, Norah. "Pratt, E. J." In *The Oxford Companion to Canadian History and Literature*. Toronto: Oxford Univ. Press, 1967, pp. 660-61. Rev. *Supplement to the Oxford Companion to Canadian History and Literature*. Ed. William Toye. Toronto: Oxford Univ. Press, 1973, pp. 269-70.

Story presents biographical information on Pratt, indicates some of the major honours bestowed upon him, succinctly summarizes his works revealing their major themes. Quoting from Birney's critical evaluation of Pratt, she notes how Frye shares in "this appreciation of the directness and simplicity of Pratt's work." The *Supplement* updates the books of criticism available on the poet.

C87   Gustafson, Ralph. "Portrait of Ned." *Queen's Quarterly*, 74 (Autumn 1967), 437-51.

A sensitive, illuminating, personal reminiscence by Gustafson of a friendship with Pratt that "goes back over a quarter of a century." He relates how he had been writing about Pratt even before meeting him for "every serious critic, of course, had to be writing about Ned; he was the figure that was bestriding the transition in Canadian poetry from worn-out romanticism of the late nineteenth century to the accuracy introduced by Yeats and Pound." Comparing Pratt to those two other writers of the time, Gustafson observed "But neither had the power and linguistics of Ned; neither had his sense of comedy and therefore his affectionate irony and alertness to the tragedy of man's nobility." His poetry depicted "the titanic struggles of beast with beast, man with ocean, and man with machines, and man with man." Gustafson includes letters received from Pratt beginning from the early forties, accompanied by explanatory commentary. The "humility and generosity of Ned" is evident as is his

strong support of Canadian writers. Gustafson includes the poem he wrote for Pratt's Commemoration Service.

C88   Buitenhuis, Peter, ed. and introd. *Selected Poems of E. J. Pratt*. Toronto: Macmillan, 1968, pp. xi-xxx.

Although Pratt has become a well-known poet, the small amount of critical material that is available tends to misinterpret or misplace the emphasis of his work. "The evolutionary process early became and always remained the central metaphor in Pratt's work ... and persisted in Pratt's work long after it had ceased to have much force for the twentieth-century poetic and philosophical mind." Buitenhuis criticizes Sharman's interpretation of *Brébeuf and His Brethren* as a statement of Pratt's atheism and argues that it is "an affirmation of the continuity of history and the transforming power of belief." Although his philosophy may be dated, the enduring qualities of his poetry may best be seen in the narratives, especially *Brébeuf*. Here the "strength of design" and Pratt's "tremendous narrative energy" exemplify "the way in which he marries his technique to his theme." Buitenhuis theorizes that Pratt's "literary isolation" from contemporary events and literary trends allowed him to develop to become the Canadian "myth and image-maker."

C89   Wilson, Milton. "Pratt's Comedy." *Journal of Canadian Studies*, 3, No. 2 (1968), 21-30.

In his analysis of Pratt's poetry, Sutherland noted that the hero frequently tended to be identified with the enemy and Wilson observes that often the quarrels are "family quarrels and at times the opponents even start to look like mirror images of each other." Frank Scott also has posed the question: "then is priest savage, or Red Indian priest?" Wilson states that "the myths and sciences in terms of which he imagines his uncles and his cousins and his aunts slaughtering and signalling one another are a distinctive mixture of the biological and mechanical and the classical." The critic's main concern is to deal with Pratt's "sense of comedy and the way in which these themes contribute to it." *The Witches' Brew* Wilson calls a "kind of scientific-cum-theological-cum-literary farce" and in "The Great Feud" "the comedy ranges from academic wit to low farce. But the themes ... are desperate and inescapably relevant." To further his thesis, Wilson analyzes *The Witches' Brew* and "The Great Feud" with reference to setting, situation, and unique characters. The essay concludes with a "coda" to "The Truant" in which the Panjandrum "assumes the airs of a Fascist dictator right from the start." At the climax of the truant's curse, we get both "a human affirmation and also the death of god, this god."

C90 Frye, Northrop. "Silence in the Sea." The Pratt Lecture, 1968. St. John's, Newfoundland: Memorial University, 1969. 14 pp. Rpt. in *The Bush Garden: Essays on the Canadian Imagination.* Toronto: House of Anansi, 1971, pp. 181-97. *EJP.*

According to Frye, Pratt takes on many of the characteristics "of the poet of an oral and pre-literate society." In such a society the function of the poet was as teacher, scientist, historian, keeper of traditions, heroic legends, myths of its gods, religious and social rituals. "The poet had a central social function from which he has since been dispossessed." Recently there has been a revival of oral poetry, with rise of the "communication media other than the book" and "one would think that some poets might become, once again, spokesmen for their communities, their tales and proverbial philosophies becoming a part of ordinary verbal culture." Christianity has always been both "revolutionary and an institutionalized religion." This contradiction became for Pratt "a fundamental cleavage in Christianity which runs all through his work." At the centre of Pratt's religion "is the enduring, resisting and suffering Christ..." ranged against "the dead God of fatality, the mindless,

pointless world." In Pratt's poetry the separation between "conscious and mindless worlds" is imaged or is often shown as "the conflict between spirit and the nature of man." Pratt tried in his poetry to "unite the real man with real nature." During his life through his poetry Pratt "took his place at the centre of society where the great myths are formed, the new myths where the hero is man the worker ... and where the poet ... is shaping also a human reality which is greater than the whole objective world ... because it includes the infinity of human desire."

C91 Smith, A. J. M. "Some Poems of E. J. Pratt: Aspects of Imagery and Theme." The Pratt Lecture, 1969. St. John's Newfoundland: Memorial University, 1969, 20 pp. Rpt. in *Towards a View of Canadian Letters: Selected Critical Essays 1928-1971.* Vancouver: Univ. of British Columbia Press, 1973, pp. 99-114. *EJP.*

Pratt's poetry is of "epic proportion" because he is "fascinated with magnitude ... immense strength ... incredible power...." The poems are long but they "are as long as they need be." His imagery "is functional ... and contributes something essential." Smith uncritically and approvingly continues to explore some of Pratt's images more closely. He finds that "Aspects of ... (the struggle for power or survival) provide the theme of all Pratt's best and major poems...." "Most of the poems . . . have philosophical and religious overtones...." Vincent Sharman is doing "an injustice to Pratt by misreading or neglecting some of his most important poems" and thus attributing to Pratt a "purely humanistic and sadly disillusioned view" rather than seeing "an affirmation of faith ... among Pratt's finest poems." In fact in this grand world with monsters organic and inorganic "that beset the paths of men . . . survival depends on the strength and cunning . . ." displayed to "watch and defeat their antagonists. It would be a meaningless universe were it not for the one inexplicable (miraculous) intervention symbolized by the Rood." Pratt is a poet in the

"English tradition" and the poets Smith "thinks of when reading" him are Hardy, Masefield, and Chaucer.

C92   Gibbs, R. J. "Living Contour: The Whale Symbol in Melville and Pratt." *Canadian Literature*, No. 40 (Spring 1969), pp. 17-25.

The whale in *Moby Dick* is "given size by the size of the book." Pratt's "The Cachalot" is "a minnow by comparison ... [although] the sense of size in the central image is not wanting." Poetry can telescope meaning using formal methods. Gibbs does not "pretend for 'The Cachalot' the measurements of *Moby Dick*" but only that both succeed in "making a mythic or epic image, larger even than life." John Sutherland's pioneer work on the symbolic approach to Pratt's poetry is considered a "perceptive guide" although the critic is not willing "to follow Sutherland all the way." Sutherland, who discovered an "ambivalence" in the poem, gave a highly individualistic interpretation. "Pratt's whale . . . is . . . a Christ-symbol. . . . Similar discoveries followed by similar courses are not hard to come by among Melville's critics." Melville's Ishmael "can peer into metaphysical depths denied Pratt [while] Pratt is able to look into physical depths ... denied Melville." "Symbolic meaning is inherent in the artistic process itself ..." and the critic warns against other critics who through symbolist speculation "will end by creating [their] own book." This is all right "as long as [they don't] make the reader forget the book he started from." The point is to go "a-whaling yourself."

C93   Frye, Northrop. "Ned Pratt." In *Canada: A Guide to the Peaceable Kingdom*. Ed. William Kilbourn. Toronto: Macmillan, 1970, pp. 299-303.

Pratt has emerged as "a kind of unofficial laureate" of Canadian poetry. "He is much more of a spokesman than a critic of public opinion and generally accepted social reactions." Both his religious beliefs and his personality are evident in his poetry, particularly in "The Depression Ends." "At one pole of human life is a cross, at the other is a last supper; and these two poles give position and meaning to every thing that occurs between them."

C94   Jones, Douglas G. "The Courage to Be." In *Butterfly on Rock: A Study of Themes and Images in Canadian Literature*. Toronto: Univ. of Toronto Press, 1970, pp. 111-23.

In an examination of Pratt's philosophy of nature and man's place in the cosmos, Jones finds that "clearly Pratt's initial impulse is to delight in nature and her powers, however prodigious or violent" and that "his poetry implies that life, especially human life, finds its fulfillment in a partnership with the elemental forces of nature." Pratt describes man caught in a struggle with the forces of nature, with the same objectivity and "impersonal sympathy" that he describes the ship or the iceberg that is also part of the conflict. It is only by acting with courage and in a "spirit of self sacrifice" that man can "oppose nature without adding to her destructive violence. Only in this spirit can he claim a superiority to the forces of nature or to a mere God of power." There is much irony in Pratt's work. "Generally, Pratt's poetry implies that whenever man attempts to improve the world or add to his own stature by means of force he fails. His efforts to annihilate nature's imperfection, whether in the name of reason or in the name of morality, always end in irony and in a holocaust of destruction." His irony is never bitter "because Pratt looks upon the folly of mankind from that more comprehensive view in which man is but one creature in the cosmic whole."

C95   Davey, Frank. "E. J. Pratt, Apostle of Corporate Man." *Canadian Literature*, No. 43 (Winter 1970), pp. 54-66.

Pratt's "vision" is an "area of dispute" among Pratt scholars who find him ranging from Christian humanist to atheist. Frye's comment that Pratt is a "spokesman rather than a critic of public opinion and generally accepted social reaction" has been forgotten except by Cogswell. His poetry and his worldview have bewildered Pratt critics because, as Pacey has observed, "a good deal of the ambiguity in Pratt is not deliberate but involuntary, and there is not only confusion among critics but also confusion in the poet." The "deceptively simple" poems do not mask "something more complex." "Power ... is one of the keys to Pratt's uncomplicated vision ... the power he respects and eulogizes is nearly always power wielded or shared in the here and now by material inhabitants of this world. Divine power is contrastingly unimpressive to Pratt." "Pratt admires . . . the loyalty [which causes] the submission of individual will to group projects significantly greater than oneself." These observations are supported from Pratt's poems. Today, "glory," of the kind Pratt envisaged, is only possible in the larger corporations. It is through corporate action that the loyal employees can realize both "effective and individual power." Pratt was "a committed and uncritical spokesman for the values of industrial man" and he believed "the machinery of technology and the machinery of social organization as man's best way to salvation." Davey concludes that Pratt's "poetry reads strangely like a celebration of the possibility of a 'brave new world.'"

C96   Djwa, Sandra. "Canadian Poetry and the Computer." *Canadian Literature*, No. 46 (Autumn 1970), pp. 47-51.

A critical reader of English Canadian poets notes that there are continued repetitions of certain words or phrases. Are these related to "a world view, a myth or a cosmology?" Is there continuity in these myths or diction among Canadian poets since the 1880s? Computer frequency counts of words used in the poetry of fourteen Canadian poets from the 1880s on, was seen as a method to attempt to answer the above questions. Patterns appear when the computer printouts are compared and there is some continuity connected with these words in Canadian poetry. "Pratt's encompassing metaphor appeared to be that

of 'blood' rather than the expected 'sea' or 'water.'" This is unique when compared to other poets. Djwa believes that since there are some demonstrable historical lines of poetic continuity "we need to re-evaluate ... the question of the continuity of Canadian poetry" for no poet's works "emerge from a cultural vacuum, but are intimately related to the development of writing in Canada."

C97   Livesay, Dorothy. "The Documentary Poem: A Canadian Genre." In *Contexts of Canadian Criticism: A Collection of Critical Essays*. Ed. Eli W. Mandel. Patterns of Literary Criticism, No. 9. Chicago: Univ. of Chicago Press, 1971, pp. 277-79.

The Roosevelt and the Antinoe is an example of Pratt's excellence as a documentarian. His knowledge of the sea, his extensive research, his compelling "power over language," and "his sense of 'cliff-hanging'" combine to illustrate his theme: "In a time of crisis men of all races work together as a communal unit—'the breed' against implacable nature."

C98   Gibbs, Robert. "A Knocking in the Clay." Paper presented at the Annual Meeting of the Association of University Teachers of English, May 1971. St. John's, Newfoundland. Rpt. in *Canadian Literature*, No. 55 (Winter 1973), pp. 50-64.

Gibbs examines Pratt's "philosophical-lyrical drama" *Clay*. Although Pratt considered *Clay* a failure, Gibbs finds passages in it that show the promise of what he would do in the future—"such verse as this from a young poet bears the mark of no ordinary command and no ordinary imagination." He feels that "its chief interest for us lies in certain relations it reveals between the writer and his material." The cosmic irony which is his central concern in this poem is a recurring theme in his later poetry and he becomes more successful in presenting it in a poetic way rather than rhetorically. "Although the play fails in total conception and realization, it does confront aspects of himself and of the external world that would always be of deep concern to Pratt."

C99   Atwood, Margaret. "Nature the Monster" and "First People." In *Survival: A Thematic Guide to Canadian Literature*. Toronto: House of Anansi, 1972, pp. 58-60, 93-95.

Atwood suggests that if a central image or symbol could be chosen for Canada (and Canadian literature) it might be survival. As a consequence of this, "preoccupation with one's survival is necessarily a preoccupation with the obstacles to that survival." One of these obstacles is Nature. Atwood's position is that Pratt is an example of a writer for whom Nature is hostile and "consistently destructive." In *The Titanic* we "are dealing with a war-with-Nature or let's fight attitude that goes with 'Nature is hostile.'" In *Towards the Last Spike* Nature is portrayed as "Female Nature-Monster." However "*Brébeuf and His Brethren* is the all-Canadian poem: it's about a French Catholic priest killed by Indians, as seen by a white English-speaking Protestant from Newfoundland." In this poem, the Indians are allied with hostile, destructive nature and "Pratt dwells consistently not only on the more disagreeable aspects of Nature but on those of the Indians as well.... His experience of the Canadian wilderness is like a city-dweller's nightmare of a canoe trip ... the description of life with them [the Indians] reads like a cross between a slum-clearance proposal and an antacid ad."

C100   Macpherson, Jay. *Pratt's Romantic Mythology: The Witches' Brew*. The Pratt Lecture, 1972. St. John's: Memorial University, 1972.

The Witches' Brew is examined from the point of view of the development of imagery from the early manuscripts to the final printed poem. Macpherson also relates *The Witches' Brew* to the other two "extravaganzas"—*The Depression Ends* and *The Truant*—showing how certain ideas which appear only in the manuscript form of *The Witches' Brew* reappear later in these two poems. Images such as drowned volcanoes, witches, cats, and sparks recur in romantic writers such as Blake, Byron, Shelley, and Goethe as well as Milton and Shakespeare. Macpherson shows how Pratt develops these images in the manuscripts and eventually refines or abandons ideas, although she suggests that Pratt is more interested in words and phrases than in making sense. *The Witches' Brew* is a very Canadian poem for three reasons— "first, its sexlessness; second, its cheerfully Robinson Crusoe attitude towards the flotsam and jetsam of literary tradition...; third, its fascination with the spectacle of life displaying its energies in a fundamentally alien universe."

C101   New, William. "The Identity of Articulation: Pratt's *Towards the Last Spike*." In *Articulating West: Essays on Purpose and Form in Modern Canadian Literature*. Toronto: new press, 1972, pp. 32-42. Rpt. in *The Literary Half-Yearly*, 13, No. 2 (July 1972), 137-48.

Towards the Last Spike is an example of how Pratt contrasts myth and fact in his poetry. The poem is more than just a "political parable," it also illustrates the "tension and . . . the ambivalent relationship between man and land." Another important aspect of the poem is language—"For Pratt ... to mark the movement towards national consciousness, towards 'the last spike,' is to mark a poetic quest for linguistic method (and thus meaning), which again forces the visionary imagination and expediency to collide." New quotes extensively from the poem to show Pratt's use of language to dramatize the tensions in the situation, until "the inaugural sounds of nationality and poetry are then uttered together, for the poet in search of a language and the country in search of its image and voice."

C102   Sutherland, John. "E. J. Pratt: Application for a Grant." In his *John Sutherland: Essays, Controversies and*

Poems. Ed. and introd. Miriam Waddington. New Canadian Library, No. 81. Toronto: McClelland and Stewart, 1972, pp. 172-77.

According to Sutherland, Pratt is the most important Canadian poet, but he has been neglected by critics. He feels criticism is now needed to show that "this poetry possesses the qualities of complexity and of depth which have so often been denied to it." In this article Sutherland is asking for assistance to continue a study of Pratt's poetry in which he examines the idea that the "strength" or power which is a central idea in Pratt's poetry must be thought of in religious terms. "It is the Christian truths which are most fundamental to his work and it is these which I would stress in my analysis."

C103 Sutherland, John. "E. J. Pratt's Right Hand Punch." In his *John Sutherland: Essays, Controversies and Poems*. Ed. and introd. Miriam Waddington. New Canadian Library, No. 81. Toronto: McClelland and Stewart, 1972, pp. 164-65.

Sutherland claims that "E. J. Pratt is almost alone among the present writers in being able to deliver a right-hand blow." Pratt's work "evokes a direct and enthusiastic response from the reader." His strength is in his narrative poetry. He needs to develop his theme on a large scale. "He does not possess the power for the striking individual line or the varieties of sensuous texture that characterize the lyrical poet."

C104 Sutherland, John. "Ironic Balance." In his *John Sutherland: Essays, Controversies and Poems*. Ed. and introd. Miriam Waddington. New Canadian Library, No. 81. Toronto: McClelland and Stewart, 1972, pp. 169-72.

Pratt's best poems "depend on an ironic balance" between delight in the existence of strength and a realization of its destructive powers. This is best illustrated in *The Titanic*. In *Towards the Last Spike* the symbolism is obscured by the clash of personalities.

C105 Sutherland, John. "Newfoundland Attitudes." In his *John Sutherland: Essays, Controversies and Poems*. Ed. and introd. Miriam Waddington. New Canadian Library, No. 81. Toronto: McClelland and Stewart, 1972, pp. 166-69.

Pratt occupies a unique position among Canadian poets, in that he is the first to be completely free of past "literary influences." "The Cachalot" which is a complete break with the traditions of the past gives "symbolic expression to the poet's internal conflict." Pratt deals with forces of power in the world with "unbounded optimism" rather than with the intellect. In doing this he also separates himself from most modern poets.

C106 Thomas, Clara. "Edwin John Pratt 1882-1964." In *Our Nature, Our Voices: A Guidebook to English-Canadian Literature*. Our Nature—Our Voices, Vol. I. Toronto: new press, 1972, pp. 95-101.

In her biographical sketch, Thomas shows how lengthy and varied was Pratt's "career-apprenticeship." She contends that the "Darwinian theory, which so radically altered the tight doctrinal world of his youth, liberated his imagination and excited him always." The themes of his major works and the range of his narrative mode made him a "virtuoso" poet. Pratt not only held a "special position among poets" but also "in the general cultural consciousness of Canada." In *Towards the Last Spike*, he transcended the real "to the truly mythic in our history."

C107 Djwa, Sandra. "Milton and the Canadian Folk Tradition: Some Aspects of E. J. Pratt's *The Witches' Brew*." *The Literary Half-Yearly*, 13, No. 2 (July 1972), 56-71.

In *The Witches' Brew*, along with "farce, hyperbole, fantasy and a most irreverent delight" there is "eating, drinking and fighting" to equal the Newfoundland folk song "The Killigrew's Soiree." In it Pratt has turned "upside down" the world of his previous poetry, as well as making a "parody of [his]

... earlier religious concerns." Pratt was delighted with the puzzle he had created for his critics with this comic epic. *The Witches' Brew* "is the comic and demonic obverse of Milton's *Paradise Lost*." An excerpting, retelling, and interpreting of the poem follows with comparisons to earlier Pratt poems and the comic ballads of Newfoundland folk song writer Johnny Burke. "The relation of *The Witches' Brew* to (Burke's) 'Kelligrew's Soiree' is the continuity of the Newfoundland folk tradition." It relates to "pulpit oratory, the hymn, and the folk song," and in turn is "a reflection of the pattern of Newfoundland speech rhythmic patterns which Pratt himself retained all of his life." The poem "is uneven and not entirely successful in its attempt to unite its two discordant elements of Milton's thought and Newfoundland song...."

C108 Djwa, Sandra. "E. J. Pratt and Evolutionary Thought: Towards an Eschatology." *The Dalhousie Review*, 52 (Autumn 1972), 414-26.

"Pratt was a sensitive man greatly troubled by the Victorian conflict between Science and Religion [... evolution and ethics] and his poetry continually explores the possibility of finding some acceptable compromise between the two." His own philosophy, as expressed in his poetry, shows a development suggesting "a series of evolutionary parables in which ethical man ... is pitted against T. H. Huxley's 'cosmic process' [evolution]." In his attempt to make man more equal to this struggle, "Pratt continually suggests that it is human 'will,' the courage and determination to accomplish a heroic act ... which established an ethical frame of reference that suggests the existence of a spiritual world." In trying to classify Pratt, Djwa finds that "he is a transitional Victorian, firmly rooted in the evolutionary ethic of the 1890s, and working out a fairly complex evolutionary structure. . . . Pratt is attempting a compromise between the old teleology of received religion and the Darwinian world without design, ultimately insisting that design resides within the organism, within the blood and nerve cells of man."

C109 Waterston, Elizabeth. *Survey: A Short History of Canadian Literature*. Methuen Canadian Literature. Toronto: Methuen, 1973, pp. 93-98, 117-19.

Waterston's *Survey* "proposes to explore some of the 'hows' and the 'whys' of Canadian art." She includes Pratt among the Canadian novelists and poets who "opened their art to themes and scenes previously censored as unpleasant or improper" and who wrote "with a thinner music of ironic resistance and endurance." Pratt's work is briefly surveyed, pointing out themes and styles from his early poems, "turbulent with sea, storms, and tidal struggles" to his later works showing "religious conviction set against savagery in the forest, and then to human organizing ability conquering rock, space, and height."

C110 Djwa, Sandra. "The Civil Polish of the Horn: E. J. Pratt's *Brébeuf and His Brethren*. *Ariel*, 4 (July 1973), 82-102.

"It is generally agreed that E. J. Pratt is Canada's major poet and that *Brébeuf and His Brethren* ... is the most significant poem yet written in Canada." The poem has been described as a "Christian epic," or as an "heroic epic." Other critics claim Pratt's philosophy is "atheism" or "reverent agnosticism." This dichotomy can be resolved, Djwa believes, by seeing that the subject "supremely transcendent 17th century Christianity of Brébeuf," is in contradiction with "the human-centered, turn-of-the-century 'New theology' of Pratt, the poem's maker." Djwa attempts to explain Pratt's philosophy through a well-documented insight into his life and an in-depth study of the poem. Pratt is able by focussing upon "the human and upon the evolution of man, of society, and of religion" to produce "a paradigm of all ethical men at all times of crisis," instead of keeping the poem in "its religious particularity of one man at one time." The poem, experienced as a whole, is a convincing religious epic but focusing on major scenes reveals some ambiguity. Djwa shows it is "an exposition of Pratt's own vision of the religious life and his admiration for the struggle of the dedicated man of faith." Revealed is Pratt's "progressive but somewhat unorthodox 'New theology'" which might explain why he probably was right in believing "that he would not have been well suited for the conventional United Church pulpit of 1917."

C111 Sproxton, Birk E. "E. J. Pratt as Psychologist, 1919-1920." *Canadian Notes & Queries*, No. 14 (1974), pp. 7-9.

Sproxton has studied Pratt's psychological work for the period 1919 to 1920, as represented in "Clay" and other poems. Several critics have underestimated E. J. Pratt as psychologist.

C112 Djwa, Sandra. "Litterae ex machina." *Humanities Association Review*, 25, No. 1 (Winter 1974), 22-31.

Using a computer to manipulate the input of themes from seven representative Canadian poets (1875-1960), Djwa found the image of nature is directly connected to Darwinian theory rather than to any reaction of Canadian poets to the concept of environment as a threatening wilderness. Darwinism was the main influence on Canadian Romanticism from the first and continued through the social Darwinist "northern" vision of the 1920s. Djwa considers Pratt's work in the light of this computer derived theory.

C113 Davey, Frank. "E. J. Pratt: Rationalist Technician." *Canadian Literature*, No. 61 (Summer 1974), pp. 65-78.

"Pratt's concept of poetic form and language are precisely of that rationalist kind [found] in the works of A. J. M. Smith." Pratt believes in "the myth of poetic objectivity... [he] stand[s] outside rather than inside his poetic materials, shaping them through sensibility and intelligence, rationally confronting problems of convention, language, and form." Pratt appears interested in measurable reality. His poems are full of "miles, tonnages, names, quotations, that which can be weighed, cited, documented.... Material reality is assumed to contain ... the whole." On the other hand "if an event is not totally knowable,... one must fake total knowledge...." This latter can be a danger since the subject may be "unfairly treated; the metaphor has said far less than needed to be said while pretending to say all." The critic believes that throughout Pratt's career "in both lyrics and narratives, Pratt was an impersonal, manipulative, synthesizing, rationalist craftsman." Pratt is in the "cosmopolitan-traditionalist stream... guarded since the fifties by the criticism of Northrop Frye." Pratt was throughout his work "an apologist for the Pelagian view of man—that view in which mankind can, by social co-operation, discipline, vigilance, the application of reason, and the suppression of individualism overcome any difficulty... corporate man can be the rationalist craftsman of his own destiny."

C114 Ross, Malcolm. "Pratt, Edwin John." *Encyclopedia Canadiana*, 1975.

A brief article including biographical information, a critical evaluation, a listing of Pratt's works, and critical references to 1958. Ross contends that "there would seem to be little doubt that the poetry of E. J. Pratt is our largest Canadian achievement in verse and that it will find a secure place in the literature of our tongue."

C115 Birbalsingh, F. "Tension of His Time." *Canadian Literature*, No. 64 (Spring 1975), pp. 75-82.

Pratt's poetry can be divided into three groups on the basis of their philosophical outlook: "those describing a world in which God's primacy is undisputed; those in which this primacy is challenged by man; and those in which the challenge of God by man is satisfactorily reconciled." In the first group, "New-foundland" and "From Stone to Steel" pass the test. In the second category, many of the poems are failures because "the poet's religious point of view is directly contradicted by his scientific outlook, and the result is ambivalence or incoherence." "The Cachalot" and "The Truant" are examples of this type of failure. In "the third group...Pratt offers a solution to the underlying conflict between religion and science." *Brébeuf and His Brethren* is a total success from this point of view." "Pratt finally succeeds in demonstrating the view of life that he held throughout his career...in a harmoniously working, God-controlled universe." Pratt had a simple, conventional view of life which was consistent with his background and the "social and historical circumstances" of his "formative years." *Brébeuf*, his best work, remains "the greatest... [and] the most complete Canadian narrative."

C116 Collins, Robert G. "E. J. Pratt: The Homeric Voice." *Review of National Literatures*, 7 (1976), 83-109.

The most considerable Canadian poet up to the 1960s according to George Woodcock was the "literary conservative E. J. Pratt" whose forte was large mock epics "in Hudibrastic verse." Collins sees a militancy in the new generation of writers, and claims that the "old conservatism" provides a strong foundation for development. What has been noted since Homer's time is the need to know where one comes from, one's heroic tradition. This is "the basis of a distinct culture," the inspiration for each new generation, the chief means of bringing "anonymous masses together as a nation." In Canada "where can a unifying tradition be found?... Pratt... is the one to whom we turn for an answer." Following Frye and his interpretation of Pratt as Canada's epic poet, Collins surveys and confirms Frye's arguments adding arguments of his own from Pratt's background and his poems. Pratt's weaknesses and strengths are explored and revealed: "There remain the great poems silently chanting within the covers of

the Collected Pratt." A closer scrutiny is made of Canada's *Aeneid, Brébeuf and His Brethren*, of which Collins concludes, "Pratt's treatment of the narrative of the early heroes amply justifies his role as national poet of Canada." Collins quotes Barker Fairley (1926), who noted the uniqueness of Pratt's work and claimed "almost for the first time in Canadian poetry" a Canadian voice.

C117 Enright, Robert. "Knockers on the Iron Door: A Report on the E. J. Pratt Symposium at the University of Ottawa, Spring, 1976." *CV/II*, No. 2 (May 1976), pp. 3-5.

An entertaining, critical report from the E. J. Pratt Symposium. Fred Cogswell, Ralph Gustafson, and Carl Klinck chorused the "touchstone for the Symposium," Pratt's attention to craftsmanship, "taking the stuff of life and giving it imaginative form." Germaine Warkentin "concentrated on the 'essential Pratt' as he revealed himself in the lyrics" while Robert Gibbs argued there is much subjectivity in the lyrics and that they "function as artistic resolutions in a world that remains intellectually unresolved." Sandra Djwa, Peter Stevens, and Peter Buitenhuis dealt with modernism, language, and Pratt and the sea respectively. Glenn Clever "preferred to keep his analyses [of war poetry] general." Enright found the poetry reading "Perhaps the most interesting event of the symposium."

C118 Middlebro', Tom. "A Commentary on the Opening Lines of E. J. Pratt's *Towards the Last Spike*." *Studies in Canadian Literature*, 1, No. 2 (Summer 1976), 242-43.

Towards the Last Spike is "modelled on the documentary" opening with "a statement of theme" followed by "a succession of particular examples" which the reader himself must "forge into a life-line of meaning."

C119 Gibbs, Robert. "Poet of Apocalypse." *Canadian Litera-*

ture, No. 70 (Autumn 1976), pp. 32-41.

"Any work of the imagination is a kind of apocalypse,... generally [with] ... the alpha-and-omega scope [of] the last book of the New Testament." Gibbs examines *The Witches' Brew* and *The Great Feud* as the work of the "Poet of Apocalypse." In *The Witches' Brew*, Tom, the cat from Zanzibar, and "the central figure of the poem,... symbolizes an imagination freed to rove through the cosmos, to illuminate its dark places with his fiery tail.... Tom ... bodies forth the very spirit which is the poem's impulse." The female ape "represents the glimmerings of reason and of moral responsibility." Her freedom is the freedom of man in Pratt's universe, the "freedom to work out his own destruction as well as his salvation." The doubling back of evolution is represented by Tyrannosaurus Rex who becomes "the repository of sleeping potential of destructive energy." Thus he "symbolizes the whole of creation and its suffering." Since "no choice, no moral decision, no glimmering of love or sympathy has motivated [Tyrannosaurus Rex] he can't be thought of as a Christ-symbol as Sutherland has claimed. Pratt sees "nature as controlled and driven by impulses that contain their opposites."

C120 Buitenhuis, Peter. "E. J. Pratt." In *The Canadian Imagination: Dimensions of a Literary Culture*. Ed. David Staines. Cambridge: Harvard Univ. Press, 1977, pp. 46-68.

This essay, in a collection for the American reader, states that although Pratt is considered "Canada's most significant poet" he is barely known in the United States. Buitenhuis briefly describes Pratt's youth and years at Victoria College, the "quintessence of the Ontario mind, bourgeois, austere, dry, with a tradition both strongly theological and liberal." The critic believes that the evolutionary theory, which was "the central metaphor of his work ... probably had a good deal to do with his decision to leave the ministry." *Brébeuf*, Pratt's greatest poem, is "about the whole French imperial effort in New France." His incisive analysis shows the numerous ironies in the poem, its "mosaic form," and the shortcomings of W. T. Scott's criticism. Turning to Pratt's earlier epics, he notes how important are the sea and the power struggles. Buitenhuis, who has had naval experience himself, shows how "Pratt makes the point, perhaps the central point of modern war, that the ultimate victory is achieved not by the Nelson touch but by the combined, unrelenting tasks of many men. And he skilfully draws together the themes of *Behind the Log* in a complex web of imagery of writing, type, blood, body, and machinery." Smith called Pratt "the only Canadian poet who has mastered the long poem" and Buitenhuis believes that even the shorter works become "versions of the heroic." Buitenhuis concludes that "Canada did not find an adequate myth-and-image-maker in Canadian poetry until E. J. Pratt appeared."

C121 Innis, Kenneth. "'The History of the Frontier Like a Saga': Parkman, Pratt, and the Jesuit Enterprise." In *The Westering Experience in American Literature: Bicentennial Essays*. Ed. Merrill Lewis and L. L. Lee. Bellingham, Wash.: Bureau for Faculty Research, Western Washington Univ., 1977, pp. 179-88.

Innis states that "By comparing the poem with the historical account that appears to be its major source I hope to bring out some Canadian-American differences in focus and emphasis...." Innis presents a brief historical background, emphasizing the distinctness of the Canadian "Westering" experience which was affected by Canada's northern locale. The movement Westward took place not so much by covered wagons but by birchbark canoes containing "Indian and Jesuit, as well as pragmatic Scottish trader." The critic believes that Parkman, who devoted much attention to his style of writing, lacked objectivity in his recording of events and that he "does not provide ... a useable version of the heroic origins of the country" the way Pratt does in *Brébeuf*. Innis goes on to examine Pratt's and Parkman's presentation of the Indians and Jesuits. Although Pratt includes ironies about the Jesuits, they still "remain types of human endurance, of heroic charity, paladins of faith who are finally beyond the range of tragedy and of critical irony." For Parkman the Jesuits were a "systematized contradiction...alien and other, their form of faith a pathetic fallacy, and their quixotic plan of embracing Indians as brothers in Christ and children of France a basic misreading of aboriginal nature and its possibilities."

C122 Laakso, Lila. "E. J. Pratt: A Preliminary Checklist." *Canadian Library Journal*, 34, No. 4 (Aug. 1977), 273, 275, 277-79, 281-83, 285, 287-91, 293-94.

C123 Marshall, Tom. "The Major Canadian Poets: E. J. Pratt." *The Canadian Forum*, Oct. 1977, pp. 19-21. Rpt. (rev.) "Weather: E. J. Pratt." In *Harsh and Lovely Land*. Vancouver: Univ. of British Columbia Press, 1979, pp. 34-40.

Pratt who "set out...to be Canada's national poet" can be regarded as Canada's Whitman and Melville because "Like Melville, he questioned man's fate. Like Whitman, he combined a national vision with a sense of man's place in the universe at large. It is this larger vision, the Canadian 'long view,' that informs his best work." Marshall sees Pratt as a Christian poet and Christ for him "symbolizes the ultimate goal of evolution and human development." In "The Truant" Pratt says the "traditional notion of God...has got to go." God is evolving "through us and our developing consciousness." Pratt's Christ then becomes "an image of man's potential future." After a closer study of *The Titanic*, *Brébeuf*, and *Towards the Last Spike*, Marshall concludes that the shorter poems, especially "Silences" and "The Truant," are more successful than the long narratives. Grove and Pratt pictured Canada in transition and therefore are "the important writers of the time. They wrestled with facts and dreams, Europe and America, nature and culture,

environment and the machine, the Darwinian theory and the vision of a Utopian future."

C124 Darling, Michael E. "E. J. Pratt's Contribution to 'Canadian Comment.'" *Canadian Notes & Queries*, No. 21 (July 1978), pp. 10-11.

The author lists articles written by Pratt in *Canadian Comment* during the period from July 1933, when he joined the editorial board, until March 1936. Among the "Literature" columns, Pratt was either celebrating "a date in literary history — the tercentenary of Samuel Pepys — or discussing the subject of a recent book — Arthur Bryant's biography of Macaulay, or a newly discovered Dickens Manuscript." Darling lists the writings chronologically.

C125 Whalley, George. "Birthright to the Sea: Some Poems of E. J. Pratt." *Queen's Quarterly*, 85 (Winter 1978-79), 578-94. Delivered at the Pratt Memorial Lecture, Memorial University, St. John's, Newfoundland, 1977.

Whalley wishes "to search out a little the specific quality of Pratt's poetry where it is of greatest intensity and of most complex human and emotional implication." A poem's definition and force is not only in the subject-matter but in "something intrinsic, with its roots in what has been experienced to the bone." Whalley defines three kinds of sea poems by Pratt: "a) poems that engage directly the way of life of fishermen and their people; b) poems that recount memorable events at sea; c) fables in which sea-creatures are depicted and celebrated . . . ." "Verbal tone and articulation" are more important than subject matter and theme in typing Pratt's poems, Whalley thinks. For instance, in the Extravaganzas Pratt "sets vibrating a string of peculiar timber, a sound of distinctive potency." In the epic manner, Pratt's masculine characters are "courageous, enduring, strong and skillful . . . [as well as] compassionate, patient, self-sacrificing, unassuming, hospitable, reticent . . . ." Pratt's poetry has the imprint "of the people he had grown up among . . . [and] his poetry . . . often sprang from — his birthright to the sea."

C126 O'Flaherty, Patrick. "Emigrant Muse." In *The Rock Observed: Studies in the Literature of Newfoundland.* Toronto: Univ. of Toronto Press, 1979, pp. 111-26.

O'Flaherty recounts the setting — Newfoundland around the turn of the century — and the story of Pratt's first twenty-five years. Pratt, having established himself in Toronto, "did not attempt, much less achieve, a comprehensive statement about his [Newfoundland] homeland." Pratt was, "without question, Newfoundland's finest poet." Still, his "poetry showed no interest in Newfoundland history, . . . no interest in exploring the distinctive traditions and habits of speech of his people, . . . [no] genuine curiosity about the outport way of life, . . . no examination of the mechanics of fishing and sealing, . . . [and] no detailed study of individual fishermen." Although he "pays lip service to the heroism inherent" in the common man, he shows no "intelligent interest in such men." Although Pratt became a "fine Canadian poet," what he would have done if he had "turned his great talent upon the materials supplied by his own people, must be left to conjecture."

C127 Brandeis, Robert C. "Crumbling Pages: The E. J. Pratt Collection — Restoration and Preservation." *Vic Report*, 7, No. 3 (Summer 1979), 8-9.

The Victoria University Library's "collection of E. J. Pratt manuscripts and printed works is the most comprehensive in Canada." It contains "all the published works of the poet, . . . a substantial number of notebooks, working papers, correspondence, rough drafts of poems and lecture notes." The Library has undertaken a restoration and preservation program to save these invaluable manuscripts. The process is described and a plea is made for the preservation of other similar "unique and valuable materials . . . of our national and cultural heritage."

C128 Love, C. C. "The Evolution of a Pratt Poem." *Vic Report*, 7, No. 3 (Summer 1979), 10.

The Pratt manuscripts provide a possibility "to see the mind of the poet at work and to understand his ideas and his imaginative presentation of them." The poem "Erosion," in three versions, is used as an example: the first and second versions, not usually available, can be compared with the final version.

Theses and Dissertations

C129 Dorothy Marie, CND, Sister. "The Epic Note in the Poetry of Edwin John Pratt." M.A. Thesis Ottawa 1956.

"A careful analysis of four of the major narrative poems of Edwin John Pratt" to "evaluate the various aspects of epic treatment in presentation of the material." After a short introductory biographical sketch of Pratt and a chapter on the definition of epic the author tackles Pratt's *Brébeuf and His Brethren* which is said to reflect "the folk epic tradition" as well as having the "classic elements of style." *The Titanic*, *The Roosevelt and the Antinoe*, and *Dunkirk* are similarly treated if in less detail.

C130 Dorothy Marie, CND, Sister. "The Poetic Imagery of Edwin John Pratt." Diss. Ottawa 1958.

This is a study of the imagery in Pratt's poetry. The "record left by the poet in the imagery that he employs is an unconscious or even a reluctant one"; the author believes the poet's "message to mankind" may be hidden "yet startlingly revealed in his imagery." Pratt calls "a spade a spade," nevertheless "his poetry contains images of strength and beauty that fashion forth a whole world of hidden analogies which can enrich Canadian poetic themes." Since poetry reaches the reader on several levels — the intellectual, the sensuous, and the emotional — the author has used these as divisions in her study. A "new poetic evaluation" using imagery in Pratt's poems is also attempted.

C131 Mary Rosalinda, Sister. "*Brébeuf and His Brethren*: A Great Canadian Poem." M.A. Thesis Ottawa 1959.

The author claims that the "detailed study" of Pratt's *Brébeuf and His Brethren* is the first lengthy analysis of the poem. Pratt's life as related to possible influence on the poem is revealed. The literary evaluation is through "textual analysis," comparison with other Canadian poems by Johnson, Lampman, Pickthall, and Sullivan, and an analysis of criticisms of the poem. The validity of the sources for the poem is evaluated as are Pratt's accuracy of reporting. The theme under "sense, feeling, tone and intention," the texture according to "diction and imagery," the "inspiration" both "intellectual and emotional" are all "carefully studied." Until the present thesis "No one has attempted to weight the body of critical opinion [for] . . . a just evaluation of the poem." In conclusion, Sister Mary Rosalinda finds that the poem "expresses Pratt's compassion and sympathy towards his fellowmen, that this poem is a sound portrayal of Canadian history, true in feeling and in expression to the source from which it was drawn, the *Jesuit Relations*."

C132 Paisley, Alixe Catherine. "Epic Features of *Brébeuf and His Brethren* by E. J. Pratt." M.A. Thesis Assumption Univ. of Windsor 1960.

In her Introduction Paisley tells of a personal interview she had with Pratt on the form and the content of *Brébeuf and His Brethren*. Although *Brébeuf* is considered to be Pratt's greatest work, it has not yet been given the detailed study it deserves. *Brébeuf* fits into the tradition of the fourteenth-century English literary epics. In providing historical background to *Brébeuf*, Paisley shows the religious zeal of the time, the relationship of priest and soldier, and priest and Indians in New France. Brébeuf's qualities as hero are examined; the elements of unity of action,

character, plot, and Pratt's "poetic powers" are probed. The final chapter deals with the themes in Pratt's major poems, showing parallels with *Brébeuf*.

C133 Sharman, Vincent Douglas. "Patterns of Imagery and Symbolism in the Poetry of E. J. Pratt." M.A. Thesis British Columbia 1963.

Sharman's stated purpose is to trace the patterns of images and symbols in Pratt's poetry in order to "discover their relation to Pratt's main themes of man and the mechanical universe, and to reveal his view of man." Starting with Pratt's lyrics and "less successful narratives" Sharman finds that in them the image patterns are sea, ships, machinery, light, religion, and heroics. These reveal "man as surrounded by death" which man fights with his reason (machines) and with his feelings "which may lead him to sacrifice himself so that others may live." A study of *The Roosevelt and the Antinoe* by Sharman reveals it as "Pratt's greatest conflict between man and death." Through interpreting the patterns of images in the poem Sharman finds that for Pratt "the power of men acting for others' benefit transcends the power of the natural universe" and that "God is uncaring of men." Sharman turns to "*The Titanic* in which fate . . . is the antagonist." The *Brébeuf and His Brethren* image patterns of fire, religion, and hero reveal that Pratt thought "the Jesuits are misguided." Kindness and charity lose out to religious abstractions in the Jesuit illusion on the question of men's welfare. Both Jesuits and most of the Indians " . . . devote their energies to death rather than life . . . in extreme . . . misdirection of the human will to succeed." Sharman concludes with a discussion of Pratt's "total image of man."

C134 Conrad, S. C., Brother. "The Dialectic of Love and Ferocity in the Shorter Poems of E. J. Pratt." Thesis Ateneo de Manila 1964.

Brother Conrad claims he is attempting to study Pratt's shorter poems "in order to discover the underlying theme which gives them unity," since "Pratt's lyrics appear simple but contain a deep meaning [and] ... the poet makes it a point not to offer any direct philosophical generalizations." Following Sutherland, Conrad feels the important themes in Pratt's poetry are "the internecine conflict, the conflict between the 'heroic' and the 'demoniac' selves in man" and "the value of Christ-like self-sacrifice as the only possible means of resolving this conflict." This study of "the dialectic of love and ferocity," a title taken from Frye's introduction to the *Collected Poems*, is not a novel attack. It probes the shorter poems instead of the narratives. Conrad's method of analysis, "thematic exegesis," is also claimed to be a new approach in Prattian criticism. Following an examination of the sea poems, in which the author has attempted to define Pratt's "concept of man's origin, evolution, and existential condition," Conrad elucidates "the central theme — The Dialectic of Love and Ferocity." He concludes with an evaluation of Pratt's shorter poems. The lyrics show the dialectic struggle within man, "his demoniacal compulsion to destroy himself," and his "spark divine" which can redeem him. The synthesis of ferocity and love, the resolution of man's dilemma, is found in Pratt to be the "seeking to emulate the sacrificial life of Christ."

C135   Desjardins, Maurice A. "A Study of E. J. Pratt's *Brébeuf and His Brethren*." M.Phil. Thesis Toronto 1968.

In his study of the sources of *Brébeuf and His Brethren*, Desjardins does not propose to examine each line's origin. He believes much can be traced back to the primary and secondary sources although it is impossible to decide exactly which sources Pratt used and in what order since he consulted *The Jesuit Relations* and read historians Parkman, Jones, Wynne, Paquin, and Devine. Checking *The Jesuit Relations*, Desjardins finds that very little is taken directly except "Brébeuf's and Joque's long letters." He finds "much historical data unaccoutted for, and certain discrepancies which are startling." Some of the great sections of the poem, "the initial vision at Bayeux, Brébeuf's meditation at Rouen, Paris and Rennes, the prophetic Mass, and his reverie before the martyrdom," are not in the sources quoted. His aim in the thesis is to determine how Pratt used all the materials. From this study emerges "a clearer picture of his great narrative skill, his dramatic inventiveness, his symbolic use of place and dates quite unexpected, his wrestling with historical characters deeply animated with religious thought which [though he pays lip service to Catholic ritual] is very different from his own." Desjardins' section on religion in the poem and in the sources covers structure, imagery, and whether religion is "the core or the surface of the poem." He believes that "the primary theme suffers from a split in beliefs between hero and poet that no rhetoric can conceal."

C136   Mahoney, Helen, CND, Sister. "Edwin John Pratt: Canadian Poet." M.A. Thesis Villanova 1968.

Sister Mahoney's purpose "is to add to the increasing prestige of the poet, Edwin John Pratt, by making better known this man whose wisdom found expression in his art." A chapter on Pratt's Newfoundland years as a child and youth is followed by personal details of his days at Victoria College. His poem *Rachel* and the play *Clay* were written at this time. Both proved failures but turned Pratt from philosophy and psychology leading him "to seek the concrete, the intuitive, the emotional approach." This is a folksy, sometimes interesting, and revealing storytelling of Pratt's life culled from many sources.

C137   Tietze, Edna Elizabeth. "Edwin John Pratt and the Epic Quality of His Poetry." M.Phil. Thesis Waterloo 1968.

A biographical introduction to the poet is presented in the first chapter. Pratt's philosophy of life was of "a process of evolution determined by the interaction of human, mechanical, and natural dynamics." By reference to the *Iliad, Aeneid, Beowulf,* and *Paradise Lost,* the author in this thesis "will strive to develop a definition of epic and to place Pratt's work within that definition." She discusses epic mode in setting, theme, character, and action with specific examples drawn from Pratt's works showing the epic devices he used. "The way in which Pratt expands from the specific to the universal" is examined and illustrations of how Pratt "fuses the three powers by describing natural things in human terms, mechanical things in natural terms, human beings in natural and mechanical terms, and combinations of these" are given. Pratt's hero is modelled on the Christian rather than the classical epic and "Brébeuf emerges as the finest example of Pratt's epic hero acting out the epic mode." Pratt, the epic poet, expresses his "cosmic themes" in "language of simple grandeur and straight-forward narrative."

C138   MacLeod, Denise Anne. "The Narrative Technique of E. J. Pratt." M.A. Thesis Mount Saint Vincent 1969.

MacLeod sets as her problem the demonstration of "Pratt's mastering of the narrative form in poetry." To do so she surveys critical standards as applied to poetry in general and Pratt's in particular. The characteristics, tradition, and validity of the narrative form are determined and traced. Pratt's poetry as narrative is compared to the "principles established" by the author from her study. In conclusion she believes she has shown that "his poetry is of stature, [and that he]... has had the integrity and the ability to work at the form [narrative] until he succeeded in creating something of lasting value."

C139   Gibbs, Robert J. "Aspects of Irony in the Poetry of E. J. Pratt." Diss. New Brunswick 1970.

Gibbs finds that "Irony is pervasive in E. J. Pratt's poetry affecting...theme and design...diction and movement." The reasons for Pratt's irony are a "native reticence about personal feelings, a distrust of closed systems of thought and belief, and...the capriciousness of natural forces in human fortunes." Unresolved tensions in his poetry are created by the combination of the above negatives with "exuberant optimism," "joy in physical being," "fascination with natural mechanics and human technology,...and Christian ideals." In the early poems irony "is external and deliberate." In such poems as "The Cachalot," "The Shark," and "Silences" irony becomes an interplay between "alazonic exuberance and emotional detachment." Irony in *The Witches' Brew* appears "as tension between rhetorical pattern and the released imagination." Gibbs examines irony in other Pratt narratives and lyrics including *The Roosevelt and the Antinoe, The Titanic,* "The Truant," *Brébeuf and His Brethren.* From this study the author believes that irony is "more or less present and essential to the greater part of [Pratt's] work."

C140   Stonehewer, Lila Lavinia. "An Interpretation of Symbols in the Work of E. J. Pratt." M.A. Thesis McGill 1970.

"The intriguing aspect of the poetry of E. J. Pratt is the complexity underlying the apparent simplicity." In this thesis, Stonehewer examines Pratt's use of the Titan symbol in *The Witches' Brew, The Great Feud, The Cachalot, The Titanic, Brébeuf and His Brethren,* and some of the shorter poems illustrating how he creates a mythology around it. She divides her thesis into sections dealing with the comic, tragic, and double vision. Using Richard Chase's definition of myth, the writer shows that Pratt's mythology "attempts to bridge the gap between the daylight world of literalities and the night impulses of life." His Titan symbol is connected with man's "eternal search for meaning and his Quixotic refusal to bow before the laws of the universe." Pratt's philosophy, influenced by "primitivism, evolution, religion and psychology" reflected the interrelationship of things in the universe.

C141 Thorpe, John B. M. "Man and Religion in the Poetry of E. J. Pratt." M.A. Thesis McGill 1970.

Thorpe attempts "to define Pratt's philosophy of man, and to determine whether this self-sacrificial human quality is based on inborn natural courage; is an automatic human reaction; or is prompted by some mystical or religious belief." The writer follows Pratt's development of the theme of man and his religion from *Newfoundland Verse* to *Towards the Last Spike.* Thorpe shows that "in Pratt's view, the importance of religion is proportional to the way in which it stimulates each individual to action, or makes the trials of life easier to bear" but that it is not dependent upon the church. The change in emphasis occurred through several volumes of his work — in the earlier poetry, and particularly in *The Iron Door*, "Pratt considered man in relation to God and religion. God was the starting point" whereas in "The Truant," "God is seen in relation to man, and it is man who has become the point of reference." As *genus homo* points out, "man was largely responsible for creating his God." Pratt's work celebrates human potential and heroism and "explores and encompasses a quintessential element of man."

C142 Clark, James Murray. "E. J. Pratt and the Will to Believe: An Examination of His Unpublished *Clay* and His Poetry." M.A. Thesis New Brunswick 1971.

The centre of Pratt's work is "a desperate struggle to possess the will to believe in the meaningfulness of existence." Pratt's early years were a continuous testing of the belief in a "benevolent God of justice and mercy" first by the "endless tragedy" of the Newfoundland fisherman in his struggle against nature's hostility and later at the University of Toronto by the scientific view of existence. Pratt's poetry reflects this intense ideological struggle going on in him. First in "Clay" where the standard, nihilistic, mystical, and humanistic views are put to battle and although doubt loses out and a positive ending is accomplished, Pratt is unable "to maintain the will to believe" by the time of the writing of *Newfoundland Verse.* From then on, Clark sees in Pratt's poetry the freeing of "himself from the need for God" and the turning "to the world of man to build a will to believe in a humanistic faith." Man has a double battle: he must maintain his humanity against the inhuman forces in himself and he must believe man can understand nature and "direct his evolution through consciously willed moral action." Pratt's "poetry is a record of his struggle with the problem of belief, a struggle in which he takes on the anguish of being and emerges with a defiant will to believe."

C143 Coles, Baxter Matthew. "Man As Hero: A Study of E. J. Pratt's Concept of Heroism." M.A. Thesis Acadia 1971.

Coles's aim is to show Pratt's concept of heroism which is found in both his narrative and shorter poems. "Pratt saw man as a potentially heroic being, who rises to heights of true heroism when required to do so"; the source of all heroism being "within man himself." This he learned from his early experiences among the people of Newfoundland who exhibited, as part of their daily lives, "courage, endurance, self-sacrifice, resourcefulness, kindness and compassion." Coles quotes from Pratt who in 1941 expressed the view that a poet's role was to interpret events within his world: "The world today provides a background which, appalling though it be, yet vibrates with poetic appeal. The events at Canton, Barcelona, Munich, and Coventry clamour for the attention of the artist as well as the statesman and soldier." His poem "Still Life" expounds this view. Devotion to a cause in itself does not necessarily produce heroes as illustrated by the Nazis who were not heroes "because their aim is evil, and harmful to mankind . . . and drag him back toward his brutal and uncivilized past." Coles examines several of Pratt's works showing how he portrays "ennobling human attributes" in man in his battle against nature and opposing odds.

C144 Mensch, Fred. "Aspects of Heroism and Evolution in Some Poems by E. J. Pratt." M.A. Thesis Simon Fraser 1972.

In Pratt's poetry, heroism exists only as part of evolution. Heroism arises if man can establish "an order that is based on ethics and a 'brotherhood of man' as well as ... strong, instinctual emotions that keep him aware ... of his evolutionary origin." Pratt's early poetry emphasizes instinctive feeling which when united with ethical compassion makes up "The most significant factor defining heroism." In *The Titantic*, "the ship symbolizes a society living under an all-encompassing illusion" which almost denies the "possibility of an ideal synthesis." This shows Pratt's development away from the ideal integration in the man-nature, logic-emotion, dichotomy of "feeling for the environment and compassion for other life" earlier exhibited in *The Roosevelt and the Antinoe*. In *Brébeuf and His Brethren* the paradoxes within Brébeuf who "gives the Indians 'roar for roar,' yet finds the source of his strength in the vision of the cross," express man's possible contradictory extremes. This dichotomy cannot be resolved by one or the other alone for both extremes, "evolution and Christian ethics, ... can be equally destructive if allowed to dominate." Pratt's answer is a gradual synthesis of these extremes when at a state of equal tension. This is "the core of Pratt's belief in heroism."

C145 Broad, Margaret. "The Nature of the Evolution of Man in Relation to the Problem of Immortality in the Poetry of E. J. Pratt." M.A. Thesis McGill 1975.

Darwinism and scientific determinism affected Pratt's ability to believe in God. Broad sees, however, Pratt's concern over man's spiritual life in the modern world. The solution lies in man endeavouring to live in "harmony with Nature and the Creator ... [and it] implies Pratt's underlying faith in a supreme mind behind evolution and suggests his belief in immortality in the specific sense of a privilege conditional upon the nature of man's earthly existence."

C146 Hunt, Peter R. "Two Catholic Epics of the Twentieth Century: E. J. Pratt's *Brébeuf and His Brethren* and James McAuley's *Captain Quiros*." M.A. Thesis New Brunswick 1975.

E. J. Pratt's *Brébeuf and His Brethren* and James McAuley's *Captain Quiros* are analyzed and compared as "Two Catholic Epics of the Twentieth Century." Although the poems are "different in outlook and style," they both deal with counter-reformation men, both try to bring out the meaning and significance of the heroic actions they depict, both have remained true to their sources, both poets have been inspired by "'Classical' and Christian humanist values" as revealed in their poems, and both using mainly the European and epic traditions, represent a "creative symbiosis" between Europe and Australia on the one hand, Europe and Canada on the other. McAuley's skepticism toward Quiros' utopian scheme causes a pessimism to creep into his poem. Pratt is considered to have "achieved dramatic objectivity." The author finds *Captain Quiros*, "has a vision, coherence and power unrivalled by any of Pratt's long narratives before *Brébeuf and His Brethren* [whose] historical sweep and depth are greater, [and whose] "intensity and focus are better sustained than *Captain Quiros*."

C147 Beckmann, Susan. "Pratt on Pratt: The Prose Commentaries of E. J. Pratt." Diss. Toronto 1977.

For the first time in "Pratt on Pratt: The Prose Commentaries of E. J. Pratt," the texts of "introductory, explicative and evaluative material written by the poet about his own work" are made known. The holdings of the E. J. Pratt Collection at Victoria University Library, where the prose commentaries are housed, are reviewed in the Introduction. A survey of Pratt scholarship to date, and "new bibliographical information about the genesis and development of the poems," are included. The commentaries "document the mind of Pratt the story-teller... reveal a good deal of his warm and lively personality... provide... the outline of Pratt's poetic theory... [and] furnish us with the poet's own description of his methods of research and writing."

C148 Maggs, W. Randall. "Tradition and Technology in the Poetry of E. J. Pratt." Diss. New Brunswick 1977.

The ability to successfully represent the modern age through "mechanistic devices" in his poetry is one of Pratt's most notable achievements, nevertheless his "outport heritage" continued strongly throughout his poetry and both his "strengths and weaknesses as a poet may be mainly attributed" to this early influence for "he never violated the spirit of... [the outport balladeers] tradition." The author, attempting to understand better the influence of Newfoundland life on Pratt's philosophy and poetry, has studied the work of Szwed and other writers concerned with Newfoundland experience. He finds that all other influences are of secondary importance, "The Elizabethan,... epic tradition,... Masefield,... Sandburg, T. S. Eliot,... T. H. Huxley, ... Wilhelm Wendt, Darwin, ... J. C. Smuts." "Pratt's sensibilities had been substantially shaped in those first twenty-five years of his life." None of the other influences changed his "way of thinking"; they only reinforced the "values of his past and helped him to develop his poetic themes based on these values."

Interviews

C149 Rowland, Nancy. "A Poet at Work." *Acta Victoriana*, 70 (Oct. 1945), 36-37.

This article is a student's report of an interview with Professor Pratt in 1945. Pratt had spent his summer aboard Canadian destroyers getting back-ground material for a poem based on the exploits of the destroyer Skeena in 1941. (The product was "Behind the Log.")

C150 Bentley, Allen. "Dinner with E. J. Pratt." *Acta Victoriana*, 79 (March 1955), 5-10.

Based on an interview with Pratt, Bentley surveys the development of Canadian poetry from regionalism to nationalism and shows the role that nature has played in it. These trends reflect also in Pratt's poetic development. He "synthesizes the two conflicting trends" and utilizes the "dynamic conception of nature" to embody the "spirit of Canada" in his narrative epics. Bentley refers to a number of works to support his thesis. One of the few direct quotes from the poet reveals his philosophy on writing: "My ground rule for writing poetry is the golden mean. The poet speaks clearly, with accuracy, but also deeply, and he demands intelligence to make his readers aware of the greatness of his subject. He chooses a theme of universal significance for serious poetry, and makes it concrete by nailing it down with information and numbers of precise examples." On matters of form, Pratt believed that the narrative epic seemed "to be best adapted for sketching the Canadian element. And the struggle of man against Nature has always been my theme." From Pratt, "the stream passes to Earle Birney, so Pratt believes."

C151 Hambleton, Ronald. "E. J. Pratt, an Experience of Life." *CBC Times*, 6-12 March, 1955, p. 3. 20-26 March, 1955, p. 3.

An abridged text of Ronald Hambleton's interview with Pratt which was broadcast on CBC Trans-Canada in the series "An Experience of Life." The interview focuses on fate, irony, and tragedy with particular reference to *The Titanic*. Pratt contrasts the tragedies of Brébeuf and the Titanic: "When Brébeuf and Lalemant were destroyed by the Indians, it was they, the two Jesuits, who chose to be. It was free will entirely. But when two thousand people died with the Titanic, there was no free will."

Audio Recordings

C152   "Complimentary Dinner to E. J. Pratt." Speakers: Mrs. Pratt, Prof. Frye, Leonard Brockington. 10 Oct. 1953. Audio tape reel-to-reel.

C153   Noseworthy, C. *A Profile of Canadian Poet E. J. Pratt*. Phonodisc. Recorded by VOCM, St. John's, Newfoundland. 1 April 1958.

C154   "Service of Commemoration for Professor E. J. Pratt at Convocation Hall, Univ. of Toronto." 28 April 1964. Audio tape reel-to-reel.

C155   "The Naming of the E. J. Pratt Library." 7 March 1968. Tape recording.

C156   "E. J. Pratt Remembered." By Bob Patchell, Grace Irwin, David Knight, Chris Love. Moderated by Sandy Johnson. Toronto, 1978. 1 cassette. Recorded 16 Jan. 1978 at Wymilwood's Music Room.

Awards and Honours

C157   Elected to Royal Society of Canada in 1930.

C158   Governor-General's Award for *The Fable of the Goats and Other Poems* (1937).

C159   Governor-General's Award for *Brébeuf and His Brethren* (1940).

C160   Royal Society's Lorne Pierce Medal for distinguished service to Canadian literature (1940).

C161   LL.D., University of Manitoba, Winnipeg, Manitoba (1945).

C162   In the King's Honour List in 1946, named Companion of the Order of St. Michael and St. George.

C163   DCL., Bishop's University, Lennoxville, Quebec (1949).

C164   LL.D., McGill University, Montreal, Quebec (1949).

C165   LL.D., Queen's University, Kingston, Ontario (1949).

C166   Governor-General's Award for *Towards the Last Spike* (1952).

C167   University of Alberta gold medal for literature based on cultural contribution of a distinguished career (1952).

C168   The University of Toronto awarded him an Honorary LL.D. "at the termination of his teaching duties" (1953).

C169   LL.D., Assumption College, Windsor, Ontario (1955).

C170   LL.D., University of New Brunswick, Fredericton, New Brunswick (1957).

C171   LL.D., University of Western Ontario, London, Ontario (1957).

C172   Canada Council paid tribute to him on his seventy-fifth birthday, by awarding him $1,000 (1958).

C173   Civic Award of Merit in Toronto (1959).

C174   Canada Council Medal for distinction in the field of literature (1961).

C175 LL.D., Memorial University of Newfoundland, St. John's, Newfoundland (1961).

D   Selected Book Reviews

Newfoundland Verse

D1   Ivanhoe [W. T. Allison]. "Lively Verse by a Newfoundland Poet." *The Winnipeg Tribune*, 30 April 1923. *EJP* (See C3).

It is a great pleasure to pick up a volume of poetry of a new Canadian poet in which "we find vigorous red-blooded verse." Since Pratt was born in Newfoundland rather than in Ontario, where "academic dryrot would probably have sapped his lyric vitality years ago," his *Newfoundland Verse* "has the suppleness of a herringbone and the freshness of sea-kelp."

D2   Morgan-Powell, S. "Newfoundland Verse from a Poet of Inspirational Power." *The Montreal Star*, 5 May 1923, p. 15. *EJP.*

For *Newfoundland Verse* Morgan-Powell gives "a hearty thanks—there are no attempts at that wretched stuff miscalled 'free verse.'" Pratt "has the courage to adhere to the recognized conception of poetry."

D3   Rev. of *Newfoundland Verse*. *Globe* [Toronto], 12 May 1923, p. 26.

Pratt in his first published book of poems, *Newfoundland Verse*, is heard as "a new voice with vigour and music, colour and understanding." Newfoundland is honoured, for "the first time ... the island

finds dignified and fitting expression in the medium of verse."

D4   Pierce, Lorne. Rev. of *Newfoundland Verse*. *Christian Guardian*, 94, No. 21 (23 May 1923), 22.

In *Newfoundland Verse* we "have for the first time a truly Newfoundland epic" written by "A new voice [which] has come among us, as sure in its finished craftsmanship as it is in its choice of material, its unerring emphasis on truth, its acute appreciation of beauty, its inevitable resonance with the voice of life."

D5   Knox, R. S. Rev. of *Newfoundland Verse*. *The Canadian Forum*, June 1923, pp. 278-79. *EJP.*

The reviewer derides subjective poetry: "the fashionable cult is still of the inward vision." "To those ... who still find pleasure in a more objective utterance" as well as "bright display of scenes and actions," Pratt's *Newfoundland Verse* is welcome

The narratives are the "great things in the volume" and "Mr. Pratt lifts himself to a place among the best of recent storytellers in verse."

D6   Rev. of *Newfoundland Verse*. *Canadian Magazine*, 61 (June 1923), 192-93.

The reviewer relates one of the poems to Prof. W. H. Greaves's Toronto home. This is of interest since Greaves was one of the first to read Pratt's poems in public, "chiefly in Toronto University circles." In *Newfoundland Verse* Pratt "possesses a sixth sense in word values" and uses successfully the "form" that "appeals to him." The author cites several "particularly fine" poems and concludes that this collection "establishes Dr. Pratt as a poet of rank."

D7   Phelps, Arthur L. Rev. of *Newfoundland Verse*. *Christian Guardian*, 94, No. 25 (20 June 1923), 12, 19.

"Vitality and variety" are found in Pratt's *Newfoundland Verse* by Phelps. The sea, the folk, the heart of the island cry out from the poems Pratt has fashioned. Phelps finds "Come Not the Seasons Here" the peak poetical achievement of the book and interprets it as "the author's comment on the war."

D8   Rev. of *Newfoundland Verse. Acta Victoriana*, 48 (Oct. 1923), 12-14.

Although critical of some of the pomposity and sentimentality of the verse, the reviewer concludes that "these faults, however, cannot detract much from the unusually sound merits of the poems."

The Witches' Brew

D9   Brown, E. K. Rev. of *The Witches' Brew. Acta Victoriana*, 50 (Feb. 1926), 12-13. *EJP*.

A brief, articulate review comparing Pratt's marine poetry to that of Masefield. Mr. Brown continues with another comparison: "*The Witches' Brew* is, in several respects, a Byronic poem." Because the subjects of the poem are "marine or fabulous," *The Witches' Brew* is more successful than Pratt's earlier comic verse.

D10   Deacon, William Arthur. "Debauching a Fish." *Saturday Night*, 6 Feb. 1926, p. 8.

William Arthur Deacon finds *The Witches' Brew* unique not only in Canadian literature but he does not "know in the whole realm of literature any precedent for it." It is an "imaginative orgy,...[a] magnificent fooling," and it took a poet combining "dramatic power...humour [and] a real feeling for the sea" to produce it.

D11   M., F. J. Rev. of *The Witches' Brew. The Canadian Forum*, April 1926, pp. 218-19.

"*The Witches' Brew* is a piece of extravagance tossed off in a fit of high spirits by a highly imaginative man."

The plot is outlined and although the reviewer does not believe this poem is equal to Pratt's "The Cachalot," "it has an Aristophanic humour and a kind of imagination unique in Canadian poetry."

D12   Hurley, John. Rev. of *The Witches' Brew. Winnipeg Free Press*, 3 May 1926, p. 9. *EJP*.

The Witches' Brew is "an extremely diverting and well written narrative poem." Such words and phrases as "rollicking," "reeling with mirth," "gay," "infinite gusto," "delicious nonsense" are used to describe the poem. The critic wonders at the topic matter for the poem of "a professor of a religious college in Toronto, a prohibition city." He concludes that perhaps Pratt is suffering from a "suppressed complex."

Titans

D13   DeWitt, N. W. Rev. of *Titans. Acta Victoriana*, 51, No. 3 (Dec. 1926), 33-35.

In a rambling criticism which includes the statement that nature "creates" poets but "chance" and "the clumsy intelligence of man" find a place for the talent to "take root and grow," the critic praises and in a friendly manner gives an inside peek into Pratt, the poet, as well as generally reviewing the *Titans*. Pratt's poetry "is simple and unaffected," and the "ease with which he tosses about...big words" is amazing. A final tongue-in-cheek warning that Pratt's "real business is golf," not poetry or teaching English. (The reviewer was a golfing partner of Pratt.)

D14   Pierce, Lorne. Rev. of *Titans. The New Outlook*, 3, No. 3 (19 Jan. 1927), p. 26. *EJP*.

The reviewer recounts the story line of "The Great Feud." The other narrative in the book, "The Cachalot," he finds "is an extravaganza of boisterous nonsense and riotous diablerie." In these poems, by using iambic tetrameter combined with the "independent use of quantity and stress," Pratt produces "a fast flowing narrative style which never tires."

D15 Rev. of *Titans*. *Globe* [Toronto], 8 Jan. 1927, p. 18.

A short favourable review of *Titans* ending with an excerpt from "The Great Feud."

D16 Ivanhoe [W. T. Allison]. "A Pleiocene Armageddon." *The Winnipeg Tribune*, 13 Jan. 1927, p. 4.

Ivanhoe finds Pratt "rises upon Canadian contemporary poetry like a new dawn" because of the originality he shows in "conception, rhyming facility, descriptive power and conduct of narrative."

D17 "Brobdingnag Outdone." *Toronto Daily Star*, 15 Jan. 1927, p. 7.

A favourable review of "The smallest book with the greatest number of monstrosities." "The Cachalot is a magnified version of Moby Dick the great whale." "The Great Feud" is a tale of Tyrannosaurus Rex in a "Pleiocene Armageddon."

D18 Fairley, B. Rev. of *Titans*. *The Canadian Forum*, Feb. 1927, pp. 148-49. *EJP*.

"In this most unusual volume of verse we find the work of a poet who is more at home with whales, octopuses, and dinosaurs than with his fellowmen." A unique Canadianism, "almost for the first time" is recognized by Fairley in Pratt's work.

D19 "Professor Pratt Writes Masterly Poems." *University Monthly*, March 1927, pp. 270-71.

After examining "The Cachalot" and "The Great Feud" the critic answers the questions "whether Canada has a National spirit...[and whether it is] expressed in poetry" both with yes, and yes by Pratt.

The Iron Door

D20 Ivanhoe [W. T. Allison]. "The Riddle of Death." *The Winnipeg Tribune*, 7 Oct. 1927, p. 4.

In writing *The Iron Door* Pratt "has turned to serious things" in attempting to answer the question, "If a man die shall he live again?" Although the poem bears no resemblance to religious poems, containing only three mentions of God and none of Christ, it is "deeply religious," making an argument for the "immortality of the soul."

D21 Creighton, J. H. "An Original Note in Canadian Poetry: The Poems of Mr. E. J. Pratt." *New Outlook*, 3, No. 48 (30 Nov. 1927), p. 6.

Creighton finds Pratt "The most original poet in Canada at present....Vigour...straightforwardness ...boldness... [and] vividness" characterize *Newfoundland Verse*. Creighton believes *The Iron Door* is breaking "entirely new ground." The mysteries of "death and immortality" are probed. Creighton interprets the poem to be "a statement of faith in God and immortality."

D22 "The Last Impregnable Retreat." *Saturday Night*, 22 Oct. 1927, p. 10.

The Iron Door is "a lengthy poem on death that is more intuitive than philosophical."

D23 "A Powerful Ode." *Globe* [Toronto], 29 Oct. 1927, p. 19.

A short study, with excerpts from the poem. *The Iron Door* has "vision, dignity and symbolic beauty... [which] add a distinct and powerful note to Canadian poetry."

D24 G., H. P. Rev. of *The Iron Door*. *Acta Victoriana*, 52, No. 2 (Nov. 1927), 26-27.

Although Professor Pratt "obtained his Ph.D. degree for a treatise on eschatology," this poem "shows little trace of metaphysical or theological influence." The reviewer proceeds to outline the theme of the ode, the character's search and plight. He concludes that "For boldness of imagery, richness of cadence and imaginative penetration this ode makes a distinct contribution to modern poetry."

D25 Macdonald, J. F. Rev. of *The Iron Door. The Canadian Forum*, Dec. 1927, p. 476.

Brief summary of Pratt's "vision of the grim barrier that prevents our getting even a glimpse of the life beyond." Although the reviewer admits the ode is a powerful work, it "leaves one feeling that Pratt has not yet found the subject in which he can use his full power with perfect sincerity." The sincerity is lacking: "the thought and the emotion are not perfectly fused."

The Roosevelt and the Antinoe

D26 "Heroic Poem of Rescue at Sea Delights Hart House Audience." *Mail* [Toronto], 19 Oct. 1929, p. 4.

With *The Roosevelt and the Antinoe* Pratt has achieved "for the first time in full measure, that high and secure place in Canadian literature, of which his first book, *Newfoundland Verse*, bore the promise in 1923." A short survey of Pratt's pre-1929 published poetry follows. The reviewer ends on a conservative note: "No one in Canada is doing anything like it. It cannot be done better; but we need more of it, very much more of precisely the same sort of poems."

D27 Deacon, William Arthur. "Pratt Makes Great Epic Poem Out of Stern Stuff of Life." *The Mail and Empire*, 8 March 1930, p. 11.

The Roosevelt and the Antinoe is a masterpiece "ranking among the greatest English narrative poems of all time." No praise seems great enough for the poem: "It is a magnificent poem, the exalted but natural climax of Pratt's career begun seven years ago."

D28 H., M. O. "Pratt's Epic of the Sea." *Globe* [Toronto], 15 March 1930, p. 7.

Favourable review of "a great epic of the sea, whose truth, imagery and sustained poetical strength will merely place E. J. Pratt among the major poets of Canada. It is a narrative poem which will live for its art, and its drama."

D29 Norwood, Gilbert. Rev. of *The Roosevelt and the Antinoe. Saturday Night*, 5 April 1930, p. 3. *EJP*.

Pratt reveals an "originality of spirit, technique and outlook" in "this remarkable work." The critic heaps praise on praise: "Homer"-like; "Virgilian"; "recall[s] Victor Hugo"; like the "finest work of Kipling"; "his verse technique is consummate"; "splendidly appropriate"; "perfectly fitted to his subject-matter and his method"; "a notable use of prose"; "a vivid and penetrating rhetoric"; "truly sublime realism"; and "articulate" through "masterly paragraph-construction." And with a close to the poem that defies "anticlimax," the critic asks, "Has anything nobler been written in our time?"

D30 P., C. "An Epic of the Sea." *Manchester Guardian*, 5 Aug. 1930, p. 5.

In *The Roosevelt and the Antinoe* Pratt "has done vastly more than versify." From the log of events "He has revisioned and recreated the moments of that eternal vigil.... Altogether, the poem is a worthy memorial of one of the greatest achievements in the chivalry and valour of the sea."

Many Moods

D31 Marquis, T. G. "Original Verse." *Saturday Night*, Dec. 1932, p. 9.

"The latent possibilities of familiar things" are seized on and revealed by Pratt in *Many Moods*. The verse is a "robust, original, and powerfully imaginative interpretation of life and nature." High ethical values, mordant satire, and riotous imagination are exhibited in the "masterpiece" of the collection, "The Depression Ends."

D32 R., E. Rev. of *Many Moods. Dalhousie Review*, 12 (Jan. 1933), 561-62.

Pratt has not imitated other writers. "It shows that Canadian poetic literature is...standing upon its own feet ... (when we have a writer) who not only by his subject matter but by his mode of thought ... [and] emotional reactions is independent of external standards." "A hardness of treatment, a resolute avoidance of ... the sentimental" give Pratt's poems an "intense virility" which is characteristic.

D33 C., G. H. Rev. of *Many Moods. Queen's Quarterly*, 40 (Feb. 1933), 168-69.

Pratt is "less certainly impelled" in his short reflective poems or pure lyric as opposed to his narratives but in *Many Moods* several short poems are "full of gusto and gustation, ... [have] romantic understanding, ... [are] finely fashioned, ... [and] stand the test of repeated re-readings."

The Titanic

D34 McInnis, Edgar. Rev. of *The Titanic. Saturday Night*, 16 Nov. 1935, p. 6.

Two themes run through all of Pratt's best poems: "an interest in monsters ... [and] an interest in the sea." In *The Titanic*, happily, both these themes are combined.

D35 Morgan-Powell, S. Rev. of *The Titanic. Montreal Daily Star*, 23 Nov. 1935.

Although "Heroic poetry is the most difficult of all verse forms to write," it provides "unlimited scope." It has attracted few, but includes "the world's greatest poets." Canadian poetic output "has been conventional, alike in theme and in form," with few attempting successfully the heroic form. Pratt is an "outstanding exception." A critical study of *The Titanic* proves this point and makes up the body of the review. Powell concludes that *The Titanic* is "A great poem, written as it should be, as great drama."

D36 Brown, E. K. Rev. of *The Titanic*. "Letters in Canada: 1935, Poetry." *University of Toronto Quarterly*, 5

(April 1936), 364-65. Rpt. in *Responses and Evaluations: Essays on Canada*. Ed. and introd. David Staines. New Canadian Library, No. 137. Toronto: McClelland and Stewart, 1977, pp. 145-48.

Brief favourable review which points out how subject matter of the "foreknown catastrophe" imposed a particular "mode" on the poet. The poem exhibits Pratt's "emotional range," "his rhythms and his imagery," his knowledge of the sea, and his use of technical terminology. The poker-game and dinner descriptions should have been shortened in order to depict "a few more of the rapid memorable pictures of individual passages in the time of crisis."

D37 Rev. of *The Titanic. Dalhousie Review*, 16 (1936-37), 126.

Pratt gives the sinking of the Titanic "the dignity of Greek drama." This short favourable review concludes with: "This is a poem not to be missed."

Fable of the Goats and Other Poems

D38 Rev. of *Fable of the Goats and Other Poems. The Canadian Forum*, Dec. 1937, pp. 321-22.

In this "markedly different work there is much experimentation in technique and ... awareness of the structure and problems of contemporary society." Allegorically Pratt's theme is "the conflict of national interests and ambitions." "He has written a poem in which the fierce bounding temperament is subdued to the purest form of Christian temper; the temperament has remained heroic for it has subdued itself." "Silences," among the other poems, "is most ... striking and impressive." "This collection continues to prove that, in creative force, in sweep of imagination, ... rhetoric and narrative, ... [Pratt] is the first of Canadian poets."

D39 "Poet's Progress." *The Globe and Mail*, 11 Dec. 1937, p. 27.

Although "miscellaneous pieces," the *Fable of the Goats* "is deeply impressive in its evidence of further growth." "There is no mere verbiage" in this book with all poems "finished with the finality of great art."

D40   Clarke, George Herbert. Rev. of *Fable of the Goats and Other Poems. Queen's Quarterly*, 45, No. 1 (1938), 126-27.

    The *Fable of the Goats* contains a "spirit of satire" which "derides the social and political follies of our time lest it should weep at them. It indicts and exposes and even condemns, but it does not despair."

D41   Brown, E. K. Rev. of *Fable of the Goats and Other Poems. University of Toronto Quarterly*, 7 (April 1938), 340-41. Rpt. in *Responses and Evaluations: Essays on Canada*. Ed. and introd. David Staines. New Canadian Library, No. 137. Toronto: McClelland and Stewart, 1977, pp. 161-63.

    This is "the most important book of poetry published by a Canadian in 1937." The collection shows Pratt's "daring experimentation in techniques and a keen awareness of the structure and diseases of contemporary society." The allegory: "wild creatures exemplify human traits, first greed, ambition, pugnacity, then peace and conciliation." The rhyming tetrameter is retained in the *Fable of the Goats* while the metre and mood in the "striking and moving" poem "Silences" are quite new to Pratt's work.

D42   "Men, Goats, and E. J. Pratt." *Daily News* [St. John's], 11 Feb. 1939.

    Using the parable, or fable form with its inherent possibility for condemning satire, Pratt, in the *Fable of the Goats*, exposes the stupidities and futilities of war.

Brébeuf and His Brethren

D43   "Poem Enshrines Martyrs with Halo of New Beauty." *Toronto Daily Star*, 20 July 1940, p. 9.

The reviewer refers to *Brébeuf and His Brethren* as Pratt's "Canadian Aeneid" in which the poet depicts death "with sublimity." The "artistry is complete" in the poet's description of suffering in his "latest masterpiece."

D44   Deacon, William Arthur. "A Peak of Canadian Heroism." *The Globe and Mail*, 27 July 1940, p. 20.

    After "seventeen years of inspired effort" and ten volumes of verse, "Pratt is now at the peak of his power." In his verse the "dramatic qualities...are dynamic. His vocabulary is objective, his rhythms positive." In his *Brébeuf and His Brethren* "the theme is on so exalted a plane that the poet outdoes himself in restraint." Deacon finds the poem "a truly great piece of work." He also calls for more use of Canadian history to provide poetic inspiration;...as for these rich resources, "the surface has barely been scratched."

D45   Edgar, Pelham. "A Vivid Poetic Impression of the Canada of 300 Years Ago...." *Ottawa Journal*, 10 Aug. 1940, p. 21.

    Edgar rates *Brébeuf and His Brethren* as "the greatest poem of [Pratt's]...career." Pratt has been able to set aside his own philosophy to write about "systems of thought that are naturally alien to his disposition." Pratt's discipline, hard work, and objectivity have produced "the greatest Catholic poem of modern times."

D46   Benson, Nathaniel A. Rev. of *Brébeuf and His Brethren. Canadian Poetry Magazine*, 5 (Sept. 1940), 40-43.

    The reviewer related Pratt's writing career as success on success until *Brébeuf and His Brethren*, "Ned Pratt's crowning achievement.... [He is] the finest poet of his own generation." *Brébeuf and His Brethren* is briefly described as "the tremendous stories of the superhuman labours and sufferings, of the glorious lives, and martyrdom of Fathers" of the

Huron Mission. No criticism of any kind is made throughout this most favourable review.

D47 Birney, Earle. Rev. of *Brébeuf and His Brethren*. *The Canadian Forum*, Sept. 1940, pp. 180-81.

Here is "the same narrative verve and dramatic intensity, founded on a fine factual assimilation of his subject, which have helped to make him not only Canada's most remarkable poet but also the finest poet of the sea writing today in the English language." "Technical brilliance,...flashing imagination... panoramic eye [and] a restraint and a simplicity" are revealed as are "enthusiasm for mankind in its moments of courage, endurance, comradeship and self-sacrifice." Deeds and characters are "heightened into the grand." Birney believes that in "some ways" *Brébeuf* is Pratt's best work although it is not "illustrative of his manifold talents."

D48 Clarke, George Herbert. Rev. of *Brébeuf and His Brethren*. *Queen's Quarterly*, 47 (Winter 1940), 483.

"*Brébeuf and His Brethren* is a stirring narrative poem written in flexible blank verse." Pratt follows with "close fidelity" the factual data of the history. The form shows workmanship which is "generally... sound and strong, save in a few instances — the somewhat too prosaic tone." In conclusion, the poem is found to be "even subtler in its feeling and richer in its humanity...than his...sagas of the sea."

D49 Haines, Lloyd. "*Brébeuf and His Brethren* and Dr. Pratt." *Acta Victoriana*, 65 (Jan. 1941), 6-8.

"E. J. Pratt's distinction is largely a distinctness: there is no one else quite like him." Pratt seems to be obsessed with "That cold, steely, blazing, indomitable, godlike part of man — heroism." He makes the reader suffer "a dozen deaths up and down the St. Lawrence and Great Lakes" in *Brébeuf and His Brethren*, a "marvellously executed" narrative of heroism. The book abounds with scholarly data: geographical,

historical, geological, botanical, astronomical, theological. The iambic pentameter conveys "a vast variety of feeling" yet helps maintain "a superb unity of tone."

D50 Brown, E. K. Rev. of *Brébeuf and His Brethren*. *University of Toronto Quarterly*, 10 (April 1941), 283-86. Rpt. in *Responses and Evaluations: Essays on Canada*. Ed. and introd. David Staines. New Canadian Library, No. 137. Toronto: McClelland and Stewart, 1977, pp. 188-91.

The choice of a subject from Canada's past "by our noblest living poet is a white milestone in the development of Canadian literature." Pratt faithfully depicts the heroic epic of the Jesuit Martyrs aiming "not at the realization of human figures but at the communication of epic emotion." A "multitude of great images are contained in this quiet, meditative narrative written in blank verse." "Along with craftsmanship of the most considered fineness" Pratt gives us "loftiness and calm."

Dunkirk

D51 "Celebrates a Glorious Defeat." *The Globe and Mail*, 25 Oct. 1941, p. 10.

Dunkirk was hurried to press so that the event would be "fresh in memory"; this did not allow time to collect "sufficient detail, sift it for authenticity, weave it into an artistic pattern" to do justice to a book-length narrative. *Dunkirk* is "fleeting impressions of the rag-tag armada...who sailed to save the army."

D52 Birney, Earle. Rev. of *Dunkirk*. *The Canadian Forum*, Dec. 1941, pp. 278-79.

"Within the limits of the space and the view, [Pratt] has done a fine job" in recounting the withdrawal from Dunkirk. There are no "cheap patriotics," "fuzzy political moralizing." The poem contains "some of the high spirits of *The Witches' Brew,* and the *Titans*" and "Pratt's peculiarly accurate and intense portrayal of the sea." Pratt is "among the top dozen poets of the English tongue today" and with this work he has "made another step toward the writing" of his great epic which will fuse "all his varied gifts" and explore "a rich and indigenous theme."

D53 Brown, E. K. Rev. of *Dunkirk*. *University of Toronto Quarterly*, 11 (April 1942), 288-89. Rpt. in *Responses and Evaluations: Essays on Canada*. Ed. and introd. David Staines. New Canadian Library, No. 137. Toronto: McClelland and Stewart, 1977, pp. 198-99.

Although "*Dunkirk* is not one of his principal works ... [it is] a brilliant experiment." It contains an "evergrowing sympathy with man which ... [gives] ... a sense for the tragic formerly lacking to his approach.... [It] enables him to communicate pity and terror." The poem contains "humour and tragedy, the heroic and the pathetic [which] jostle one another with rugged effectiveness."

Still Life

D54 Rev. of *Still Life*. *The Globe and Mail*, 18 Dec. 1943, p. 11.

Pratt's reputation, twenty years after *Newfoundland Verse*, is so great that it is unnecessary "to deal exhaustively with his new poems in *Still Life*." Several of the poems, "The Radio in the Ivory Tower," "The Submarine," "The Dying Eagle," and "Still Life" are dealt with sketchily. The critic finds *Still Life* is "a worthy successor to great predecessors."

D55 Clarke, George Herbert. Rev. of *Still Life*. *Queen's Quarterly*, 51 (Spring 1944), 115.

There are fifteen poems in this collection of lyrics, satires, and narratives. They show off the poet's "bright energy of fancy, variety in diction and cadence, and a firmly woven texture." Worth mention are the satires, "The Truant" and "The Radio in the Ivory Tower," and special mention of the narrative "The

Dying Eagle," which is "The most striking" and "successful" poem in the collection.

D56 Brown, E. K. Rev. of *Still Life*. *University of Toronto Quarterly*, 13 (April 1944), 306-08. Rpt. in *Responses and Evaluations: Essays on Canada*. Ed. and introd. David Staines. New Canadian Library, No. 137. Toronto: McClelland and Stewart, 1977, pp. 221-22.

From this collection of lyrics and narratives Brown selects a number for particular mention. "Pratt has never been happier as a lyrist than he is" in "Come Away, Death" and "The Invaded Field." Irony, a device new to Pratt, is used in "Still Life," "his most sustained study in irony, an assault dangerously polite upon the dwellers in ivory towers." "The Truant" is the poem which most impresses the reviewer; it contains a "powerful Hitler-symbol; and indeed everywhere in the volume war is either a theme or a substantial part of the framework of feeling."

D57 M., B. Rev. of *Still Life*. *Dalhousie Review*, 24 (April 1944), 118.

"Still Life" and "Missing: Believed Dead: Returned," the shorter poems, are considered among the best in the collection. "When a poem goes beyond twenty lines, the demons of verbosity, banality and flatness try to throttle Prof. Pratt's gift for poetry." His work is criticized as thoughtless and "words and lines follow one another in a ceaseless and meaningless flow."

Collected Poems

D58 "A Prattian Convert." *Acta Victoriana*, 69 (Fall 1944), 38-42.

Pratt uses "concrete experience," "national and contemporary subjects" with the "cool observation of a sympathetic but impartial outsider." The poetry's strength is in Pratt's "treatment and vision." He returns "to nature and forces as yet unleashed by civilization, to draw his contrast, to point out the unrelenting cruelty of irony." Subjects are large in his narrative poems; in his extravaganzas it is his humour. Strength and irony, major components of his verse, give way to "delicacy of feeling" in his lighter lyrics. The reviewer concludes by revealing his own prejudices, understanding, and eventual acceptance of the necessity of wartime verse.

D59 Deacon, William Arthur. "Pratt's Definitive Edition Symbol of Poetic Leadership." *The Globe and Mail*, 21 Oct. 1944, p. 21.

The only poet who was not censured in Brown's critical work *On Canadian Poetry* was correctly Pratt, "the one exception to our mediocrity." Fittingly, Pratt now at "the highest level of his career" offers his work in comprehensive form bringing together "in one volume...the best of his works.... At 61,...Pratt is now free of his past" and the critic predicts tentatively that he will "speak out of the convictions of his head and the promptings of his heart."

D60 Morgan-Powell, S. "New Edition of Poems by E. J. Pratt." *Montreal Star*, 4 Nov. 1944, p. 22.

On the publication of *The Collected Poems of E. J. Pratt*, Morgan-Powell assesses Pratt as "the only major poet in the Dominion." Two of Pratt's narratives, *The Titanic* and *Brébeuf and His Brethren*, have never been equalled by any writing on these themes. Morgan-Powell is astounded by Pratt's range, "That the same man could have written *Brébeuf* and *The Witches' Brew* is well nigh unbelievable." Pratt is unequalled in Canadian letters for his "song" is "more authentic Canadian" and he "has penetrated deeper into the heart and soul of Canada" than any other poet or prose writer.

D61 Mackay, L. A. Rev. of *Collected Poems. The Canadian Forum*, Dec. 1944, pp. 208-09. *EJP*.

The collection of Pratt's poems makes clear the reasons why Pratt is considered "the greatest of the contemporary Canadian poets, and one of the chief figures in contemporary poetry written in English anywhere." Throughout "one idea is dominant, the idea of heroic combat...the elation of sheer enormous brute conflict has been exalted and humanized...into the heroic struggle of mankind against hostile material, human, and spiritual forces." From the collection it is obvious that "Pratt's gift is...epic rather than lyric.... [He] has developed a highly individual and effective technique." His is a poetry of "energy rather than delicacy."

D62 K., W. Rev. of *Collected Poems. Canadian Poetry Magazine*, 8 (Dec. 1944), 38-39.

The *Collected Poems* allows me to "gaze with admiring eyes at the solid totality of his output." In general the style is "masculine"; this is accomplished by an "impelling vigour," and "intense and controlled power." A wide ranging erudition and intellectuality are other marked qualities of his work which help to give his poetry what Canadian poetry has often lacked, content.

D63 Brown, E. K. Rev. of *Collected Poems. University of Toronto Quarterly*, 14 (Jan. 1945), 211-13.

The reviewer of Pratt's *Collected Poems* finds that he has "wisely...sifted [his] earlier collections" and that in all "the effect on the general reader [will] be much stronger than any that Mr. Pratt's work has yet had." He believes the reasons why "such a large body of great poetry has gone so little noticed" are firstly "as a people we are not sensitive to the quality of poetry or appreciative of its importance in the national life." Secondly he finds that the Canadian critics, especially academic critics, are too conservative and have failed to recognize and perpetrate the "genius" of Pratt.

D64 Rev. of *Collected Poems. Saturday Review of Literature*, 28 April 1945, p. 11.

"Pratt is a poet highly sensitive to time as a controlling element in human affairs." A comparison with Thomas Hardy is made on the basis of Pratt's "outline of human events against the flare of time and space." Pratt's "versification is exuberant and usually skilful." The critic agrees with Bénet that Pratt "has enough vitality for ten poets. He has also an alert sensitiveness to dramatic contrast, a sweeping view of time, and an abiding interest in the children and victims of time."

They Are Returning

D65   Rev. of *They Are Returning. Canadian Poetry Magazine*, 9 (Sept. 1945), 32-33.

"Canada's chief living poet" has penned "with modern vigour and brevity, the Iliad and Odyssey . . . of the young men in Canada's armed forces." A short analysis of the form used in the poem concludes this brief favourable review.

D66   Daniells, Roy. Rev. of *They Are Returning. The Canadian Forum*, Oct. 1945, pp. 168-69.

"*They Are Returning* is one more proof that poetic imagination can, at will, dispense with the materials of detailed realism."

Behind the Log

D67   "Wolf-Pack Attacks Convoy Guarded by Canadian Navy." *The Globe and Mail*, 6 Dec. 1947, p. 10.

"The sea and especially its hazards," have always provided inspiration for Pratt. Returning to this theme again in *Behind the Log*, "Pratt has added one more masterly achievement to those that have already brought him fame."

D68   L., A. N. Rev. of *Behind the Log. The Gazette* [Montreal], 13 Dec. 1947, p. 24.

Throughout Pratt's poetry there is one constant symbol — the sea. Heroism of man at sea is his favourite theme. In *Behind the Log* an "epic battle on the water" is again related. Pratt, according to A. N. L., is able, "in this age of the impatient reader . . . to keep the reader's interest throughout" by combining dramatic dialogue and narrative description.

D69   R., W. Rev. of *Behind the Log. Canadian Poetry Magazine*, 11 (March 1948), 41-42.

A brief attack on "certain critics [who] have offered disparaging comments on Pratt's writing as pedestrian in its realism, and as seeking compensation for an inner uncertainty by virility of diction and 'gigantism' of imagery." They have missed the "evocative imagery," the "social satire," the able craft of "the long line . . . [and] the tone values of words" and ignored the honoured position Pratt has earned as a narrative poet.

D70   Brown, E. K. Rev. of *Behind the Log. University of Toronto Quarterly*, 17 (April 1948), 258-60. Rpt. in *Responses and Evaluations: Essays on Canada*. Ed. and introd. David Staines. New Canadian Library, No. 137. Toronto: McClelland and Stewart, 1977, pp. 264-67.

The background for *Behind the Log* is related. The poem itself has "the familiar Pratt rhythms recur[ring] with undiminished power." "The core of the poem . . . [the third block] draws on his greatest resources of style," which is "assuming a new austerity." "The danger incurred in the new style is the danger of prosaism [and there are] . . . some lines . . . in which the manner lapses into the prosaic." If the "beautiful quiet close . . . has a fault that is its brevity."

D71   Gustafson, Ralph. Rev. of *Behind the Log. The Canadian Forum*, June 1948, p. 69.

Behind the Log contains "many of the long-admired qualities of Pratt." Although the book "does not equal, as poetry, the earlier narratives of Pratt" it still "effectively reminds Canadians that in Pratt they have not only a great narrative poet but almost the only one writing in English to-day."

D72 Bates, Ronald. Rev. of *Behind the Log. Acta Victoriana*, 72 (Summer 1948), 19-20.

The whole review is a mild attack on narrative poetry and thus on Pratt's *Behind the Log* which is the subject of review. The poem has "certain shortcomings which are, perhaps, inherent in the form." Pratt is unable to give the poem "emotional unity" through the "infusion of the more specifically poetic" and therefore *Behind the Log* "has to fall back on the purely narrative link for its unity, which is not enough, poetically." The final damning: "one should bear in mind the limitations of narrative poetry for our age."

D73 Clarke, George Herbert. Rev. of *Behind the Log. Queen's Quarterly*, 55 (Summer 1948), 229-30.

Behind the Log contains some of the "narrative vigour" of his longer sea poems, "but hardly their characteristic thrust." Factual points which Pratt "scrupulously" relates impose "too close a collaboration, in movement and diction alike, between actuality and purely imaginative processes that must fashion and empower any given work of art."

Ten Selected Poems

D74 Morgan-Powell, S. Rev. of *Ten Selected Poems. Montreal Daily Star*, 30 Aug. 1947, p. 14.

A brief review of a volume which shows Pratt's narrative ability as well as "his right to be regarded as a poet of national stature in terms both of subject-matter and style."

D75 "Pratt's Poems for School Use." *The Globe and Mail*, 6 Sept. 1947, p. 10.

The volume, "well annotated for school use, offer[s] the general reader a bargain" and the notes and definitions are useful for every one. The few shorter pieces included in addition to the narratives give the reader a "fair idea of the poet's scope."

D76 Brown, E. K. Rev. of *Ten Selected Poems. University of Toronto Quarterly*, 17 (April 1948), 260-61. Rpt. in *Responses and Evaluations: Essays on Canada*. Ed. and introd. David Staines. New Canadian Library, No. 137. Toronto: McClelland and Stewart, 1977, p. 267.

Ten Selected Poems is for school use, but the volume provides "an excellent sampling of Mr. Pratt's work for the general Canadian reader." Included are "The Cachalot," "The Titanic," "Brébeuf and His Brethren," and "Dunkirk."

D77 M., C. R. Rev. of *Ten Selected Poems. Telegram* [Toronto], 16 April 1948.

Ten Selected Poems "seems designed especially for those who enjoy the companionship of poetry in precious free moments of brimming days though actually it was prepared originally for schools."

Towards the Last Spike

D78 Rev. of *Towards the Last Spike. Toronto Daily Star*, 28 June 1952, p. 5.

"It is a happy chance that [Pratt] is the first one to seize upon perhaps the greatest epic of Canada's industrial development and commemorate it in" his poem *Towards the Last Spike*. "With full drama and poetic power" the poet has successfully told the great tale of the building of the "parallels of steel ... from coast to coast toward the last spike that served as a linchpin for a nation."

D79 Morgan-Powell, S. Rev. of *Towards the Last Spike. The Montreal Star*, 5 July 1952, p. 14.

In verse panorama Pratt has taken as theme, "one of the greatest events in the history of Canada ... perhaps the most important development in the story of world transportation ... the completion of a monument of empire-building," the building of the C.P.R. Morgan-Powell tells the story through long quotes from the poem and short explanatory injections. He also tries to convey the appreciation and approval the nation owes Pratt for his outstanding contribution to "its cultural growth and well-being."

D80 Deacon, William Arthur. "How the Crazy Canadians Built the Pacific Railway." *The Globe and Mail*, 12 July 1952, p. 12.

The critic awes at the irrational inspiration of the "builders of Canada" brought to life by Pratt in *Towards the Last Spike*. Pratt has "positive convictions about life" and also "a philosophy of literature." *Towards the Last Spike* is "one more proof of his lifelong fidelity to his own ideals."

D81 T., F. "Fine Narrative Poem by Pratt Describes Building of CPR." *Ottawa Journal*, 26 July 1952, p. 17.

With "a theme as broad as Canada itself," *Towards the Last Spike*, building the CPR, Pratt "has once again painted a vivid word picture with imagination and humour."

D82 P., R. "E. J. Pratt's Epic Poem Worthy of Its Subject." *Winnipeg Tribune*, 26 July 1952, p. 9.

The "great Canadian epic," building the CPR, is the worthy subject of Pratt. He catches "the rhythm of one of our most striking national characteristics — an enthusiasm for large-scale physical action of a constructive purposeful character."

D83 Collin, W. E. Rev. of *Towards the Last Spike. Canadian Poetry Magazine*, 16 (Autumn 1952), 29-30.

A short, highly appreciative, review of Pratt's *Towards the Last Spike*. "It is not enough to say that he [Pratt] has an heroic conception of life." He is able to observe, relate and moreover "live the heroic act" and perform "even their [the characters'] mental acts of reflection, even their dreams."

D84 Pacey, Desmond. Rev. of *Towards the Last Spike. The Canadian Forum*, Oct. 1952, p. 164.

The theme is the conflict between the "passionate, the instinctive,...the primitive...and the logical, the intellectual, and the sophisticated." Pratt writes "compactly, antithetically, in clear hard phrases." In this work Pratt is favourably compared to Dryden because of "the disciplined economy of statement" and the "penetrating character analysis." Although Pacey finds minor flaws in the work, and finds it lacking when compared to the "finest passages" in *Brébeuf and His Brethren*, he concludes that "in depth and clarity of characterization, and in significance of theme, it marks a definite step forward in Pratt's development."

D85 Stewart, Walt. Rev. of *Towards the Last Spike. Acta Victoriana*, 77 (Dec. 1952), 25-27.

"*Towards the Last Spike* is not the best modern poem in the world...it is the work of a first-class craftsman on a first-class theme, and a competent, occasionally outstanding, job." Although blank or free verse "is the only appropriate medium for Pratt's theme," it is not Pratt's "aptest medium." Pratt writes unemotionally from knowledge and with "the casual air of a browser." He is interested in "man's struggle against himself, and in commenting on that struggle for the enlightenment of all mankind." Narrative poetry, "requires dramatic structure.... There is no plot...no proper climax" in *Towards the Last Spike*.

D86 Frye, Northrop. Rev. of *Towards the Last Spike. University of Toronto Quarterly*, 22 (April 1953), 270-73. Rpt. "Letters in Canada: Poetry, 1952-1960 (Pratt's 'Spike' and Birney's 'Trial' 1952)." In *Masks of Poetry: Canadian Critics on Canadian Verse*. Ed. A. J. M. Smith. New Canadian Library, No. 3. Toronto: McClelland and Stewart, 1962, pp. 97-101. Rpt. in *The Bush Garden: Essays on the Canadian Imagination*. Toronto: House of Anansi, 1971, pp. 10-17.

Frye uses Pratt's *Towards the Last Spike* and

Birney's *Trial of a City* to demonstrate "the theory of cultural containment." According to Frye "there would be nothing distinctive in Canadian culture at all if there were not some feeling for the immense searching distance, with the lines of communication extended to the absolute limit...." "The horizon-focussed perspective" and an interest in the "problems of communication" are common elements in the work of other Canadian artists, writers, and thinkers, including Pratt. His theme in *Towards the Last Spike* — "the epic art of communication in Canadian history [is] fantastically difficult" but Pratt has shown great ingenuity in dealing with the problems.

The Collected Poems of E. J. Pratt

D87 Deacon, William Arthur. "35 Years of Pratt." *The Globe and Mail*, 6 Dec. 1958, p. 24.

This is a revised and extended *Collected Poems* that can be termed a "Definitive rather than [a] second edition." Although it is generally believed that most of Pratt's heroic narratives can be "understood at a glance" critical studies of Pratt's work "reveal subtlety — meaning within meanings" and therefore Frye's introduction "will aid readers to a richer comprehension."

D88 Elliott, John K. "Clarity, Variety in New Pratt Collection." *London Free Press*, 13 Dec. 1958, p. 20.

The Collected Poems of E. J. Pratt shows that the bridge between the "common reader" and poetry "has not been completely destroyed." Although "complicated" and "scholarly," Pratt's verse is "clear."

D89 Bruce, Charles. Rev. of *The Collected Poems of E. J. Pratt*. *Telegram* [Toronto], 20 Dec. 1958, p. 34.

Bruce finds that "The Truant" "is the distillation of Pratt's view of life" and that his earlier verse "is feeling its way toward" its statement, while the "later verse is in some measure an explication of its theme."

For all the collected verse there is a "central thread: That Man's hope lies in his refusal to be ruled by brute strength and blind force,... and that his battle with blind force and with himself is an endless, hazardous, tragic and heroic business."

D90 McPherson, Hugo. "With a Wide-Angle Lens He Viewed Great Themes." *Toronto Daily Star*, 20 Dec. 1958, p. 26.

Pratt is both "admired by exacting critics on the one hand and a wide public on the other." He compares to only Robert Frost among Americans in being a success in his own country. Pratt has achieved this popularity with a difference, "with quiet independence" snubbing "all of the literary fashions of his day.... Pratt turned boldly to full-scale narrative poems." In opposition to subjective personal poetry he "adopted the impersonal wide-angled lens of the narrator." *The Collected Poems of E. J. Pratt* is reviewed and proves McPherson's thesis. Pratt has become society's spokesman and prophet, dealing not with the local and personal but with mankind's timeless problems as revealed in Canadian life."

D91 Rev. of *Collected Poems of E. J. Pratt*. *Ottawa Journal*, 20 Dec. 1958, p. 46.

The differences between first and second editions of *Collected Poems* are listed. The reviewer agrees with Frye that Pratt's work has "a stature and authority that reaches beyond Canada."

D92 Little, Andrew. "Canadian Poet." *The Gazette* [Montreal], 27 Dec. 1958, p. 19.

A short chronicle of Pratt's life and career is followed by a description of *The Collected Poems*. Pratt is found to have "displayed a quality in editing which is only surpassed by his ability as a poet."

D93 Daniells, Roy. Rev. of *Collected Poems*. *Dalhousie Review*, 39 (Spring 1959), 112-15.

The new and enlarged edition "fills a long felt need." Frye's illuminating introduction is a "chart" to guide the reader through a "voyage of fresh discovery" for Pratt is "still startlingly unique." "Come Not the Seasons Here" is "memorable of the shorter poems" and Daniells points to the development of Pratt's language "which now like a forest enfolds the action of Brébeuf." He shows how irony prevails in Pratt's work, how it contains "pity for poverty and suffering," how he "draws habitually on the immemorial and the cosmic for the ingredients of his dominant image patterns," and how "pervasive" the sea image has been throughout.

concludes with: "It is dangerous to assume that because Pratt chose not to adopt the poetic styles of his contemporaries, he was somehow 'dated' or 'out of touch' with reality, or less poetic than the free-verse poets of his day."

D94 Watt, F. W. "Edwin John Pratt." *University of Toronto Quarterly*, 29 (Oct. 1959), 77-84.

In an excellent critical analysis, Watt surveys Pratt's works from *Newfoundland Verse*, with its "strength and originality," through to the present volume which "remains easily the most impressive yet produced by a Canadian poet." Watt shows how Pratt was always involved in his world. "Liberal, humanitarian, Christian" were the features of Pratt's work and his heroes were set in "a world brought to a crisis where action is necessary at once." Watt praises the "energy, wit, . . . verbal exuberance, strength of feeling" in the verse and expresses his few reservations. Frye's Introduction is "witty, vital, and penetrating critical exposition."

Selected Poems

D95 Macmillan, Duane J. Rev. of *Selected Poems. The Canadian Forum*, July 1968, p. 93.

This anthology was prepared to make the poet's work more accessible, to provide a bibliography of selected secondary material and a "critical apparatus for understanding Pratt's work." The reviewer questions some omissions, and the abridgement of *Towards the Last Spike*. While praising parts of the analysis, she criticizes some of Professor Buitenhuis' statements and

Index to Critics Listed in the Bibliography

Al Purdy
An Annotated Bibliography

Marianne Micros

Introduction

Al Purdy has been writing poetry since the 1930s and has been an important Canadian figure since the early 1960s, at which time he became the most popular, and possibly most influential, of the poets in Canada. His first publication, *The Enchanted Echo* (1944), contains poems that are romantic, traditional, rhymed, and filled with clichés. Purdy now calls that book "crap," but it reveals the sentimental idealist that is still hidden inside the often cynical-sounding Purdy. That romantic side surfaces now and again in his later poems, and is always there beneath the realism, prompting the poet to seek the continuities that give life meaning and make love possible, continuities between past and present, Eskimo and urban white man, ancient Egyptian and modern Canadian, man and woman, man and man.

In his books of the 1950s, *Pressed on Sand*, *Emu, Remember!*, and *The Crafte So Longe to Lerne*, Purdy's mature style began to evolve. His poems were becoming looser, more natural, more conversational, more realistic, and highly original. Purdy forsook traditional poetic diction for a voice entirely his own, a voice that is unmistakeable, in spite of all its imitators. With *Poems for All the Annettes* (1962) and *The Cariboo Horses* (1965, and winner of the Governor-General's Award in 1966), Purdy found his unique style. His long, rambling "open form" is appropriate to his subjects: the ordinary man, everyday life, Purdy's home area and other parts of Canada, the presence of the past, and the disjointed quality of life. His style reflects that continuous search for truth which never leads to any fixed statement, but is always evolving and changing. Many of Purdy's poems follow the workings of the mind in its process of observation, thought, conclusion, alteration of the conclusion, new observations.

In writing about the everyday and the ordinary, and in beginning with particular objects or events and leading up to general, universal ideas, Purdy began a new movement in Canadian poetry. As he surpassed his previous work with *North of Summer* (1967), with some of the poems in *Wild Grape Wine* (1968), and with the revised versions of *Poems for All the Annettes* (1968, 1973), he became the number one poet in Canada, an idol for younger poets, and the object of interest as much for his rough, direct, and earthy personality as for his poems.

He has continued writing and publishing fine poems, often travelling in search of new subject matter, but always ending up back home in Ameliasburg, Ontario. In the 1970s, he has become more of a public poet, writing on political and social issues, satirizing modern institutions, showing the horrors of war and repressive governments, and profiling some of the world's heroes and anti-heroes. Critics find some of these poems flawed; some say Purdy is resting on his reputation, relying on his image. Although it is true that some of the poems are weak, others are superb, showing Purdy's concern for human beings, and displaying his trademark—a tone of sceptical cynicism, harsh mockery, ironic humour, but gentle hope. The poems of 1977 and 1978 show more of the sentimental side of Purdy, as he observes man's fumblings and his own inadequacies. Purdy fears that he is growing old, and feels that he is winding down his career, but he keeps writing, and there will be much to add to this bibliography. His recent book, *Being Alive* (1978), is an excellent selection of previously published poems (with minor revisions), representing the best of Purdy for the past twenty years.

In spite of the lavish praise given to Purdy by many reviewers, others have been critical of his lack of organization, sloppiness, and cacophony. But most of these so-called flaws are purposeful on Purdy's part. He is writing about life, and life is never fixed or static. As well, the poems are not as disorganized as they seem, but contain subtle organizing principles which structure, loosely, the experience about which Purdy is writing, and cause an intended effect on the reader. Sometimes Purdy begins with a seemingly inconsequential object or event, discusses it, compares it to objects and events of other times and places, raises it to the level of myth or universal significance, then slams the reader back to earth at the end of the poem. Other devices used include the ironic juxtaposition of contrasting items, and the cataloguing of rambling thoughts leading up to a final realization of a harsh or sad reality. Critics are beginning to realize that Purdy's apparent laziness and carelessness are only a pose. He has taken the care to revise his poems countless times, as is indicated in Section B of this bibliography, to work on line divisions and pauses, to find the word that is exactly right and to put it in the right place. He has made the effort to contribute poems and prose pieces to many magazines, even obscure ones, and has worked as a critic himself, writing a great number of articles and reviews. Nor is Purdy the everyday, common man that he purports to be. Although he is self-educated, his learning is vast, and he brings into his poems information on a variety of subjects.

Purdy is a popular poet for many reasons, but especially because he is dealing with the emotions, aspirations, and fears of the "little guy." Beneath the humour and roughness is always the sentiment, and between the lines written by critics is personal feeling for the poetry, no matter how learned or how casual the analysis. Many reviewers refuse to dissect these poems with which they have identified to such a degree, and prefer to speak of Purdy the man, or generally praise his works. Those who do evaluate the works usually return to the fun or the impact of the poems themselves. Other than the reviews, there has been little critical work done on Purdy, with a few exceptions: for example, the book by George Bowering, and articles by Peter Stevens and Dennis Duffy. But the tendency on the part of many to minimize Purdy's work as merely popular seems to be over, and more serious studies of the meaning and form of the poems are now being undertaken. In recent articles, review articles, and theses (see Part II), the writers look beneath the surface to find significance in Purdy's poetry.

* * *

In preparing this bibliography it was necessary to peruse,

issue by issue, a large number of periodicals. Al Purdy has published extensively in magazines, but there has previously been no complete record of these appearances in a Purdy bibliography or in a periodical index. Purdy's work has also been published in some short-lived and little-known magazines, most of which are not available at libraries.

Early books by Purdy were also difficult to find. In the 1930s he printed and bound several collections of his poetry. Many of the early published books were printed in limited editions, and several poems appeared as limited broadsheets.

Fortunately, most of the early books plus a few broadsheets are part of the special collections of the Rare Book Room of the D. B. Weldon Library at the University of Western Ontario, and librarian Beth Miller was most informative and encouraging. She also showed me a catalogue of Purdy books available from William Hoffer, a bookseller in Vancouver; Hoffer lists several broadsides, books, journals, and unpublished material.

I received valuable information from the libraries which have bought Purdy manuscripts; the largest collections are held by the University of Saskatchewan Library, and by the Douglas Library at Queen's University, Kingston, Ontario. These materials include the books bound by Purdy in the 1930s (University of Saskatchewan Library), broadsides, plays, some of the obscure journals, manuscripts of books, letters, and unpublished work. In addition, a great deal of bibliographical and editorial information was provided by my husband, J. R. (Tim) Struthers.

Of course, the person who helped me most was Al Purdy himself, who, on my visit to Ameliasburg, shared with me his personal collection of his publications and gave me information concerning forthcoming book and periodical publications.

Part I

Works by Al Purdy

A   Books (Poetry, Prose, Books Edited, Broadsides) and Manuscripts

Poetry

A1   *The Enchanted Echo*. Vancouver: Clarke and Stuart, 1944. 62 pp.

A2   *Pressed on Sand*. Toronto: Ryerson, 1955. 16 pp.

A3   *Emu, Remember!*. Fredericton: Fiddlehead Poetry Books, 1956. 16 pp.

A4   *The Crafte So Longe to Lerne*. Toronto: Ryerson, 1959. 23 pp.

A5   *The Blur in Between: Poems 1960-61*. Toronto: Emblem Books, 1962. 21 pp.
Illustrated by R. V. Rosewarne.

A6   *Poems for All the Annettes*. Toronto: Contact, 1962. 64 pp.
Toronto: House of Anansi, 1968. 101 pp.
Toronto: House of Anansi, 1973. 108 pp.

A7   *The Cariboo Horses*. Toronto: McClelland and Stewart, 1965. 112 pp.

A8   *North of Summer*. Toronto: McClelland and Stewart, 1967. 87 pp.

A9 *Wild Grape Wine*. Toronto: McClelland and Stewart, 1968. 128 pp.

A10 *Love in a Burning Building*. Toronto: McClelland and Stewart, 1970. 88 pp.

A11 *The Quest for Ouzo*. Trenton, Ont.: M. Kerrigan Almey [1971]. N. pag.

A12 *Hiroshima Poems*. Trumansburg, N.Y.: Crossing, 1972. N. pag.

A13 *Selected Poems*. Introd. George Woodcock. Toronto: McClelland and Stewart, 1972. 127 pp.

A14 *On the Bearpaw Sea*. Burnaby, B.C.: Blackfish, 1973. N. pag.
Illustrated by Jean Wong.

A15 *Sex and Death*. Toronto: McClelland and Stewart, 1973. 126 pp.

A16 *In Search of Owen Roblin*. Toronto: McClelland and Stewart, 1974. N. pag.

A17 *The Poems of Al Purdy: A New Canadian Library Selection*. Poets of Canada, No. 10. Toronto: McClelland and Stewart, 1976. 61 pp.

A18 *Sundance at Dusk*. Toronto: McClelland and Stewart, 1976. 111 pp.

A19 *A Handful of Earth*. Coatsworth, Ont.: Black Moss, 1977. 62 pp.

A20 *At Marsport Drugstore*. Sutton West, Ont.: Paget, 1977. 62 pp.

A21 *Moths in the Iron Curtain*. Cleveland: Black Rabbit, 1977. N. pag.

Sutton West, Ont.: Paget, 1979. 45 pp.
Includes photographs.

A22 *No Second Spring*. Coatsworth, Ont.: Black Moss, 1977. N. pag.

A23 *Being Alive: Poems 1958-78*. Toronto: McClelland and Stewart, 1978. 208 pp.

Prose

A24 *No Other Country*. Toronto: McClelland and Stewart, 1977. 187 pp.
Includes "Aklavik on the Mackenzie River," "Angus," "Argus in Labrador," "Bon Jour" (B423), "Cougar Hunter" (B436), "Dryland Country" (B447), "Harbour Deep" (B444), "'Her Gates Both East and West'" (B424), "Imagine a Town," "Introduction: The Cartography of Myself" (B422), "The Iron Road" (B415), "Lights on the Sea: Portraits of BC Fishermen" (B429), "Malcolm Lowry," "Norma, Eunice, and Judy" (B431), "Poets in Montreal" (B440), "Seven-League Skates: An Interview with Brian Glennie" (B437), "Streetlights on the St. Lawrence" (B433).

Books Edited

A25 ----------, ed. *The New Romans: Candid Canadian Opinions of the U.S.* Edmonton: Hurtig, 1968. 172 pp.

A26 ----------, ed. *Fifteen Winds: A Selection of Modern Canadian Poems*. Toronto: Ryerson, 1969. 157 pp.

A27 ----------, ed. *I've Tasted My Blood: Poems of Milton Acorn*. Toronto: Ryerson, 1969. 136 pp.

A28 ----------, ed. *Storm Warning: The New Canadian Poets*. Toronto: McClelland and Stewart, 1971. 152 pp.

A29 ----------, ed. *Storm Warning 2: The New Canadian*

Poets. Toronto: McClelland and Stewart, 1976. 159 pp.

A30 ----------, ed. *Wood Mountain Poems*. By Andrew Suknaski. Toronto: Macmillan, 1976. 128 pp.

Broadsides

A31 *The Old Woman and the Mayflowers*. Ottawa: Blue R [1962].

A32 *Nine Bean-rows on the Moon*. N.p.: n.p., n.d.
    The suppressed first state.

A33 *Interruption*. Willowdale, Ont.: Fiddlehead, n.d.

A34 *Spring Song*. Willowdale, Ont.: Fiddlehead, 1968.

A35 *The Winemaker's Beat-étude*. Willowdale, Ont.: Fiddlehead, 1968.

A36 *The Peaceable Kingdom*. N.p.: n.p., n.d.

A37 *Lament for Robert Kennedy*. N.p.: n.p., n.d.

A38 *The Horseman of Agawa*. N.p.: n.p., 1970.

A39 *Nine Bean-rows on the Moon*. N.p.: n.p., 22 March 1970.

A40 *Scott Hutcheson's Boat*. Prince George, B.C.: Caledonia Writing Series, 1973.

(The above broadsides are available from William Hoffer, Bookseller, 4529 W. 10th Avenue, Vancouver, B.C., V6S 2J2.)

Manuscripts

A41 Al Purdy Papers
    Douglas Library

Queen's University
Kingston, Ontario

Boxes 1-3:
Correspondence.

Boxes 4-6:
Manuscripts — poetry, fiction, book reviews, articles.

Box 7:
Miscellaneous manuscripts.

Boxes 8-9:
Manuscripts and correspondence concerning *The New Romans*.

Box 10:
Galleys, clippings, manuscripts, and correspondence concerning *The New Romans*, *North of Summer*, *Poems for All the Annettes*, and *Wild Grape Wine*.

Box 11:
Material concerning *Wild Grape Wine*, *Fifteen Winds*, and *I've Tasted My Blood*.

Box 12:
Material concerning *I've Tasted My Blood*, biographical material, Earle Birney material, poems by other authors, miscellaneous material, and Scrapbook.

Box 13:
Tape recordings.

Box 14:
Books and periodicals.

A42 Al Purdy Library Papers
    University of Saskatchewan Library
    Saskatoon, Saskatchewan

Box 1:
Manuscripts.

Box 2:
Published materials.

Box 3:
Reviews of Purdy's work.

Box 4:
Articles on Purdy.

Box 5:
Notes on the first Purdys in Canada.

Box 6:
Photographs.

Box 7:
Tape recordings of Purdy's poems.

Box 8:
Material by others.

Box 9:
Correspondence.

Box 10:
Material concerning *The Quest for Ouzo.*

Box 11:
Oversize material.

A43   University of British Columbia Library
University of British Columbia
Vancouver, British Columbia

      A manuscript of "Yehl the Raven, and other Creation Myths of the Haidas" and five letters to Doug Kaye, 1968-71.

A44   Lakehead University Library
Lakehead University
Thunder Bay, Ontario

      Manuscript for play "Point of Transfer," and drafts of several poems.

A45   Thomas Fisher Rare Book Library
University of Toronto
Toronto, Ontario

      Drafts of poems and plays; several tape recordings of Purdy's books of poems, articles, and a short story.

A46   William Hoffer, Bookseller
4529 W. 10th Avenue
Vancouver, British Columbia

      A catalogue is available from Mr. Hoffer, who sells Purdy's books and manuscripts. His collection includes books (some of them rare), broadsides (see A31-A40), anthologies, periodicals, manuscripts, and unpublished material.

A47   Al Purdy
Ameliasburg, Ontario

      This collection includes eighteen boxes of Purdy's manuscripts, as well as correspondence, proofs of books, and tapes.

Poetry

B Contributions to Periodicals and Books (Poetry, Selected Anthology Contributions, Short Stories, Articles, Reviews, Letters, Introductions), Audio Recordings, Film, and Radio and Television Plays

Note: When an item is reprinted in one of Purdy's books, this fact is noted in the entry through one of the following abbreviations:

B1 "Dramatis Personae." *Canadian Poetry Magazine*, 8, No. 2 (Dec. 1944), p. 39. *EE*.

B2 "Lay of the Last Mariner." *Canadian Poetry Magazine*, 8, No. 4 (June 1945), 27-28. *EE*.

B3 "Definition." *Canadian Poetry Magazine*, 9, No. 2 (Dec. 1945), 29.

B4 "The Hill Farm." *The Canadian Forum*, Dec. 1945, p. 207.

B5 "Dust." *Canadian Poetry Magazine*, 10, No. 1 (Sept. 1946), 29-30.

B6 "Small Boys." *The Canadian Forum*, Dec. 1947, p. 210.

B7 "Defence Counsel." *The Canadian Forum*, Aug. 1948, p. 115.

B8 "Druids." *The Canadian Forum*, Aug. 1948, p. 116.

B9 "Identity." *The Canadian Forum*, Aug. 1948, p. 116.

B10 "Reaction." *The Canadian Forum*, Aug. 1948, p. 116.

B11 "Mallards." *The Canadian Forum*, Sept. 1948, p. 140.

B12 "Night Errant." *Canadian Poetry Magazine*, 12, No. 1 (Sept. 1948), 15-16.

B13 "The Old Barn." *The Canadian Forum*, Sept. 1948, p. 140.

B14 "Abstract Plans." *The Canadian Forum*, Oct. 1948, p. 160.

B15 "Wind Bell." *Saturday Night*, 16 Oct. 1948, p. 33.

B16 "Biased Analysis." *Canadian Poetry Magazine*, 12, No. 2 (Dec. 1948), 14-15.

B17 "The Crosstown Bus." *The Canadian Forum*, Dec. 1948, p. 210.

B18 "Requiem for Whom?" *Saturday Night*, 25 Dec. 1948, p. 10.

B19 "The Bandit." *Canadian Poetry Magazine*, 12, No. 3 (March 1949), 15.

B20 "Childhood." *Canadian Poetry Magazine*, 12, No. 3 (March 1949), 17.

B21 "The Hired Man." *Canadian Poetry Magazine*, 12, No. 3 (March 1949), 17.

B22 "The Rattlesnake." *The Canadian Forum*, March 1949, p. 284.

B23 "Forgotten Music." *The Canadian Forum*, May 1949, p. 43.

B24 "Night Alarm." *The Canadian Forum*, May 1949, p. 43.

B25 "Winter Harbour." *Canadian Poetry Magazine*, 12, No. 4 (Summer 1949), 17.

B26 "Farm Grandmother." *The Canadian Forum*, Sept. 1949, p. 137.

B27 "The Blind Fiddler." *Canadian Poetry Magazine*, 13, No. 1 (Fall 1949), 21.

B28 "Living Ice." *The Canadian Forum*, Nov. 1949, p. 187.

B29 "Poem." *Canadian Poetry Magazine*, 13, No. 2 (Christmas 1949), 11.

B30 "Wood Road." *Saturday Night*, 27 Dec. 1949, p. 25.

B31 "Weddell." *Canadian Poetry Magazine*, 13, No. 3 (Spring 1950), 5-7.

B32 "Spanish Hilltop." *The Canadian Forum*, June 1950, p. 67.

B33 "Concerning Cracksmen." *The Canadian Forum*, Sept. 1950, p. 137.

B34 "Red Landscape." *The Canadian Forum*, Sept. 1950, p. 137.

B35 "Canadian." *Canadian Poetry Magazine*, 14, No. 1 (Autumn 1950), 4-5.

B36 "Mary the Allan." *Canadian Poetry Magazine*, 14, No. 1 (Autumn 1950), 6-7. *PS* (revised).

B37 "The Extroverts." *Canadian Poetry Magazine*, 14, No. 2 (Winter 1950), 26.

B38 "Overheard: 1865." *The Canadian Forum*, Jan. 1951, p. 235.

B39 "Operation Pipeline." *The Canadian Forum*, March 1951, p. 283.

B40 "Remembrance." *Canadian Poetry Magazine*, 14, No. 3 (Spring 1951), 7.

B41 "Paul Kane." *The Canadian Forum*, May 1951, p. 43.

B42 "Eighteenth Century Foot-note." *Canadian Poetry Magazine*, 14, No. 4 (Summer 1951), 10.

B43 "Joe Barr." *Canadian Poetry Magazine*, 14, No. 4 (Summer 1951), 16-17. *WGW* (revised).

B44 "Trading Post." *Canadian Poetry Magazine*, 14, No. 4 (Summer 1951), 17.

B45 "The Haymakers." *The Canadian Forum*, July 1951, p. 89.

B46 "The Baritone." *The Canadian Forum*, Aug. 1951, p. 105.

B47 "Samuel Champlain." *The Canadian Forum*, Sept. 1951, p. 125.

B48 "The Old Time." *Canadian Poetry Magazine*, 15, No. 1 (Autumn 1951), 10-11.

B49 "Poem." *The Canadian Forum*, Oct. 1951, p. 150.

B50 "Bed-Time Story." *Canadian Poetry Magazine*, 15, No. 3 (Spring 1952), 10-11.

B51 "Departure." *Canadian Poetry Magazine*, 15, No. 4 (Summer 1952), 12-13.

B52 "Epitaph." *Canadian Poetry Magazine*, 15, No. 4 (Summer 1952), 27. Rpt. in *Teangadoir*, 5, No. 3, Ser. 2 (1 March 1962), 94. Rpt. in *Canadian Author & Bookman*, 39, No. 4 (Summer 1964), 5. *PA62* (revised).

B53 "Exercise." *Canadian Poetry Magazine*, 16, No. 1 (Autumn 1952), 25.

B54 "The Gambling Man." *Canadian Poetry Magazine*, 16, No. 3 (Spring 1953), 20.

B55 "Soliloquy." *Canadian Poetry Magazine*, 16, No. 3 (Spring 1953), 23-24. *PS*.

B56 "Memorial." *The Canadian Forum*, May 1953, p. 43.

B57 "Retrospection." *The Canadian Forum*, May 1953, p. 43.

B58 "Alternately." *Canadian Poetry Magazine*, 17, No. 1 (Autumn 1953), 24.

B59 "Meander." *Canadian Poetry Magazine*, 17, No. 1 (Autumn 1953), 24-25. *PS*.

B60 "Contrivance." *The Fiddlehead*, No. 19 (Nov. 1953), p. 3. Rpt. in *The Canadian Forum*, Jan. 1955, p. 231.

B61 "Anachronism." *Canadian Poetry Magazine*, 17, No. 2 (Winter 1953-54), 34.

B62 "Autumn Preference." *Canadian Poetry Magazine*, 17, No. 2 (Winter 1953-54), 33.

B63 "Landscape." *The Fiddlehead*, No. 20 (Feb. 1954), p. 10.

B64 "For the Record." *The Canadian Forum*, April 1954, p. 17. *PS*; *PA68* (revised); *PA73*.

B65 "Indian Fisherman along the Skeena." *Canadian Poetry Magazine*, 17, No. 4 (Summer 1954), 7.

B66 "Lexicon." *Canadian Poetry Magazine*, 17, No. 4 (Summer 1954), 6.

B67 "Portrait of Sir William Cornelius Van Horne."

Canadian Poetry Magazine, 17, No. 4 (Summer 1954), 8-9.

B68 "The Pumpmaker: 1925." *Canadian Poetry Magazine*, 17, No. 4 (Summer 1954), 7-8.

B69 "As a Young Man." *The Canadian Forum*, Nov. 1954, p. 186. *PS*.

B70 "Late Arrival." *The Fiddlehead*, Nos. 23-24 (Feb. 1955), p. 11.

B71 "Spokesman for the Andeans." *The Fiddlehead*, No. 25 (May 1955), pp. 5-6.

B72 "Artist's Model." *The Canadian Forum*, July 1955, p. 87.

B73 "I See No Hand." *The Canadian Forum*, Oct. 1955, p. 164.

B74 "Parable." *The Canadian Forum*, Oct. 1955, p. 165.

B75 "Postscript." *The Fiddlehead*, No. 26 (Nov. 1955), p. 14. *ER*; *CH* (revised); *PA62* (revised); *LBB* (revised); *BA*.

B76 "Complex." *The Canadian Forum*, Jan. 1956, p. 234.

B77 "Seasonal Malady." *The Canadian Forum*, April 1956, p. 18. *PS*.

B78 "In a Far Country." *The Fiddlehead*, No. 28 (May 1956), p. 29. Rpt. in *The Fiddlehead*, No. 50 (Fall 1961), p. 48.

B79 "Aunt Cassie." *The Canadian Forum*, Jan. 1957, p. 233.

B80 "Political Meeting." *The Canadian Forum*, April 1957, p. 23.

B81 "Small Town at Night." *The Canadian Forum*, April 1957, p. 23.

B82 "Love Song." *The Canadian Forum*, June 1957, p. 65.

B83 "Word-Symbols." *The Canadian Forum*, June 1957, p. 69.

B84 "Gilgamesh and Friend." *The Canadian Forum*, July 1957, p. 86. *CLL*; *PA68* (revised); *PA73*.

B85 "Indictment." *The Canadian Forum*, Aug. 1957, p. 108. *ER*.

B86 "Lovers." *The Canadian Forum*, Aug. 1957, p. 108.

B87 "Tomatoes." *The Fiddlehead*, No. 33 (Aug. 1957), pp. 6-7.

B88 "Testament." *The Canadian Forum*, Sept. 1957, p. 134.

B89 "Vestigia." *The Canadian Forum*, Sept. 1957, p. 134. *CLL* (revised); *PA68* (revised); *PA73*; *LBB* (revised).

B90 "Wash Day Helper." *The Canadian Forum*, Sept. 1957, p. 134.

B91 "Pre-Epitaph for Love." *The Fiddlehead*, No. 34 (Fall 1957), p. 29.

B92 "Annette." *The Canadian Forum*, Oct. 1957, p. 159.

B93 "Early Winter Morning." *Delta*, No. 2 (Jan. 1958), pp. 22-23.

B94 "Incognito." *The Fiddlehead*, No. 36 (Spring 1958), p. 39.

B95 "At the Mardi Gras." *The Canadian Forum*, April 1958, p. 14.

B96   "If Birds Look In." *The Canadian Forum*, April 1958, p. 14.

B97   "Night Song for a Woman." *The Canadian Forum*, April 1958, p. 14. *BB*; *PA68* (revised); *PA73*; *LBB* (revised); *BA* (revised).

B98   "Palimpsest." *The Canadian Forum*, April 1958, p. 14. *CLL*.

B99   "Stencils." *The Canadian Forum*, April 1958, p. 14.

B100   "Where the Moment Is." *The Canadian Forum*, June 1958, p. 64. *CLL* (revised); *PA68* (revised); *PA73*; *LBB* (revised).

B101   "Incantation." *The Fiddlehead*, No. 37 (Summer 1958), pp. 24-25.

B102   "Rougeau, Oct. 30, 1955." *The Fiddlehead*, No. 38 (Fall 1958), p. 20. Rpt. in *The Fiddlehead*, No. 50 (Fall 1961), p. 49.

B103   "At Evergreen Cemetery." *The Canadian Forum*, Dec. 1958, p. 205. *CLL*; *PA68* (revised); *PA73*.

B104   "Passport." *Yes*, No. 8 (Winter 1958-59), n. pag. *CLL*.

B105   "The Death of Animals." *Yes*, No. 9 [1959?], n. pag. *BB*; *PA68* (revised); *PA73*.

B106   "Visitors." *Delta*, No. 6 (Jan. 1959), p. 23.

B107   "Canadian New Year Resolutions for 1959." *Delta*, No. 7 (April 1959), p. 2. *CLL*.

B108   "The Dutch Masters." *Delta*, No. 7 (April 1959), p. 1.

B109   "Rain Poem?" *The Canadian Forum*, April 1959, p. 10. *CLL*.

B110   "From the Chin P'ing Mei." *Combustion*, No. 10 (May 1959), p. 2. Rpt. (revised) in *The Canadian Forum*, Oct. 1959, p. 155. *CLL*; *PA68* (revised); *PA73* (revised); *LBB*; *SP*; *BA*.

B111   "Indian Reservation: Caughnawaga, 1957 (after A. M. Klein)." *Combustion*, No. 10 (May 1959), pp. 1-2.

B112   "Love Song." *Combustion*, No. 10 (May 1959), p. 1. *CLL*; *LBB*; *PA73*.

B113   "Olympic Room." *The Canadian Forum*, May 1959, p 41. *CLL*.

B114   "Personal." *Combustion*, No. 10 (May 1959), p. 2.

B115   "After the Rats." *The Canadian Forum*, June 1959, p. 60. *CLL* (revised); *PA68* (revised); *PA73*.

B116   "Old Woman." *Canadian Poetry Magazine*, 23, No. 1 (Fall 1959), 11-12.

B117   "Driftwood Logs." *The Canadian Forum*, Nov. 1959, p. 192. *CLL*.

B118   "Waiting for an Old Woman to Die." *The Canadian Forum*, Nov. 1959, p. 182. *CLL*.

B119   "Towns." *Delta*, No. 10 (Jan.-March 1960), pp. 1-2.

B120   "And We Shall Build Jerusalem." *The Canadian Forum*, April 1960, p. 13. Rpt. "And We Shall Build Jerusalem—in Montreal." In *The Human Voice*, 2, No. 3 (Aug. 1966), n. pag. *BB*.

B121   "Decree Nisi." *The Canadian Forum*, April 1960, p. 12. Rpt. in *The Human Voice*, 2, No. 3 (Aug. 1966), n. pag. *BB*; *PA68* (revised); *PA73*.

B122   "In Ellesmereland." *The Canadian Forum*, April 1960,

p. 13. Rpt. in *The Human Voice*, 2, No. 3 (Aug. 1966), n. pag. *BB* (revised).

B123 "Pause." *The Canadian Forum*, April 1960, p. 13. *BB*; *PA68* (revised); *PA73*; *BA*.

B124 "The Study of Islands." *The Canadian Forum*, April 1960, pp. 12-13.

B125 "Dimensions." *The Tamarack Review*, No. 16 (Summer 1960), p. 62.

B126 "Short History of X County." *The Tamarack Review*, No. 16 (Summer 1960), pp. 63-64. *CLL*.

B127 "How to Say What You Mean (or Vice Versa)." *Delta*, No. 12 (Sept. 1960), p. 16.

B128 "Plumbing." *The Canadian Forum*, Sept. 1960, p. 136.

B129 "Winter Walking." *The Canadian Forum*, Sept. 1960, p. 129. Rpt. in *The Human Voice*, 2, No. 3 (Aug. 1966), n. pag. *BB*; *PA68* (revised); *PA73*.

B130 "Gawd, the Eumenides." *Delta*, No. 13 (Dec. 1960), p. 22. Rpt. in *The Human Voice*, 2, No. 3 (Aug. 1966), n. pag. *BB*.

B131 "Miss Adventure." *Delta*, No. 13 (Dec. 1960), p. 26. *PA62* (revised); *PA68* (revised); *PA73*; *LBB* (revised).

B132 "A Second Look at the Teepee." *The Canadian Forum*, Jan. 1961, p. 229.

B133 "The Old Woman and the Mayflowers." *Delta*, No. 14 (March 1961), pp. 20-21. *BB*; *PA68* (revised); *PA73*; *BA*.

B134 "On Canadian Identity." *Queen's Quarterly*, 68 (Summer 1961), 314-15. *PA62* (revised).

B135 "Dudek's Crazy Theory Refuted (Or Proven Maybe)." *Delta*, No. 15 (Aug. 1961), pp. 22-23.

B136 "Eli Mandel's Sunday Morning Castle." *Delta*, No. 14 (Aug. 1961), pp. 21-22. *PA62* (revised); *PA68* (revised); *PA73*.

B137 "Mind Process Re a Faucet." *Delta*, No. 15 (Aug. 1961), pp. 23-24. *PA62* (revised); *PA68* (revised); *PA73*.

B138 "Evergreen Cemetery." *Evidence*, No. 5 (1962), pp. 42-44. *PA62* (revised); *PA68*; *PA73*; *SP* (revised); *BA*.

B139 "The Great Man." *Yes*, No. 10 (Jan. 1962), n. pag.

B140 "The Listeners." *Evidence*, No. 5 (1962), pp. 46-47. *PA62* (revised); *PA68* (revised); *PA73* (revised); *LBB* (revised).

B141 "O Recruiting Sergeants." *Evidence*, No. 5 (1962), pp. 40-41. *PA62* (revised); *PA68* (revised); *PA73*; *BA*.

B142 "Policeman." *Evidence*, No. 5 (1962), p. 45. *CH*.

B143 "Portrait." *Evidence*, No. 5 (1962), pp. 39-40. *CH* (revised).

B144 "On the Apotheosis of Miss Monroe." *Evidence*, No. 6 [1962?], pp. 77-78.

B145 "Spring Song." *Mountain*, No. 2 [1962?], n. pag. [poem no. 39]. *PA62*; *WGW* (revised); *SP* (revised); *BA* (revised).

B146 "Collecting the Square Root of Minus One." *The Canadian Forum*, Feb. 1962, p. 255. *PA62*; *PA68* (revised); *PA73*; *SP*.

B147 "For Norma in Lieu of an Orgasm." *The Canadian Forum*, Feb. 1962, p. 254. *PA62*; *PA68* (revised); *PA73*; *LBB*; *BA*.

B148 "Poem for One of the Annettes." *The Canadian Forum*, Feb. 1962, p. 254. *PA62*; *PA68*; *PA73*; *LBB*; *SP*; *BA*.

B149 "The Widower." *The Canadian Forum*, Feb. 1962, p. 254. *PA62*; *PA68*; *PA73*; *LBB* (revised).

B150 "Remains of an Indian Village." *Teangadoir*, 5, No. 3, Ser. 2 (1 March 1962), 92-94. Rpt. in *Queen's Quarterly*, 74 (Spring 1967), 70-71. *PA62*; *WGW* (revised); *PAP*; *BA*.

B151 "Biography." *The Canadian Forum*, April 1962, p. 16. Rpt. in *The Human Voice*, 2, No. 3 (Aug. 1966), n. pag. *BB*; *PA68* (revised); *PA73*.

B152 "Love Poem." *The Outsider*, 1, No. 2 (Summer 1962), 53-54.

B153 "The Machines." *The Canadian Forum*, July 1962, p. 91. *BB* ("Machines"); *CH* (revised).

B154 "Douks Disrobe as Dief Declaims." *The Sheet*, 5 (Sept. 1962), 3.

B155 "Country Snowplow." *The Bloody Horse*, 1, No. 1 (Jan. 1963), 19. *CH*.

B156 "Critique." *The Canadian Forum*, Jan. 1963, p. 240.

B157 "My Grandfather Talking—30 Years Ago." *The Canadian Forum*, Jan. 1963, p. 240. *CH*; *SP* (revised); *OR*; *PAP*; *BA*.

B158 "Pickets." *The Bloody Horse*, 1, No. 1 (Jan. 1963), 22.

B159 "Potter." *The Bloody Horse*, 1, No. 1 (Jan. 1963), 20-21. *CH*.

B160 "To an Ex-Wife." *The Bloody Horse*, 1, No. 1 (Jan. 1963), 18. *CH*; *LBB*.

B161 "The Country North of Belleville." *The Tamarack Review*, No. 27 (Spring 1963), pp. 64-66. *CH*; *SP* (revised); *PAP*; *BA*.

B162 "Indian Summer." *The Tamarack Review*, No. 27 (Spring 1963), p. 66. *PA62*; *PA68* (revised).

B163 "Necropsy of Love." *The Tamarack Review*, No. 27 (Spring 1963), p. 63. *CH*; *LBB*; *SP*.

B164 "Postscript." *The Tamarack Review*, No. 27 (Spring 1963), pp. 69-70. *ER* (revised); *CH* (revised); *PA62* (revised); *LBB* (revised); *BA*.

B165 "Transient." *The Tamarack Review*, No. 27 (Spring 1963), pp. 67-68. *CH* (revised); *SP* (revised); *PAP*; *BA* (revised).

B166 "Rural Henhouse." *Delta*, No. 21 (May 1963), pp. 24-25. *PA62* (revised); *PA68*; *PA73*.

B167 "The Gift of a Water Colour." *Amethyst*, 2, No. 4 (Summer 1963), 36.

B168 "The Old Girlfriend." *Volume 63*, No. 1 (Dec. 1963), p. 49. *CH*; *LBB* (revised).

B169 "Ballad of the Despairing Wife." *Evidence*, No. 8 [1964?], pp. 79-80. *CH*; *LBB* (revised).

B170 "The Cariboo Horses." *Evidence*, No. 8 [1964?], pp. 69-70. Rpt. in *Hobi Ahi*, May 1969, p. 1. *CH* (revised); *SP*; *PAP*; *BA*.

B171 "Homo Canadensis." *Evidence*, No. 8 [1964?], pp. 73-74. *CH* (revised).

B172 "In the Wilderness." *Evidence*, No. 8 [1964?], pp. 65-68. *CH*.

B173 "The Madwoman on the Train." *Evidence*, No. 8 [1964?], pp. 77-78. *CH* (revised).

B174 "Music on a Tombstone." *Evidence*, No. 8 [1964?], p. 76. *CH*; *LBB*.

B175 "A Power." *Evidence*, No. 8 [1964?], pp. 75-76. *CH*.

B176 "To an Attempted Suicide (at Sunnybrook Military Hospital)." *Evidence*, No. 8 [1964?], pp. 71-72. *CH* (revised).

B177 "Winter at Roblin Lake." *Evidence*, No. 8 [1964?], p. 78. Rpt. in *New American and Canadian Poetry*, No. 3 (April 1967), p. 16. *CH*; *LBB*; *SP*; *PAP*; *BA*.

B178 "Mountain Lions in Stanley Park." *The Canadian Forum*, Jan. 1964, p. 240. *CH* (revised).

B179 "Late Rising at Roblin Lake." *The Canadian Forum*, Feb. 1964, p. 255. *CH*; *SP*; *PAP*.

B180 "The Viper's Muse." *The Canadian Forum*, Feb. 1964, p. 245. *CH* (revised); *BA*.

B181 "Notes on Painting." *Delta*, No. 23 (March 1964), pp. 25-27. *CH* (revised).

B182 "Helping My Wife Get Supper." *Canadian Author & Bookman*, 39, No. 4 (Summer 1964), 5. *CH*; *LBB*; *SP*.

B183 "Method for Calling Up Ghosts." *Canadian Author & Bookman*, 39, No. 4 (Summer 1964), 4. *CH*; *BA* (revised).

B184 "Observer." *Canadian Author & Bookman*, 39, No. 4 (Summer 1964), 4. *CH* (revised).

B185 "Sunday Swim." *Canadian Author & Bookman*, 39, No. 4 (Summer 1964), 4. *CH*.

B186 "Homemade Beer." *Prism International*, 4, No. 2 (Autumn 1964), 45. *CH*; *LBB*; *SP*; *PAP*; *BA*.

B187 "Lu Yu (A.D. 1125-1209)." *The Tamarack Review*, No. 33 (Autumn 1964), p. 12. Rpt. in *New American and Canadian Poetry*, No. 3 (April 1967), p. 16. *CH*.

B188 "Malcolm Lowry." *The Tamarack Review*, No. 33 (Autumn 1964), pp. 18-19. *CH*.

B189 "Old Alex." *The Tamarack Review*, No. 33 (Autumn 1964), pp. 12-13. *CH*; *SP* (revised); *PAP*; *BA*.

B190 "Percy Lawson." *The Tamarack Review*, No. 33 (Autumn 1964), pp. 16-17. *CH*; *SP*; *PAP*.

B191 "Roblin Mills." *The Tamarack Review*, No. 33 (Autumn 1964), p. 11.

B192 "Snow at Roblin Lake." *The Tamarack Review*, No. 33 (Autumn 1964), p. 10. *CH*.

B193 "A Very Light Sort of Blue Faded from Washing?" *The Tamarack Review*, No. 33 (Autumn 1964), pp. 14-15. *CH* (revised).

B194 "Wilderness Gothic." *Prism International*, 4, No. 2 (Autumn 1964), 44. *WGW*; *SP*; *PAP*; *BA*.

B195 "Night Woman." *Canadian Poetry Magazine*, 28, No. 1 (Nov. 1964), 4-5.

B196 "Roblin's Mills: Circa 1842." *Canadian Poetry Magazine*, 28, No. 1 (Nov. 1964), 3-4. Rpt. "Roblin Mills Circa 1842." In *Hiram Poetry Review*, No. 3 (Fall-Winter 1967), pp. 24-27. *WGW*; *SP* (revised— "Roblin's Mills (2)"); *OR*; *BA*.

B197 "Beaudoin (1960)." *Island*, Ser. 2, 8, No. 2 (17 Dec. 1964), 45. *WGW* (revised).

B198 "Complaint Lodged with L.C.B.O. by a Citizen in Upper Rumbelow." *Island*, Ser. 2, 8, No. 2 (17 Dec. 1964), 44. *CH*; *SP* (revised) *PAP*; *BA* (revised).

B199 "Hunting Season." *Island*, Ser. 2, 8, No. 2 (17 Dec. 1964), 48. *WGW* (revised).

B200 "What It Was." *Island*, Ser. 2, 8, No. 2 (17 Dec. 1964), 46-47. *CH* (revised); *BA* (revised).

B201 "Fidel Castro in Revolutionary Square." *The Canadian Forum*, Jan. 1965, pp. 229-30. *CH*; *SP* (revised); *PAP*; *BA*.

B202 "Shoeshine Boys on the Avenida Juarez." *The Canadian Forum*, Jan. 1965, p. 229. *WGW* (revised); *BA*.

B203 "Thank God I'm Normal." *The Canadian Forum*, Jan. 1965, p. 230. *CH*.

B204 "The Wine-maker's Beat-étude." *The Canadian Forum*, Jan. 1965, p. 230. Rpt. "The Wine-maker's Beat-Étude." In *New American and Canadian Poetry*, No. 1 (Sept. 1966), pp. 26-27. Broadside. *WGW*; *SP*; *PAP*; *BA*.

B205 "Cronos at the Quinte Hotel." *Quarry*, 14 (March 1965), 9-10. *CH* (revised).

B206 "Death of John F. Kennedy." *Quarry*, 14 (March 1965), 6-8. *CH* (revised); *SP* (revised).

B207 "The Beach at Veradero." *Volume 63*, No. 3 (Summer 1965), p. 4. Rpt. in *Evidence*, No. 10 [1967?], p. 77. *WGW*.

B208 "Hockey Players." *Volume 63*, No. 3 (Summer 1965), pp. 7-8. *CH*; *SP* (revised); *BA*.

B209 "John." *Volume 63*, No. 3 (Summer 1965), p. 5. *CH*.

B210 "Old Settler's Song." *Volume 63*, No. 3 (Summer 1965), p. 6. Rpt. in *Hobi Ahi*, May 1969, p. 1. *CH*.

B211 "I Think It Was Wednesday." *Poet*, 6, No. 4 (July-Aug. 1965), 14-17. *CH*.

B212 "Death of a Young Poet." *Ole*, No. 3 (Nov. 1965), n. pag. *WGW* (revised).

B213 "Mr. Greenhalgh's Love Poem." *Delta*, No. 25 (Nov. 1965), pp. 28-29. *PA68* (revised); *PA73*; *LBB* (revised).

B214 "Dylan." *Queen's Quarterly*, 72 (Winter 1965-66), 647. Rpt. in *Kayak*, No. 16 (1968), p. 65. *WGW*; *SP* (revised).

B215 "Skeleton by an Old Cedar." *Queen's Quarterly*, 72 (Winter 1965-66), 648. *WGW* (revised); *BA*.

B216 "The Moment Passed." *Canadian Poetry Magazine*, 29, Nos. 1 and 2 (Feb. 1966), 5.

B217 "Moose Calf of the Chilcotin." *Canadian Poetry Magazine*, 29, Nos. 1 and 2 (Feb. 1966), 6.

B218 "Return to the City." *Canadian Poetry Magazine*, 29, Nos. 1 and 2 (Feb. 1966), 6-7.

B219 "At the Movies." *The Tamarack Review*, No. 39 (Spring 1966), pp. 42-43. Rpt. in *Canadian Poetry Magazine*, 30, No. 4 (Aug. 1967), 65-66. *NS* (revised); *SP* (revised).

B220 "The Country of the Young." *The Tamarack Review*, No. 39 (Spring 1966), pp. 48-49. *NS*; *SP*; *PAP*; *BA*.

B221 "Dead Seal." *The Tamarack Review*, No. 39 (Spring 1966), pp. 40-41. *NS*.

B222 "Metrics." *The Tamarack Review*, No. 39 (Spring 1966), pp. 43-45. Rpt. in *Northern*, 4, No. 1 (Feb. 1967), 65-67. *NS* (revised).

B223 "The Northwest Passage." *The Tamarack Review*, No. 39 (Spring 1966), pp. 46-47. Rpt. in *North*, Jan.-Feb. 1968, pp. 25-27. *NS*.

B224 "Prelude." *The Tamarack Review*, No. 39 (Spring 1966), p. 39. *NS*.

B225 "When I Sat Down to Play the Piano." *The Tamarack Review*, No. 39 (Spring 1966), pp. 49-51. *NS*; *SP* (revised); *PAP*; *BA*.

B226 "Shopping at Loblaws." *Ole*, No. 4 (May 1966), n. pag. *WGW* (revised); *LBB* (revised); *BA* (revised).

B227 "Aspects." *Prism International*, 6, No. 1 (Summer 1966), 79. *NS*.

B228 "Eskimo Hunter." *Prism International*, 6, No. 1 (Summer 1966), 76. *NS*.

B229 "Odysseus in Kikastan." In "North of Summer: Arctic Poems and Prose." *Beaver*, Summer 1966, p. 23. *NS*.

B230 "The Sculptors." *Prism International*, 6, No. 1 (Summer 1966), 77-78. *NS* (revised); *SP*; *PAP*; *BA*.

B231 "Track Meet at Pangnirtung." *Prism International*, 6, No. 1 (Summer 1966), 74-75. *NS*.

B232 "The Turning Point." In "North of Summer: Arctic Poems and Prose." *Beaver*, Summer 1966, p. 19. *NS* (revised); *SP* (revised).

B233 "Two Hunters." In "North of Summer: Arctic Poems and Prose." *Beaver*, Summer 1966, p. 25. *NS*.

B234 "What Do the Birds Think?" In "North of Summer: Arctic Poems and Prose." *Beaver*, Summer 1966, p. 27. *NS*; *SP*; *BA* (revised).

B235 "St. Francis in Ameliasburg." *Intercourse*, No. 3 (Midsummer 1966), p. 3. *WGW*.

B236 "About Being a Member of Our Armed Forces." *The Canadian Forum*, July 1966, p. 80. Rpt. in *The Hiram Poetry Review*, No. 1 (Fall-Winter 1966), p. 29. Rpt. in *Canadian Poetry Magazine*, 30, No. 4 (Aug. 1967), 68. *WGW* (revised); *SP*; *PAP*; *BA*.

B237 "Dominion Day." *The Canadian Forum*, July 1966, p. 80. *WGW* (revised).

B238 "Pedestrian in Trenton, Ont." *Ole*, No. 6 (July 1966), n. pag. Rpt. in *Blewointment*, Occupation Issue (1977-78), n. pag. *HE* (revised).

B239 "Sergeant Jackson." *The Canadian Forum*, July 1966, p. 80. Rpt. in *Intercourse*, Oct. 1968, pp. 11-12. *WGW*; *SP* (revised).

B240 "William Lyon MacKenzie." *The Canadian Forum*, July 1966, p. 80. *WGW* (revised).

B241 "The Blur in Between." *The Human Voice*, 2, No. 3 (Aug. 1966), n. pag. *BB*.

B242 "Hazelton, B.C." *The Human Voice*, 2, No. 3 (Aug. 1966), n. pag. *BB*.

B243 "Autumn." *The Tamarack Review*, No. 41 (Autumn 1966), pp. 127-28. *WGW*; *BA*.

B244 "Boundaries." *The Tamarack Review*, No. 41 (Autumn 1966), pp. 134-35. *WGW*; *SP* (revised); *BA*.

B245 "Dark Landscape: Roblin Lake." *The Tamarack*

Review, No. 41 (Autumn 1966), pp. 128-30. Rpt. "Dark Landscape." In *Ole*, No. 8 (April 1967), n. pag. *WGW* (revised); *LBB* (revised); *SP* (revised); *BA*.

B246 "The Drunk Tank." *The Tamarack Review*, No. 41 (Autumn 1966), pp. 132-34. *WGW*; *SP*; *PAP*; *BA*.

B247 "My '48 Pontiac." *The Tamarack Review*, No. 41 (Autumn 1966), pp. 130-32. *WGW* (revised); *SP* (revised); *PAP*; *BA*.

B248 "South." *Delta*, No. 26 (Oct. 1966), pp. 13-15. *NS*.

B249 "Watching Trains." *The Hiram Poetry Review*, No. 1 (Fall-Winter 1966), pp. 27-28. Rpt. in *Poetry Australia*, 3, No. 16 (1967), 26-27. *WGW*; *SP* (revised); *BA*.

B250 "Arctic River." *Evidence*, No. 10 [1967?], pp. 70-71. *NS* (revised).

B251 "Canadian." *Evidence*, No. 10 [1967?], p. 73. *WGW* (revised).

B252 "Hemingway's Villa in Cuba." *Evidence*, No. 10 [1967?], p. 80.

B253 "House Pride." *Evidence*, No. 10 [1967?], p. 72.

B254 "I Guess a Poem." *Evidence*, No. 10 [1967?], pp. 74-75. *WGW* (revised).

B255 "Innuit." *Evidence*, No. 10 [1967?], p. 68. Rpt. in *The Small Pond*, Winter 1968, p. 3. *NS*.

B256 "The Liars." *Evidence*, No. 10 [1967?], pp. 78-79.

B257 "Love Poem for My Wife." *Evidence*, No. 10 [1967?], pp. 75-76. *WGW* (revised); *LBB* (revised).

B258 "Tent Rings." *Evidence*, No. 10 [1967?], pp. 69-70. Rpt. in *Arts/Canada*, 28, No. 6 (Dec. 1971-Jan. 1972), 84. *NS*.

B259 "Return from Kikastan." *Adam International Review*, Nos. 313-314-315 (1967), pp. 45-46. *WGW*.

B260 "Washday." *Evidence*, No. 10 [1967?], pp. 66-67. *NS* (revised); *SP* (revised).

B261 "U.E. Loyalist Graveyard at Saint John." *Saturday Night*, Jan. 1967, p. 46.

B262 "Over the Hills." *Saturday Night*, Feb. 1967, p. 23. *WGW* (revised); *LBB* (revised); *SP* (revised); *PAP*; *BA*.

B263 "Elegy for a Grandfather." *Queen's Quarterly*, 74, No. 1 (Spring 1967), 72-73. *ER* (revised); *WGW* (revised); *OR* (revised); *BA* (same as *WGW*).

B264 "Louisbourg Fortress." *Queen's Quarterly*, 74, No. 1 (Spring 1967) 74. *WGW* (revised).

B265 "Interruption." *The Canadian Forum*, June 1967, p. 54. Broadside. *WGW* (revised); *SP* (revised); *PAP*; *BA*.

B266 "Nothing Is Changed." *Talon*, 4, No. 3 (June 1967), 22.

B267 "The Road to Newfoundland." *The Canadian Forum*, June 1967, p. 54. *WGW*; *SP* (revised); *BA*.

B268 "My Grandfather's Country." *The Canadian Forum*, June 1967, p. 65. *WGW* (revised); *SP* (revised); *PAP*; *BA* (revised).

B269 "Ameliasburg Stew." *Hiram Poetry Review*, No. 3 (Fall-Winter 1967), pp. 24-27. *WGW*.

B270 "Arctic Rhododendrons." *Canadian Literature*, No. 31

(Winter 1967), p. 73. Rpt. in *Hobi Ahi*, May 1969, p. 2. *NS* (revised); *SP* (revised); *PAP*; *BA*.

B271 "Dream of Havana." *Kayak*, No. 16 (1968), p. 55. Rpt. "Dream of Havana 1964." In *Hiram Poetry Review*, No. 3 (Fall-Winter 1967), pp. 24-27. *WGW*; *SP* (revised).

B272 "Attempt." *Talon*, 4, No. 4 (Jan. 1968), 21. *WGW*; *BA*.

B273 "On the Avenida Juarez." *Talon*, 4, No. 4 (Jan. 1968), 21. *WGW*.

B274 "Lament for the Dorsets." *Northian*, Feb. 1968, p. 36. Rpt. in *Arts/Canada*, 28, No. 6 (Dec. 1971-Jan. 1972), 30-31. *WGW*; *SP* (revised); *PAP*; *BA*.

B275 "Further Development Saith Not." *Quarry*, 17, No. 3 (Spring 1968), 12-13. *WGW* (revised); *SP* (revised); *BA*.

B276 "News Reports at Ameliasburg." *Edge*, No. 8 (Fall 1968), pp. 49-50. *PA68* (revised); *PA73*; *PAP* (revised); *BA*.

B277 "Roblin Lake." *Edge*, No. 8 (Fall 1968), pp. 50-51.

B278 "The Jackhammer Syndrome." *The Canadian Forum*, Oct. 1968, p. 155. Rpt. in *The Outsider*, 2, Nos. 4-5 (Winter 1968-69), 140-41. *QO*; *S&D* (revised); *BA* (revised).

B279 "Married Man's Song." *The Canadian Forum*, Oct. 1968, p. 154. *LBB* (revised); *SP* (revised); *BA*.

B280 "Pandora at Roblin Lake." *The Canadian Forum*, Oct. 1968, p. 154.

B281 "Detail." *Quarry*, 17, No. 2 (Winter 1968), 3. *WGW*; *BA*.

B282 "From a Window." *Quarry*, 17, No. 2 (Winter 1968), 5-6.

B283 "House Guest." *Quarry*, 17, No. 2 (Winter 1968), 4-5. *PS* (revised); *PA68* (revised); *PA73*; *SP*; *PAP*; *BA*.

B284 "The New Romans." *Canadian Dimension*, 5, No. 7 (Dec. 1968-Jan. 1969), 14.

B285 "All of Us." *The Tamarack Review*, No. 52 (1969), pp. 41-43. *QO*.

B286 "At the Athenian Market." *The Tamarack Review*, No. 52 (1969), pp. 36-37. *QO*; *S&D* (revised); *BA* (revised).

B287 "Hellas Express." *The Tamarack Review*, No. 52 (1969), pp. 38-39. *QO*; *S&D* (revised).

B288 "Letters of Marque." *The Tamarack Review*, No. 52 (1969), pp. 39-41.

B289 "Poem." *The Tamarack Review*, No. 52 (1969), p. 35. *QO*; *LBB*; *SP*.

B290 "Johnston's on St. Germain." *Inner Space*, Spring 1969, n. pag.

B291 "Girl." *Hobi Ahi*, May 1969, p. 1.

B292 "Listening." *Hobi Ahi*, May 1969, p. 2. *NS*.

B293 "The Time of Your Life." *Canadian Literature*, No. 41 (Summer 1969), pp. 62-65. *S&D* (revised).
Includes information about the revision of this poem.

B294 "Nine Bean Rows on the Moon." *Maclean's*, Aug. 1969, p. 8. *QO*; *LBB* (revised).

B295 "Bored with Ruins." *Quarry*, 19, No. 1 (Fall 1969), 25-27. *QO*.

B296 "Ephesus." *Quarry*, 19, No. 1 (Fall 1969), 27-28. *QO*; *S&D* (revised).

B297 "The Pope's 1968 Encyclical." *Quarry*, 19, No. 1 (Fall 1969), 22-23. *QO*; *S&D* (revised).

B298 "St. Paul to the Corinthians." *Quarry*, 19, No. 1 (Fall 1969), 23. *QO*.

B299 "Street Scene." *Quarry*, 19, No. 1 (Fall 1969), 23-24. *QO*; *S&D* (revised).

B300 "Dog with Fleas." *Wascana Review*, 5, No. 1 (1970), 28-29.

B301 "Flight 17 Eastbound." *Wascana Review*, 5, No. 1 (1970), 29-30.

B302 "The Beavers of Renfrew." *The Canadian Forum*, April-May 1970, p. 7. *S&D* (revised); *BA* (revised).

B303 "Indian Rock Painting under the Cliffs of Lake Superior." *Globe Magazine*, 25 July 1970, pp. 10-11.

B304 "Poem Worth Fifty Bucks." *The Canadian Forum*, Oct. 1970, p. 248.

B305 "Floating Down the North Saskatchewan River." *Black Moss*, No. 5 (1971), n. pag.

B306 "The Peaceable Kingdom." *The Canadian Forum*, Jan. 1971, p. 358. *S&D*.

B307 "FLQ Kidnapping." *The Tamarack Review*, No. 56 (First Quarter 1971), p. 32. *S&D*.

B308 "A Graceful Little Verse." *The Tamarack Review*, No. 56 (First Quarter 1971), p. 30. *S&D* (revised); *BA*.

B309 "Ten Thousand Bromos." *The Tamarack Review*, No. 56 (First Quarter 1971), p. 31.

B310 "This Is How." *The Tamarack Review*, No. 56 (First Quarter 1971), p. 33.

B311 "Tourist Itinerary." *The Tamarack Review*, No. 56 (First Quarter 1971), p. 34. *S&D* (revised).

B312 "Along the Ionian Coast." *Blackfish*, No. 1 (Spring 1971), pp. 38-40.
With excerpts from a letter describing the location.

B313 "Literary Feuds in Montreal." *Saturday Night*, July 1971, p. 33. *S&D* (revised).

B314 "Atomic Museum." *Saturday Night*, Aug. 1971, pp. 21-22. *HP*; *S&D* (revised).

B315 "Buddhist Bell." *Saturday Night*, Aug. 1971, p. 18. *HP*; *S&D* (revised); *BA*.

B316 "In Peace Memorial Park." *Saturday Night*, Aug. 1971, pp. 20-21. *HP*; *S&D* (revised).

B317 "One Thousand Cranes." *Saturday Night*, Aug. 1971, p. 20. *HP*; *S&D*.

B318 "Survivors." *Saturday Night*, Aug. 1971, pp. 18-19. *HP*; *S&D*.

B319 "Whose Mother?" *Saturday Night*, Aug. 1971, pp. 19-20. *HP*; *S&D*.

B320 "Picture Layout in *Life* Magazine (May 8, 1970)." *Saturday Night*, Sept. 1971, p. 10. *S&D*.

B321 "Hands." *Books in Canada*, Nov. 1971, p. 24. *S&D*.

B322 "Arctic Romance." *Arts/Canada*, 28, No. 6 (Dec. 1971-Jan. 1972), 68. *S&D*.

B323 "Observing Persons." *Chatelaine*, Jan. 1972, p. 48. *S&D* (revised).

B324 "A Charm." *The Canadian Forum*, Jan.-Feb. 1972, p. 25.

B325 "8.50 a.m." *The Canadian Forum*, Jan.-Feb. 1972, p. 25. *S&D* (revised).

B326 "For Her in Sunlight." *The Canadian Forum*, Jan.-Feb. 1972, p. 25. *S&D* (revised).

B327 "Power Failure in Disneyland." *The Canadian Forum*, Jan.-Feb. 1972, p. 23. *S&D* (revised); *BA*.

B328 "Remembering Hiroshima." *The Canadian Forum*, Jan.-Feb. 1972, p. 24. *HP*; *S&D* (revised); *BA*.

B329 "Vera Cruz Hotel." *The Canadian Forum*, Jan.-Feb. 1972, p. 22.

B330 "R.C.M.P. Post." *Saturday Night*, May 1972, p. 45. *S&D*; *BA*.

B331 "The Scream." *Unmuzzled Ox*, 1, No. 3 (Summer 1972), 51-52. *PA73*.

B332 "Egotism." *Waves*, 1, No. 2 (Autumn 1972), 11.

B333 "On the Bearpaw Sea." *Waves*, 1, No. 2 (Autumn 1972), 22. *BPS*.

B334 "Iguana." *The Canadian Forum*, Sept. 1972, p. 15. *S&D* (revised).

B335 "'Old Man Mad about Painting.'" *The Canadian Forum*, Sept. 1972, p. 19. Rpt. in *New:*, Nos. 22-23 (Fall-Winter 1973-74), p. 5. *S&D* (revised); *BA*.

B336 "Portrait of Herman and...." *The Canadian Forum*, Oct.-Nov. 1972, pp. 16-17. *S&D* (revised).

B337 "Interview." *Queen's Quarterly*, 79 (Winter 1972), 470-71. *PA73*.

B338 "On Being a Love-Object." *Queen's Quarterly*, 79 (Winter 1972), 471-72. Rpt. in *Mag-5* (1973), pp. 25-26. *S&D*.

B339 "Beat Joe McLeod Off Triangle Island." *Blackfish*, Nos. 4 and 5 (Winter-Spring 1972-73), n. pag. *S&D* (revised).

B340 "You As Me and I As Her." *Mag-5* (1973), p. 26.

B341 "Some Mountains near Banff." *Saturday Night*, June 1973, p. 46. *S&D* (revised).

B342 "Chronos at Quintana Roo." *Ariel*, 4, No. 3 (July 1973), 40-41. *S&D*; *BA*.

B343 "Lampman in Heat." *Ariel*, 4, No. 3 (July 1973), 42. *S&D*.

B344 "The Listening Child (Jacques & Susanne Lanctot in Cuba)." *Saturday Night*, Aug. 1973, p. 5. *S&D*.

B345 "Melodrama." *Queen's Quarterly*, 80, No. 3 (Autumn 1973), 408-09. Rpt. in *New:*, Nos. 22-23 (Fall-Winter 1973-74), pp. 11-12. *S&D*.

B346 "Siswe Bansi is Dead." *Queen's Quarterly*, 80, No. 3 (Autumn 1973), 405-08. *S&D*.

B347 "Dead March for Sergeant MacLeod." *Saturday Night*, Sept. 1973, p. 43. *S&D*.

B348 "Depression in Namu, B.C." *New:*, Nos. 22-23 (Fall-Winter 1973-74), p. 10. *S&D*; *BA*.

B349 "Flat Tire in the Desert." *New:*, Nos. 22-23 (Fall-Winter 1973-74), pp. 6-7. *S&D.*

B350 "For Her in Sunlight." *New:*, Nos. 22-23 (Fall-Winter 1973-74), pp. 12-13. *S&D.*

B351 "Hallucinations of a Tourist." *New:*, Nos. 22-23 (Fall-Winter 1973-74), p. 7. *QO; S&D.*

B352 "Temporizing in the Eternal City." *New:*, Nos. 22-23 (Fall-Winter 1973-74), pp. 8-10. *S&D; BA* (revised).

B353 "Uncertainties." *Waves*, 2, No. 3 (1974), 11. Rpt. in *CrossCountry*, Nos. 8-9 (1977), pp. 42-43. *S&D* (revised); *SatD; AMD; BA.*

B354 "Scott Hutcheson's Boat." *Jewish Di'al-og* (Hanukah 1974), p. 17. *PA73* (revised).

B355 "Snapshot from Baffin Island." *Jewish Di'al-og* (Hanukah 1974), p. 47. *SatD* (revised).

B356 "Watergate at Floodtide." *Jewish Di'al-og* (Hanukah 1974), p. 52.

B357 "Murder of D'Arcy McGee." *Queen's Quarterly*, 82, No. 1 (Spring 1975), 74-75. *SatD* (revised).

B358 "Night Summer." *Queen's Quarterly*, 82, No. 1 (Spring 1975), 76. *SatD.*

B359 "Stopping Here." *Canadian Literature*, No. 64 (Spring 1975), p. 74. *SatD* (revised).

B360 "Excess of Having." *The Allegheny Star Route*, March 1975, n. pag. *S&D; BA.*

B361 "Rodeo." *Saturday Night*, June 1975, p. 12. *SatD; BA.*

B362 "Kerameikos Cemetery." *Canadian Literature*, No. 63 (Winter 1975), p. 51. *SatD.*

B363 "Trees at the Arctic Circle." *The Canadian Log House*, No. 2 (Spring 1976), p. 71. *NS; SP; PAP; BA.*

B364 "'I Am Searching for You.'" *The Canadian Forum*, April 1976, p. 33. *SatD* (revised).

B365 "Artifact." *The Canadian Forum*, April 1976, p. 32. *SatD* (revised).

B366 "Imagine the Andes." *The Canadian Forum*, April 1976, p. 34. *SatD* (revised).

B367 "Plaza de la Inquisicion." *The Canadian Forum*, April 1976, p. 34.

B368 "Transvestite." *The Canadian Forum*, April 1976, p. 34. *SatD* (revised).

B369 "Turkish Delight." *The Canadian Forum*, April 1976, p. 33. *SatD* (revised).

B370 "Ulysses Alone." *The Canadian Forum*, April 1976, p. 34.

B371 "Alive or Not." *Saturday Night*, May 1976, p. 81. *SatD; BA.*

B372 "Homage to Ree-shard." *The Canadian Forum*, Dec.-Jan. 1976-77, p. 27. *SatD* (revised).

B373 "Deprivations." *The Malahat Review*, No. 41 (Jan. 1977), pp. 100-01. *SatD; BA.*

B374 "Postscript to E. B. B." *Waves*, 5, Nos. 2-3 (Spring 1977), 75-76. *HE* (revised).

B375 "Fiddleheads." *Montreal Poems*, No. 3 (April 1977), pp. 5-6.

B376 "A Handful of Earth: To Rene Levesque." *The Canadian Forum*, April 1977, p. 27. Rpt. in *The Globe and Mail*, 26 Nov. 1977, p. 10. *HE*; *BA* (revised).

B377 "Llama." *Montreal Poems*, No. 3 (April 1977), pp. 3-5.

B378 "Ave Imperator." *Canadian Literature*, No. 73 (Summer 1977), p. 86. *HE* (revised).

B379 "No Second Spring." *The Canadian Forum*, Oct. 1977, p. 40. *NSS* (revised).

B380 "On the Altiplano." *Queen's Quarterly*, 84, No. 2 (Summer 1977), 229-30. *HE*.

B381 "Running." *Queen's Quarterly*, 84, No. 2 (Summer 1977), 228-29. *HE* (revised).

B382 "Starlings." *Queen's Quarterly*, 84, No. 2 (Summer 1977), 227-28. *HE*; *BA*.

B383 "On Realizing He Has Written Some Bad Poems." *Saturday Night*, Nov. 1977, p. 14. *BA*.

B384 "Bankruptcy Proceedings." *Blewointment*, Occupation Issue (1977-78), n. pag. *HE*.

B385 "Encounter in the Lobby." *Blewointment*, Occupation Issue (1977-78), n. pag. *HE*.

B386 "Funeral." *Blewointment*, Occupation Issue (1977-78), n. pag. *HE*.

B387 "I Guessa Kinda Love Poem." *Blewointment*, Occupation Issue (1977-78), n. pag.

B388 "President Nixon in Cambodia." *Blewointment*, Occupation Issue (1977-78), n. pag.

B389 "Doggerel of the Little Dog-Soul." *Mountain*, No. 3, n.d., n. pag. Poem no. 96.

B390 "Warning." *Mountain*, No. 3, n.d., n. pag. Poem no. 119.

B391 "A. Reigo." *Canadian Literature*, No. 79 (Winter 1978), pp. 127-31.

B392 "Writer-in-Rez." In *Aurora: New Canadian Writing 1978*. Ed. Morris Wolfe. Toronto: Doubleday, 1978, pp. 53-56.

B393 "Angus Unlimited." *Queen's Quarterly*, 85, No. 3 (Autumn 1978), 454-55.

B394 "Obit for Angus." *Queen's Quarterly*, 85, No. 3 (Autumn 1978), 453.

B395 "Mexico: Four Poems." *Queen's Quarterly*, 86, No. 3 (Autumn 1979), 420-24.

B396 "Spinning: For Colleen Thibaudeau." *Brick: A Journal of Reviews*, No. 7 (Fall 1979), back cover.

B397 "Ballad of the Arctic." *Beaver* (Winter 1979), p. 52.

B398 "There Is a Strength...." *The Canadian Forum*, April 1980, pp. 46-47.

Selected Anthology Contributions

B399 "At Roblin Lake," "On the Decipherment of Linear B." In *Recent Canadian Verse*. Ed. Milton Wilson. Kingston: Queen's Quarterly Publication, 1959, pp. 24-26.

B400 "Courtier's Soliloquy," "Dudek's Crazy Theory Refuted (Or Proven Maybe)," "Eli Mandel's Sunday Morning Castle," "Mind Process Re a Faucet," "Sires and

Opposites." In *Poetry 62*. Ed. Eli Mandel and Jean-Guy Pilon. Toronto: Ryerson, 1961, pp. 16-27.

B401 "Dead Seal," "Evergreen Cemetery," "What Do the Birds Think?", "Wilderness Gothic," "The Winemaker's Beat-Etude." In *Modern Canadian Verse*. Ed. A. J. M. Smith. Toronto: Oxford Univ. Press, 1967, pp. 228-36.

B402 "Arctic Rhododendrons," "The Beavers of Renfrew," "The Cariboo Horses," "Detail," "Eskimo Graveyard," "Interruption," "Lament for the Dorsets," "The Runners," "Song of the Impermanent Husband," "Transient." In *15 Canadian Poets*. Ed. Gary Geddes and Phyllis Bruce. Toronto: Oxford Univ. Press, 1970, pp. 28-42.

B403 "The Cariboo Horses," "Inuit," "Lament for the Dorsets," "Mountain Lions in Stanley Park," "Transient," "Trees at the Arctic Circle," "Wilderness Gothic." In *Five Modern Canadian Poets*. Ed. Eli Mandel. Toronto: Holt, Rinehart and Winston, 1970, pp. 39-53.

B404 "After the Rats," "Beothuk Indian Skeleton," "The Country North of Belleville," "Detail," "Elegy for a Grandfather," "Gilgamesh and Friend," "Home-Made Beer," "Innuit," "Interruption," "Lament for the Dorsets," "The Listeners," "Mice in the House," "Mountain Lions in Stanley Park," "Necropsy of Love," "On the Decipherment of Linear B," "Remains of an Indian Village," "To an Attempted Suicide," "Trees at the Arctic Circle," "Wilderness Gothic." In *Poets of Contemporary Canada, 1960-70*. Ed. Eli Mandel. Toronto: McClelland and Stewart, 1972, pp. 1-22.

B405 "The Cariboo Horses," "The Country North of Belleville," "Hockey Players," "Innuit," "Lament for the Dorsets," "Mind Process Re a Faucet," "Wilderness Gothic." In *The Evolution of Canadian Literature in English 1945-1970*. Ed. Paul Denham. Toronto: Holt, Rinehart and Winston, 1973, pp. 110-21.

B406 "Dead Seal," "Girl." In *The Norton Anthology of Modern Poetry*. Ed. Richard Ellmann and Robert O'Clair. New York: Norton, 1973, pp. 959-62.

B407 "The Cariboo Horses," "The Country North of Belleville," "Lament for the Dorsets," "Wilderness Gothic." In *The Oxford Anthology of Canadian Literature*. Ed. Robert Weaver and William Toye. Toronto: Oxford Univ. Press, 1973, pp. 402-08.

B408 "Arctic Rhododendrons," "The Cariboo Horses," "Country Snowplow," "Elegy for a Grandfather," "Elegy for a Grandfather" (revised), "Innuit," "Lament for the Dorsets," "Wilderness Gothic." In *Canadian Anthology*. Ed. Carl F. Klinck and Reginald E. Watters. 3rd ed. Toronto: Gage, 1974, pp. 457-65.

B409 "Arctic Rhododendrons," "The Cariboo Horses," "The Country North of Belleville," "Depression in Namu, B.C.," "Percy Lawson," "Poem," "Poem for One of the Annettes," "Roblin's Mills (2)," "Tourist Itinerary." In *Canadian Poetry: The Modern Era*. Ed. John Newlove. Toronto: McClelland and Stewart, 1977, pp. 200-13.

B410 "Borderlands," "The Cariboo Horses," "The Country North of Belleville," "Elegy for a Grandfather," "Freydis Eriksdottir in Greenland," "Inside the Mill," "Necropsy of Love," "Roblin's Mills," "Tourist Itinerary," "Trees at the Arctic Circle," "Wilderness Gothic." In *Literature in Canada*. Ed. Douglas Daymond and Leslie Monkman. Vol. II. Toronto: Gage, 1978, pp. 361-74.

Short Stories

B411 "The Undertaker." *The Canadian Forum*, Oct. 1963, pp. 156-59.

B412 "My Friend Julio." *The Tamarack Review*, No. 33 (Autumn 1964), pp. 40-48.

Articles

B413 "Moccasins to Oxfords: Toronto." *Habitat*, 10, Nos. 3-6, n.d., pp. 77-81.

B414 "Dormez-vous? A Memoir of Malcolm Lowry." *Canada Month*, Sept. 1962, pp. 24-26.

B415 "The Iron Road." *Canada Month*, July 1963, pp. 23-24. *NOC* (revised).

B416 "An Old Man's Memories of Indian Days." *Canada Month*, Sept. 1963, p. 11.

B417 "Leonard Cohen: A Personal Look." *Canadian Literature*, No. 23 (Winter 1965), pp. 7-16.

B418 "Canadian Poetry in English Since 1867." *Journal of Commonwealth Literature*, No. 3 (July 1967), pp. 19-33.

B419 "Purdy at 25." *Intercourse*, No. 9 (Oct. 1968), pp. 9-11.

B420 "Canfor's Lit. Section: Of Yesterday and the Day Before." *The Canadian Forum*, April-May 1970, pp. 47-48.

B421 "Why I Won't Let a U.S. Branch Plant Publish My Poetry." *Maclean's*, Jan. 1971, p. 14.

B422 "Al Purdy's Canada." *Maclean's*, May 1971, pp. 14-15. *NOC* (revised—"The Cartography of Myself").

B423 "Levesque: The Executioner of Confederation?" *Maclean's*, Oct. 1971, pp. 28-29, 83. *NOC* (revised—"Bon Jour").

B424 "A Feast of Provinces." *Maclean's*, April 1972, pp. 48-55. *NOC* (revised—"Her Gates Both East and West").

B425 "Le Canada en quelques grands bonds." *Maclean's* (French version), avril 1972, pp. 14-15, 18-20.

B426 "Verse Is Blossoming along with Nationalism across the Country." *The Toronto Star*, 25 Aug. 1973, Sec. H, p. 6.

B427 "Lowry: A Memoir." *Books in Canada*, Jan.-Feb. 1974, pp. 3-4.

B428 "The Agony of South Africa." *Maclean's*, April 1974, pp. 34-35, 83-84, 86.

B429 "Caught in the Net." *Maclean's*, May 1974, pp. 26-27, 85, 87. *NOC* (revised—"Lights on the Sea: Portraits of BC Fishermen").

B430 "A Time before the Season of Man." *Weekend Magazine*, 11 May 1974, pp. 8-9.

B431 "How the Salvation of Canadian Literature May Rest on the Good Deed of Three Toronto Prostitutes: Jim Foley's Unlikely Path to the Classroom." *Weekend Magazine*, 15 June 1974, pp. 7-9. *NOC* (revised—"Norma, Eunice, and Judy").

B432 "Let He Who Is without Gin Cast the First Stone." *Weekend Magazine*, 17 Aug. 1974, pp. 14-15.

B433 "The Rime of the Fledgling Mariner: Retracing the Route of Canada's Early Immigrants Along the St. Lawrence." *Weekend Magazine*, 10 Aug. 1974, pp. 3-9. *NOC* (revised—"Streetlights on the St. Lawrence").

B434 "Escaping the Quiet Desperation." *Weekend Magazine*, 23 Nov. 1974, pp. 24-28.

B435 "The Man Who Killed David." *Weekend Magazine*, 14 Dec. 1974, pp. 16-17.

B436 "In the Shoes of the Fisherman." *Weekend Magazine*, 28 Dec. 1974, pp. 16-21. *NOC* (revised — "Cougar Hunter").

B437 "When Your Job Is Child's Play It's Hard to Know How to Behave at Home." *Weekend Magazine*, 22 Feb. 1975, pp. 2-5. *NOC* (revised — "Seven League Skates: A Talk with Brian Glennie").

B438 "Boozy Saddles." *Maclean's*, May 1975, pp. 78-82.

B439 "King Tyee and the Salmon Princess." *Weekend Magazine*, 3 May 1975, pp. 8-10.

B440 "The Ego Has It Both Ways: Poets in Montreal." *Northern Journey*, Nos. 7-8 (1976), pp. 127-45. *NOC* ("Poets in Montreal").

B441 "Al Purdy at the Gardens." In *Zap: Hockey*. Ed. Barbara Bondar and Robert Reed. Toronto: Fitzhenry and Whiteside, 1976, pp. 3-7.

B442 "Unstrange Love: How a Bibliophile Learned to Beat Inflation by Collecting the Atomic Bomb." *Books in Canada*, May 1976, pp. 6-8.

B443 "An Unburnished One-Tenth of One Per Cent of an Event." *The Malahat Review*, No. 41 (Jan. 1977), pp. 61-64.

B444 "A Village out of Time." *The Canadian*, 12 Feb. 1977, pp. 8-10, 13. *NOC* (revised — "Harbour Deep").

B445 "The Death of a Friend." *Canadian Literature*, No. 72 (Spring 1977), pp. 94-95.

B446 "Swingin' in the Ritz." *Montreal Star*, 22 Oct. 1977, p. D4.

B447 "The Grassland Question: Who Shall Inherit the Earth: — People or Prairie Dogs?" *The Canadian*, 19 Nov. 1977, pp. 12-16. *NOC* (revised — "Dryland Country").

B448 "That Gift Can of Canadian Beef Will Be 25 Pesos, Senor." *London Free Press*, 3 March 1978, p. A2.

B449 "Padráig Ó Broin." *Poetry Toronto*, No. 51 (March 1980), n. pag.

B450 "Metre Readings." *Books in Canada*, June-July 1980, pp. 6-7.

Reviews

B451 Rev. of *In England Now*, by Ada Jackson. *Canadian Poetry Magazine*, 12, No. 3 (March 1949), 36.

B452 Rev. of *Poems of the War Years*, ed. Maurice Wollman. *Canadian Poetry Magazine*, 12, No. 3 (March 1949), 35.

B453 Rev. of *These Are Mine*, by Wendy Warfield. *Canadian Poetry Magazine*, 12, No. 3 (March 1949), 36.

B454 Rev. of *Awake in the Night*, by Marcelle Chancellor Leath. *Canadian Poetry Magazine*, 12, No. 4 (Summer 1949), 37.

B455 Rev. of *The Snow Fairies' Recitations and Verses for Children*. *Canadian Poetry Magazine*, 12, No. 4 (Summer 1949), 37.

B456 Rev. of *Where the Moment Was*, by Henry McLaughlin. *Canadian Poetry Magazine*, 12, No. 4 (Summer 1949), 37.

B457 Rev. of *High on a Hill*, by Marjorie Campbell; *Gates of Glory*, by Thomas B. Windross; and *Prairie Skyline*, by

Enid and Vesta Pickel. *Canadian Poetry Magazine*, 13, No. 1 (Fall 1949), 27-29.

B458   Rev. of *Invitation to Mood*, by Carol Coates. *Canadian Poetry Magazine*, 13, No. 3 (Spring 1950), 33.

B459   Rev. of *Spirit of Israel*, by Hyman Edelstein; *Leaves of Amber Wine*, by Edna James Kayser; *Recollections of the Gala*, by Nicholas Moore; and *Theory of Silence*, by William Pillin. *Canadian Poetry Magazine*, 14, No. 1 (Autumn 1950), 24-27.

B460   Rev. of *New Poetic Lamps and Old*, by Stanton A. Coblentz; *Within the Tavern Caught*, by Rupert Munday; *Peace and War*, by R. G. Lovell; *Time Is the Measure*, by M. E. Drew; and *Leaves in the Wind*, by William McDermott. *Canadian Poetry Magazine*, 14, No. 3 (Spring 1951), 29-31.

B461   Rev. of *Of Time and the Lover*, by James Wreford; *Moment of Visitation*, by Gustaf Davidson; *The Iron Harvest*, by Geoffrey Johnson; *What Matter What Way*, by Lilian Found; and *Dominant Seventh*, by Phillips Kloss. *Canadian Poetry Magazine*, 14, No. 4 (Summer 1951), 25-28.

B462   Rev. of *Collected Poems*, by Keith Douglas, and *I See a Light*, by David Dainow. *Canadian Poetry Magazine*, 15, No. 1 (Autumn 1951), 30-31.

B463   Rev. of *The Searching Image*, by Louis Dudek; *It Was a Plane*, by Tom Farley; *Mint and Willow*, by Ruth Cleaves Hazelton; and *Viewpoint* by Myra Lazechko-Haas. *Canadian Poetry Magazine*, 15, No. 3 (Spring 1952), 28-30.

B464   Rev. of *Angry Decade*, by Raymond Tong. *Canadian Poetry Magazine*, 16, No. 1 (Autumn 1952), 31.

B465   Rev. of *Collected Poems*, by Oliver St. John Gogarty. *Canadian Poetry Magazine*, 16, No. 2 (Christmas 1952), 30-31.

B466   Rev. of *Poems*, by Martin Gray. *The Canadian Forum*, Aug. 1958, p. 120.

B467   Rev. of *Hyphens*, by James Russell Grant. *The Canadian Forum*, Nov. 1958, pp. 190-91.

B468   Rev. of *Laughing Stalks* and *En Mexico*, by Louis Dudek. *The Canadian Forum*, Nov. 1958, pp. 187-88.

B469   Rev. of *Collected Poems, Vol. II*, by Roy Campbell. *The Canadian Forum*, Jan. 1959, pp. 238-39.

B470   Rev. of *African Genesis*, by Robert Ardrey. *The Canadian Forum*, April 1962, p. 21.

B471   Rev. of *Bridge Force*, by Frank Davey, and *For the Mean Time*, by Eugene McNamara. *Canadian Literature*, No. 14 (Autumn 1962), pp. 70-72.

B472   Rev. of *Balls for a One-Armed Juggler*, by Irving Layton. *Canadian Literature*, No. 16 (Spring 1963), pp. 81-82.

B473   Rev. of *Burglar Tools*, by Harry Howith. *Canadian Author & Bookman*, 39, No. 1 (Autumn 1963), 18-19.

B474   Rev. of *It Catches My Heart in Its Hands*, by Charles Bukowski. *Evidence*, No. 8 [1964?], pp. 137-40.

B475   Rev. of *Jawbreakers*, by Milton Acorn. *Evidence*, No. 8 [1964?], pp. 120-24.

B476   Rev. of *Tales of Nanabozho*, by Dorothy Reid. *Evidence*, No. 8 [1964?], pp. 135-36.

B477   Rev. of *The Rising Fire*, by Gwendolyn MacEwen. *Canadian Author & Bookman*, 39, No. 3 (Spring 1964), 11.

B478 Rev. of *The Colour of the Times*, by Raymond Souster. *Canadian Author & Bookman*, 39, No. 4 (Summer 1964), 15-16.

B479 Rev. of *Elephants, Mothers & Others*, by John Newlove; *Kyoto Avis*, by Roy Kiyooka; and *White Lunch*, by Gerry Gilbert. *The Canadian Forum*, Sept. 1964, pp. 142-43.

B480 Rev. of *Moving in Alone*, by John Newlove. *Canadian Literature*, No. 25 (Summer 1965), pp. 70-71.

B481 Rev. of *Near False Creek Mouth*, by Earle Birney. *The Fiddlehead*, No. 65 (Summer 1965), pp. 75-76.

B482 Rev. of *Tiptoeing on the Mount*, by Seymour Mayne. *Canadian Author & Bookman*, 40, No. 4 (Summer 1965), 17.

B483 Rev. of *A Dream of Lilies*, by Joan Finnegan. *Canadian Literature*, No. 28 (Spring 1966), pp. 70-71.

B484 Rev. of *The Collected Poems of Irving Layton*. *Quarry*, 15, No. 3 (March 1966), 40-44.

B485 "Turning New Leaves." Rev. of *Selected Letters of Malcolm Lowry*. *The Canadian Forum*, May 1966, pp. 40-41.
Signed "Al something or other."

B486. Rev. of *The Life of Dylan Thomas*, by Constantine Fitzgibbon. *The Tamarack Review*, No. 38 (Winter 1966), pp. 91-94.

B487 Rev. of *Eskimo Sculpture*, by George Swinton. *Evidence*, No. 10 [1967?], pp. 170-71.

B488 Rev. of *Smoking the City*, by Bryan McCarthy. *Evidence*, No. 10 [1967?], pp. 171-72.

B489 Rev. of *North-West Fox*, by Luke Fox. *The Tamarack Review*, No. 45 (Spring 1967), pp. 96-99.

B490 Rev. of *New Wave Canada*, ed. Raymond Souster. *Quarry*, 16, No. 3 (March 1967), 42-45.

B491 Rev. of *Small Change*, by Renald Shoofler; *Wrestle with an Angel*, by R. G. Everson; *Lost Diver*, by G. V. Downes; *Sunday Afternoon at the Toronto Art Gallery*, by John Grube; *For the Record*, by Luella Booth; *The Suspended Landscape*, by Anne Kekes; and *A Canadian Anthology*. *Ole*, No. 7 (May 1967), n. pag.

B492 "Landfall in Vinland." Rev. of *Westviking*, by Farley Mowat, and *Land under the Pole Star*, by Helge Ingstad. *Canadian Literature*, No. 33 (Summer 1967), pp. 63-67.

B493 Rev. of *Beautiful Losers*, by Leonard Cohen. *The Canadian Forum*, July 1967, p. 91.

B494 "Turning New Leaves." Rev. of *Modern Canadian Short Stories*, ed. Giose Rimanelli and Roberto Ruberto. *The Canadian Forum*, Oct. 1967, pp. 163-64.

B495 "Prose Birney." Rev. of *The Creative Writer*, by Earle Birney. *Canadian Literature*, No. 31 (Winter 1967), pp. 61-64.

B496 "Aiming Low." Rev. of *The Absolute Smile*, by George Jonas; *Phrases from Orpheus*, by D. G. Jones; *Nevertheless These Eyes*, by Roy Kiyooka; *Poems, New and Collected*, by A. J. M. Smith; *Kingdom of Absence*, by Dennis Lee; *As Is*, by Raymond Souster; *Cry Ararat!*, by P. K. Page; *Pointing*, by Lionel Kearns; *The Unquiet Bed*, by Dorothy Livesay; *Selected Poems*, by George Woodcock; *Bread, Wine and Salt*, by Alden Nowlan; and *The Making of Modern Poetry in Canada: Essential Articles on Contemporary Canadian Poetry in English*, ed. Louis Dudek and Michael Gnarowski. *The Tamarack Review*, No. 49 (Spring 1968), pp. 81-97.

B497 Rev. of *The Distance Everywhere*, by Kenneth O. Hanson; *Dimensions*, by Frederick Candelaria; and *Hunt in an Unmapped Interior* and *Canticle for Electronic Music*, by J. Michael Yates. *Northwest Review*, 9, No. 3 (Spring 1968), 121-23.

B498 Rev. of *The Absolute Smile*, by George Jonas. *The Canadian Forum*, March 1968, p. 284.

B499 "Achievement and Monument." Rev. of *Poets between the Wars*, ed. Milton Wilson. *Canadian Literature*, No. 37 (Summer 1968), pp. 72-74.

B500 Rev. of *The Young Toronto Poets*, ed. Dennis Lee. *The Canadian Forum*, Nov. 1968, pp. 181-82.

B501 "Other Vancouverites." Rev. of *From the Portals of the Mouseholes*, by Seymour Mayne; *Fires in the Temple*, by bill bissett; *Letters from the Savage Mind*, by Pat Lane; and *The Circus of the Boy's Eye*, by Jim Brown. *Canadian Literature*, No. 35 (Winter 1968), pp. 83-85.

B502 Rev. of *The Poems of James Dickey*. *Quarry*, 17, No. 2 (Winter 1968), 34-37.

B503 Rev. of *The Private Labyrinth of Malcolm Lowry*, by Perle Epstein. *The Five Cent Review*, Oct. 1969, pp. 1-3, 11-12.

B504 Rev. of *Black Night Window*, by John Newlove. *Quarry*, 18, No. 2 (Winter 1969), 43-45.

B505 "After a Hundred Years." Rev. of *Changes*, by Ronald Bates; *Homage to Mr. MacMullen*, by Richard Som-

mer; *The Gentlemen Are Also Lexicographers*, by Michael Gnarowski; *Nothing but Spoons*, by Peter Stevens; *I've Laughed and Sung through the Whole Night Long Seen the Summer Sunrise in the Morning*, by Raymond Fraser; *The Welder's Arc*, by Stuart MacKinnon; *Man: Unman*, by Glen Siebrasse; *The Gathering* and *The Ends of the Earth*, by David Bromige; *Seaweed and Rosaries*, by Al Pittman; *Man in the Glass Octopus*, by J. Michael Yates; *The Shadow-Maker*, by Gwendolyn MacEwen; and *The Silences of Fire*, by Tom Marshall. *Queen's Quarterly*, 76, No. 4 (Winter 1969), 710-18.

B506 "Poet Besieged." Rev. of *The Animals in That Country*, by Margaret Atwood. *Canadian Literature*, No. 39 (Winter 1969), pp. 94-96.

B507 Rev. of *Contemporary Poetry of British Columbia*, ed. J. Michael Yates; *The Gangs of Kosmos*, by George Bowering; *The Journals of Susanna Moodie*, by Margaret Atwood; *The Mysterious Naked Man*, by Alden Nowlan; *The Great Bear Lake Meditations*, by J. Michael Yates; and *Poemas Humanos*, by Cesar Vallejo, trans. Clayton Eshleman. *Wascana Review*, 5, No. 2 (1970), 53-63.

B508 "Betrayed by the Evening Star." Rev. of *Why Should I Have All the Grief?*, by Phyllis Gotlieb, and *The Street*, by Mordecai Richler. *Canadian Literature*, No. 44 (Spring 1970), pp. 84-86.

B509 Rev. of *Face at the Bottom of the World*, by Hagiwara Sakutaro, trans. Graeme Wilson; *Fragments of the Dance*, by Harry Howith; *John Toronto: New Poems by Dr. Strachan*, found by John Robert Colombo; and *The Dark Is Not So Dark*, by R. G. Everson. *Quarry*, 19, No. 3 (Spring 1970), 60-62.

B510 "Amazonian Travels." Rev. of *Henry Walter Bates,*

Naturalist of the Amazons, by George Woodcock. *Canadian Literature*, No. 45 (Summer 1970), p. 93.

B511 "Calm Surfaces Destroyed." Rev. of *The Cave*, by John Newlove. *Canadian Literature*, No. 48 (Spring 1971), pp. 91-92.

B512 Rev. of *Our Man in Utopia*, by Doug Fetherling, and *The Red Fox*, by Bill Howell. *Books in Canada*, Nov. 1971, p. 22.

B513 "Atwood's Moodie." Rev. of *The Journals of Susanna Moodie*, by Margaret Atwood. *Canadian Literature*, No. 47 (Winter 1971), pp. 80-84.

B514 "The Woman of Barrie." Rev. of *Touch: Selected Poems 1960-1970*, by George Bowering; *Nobody Owns th Earth*, by bill bissett; *Our Man in Utopia*, by Doug Fetherling; and *The Red Fox*, by Bill Howell. *Canadian Literature*, No. 54 (Autumn 1972), pp. 86-90.

B515 "Rock Gothic." Rev. of *Narrative of a Journey to the Shores of the Polar Sea*, by John Franklin. *Canadian Literature*, No. 51 (Winter 1972), pp. 92-94.

B516 Rev. of *The Dance Is One*, by F. R. Scott. *Books in Canada*, July-Sept. 1973, pp. 50-51.

B517 Rev. of *The Dance Is One*, by F. R. Scott; *Selected Poems*, by Ralph Gustafson; *Lies*, by John Newlove; *Headwaters*, by Sid Marty; *Hob and Other Poems*, by Michael Baldwin; and *Young and Old*, by R. S. Thomas. *Wascana Review*, 8, No. 2 (Fall 1973), 66-78.

B518 Rev. of *Riverrun*, by Peter Such. *Books in Canada*, Oct. 1973, pp. 7-8.

B519 "Farley's Fling at Fiction." Rev. of *The Snow Walker*, by Farley Mowat. *Books in Canada*, Oct. 1975, pp. 12-13.

B520 Rev. of *The Island Means Minago*, and *Poems from Prince Edward Island*, by Milton Acorn. *CV/II*, 2, No. 1 (Jan. 1976), 4-5.

B521 Rev. of *A Government Job at Last: An Anthology of Working Poems, Mainly Canadian*, ed. Tom Wayman. *Books in Canada*, Oct. 1976, pp. 24, 26.

B522 "Enduring Essentials." Rev. of *The Faroe Islanders Saga*, trans. George Johnston. *Canadian Literature*, No. 67 (Winter 1976), pp. 104-06.

B523 Rev. of *Literary History of Canada: Canadian Literature in English*, 2nd ed., Vols. I, II, and III, gen. ed. and introd. Carl F. Klinck. *Books in Canada*, Jan. 1977, pp. 9-12.

B524 "Tribute to Everson." Rev. of *Indian Summer*, by R. G. Everson. *Canadian Literature*, No. 72 (Spring 1977), pp. 80-82.

B525 "A Flooding Past." Rev. of *The Alders and Others*, by Peter Trower; *Jericho Road*, by Joy Kogawa; and *Images on Water*, by Ken Cathers. *Canadian Literature*, No. 76 (Spring 1978), pp. 126-27.

B526 Rev. of *Death of a Lady's Man*, by Leonard Cohen. *The Toronto Star*, 30 Sept. 1978, Sec. D, p. 7.

B527 Rev. of *A Border of Beauty: Arthur Lismer's Pen and Pencil*, by Marjorie Lismer Bridges. *Canadian Literature*, No. 81 (Summer 1979), pp. 132-34.

Letters

B528 Letter from Al Purdy. *Tish*, No. 4 (14 Dec. 1961), p. 2.
   A critical commentary on the first issue of *Tish*. He prefers Frank Davey's poems, because Davey, like Purdy, deals with the specific in order to get to the general.

B529 Letter from Al Purdy. *Tish*, No. 5 (13 Jan. 1962), p. 2.
Purdy disagrees with George Bowering's review of *Against a League of Liars*, by Milton Acorn.

B530 "Letter to Editor from Al Purdy." *The Canadian Forum*, July 1966, p. 86.
Purdy replies to criticisms by Ralph Gustafson, Victor Coleman, and John Mills of his review of *Lowry's Selected Letters*. He claims not to have intended criticism of Gustafson, and defends his assertion that Mills, as an academic, has little time for writing.

B531 "Written to Charles Bukowski from Al Purdy." *Open Skull*, No. 1 (1967), pp. 12-21.
Purdy writes to Bukowski in hip sixties style (crowding as many swear words in as possible), about drinking, writing, reviewing, etc.

B532 Letter from Al Purdy. *The Tamarack Review*, No. 45 (Spring 1967), p. 100.
A criticism of the review of Earle Birney's *Selected Poems* by Hayden Carruth in Number forty-two.

B533 Letter from Al Purdy to the Editor. *Books in Canada*, Nov. 1979, p. 21.

Introductions

B534 Foreword. *And Now My Pen Lies Still.* By Loretta Parker. [1945?], pp. 3-4.

B535 "Leonard Cohen." *Moment*, No. 1 (1960), p. 13.

B536 "West of Summer: New Poets from the West Coast." *The Tamarack Review*, No. 47 (Autumn 1967), pp. 23-38.
Introduction to his selection of poems from Vancouver.

B537 Introduction. *The United States of Heaven / Gwendolyn Papers / That Chainletter Hiway*, by Doug Fetherling. Toronto: House of Anansi, 1968.

B538 Introduction. *A Bukowski Sampler*, by Charles Bukowski. Ed. Douglas Blazek. Madison, Wisc.: Quixote, 1969, p. 8.

B539 Introduction. *I've Tasted My Blood*, by Milton Acorn. Ed. Al Purdy. Toronto: Ryerson, 1969, pp. vii-xv.
Concerning Milton Acorn and Purdy's meeting with him.

B540 "The Journey." Introduction to *The Quest for Ouzo*. *Black Moss*, No. 5 (1971), n. pag. *QO*.

B541 Foreword. *Tales from the Igloo*. Ed. and trans. Maurice Metayer. Edmonton: Hurtig, 1972, pp. 6-9.

B542 "New Women Poets." Selected by Al Purdy, with an introduction. *Canadian Literature*, No. 66 (Autumn 1975), pp. 87-93.

B543 Introduction. *Wood Mountain Poems*, by Andrew Suknaski. Ed. Al Purdy. Toronto: Macmillan, 1976, pp. 11-12.

B544 Introduction. *Ragged Horizons*, by Peter Trower. Toronto: McClelland and Stewart, 1978, pp. 9-12.

B545 Introduction. *Mad Women*, by Fraser Sutherland. Coatsworth: Black Moss, 1978, pp. 7-9.

B546 Introduction. *Woods and River Tales*, by Roderick Haig-Brown. Toronto: McClelland and Stewart, 1980. *NOC*.

Audio Recordings

B547 *Canadian Poets I.* [Toronto] CBC, 1967.

Two twelve-inch LP's of readings by Canadian poets, including Purdy.

B548 *Canadian Poets Reading*. [Toronto] High Barnet, n.d.
Two cassettes of readings by poets, including Purdy.

B549 *Interviews with Ten Poets*. Five cassettes. [Toronto] Ontario Institute for Studies in Education, n.d.

B550 *Al Purdy's Ontario*. 12-inch LP [Toronto] CBC Learning Systems [1973?].

Film

B551 *Roblin's Mills*. Toronto: Cinematics Canada, n.d.
A sixteen mm. nine-minute long film of the dramatized poem. Films were also made of other poems, shown on CBC TV.

Radio and Television Plays

B552 "A Gathering of Days." Prod. John Reeves. CBC Radio, 1955 and 1959. *CBC Times*, 17-23 Oct. 1959, p. 9.

B553 "The Woman of Andros." By Thornton Wilder. Adapted for CBC Radio, 1956.

B554 "The Lost Sea." By Jan de Hartog. Adapted for CBC Radio, 1957.

B555 "The Knife." By Theon Wright. Adapted for CBC Radio, 1960.

B556 "The Fall of Troy." *Shoe String Theater*, CBC TV, 1960.

B557 "Point of Transfer." *Shoe String Theater*, CBC-TV [1961?].
Performed at the Theatre in the Dell, 1962.

Adapted for CBC Radio under title: "Just Ask for Sammy," 1968.

B558 "David." By Earle Birney. Adapted for CBC Radio, 1 Jan. 1961.

B559 "Jericho's Red Brick Battlements." By Margaret Laurence. Adapted for CBC Radio, 1969.

B560 "Maple Leaves and Things Like That." CBC Radio [1970?].

Part II

Works on Al Purdy

C Book, Articles and Sections of Books, Theses, Interviews, and Awards and Honours

Book

C1 Bowering, George. *Al Purdy*. Toronto: Copp Clark, 1970. 117 pp.

   The only book written solely on Al Purdy, this is a careful study of the growth of Purdy as poet. Bowering analyzes each book of poetry chronologically, comparing the early Purdy to the mature Purdy, and looking closely at some individual poems. He traces the works from the early traditional, "romantic," and very "poetic" poetry to Purdy's open, natural, loose style. Purdy learned to start with the particular and local in seeking the universal, and to concern himself with process and search rather than closed answers. His main theme is "being alive," and his method that of "continuous discovery." Purdy comes into his own with *The Cariboo Horses* and is even better in *North of Summer*. In *Wild Grape Wine*, however, he is too willing to play the role laid out for him by the public.

   Although its brevity prevents detailed criticism, the book fulfils its purpose of providing an introduction to Purdy criticism and an excellent, overall view of Purdy and his development.

Articles and Sections of Books

C2 Sylvestre, Guy, Brandon Conron, and Carl F. Klinck, eds. *Canadian Writers*. Toronto: Ryerson, 1964, p. 125.

Biographical data with a few comments. Purdy presents trivial subjects with imaginative insight. His style is occasionally commonplace, but intense and satirical.

C3 Beattie, Munro. "Poetry (1950-1960)." In *Literary History of Canada: Canadian Literature in English*. Gen. ed. and introd. Carl F. Klinck. Toronto: Univ. of Toronto Press, 1965. 2nd ed. Toronto: Univ. of Toronto Press, 1975, III, pp. 10, 13, 24, 29, 288, 291, 292, 296, 297, 306, 311, 313.

   Purdy is mentioned briefly as a poet of promise for his *The Crafte So Long to Lerne*.

C4 "The Purdy Pigment." *Time*, 28 May 1965, p. 11. Rpt. in *The Making of Modern Poetry in Canada: Essential Articles on Contemporary Canadian Poetry in English*. Ed. Louis Dudek and Michael Gnarowski. Toronto: Ryerson, 1967, pp. 243-44.

   The author of this article refers to the opinions of critics that Purdy is the most important poet in Canada at present. He calls Purdy a "refreshingly unobtrusive painter of man and his metaphysical landscape" and finds his poetry spare and "maturely reflective." However, Purdy is criticized for his careless work, for "allowing the commonplace to mar his verse with sentimental clichés." Even in "The Country North of Belleville," Purdy's fine image goes "lurching off the page." The critic here does not understand Purdy's purpose of juxtaposing commonplace with great and universal, of using open form and colloquial diction in order to see life as it is without trapping it. A brief discussion of Purdy's life is included, with the comment that his wife has finally finished high school, after dropping out and working for years so that Purdy could write.

C5 Stone, Sheila. "Baffin Island Bid by Bard." *Montreal Star*, 10 July 1965, Sec. Entertainment, p. 5.

   This is a journalistic article, concerning Purdy's

life and travels, and containing bits of an interview. Purdy has recently been awarded a Canada Council grant and will travel to the Arctic. Purdy says that his chief theme is not Canada, but people: "Life seems so impermanent. One looks for a certain permanence in the qualities of people." He feels that ideas are more important than form, and cites his poetic influences as Yeats, Dylan Thomas, Dudek, Birney, and Layton. However, Purdy states that he is different from all his influences, that he is his own poet with his own slant on life and his own way of saying it.

C6   Stevens, Peter. "In the Raw: The Poetry of A. W. Purdy." *Canadian Literature*, No. 28 (Spring 1966), pp. 22-30.

Stevens compares "cooked" with "raw" poetry and calls Purdy "one of our best raw poets," who gives us a fresh no-nonsense approach. Stevens feels that *Cariboo Horses* is one of the best collections of Canadian poetry in a long time. Purdy's poetry is traced through three stages, from the beginning and explora-tory stage, to the central poetic upheaval, to the truly individual poetry of *The Cariboo Horses*. The theme that governs Purdy's development as a poet is "romanticism vs. the realism of the modern world," with his early poems romantic, and with *The Cariboo Horses* finding a balance of realism and romanticism, of open form and control. This is a valuable article for its discussion of Purdy's growth into a mature poet.

C7   Story, Norah. *The Oxford Companion to Canadian History and Literature*. Ed. Norah Story. Toronto: Oxford Univ. Press, 1967, p. 673.

This contains a biographical sketch and a review of the books from *The Enchanted Echo* to *The Cariboo Horses*. Purdy moves from writing traditional poetry to using varied structures and to the viewing of the universal through the commonplace.

C8   Dudek, Louis. "Poetry in English." In *The Sixties:*

Writers and Writing of the Decade. Ed. George Woodcock. Vancouver: Univ. of British Columbia Publishing Centre, 1969, pp. 111-20. Rpt. in *Readings in Commonwealth Literature*. Ed. William Walsh. Oxford: Clarendon, 1973, pp. 254-66.

Dudek does not see into Purdy's depth of purpose. He writes that Purdy, along with Cohen and Layton, exploits sex "as an entertainment come on," and Dudek describes the characteristics of Purdy's poetry as "primitivism" and as "vigor and vulgarity." Purdy, however, is a gifted poet, Dudek concedes.

C9   Jones, D. G. *Butterfly on Rock: A Study of Themes and Images in Canadian Literature*. Toronto: Univ. of Toronto Press, 1970, pp. 30-31, 168, 169-71, 174-76.

Jones briefly discusses Purdy's ambivalence, which suggests the problems of Canadian identity; Purdy's colloquial voice, seeking an answer but never finding one; the meaning of Purdy's poems, which is in the tone of the talk and in the gathering of detail, not in a conclusion; and his use of the vernacular, the spoken word.

C10   Woodcock, George. "Al Purdy." In *Contemporary Poets of the English Language*. Ed. Rosalie Murphy. London: St. James, 1970, pp. 879-81.

This contains bio-bibliographical information, statements by Purdy on his work, and critical evaluation by Woodcock.

C11   Bowering, George. "Purdy: Man and Poet." *Canadian Literature*, No. 43 (Winter 1970), pp. 24-35. Rpt. (abridged) in *Al Purdy*. Toronto: Copp Clark, 1970. (See C1).

Bowering calls Purdy "the world's most Canadian poet," and discusses the man and his popularity as a poet. He describes Purdy's physical appearance, his personality, his life, mentions his editing of *Moment* magazine with Milton Acorn, his winning of the President's Medal at the University of Western

Ontario in 1963, and his travelling.

C12 Duffy, Dennis. "In Defence of North America: The Past in the Poetry of Alfred Purdy." *The Journal of Canadian Studies*, 6, No. 2 (May 1971), 17-27.

Duffy, in this excellent article, discusses the way in which Purdy deals with the two major facts of North American experience, dispossession and discontinuity. Purdy is "an outstanding shaper of the Canadian past," who, through his sense of the past, finds metaphors for capturing the present. Purdy is able to find continuities, connections between man and his past, continuities that even overcome man's dispossession from himself—death. By making a world out of his own time and place, Purdy enables his readers to interpret their own experience.

C13 Fulford, Robert. "Purdy's Search." *Saturday Night*, Aug. 1971, p. 8.

Fulford calls Purdy a "poet-reporter" who "covers" places and then writes about them, as in his *Hiroshima* cycle.

C14 Jones, D. G. "Adam's Inventory: Aspects of Contemporary Canadian Literature." *Social Education*, 35, No. 6 (Oct. 1971), 595-601. Rpt. in *Readings in Commonwealth Literature*. Ed. William Walsh. Oxford: Clarendon, 1973, pp. 242-53.

Purdy and other Canadian poets try "to articulate the convulsive illegible world in its manifold particularities and peculiarities." Poems by Purdy are listed which contain the theme of isolation.

C15 Atwood, Margaret. *Survival: A Thematic Guide to Canadian Literature*. Toronto: House of Anansi, 1972, pp. 77, 95, 112, 123-24.

Atwood touches briefly on Purdy's work under some of the categories she sets up. Animal victims— Purdy juxtaposes animal deaths and trivial human activities. Eskimos and Indians—in *North of Summer* they are neither good nor bad, but in other poems they are victims. Ancestral totems—Purdy seeks through the remains of past cultures for roots or metaphors. Settlers—she mentions "The Country North of Belleville."

C16 Thomas, Clara. *Our Nature—Our Voices: A Guidebook to English-Canadian Literature*. Vol. I. Toronto: new press, 1972, pp. 144-49.

Thomas focusses on Purdy as a Canadian, as describing this country better than anyone else has done. Purdy's growth as a poet is traced through his books; the mature Purdy has found a genuine locale in Roblin Lake and has learned to contrapose the classical and historical "against the solid realities of the human world." Purdy's form and content are based on the process of "continuous discovery" and come from the natural world and his own experience.

C17 Woodcock, George. "On the Poetry of Al Purdy." In *Selected Poems*. By Al Purdy. Toronto: McClelland and Stewart, 1972, pp. 8-15.

Woodcock views Purdy mainly as a poet of place, and of the history of place. Because of Purdy's grasp of the nature of the land and its history, he knows the extremes of Canada. Woodcock writes that "Al Purdy's writing fits Canada like a glove; you can feel the fingers of the land working through his poems." Fortunately, Woodcock realizes that to call Purdy purely a Canadian poet would be "to do him an immense injustice," as Purdy relates Canada to all places and all times. Purdy deals with the relationship of man to nature and to art, and transfigures ordinary things into myth. This article also discusses Purdy's versatility as a poetic craftsman, his use of the long line, his technique, and his skill as a writer. Purdy is also a comic poet, who shows man as absurd as he tries to reconcile the animal and the human within him. This is a good overview.

C18 Lee, Dennis. "Running and Dwelling: Homage to Al

Purdy." *Saturday Night*, July 1972, pp. 14-16.

Lee believes that Purdy is doing for Canada what Walt Whitman did for the United States. Purdy has run around Canada and discovered that Canadians cannot master the space of their country yet are claimed by this land and are at home nowhere else. Purdy, in his poems, tries to *place* us, to locate our dwelling in time and space. He places Canada and its connections with all times and places, and, in his exploring, defines what it is to be an English Canadian human being. A letter from Robin Mathews in *Saturday Night*, September 1972, pages 31-32, criticizes Lee for comparing Purdy to an American poet when other Canadian poets could have been used instead, and says that Purdy does not feel alienated, as Lee does. Lee replies (pages 32-33) that Mathews' letter is "silly," that none of Purdy's Canadian predecessors have done for Canada what Purdy has, and only Whitman can compare with Purdy.

C19   Observer. "Al Purdy's Poetry." *Canadian Author & Bookman*, 48, No. 1 (Fall 1972), 16.

This brief article is interesting in that it shows how far Al Purdy has moved from his earlier connections with the Canadian Authors' Association and from the traditional poetry that he wrote at that time. When Purdy, in 1972, read his poetry at a CAA convention, many people found his work "not very tasteful." "Observer" tries to justify Purdy's poetry, by his discussion of "taste" as only a social phenomenon and as applying only to minor works, but Purdy is not a minor poet.

C20   Woodcock, George. "Al Purdy." *Supplement to the Oxford Companion to Canadian History and Literature*. Toronto: Oxford Univ. Press, 1973, pp. 271-72.

Biographical sketch and analysis. Woodcock stresses the importance of Purdy's travels. Although the travels help shape his work, the heart of his world is always Roblin Lake, "the symbolic omphalos of his imaginative world." Purdy is more than a "versifying geographer"; he has an historical sense and evokes "the sense of Canada as an old country resonant with echoes." In *The Crafte So Longe to Lerne*, Purdy first used open forms and began to use the here-and-now to reflect universal values.

C21   Davey, Frank. "Al Purdy." *From There to Here: A Guide to English Canadian Literature Since 1960*. Our Nature—Our Voices. Vol. II. Erin, Ont.: Porcépic, 1974, pp. 236-39.

This is a brief and general analysis, but Davey makes some important observations about Purdy's poetry. It is Purdy's personality and subjective impressions that permeate all the poems, and Purdy often presents himself in humiliating situations; this tendency to self-deprecation, however, is essential to his poetry and attractive to the reader. "In Purdy we are made to see the fate of the romantic in our materialistic society," and we can laugh at the humiliation of the romantic in a mundane world. Yet Purdy shows not despair, but joy in man's "continuing struggle to survive and understand." A very important point made by Davey is his criticism of the transformation of Purdy by Canadian nationalists into a "static caricature of some national Canadian archetype. Purdy does not deserve this, for his sense of history, especially geologic history, and of the impenetrability of cultural and inter-cultural realities, is much more sophisticated than that of most of the nationalist analysts."

C22   Stevens, Peter. "Canada." *Literatures of the World in English*. Ed. Bruce King. London: Routledge and Kegan Paul, 1974, pp. 42-60.

Although the surface of Purdy's poetry is "off-hand, colloquial, tough or prosaic by turns," the poetry is personal, Canadian in its joining of disparate elements, and has an epic strain. Characteristics of Purdy's poetry are: the deflation of romanticism with realism; descriptions of travelling, which can "transcend even the limits of the human condition";

expressions of the transience yet persistence of man; and comedy and mockery. Stevens is somewhat critical of Purdy's northern poetry, as the poet's response to the Eskimos is that of an outsider. But he praises Purdy for his ability to weld "poet, poetry and country into one whole."

C23 Doyle, Mike. "Proteus at Roblin Lake." *Canadian Literature*, No. 61 (Summer 1974), pp. 7-23. Rpt. in *Poets and Critics: Essays from* Canadian Literature *1966-1974.* Ed. George Woodcock. Toronto: Oxford Univ. Press, 1974, pp. 92-109. Rpt. (abridged) in *Contemporary Literary Criticism.* Ed. Carolyn Riley and Phyllis Carmel Mendelson. Vol. VI. Detroit: Gale, 1976, p. 428.

Purdy as a poet is very Protean, multi-faceted, and elusive, but is often able to combine several of these facets in a single poem. Doyle traces Purdy's growth as a poet, calling *Poems for All the Annettes* a landmark in his development. With *Cariboo Horses*, Purdy masters the "continuous form" to denote actions that are incomplete and always continuing. Doyle is one of the few critics to note the Platonism in Purdy's poetry in its obsession with the interpenetration of all things into one, yet Doyle recognizes that Purdy's view is also non-Platonic since the flux itself is a sufficient answer. Purdy is a very Canadian poet in his concern with the links between past and present and in his preoccupation with the way in which Canadians dwell in their homeland. Purdy will never stick to one stance, will never forget the existence of either "the shit-house or the sky." Doyle finds that, in spite of Purdy's excellence as a poet, he is often too self-conscious and too much present in his poems. Although many of the poems *display* too much Purdy but *reveal* too little Purdy, sometimes participation and self-definition merge. This is an excellent article, combining praise and criticism.

C24 *The Canadian Who's Who: A Biographical Dictionary of Notable Living Men and Women.* Vol. XIII, 1973-1975. Toronto: Who's Who Canadian Publications, 1975, p. 822.

Bio-bibliographical information.

C25 Woodcock, George. "Al Purdy." In *Contemporary Poets.* Ed. James Vinson. 2nd ed. London: St. James, 1975, pp. 1223-26.

Revised and updated from the first edition (see C10). Bio-bibliographical information on Purdy and his work, with critical evaluation by Woodcock.

C26 Colombo, John Robert. *Colombo's Canadian References.* Toronto: Oxford Univ. Press, 1976, p. 427.

Bio-bibliographical information.

C27 Woodcock, George. "Poetry." In *Literary History of Canada: Canadian Literature in English.* Gen. ed. and introd. Carl F. Klinck. 2nd ed. Toronto: Univ. of Toronto Press, 1976, III, pp. 288, 291-92, 296-97, 306, 311, 313.

Al Purdy, writing since the 1940s, became one of the most popular poets in the 1960s. Purdy writes of Loyalist Canada, of all Canada, and of Europe, Asia, and Africa as well. He grew from a "timidly traditional poet" to become "one of the most fluent and idiosyncratic of Canadian poets," and has been able "to set into verse the historical and geographical complexities that make Canada."

C28 Cohn-Sfetcu, Ofelia. "The Privilege of Finding an Opening in the Past: Al Purdy and the Tree of Experience." *Queen's Quarterly*, 83 (Summer 1976), 262-69.

Sees Purdy's arctic trees, which "use death to remain alive," as the symbols for his attempts to order his consciousness of human reality and to put himself in harmony with the patterns of the universe. It is through the psychological time of the individual, which is vertical rather than horizontal, that all things become interconnected. By descending to the level of mythical roots, Purdy emerges better able to see the relationships between all of mankind, and between man and nature. By allowing the subjective to swallow the objective, man can merge himself with other beings of all times and all places. According to Cohn-Sfetcu, Purdy, through his search for roots, has been better able to participate emotionally in the world, while transcending his objective existence at the same time.

C29   Lye, John. "The Road to Ameliasburg." *The Dalhousie Review*, 57, No. 2 (Summer 1977), 242-53.

This article discusses the various personae that Purdy uses in his poems, stating that Purdy's essential stance is sentimental and conservative. The sensitive man seeks God and recognizes the possibility of transcendence, while at the same time he is aware of the void and of meaninglessness. The solution is in the continuum of history and the continued existence of individuals, in the presence of the past. Purdy's sensitive persona stresses the individual facing a world that is flawed and full of pain, but finding comfort through history and the continuation of the human individual through mental and spiritual processes.

C30   Cohn-Sfetcu, Ofelia. "To Live in Abundance of Life: Time in Canadian Literature." *Canadian Literature*, No. 76 (Spring 1978), pp. 25-36.

Cohn-Sfectu discusses time in Grove, Avison, Richler, Aquin, and Purdy. Her comments on Purdy are essentially the same as in her article in *Queen's Quarterly* (see C28), that Purdy finds a sense of human unity by descending into mythical roots, and thus transcending the limitations of the present.

C31   Reeves, John. "A Reeves Gallery." *Books in Canada*, May 1978, cover, p. 4.

John Reeves, photographer, displays photographs of famous people and comments on them. In explaining the photograph of Al Purdy (cover), Reeves remembers driving to Al Purdy's house and arriving there in November of 1965. However, he has no memory of anything after that, including taking the photograph. The memento he has at home, some of Purdy's homemade wine, is some explanation of what happened.

C32   Adachi, Ken. "Timely Homage for a Unique Poet." *Toronto Star*, 16 Dec. 1978, p. D8.

Biography of Purdy on his sixtieth birthday.

C33   Amiel, Barbara. "Poetry: Capsule Comments on Canada." *Maclean's*, 15 Jan. 1979, pp. 49-50.

Portrait of Purdy.

Theses

C34   Wilson, Jean Lenore. "The Sense of Place and History in the Poetry of A. W. Purdy." M.A. Thesis Saskatchewan 1968.

Wilson discusses Purdy's awareness of the relationship between present and past, and traces the growth of his poetic handling of this chronologically through his poetry. She finds three aspects of his sense of place: (1) his relationship to Canada; (2) his relationship to cultural history in general; (3) his sense of place as acquired from historical, contemporary, or fictional people. Through his earlier books, Purdy wavers ambiguously, but in *The Cariboo Horses*, he "knows exactly who he is, where he is, and how he is related to both past and present history." Purdy's sense of place and history is even sharper and clearer in *North of Summer*, and Wilson shows the growth of Purdy's sense of belonging by comparing different versions of "The Turning Point." (With acknowledgement to the English Department of the University of Saskatchewan for permission to quote and abstract from this thesis.)

C35 Miller, Susan Marliss. "Myth in the Poetry of A. W. Purdy." M.A. Thesis Queen's 1971.

This is a well-written and well-researched thesis. Miller finds Purdy's central myth to be that of a "total order in which everything has a life of its own and is yet one life," and finds that Purdy has sought, and often found, the continuity of man through time and beyond the boundaries of place, culture, or race. Yet she recognizes the fact that Purdy believes in ambiguity, and is against fixing anything or pinning oneself down, believing instead in the continual becoming. Some of Purdy's poems do not lead him into myth; instead his sense of realism leads him to anti-myth at times. Miller traces Purdy's evolution through his published books, carefully discussing individual poems, and demonstrating that Purdy has developed his myth of a single order in the universe through people, nature, and the individual. The individual man, within himself, includes past, present, and future. Purdy rejects the "garrison mentality," and, in stepping out of the garrisons of race, nationality, culture, and language, he identifies with man on a universal level, and even goes beyond the boundaries of time and space. (With acknowledgement to the English Department of Queen's University for permission to abstract and quote from this thesis.)

Interviews

C36 Geddes, Gary. "A. W. Purdy: An Interview." *Canadian Literature*, No. 41 (Summer 1969), pp. 66-72. Rpt. in *20th-Century Poetry and Poetics*. 2nd ed. Ed. Gary Geddes. Toronto: Oxford Univ. Press, 1973, pp. 563-71.

This is an excellent interview, focussing on Purdy the poet rather than on Purdy the man. Purdy discusses his feelings about poetry, and talks about how and why he writes. To Purdy it is important to write out of his own life, and about people. He is "self-conscious about being self-conscious about being self-conscious," uses travelling and landscape only to awaken areas of oneself and to see one's own land in perspective, uses objects only in relation to people. He is against positive stances, believing poetry (and life) to be "a continual becoming and a changing and a moving." He mentions literary influences on him, and tells of the evolution of the poem "Roblin's Mills." Purdy writes poetry only because he likes to.

C37 "Perspective: Selection from an Interview with Al Purdy, Conducted by S. G. Buri and Robert Enright on November 11, 1975, in Winnipeg." *CV/II*, 2, No. 1 (Jan. 1976), 50-58.

This is a very interesting interview for its insight into Purdy's personality. The interviewers do not allow him to back down on any issues, and therefore capture his prejudices, anger, strong opinions, and his evasiveness on certain issues. They discuss his life, his drinking, his reading habits, literary influences on him, his latest books (Purdy feels that *Owen Roblin* doesn't quite succeed), his agnosticism, his feeling that he is growing old and must wind down his career now.

C38 "Al Purdy's Not Here to Massage Egos." *Western News* [Univ. of Western Ontario], 1 Dec. 1977, p. 5.

Purdy stresses his belief that if creative writers remain tied to the "phoney" environment of the academic world, then there is little chance that they will become great. He discusses the importance of constructive criticism for aspiring writers, his life, his recent books, the difference between writing prose and writing poetry.

Awards and Honours

C39 Canada Council Arts Awards (1959-60).

C40 President's Medal, University of Western Ontario, London, Ontario (1961).

For the poem "The Country North of Belleville," which appeared in *The Tamarack Review*.

C41 Canada Council Senior Arts Fellowship (1964-65).

C42 Governor-General's Award for Poetry (1966).
For *The Cariboo Horses*.

C43 Canadian Centennial Medal (1967).

C44 Canada Council Arts Award and Short Term Grant (1967-68).

C45 Visiting Associate Professor, Simon Fraser University, Burnaby, B.C. (1970).

C46 Canada Council Short Term Grant (1970-71).

C47 Canada Council Arts Award (1971-72).

C48 Poet-in-Residence, Loyola College, Montreal, Quebec (1973-74).

C49 A. J. M. Smith Award for *Sex and Death* (1974).

C50 Canada Council Short Term Grant (1974-75).

C51 Writer-in-Residence, University of Manitoba, Winnipeg, Manitoba (1976).

C52 Writer-in-Residence, University of Western Ontario, London, Ontario (1977).

C53 Canada Council Senior Arts Grant (1977-78).

D Selected Book and Record Reviews

Selected Book Reviews

The Enchanted Echo

D1 Kirkconnell, Watson. Rev. of *The Enchanted Echo*. *Canadian Poetry Magazine*, 8, No. 4 (June 1945), 42.
Purdy's work in this volume has zest and exuberance, but lacks discipline. Kirkconnell criticizes the poems for errors in rhyme, grammar, and style, and hopes that Purdy will be less hasty in the future, as he has genuine ability.

Pressed on Sand

D2 Pacey, Desmond. Rev. of *Pressed on Sand*. *The Fiddlehead*, No. 25 (May 1955), p. 13.
This brief review calls the book competent but colourless, as it has suffered from overcautious editing, and therefore the more audacious and exciting poems by Purdy have been excluded.

Emu, Remember!

D3 Wilson, Milton. Rev. of *Emu, Remember! The Canadian Forum*, July 1957, p. 87.
Of Purdy's earlier book, *Pressed on Sand*, Wilson says that it "had an occasional, fragmentary brilliance which compensated for its confusion of styles and uncertainty of direction," and that "an authentic idiom

kept promising to emerge out of the half-digested clichés of Laurentian primitivism." Purdy shows, in his next book, that he is a visual poet, but with more promise than solid achievement. Wilson criticizes Purdy's "combination of self-educated pedantry and self-conscious Bohemianism," but sees promise for the future, and, having seen Purdy's recent periodical verse, feels that "the future may already be upon us."

D4 Gnarowski, Michael. Rev. of *Emu, Remember! Yes*, 2, No. 3 (Feb. 1958), n. pag.

Many of these poems are obscure, unambitious, vague, and mediocre, and shouldn't have been included. Purdy has written better poems, which have been published in magazines.

D5 Hazo, Samuel J. Rev. of *Emu, Remember! The Fiddlehead*, No. 35 (Winter 1958), pp. 43-44.

Although there are some fine poems in this book, sometimes Purdy tries too hard to be clever, and the effect is contrived and calculated. Purdy is at his best when his "highly original wit is fused with a more sedate lyricism which transcends and somehow spiritualizes the poetry."

The Crafte So Longe to Lerne

D6 Wilson, Milton. Rev. of *The Crafte So Longe to Lerne. The Canadian Forum*, Feb. 1960, p. 263.

Wilson wonders why Purdy uses the style that he does, and finds that style inadequate for telling a story, writing social satire, praising, deploring, or acting too concerned. But Purdy, as a minor poet, has "a special quality that you can't find in his betters."

D7 Bromige, David. Rev. of *The Crafte So Longe to Lerne*; *Moon Lake and Other Poems*, by R. E. Rashley; and *River and Realm*, by Theresa E. and Don W. Thomson. *Canadian Literature*, No. 4 (Spring 1960), pp. 85-86.

Although Bromige appreciates the tone of quiet,

ironic understatement of the book, he finds that it is not completely successful, because of the inferior imagery, misuse of punning, wooliness of thought and expression, and a technical standard that is not well-sustained.

D8 Mandel, E. W. "Poetry Chronicle: Giants, Beasts, and Men in Recent Canadian Poetry." Rev. of *The Crafte So Long to Lerne* and sixteen other books. *Queen's Quarterly*, 67 (Summer 1960), 285-93.

Purdy's method is like that of Browning and Pound—we feel "that we are watching the poem take shape on the page at the moment of writing." Mandel calls Purdy's work "another beginning for Canadian poetry," and his master theme "creation's eternal immediacy." Purdy, like other Canadian poets, raises the question of whether man should admit to being no more than beast or accept theories that he is more.

D9 Collie, Michael. Rev. of *The Crafte So Longe to Lerne*; *River and Realm*, by Theresa E. and Don W. Thomson; *Moon Lake and Other Poems*, by R. E. Rashley; *Poems*, by Florence Wyle; *The Varsity Chapbook*, ed. J. R. Colombo; *The McGill Chapbook*, ed. Leslie L. Kaye; and *Descent from Eden*, by Fred Cogswell. *Dalhousie Review*, 40, No. 3 (Fall 1960), 433-35.

Most of the poems lack identity and are cacophonous, and the puns turn out to be "artistically gross."

D10 Nowlan, Alden A. Rev. of *The Crafte So Longe to Lerne. The Fiddlehead*, No. 49 (Summer 1961), pp. 56-57.

Calls Purdy an ambitious writer and an honest experimentalist, but finds that his straining for effect is sometimes too obvious. His poems are praised, however, for dealing with "the real stuff of experience."

D11 Hornyansky, Michael. "Festive Bards." Rev. of *The*

Crafte So Longe to Lerne and five other books. *The Tamarack Review*, No. 21 (Autumn 1961), pp. 83-84.

The reviewer responds playfully to Purdy, recreating Purdy's joyful moods and appreciating his many stances. Hornyansky believes that Purdy has mastered his style, although he has lapses.

The Blur in Between

D12   Pearson, Alan. Rev. of *The Blur in Between*. *The Canadian Forum*, April 1964, p. 21.

Pearson appreciates the book. He divides Purdy's poems among personal problems, social questions, and evocations of Canadian landscape. He calls Purdy "one of Canada's top three contemporary poets," a label that will stick to him in the near future.

D13   Percy, H. R. Rev. of *The Blur in Between*. *Canadian Author & Bookman*, 39, No. 4 (Summer 1964), 19.

These poems are not as mature as the poems of *Poems for All the Annettes* (1962), but they are still good. Percy fears that Purdy's self-consciousness about being self-conscious, his attempts at objectivity, may cause him to lose much of his warmth and compassion.

D14   Blostein, David. Rev. of *The Blur in Between* and *Poems for All the Annettes*. *Alphabet*, No. 8 (June 1964), pp. 77-79.
See D25.

D15   Wilson, Milton. "Letters in Canada: 1963." *University of Toronto Quarterly*, 33, No. 4 (July 1964), 377-78.

Although this collection is not as "striking or substantial" as *Poems for All the Annettes*, it is worth owning.

D16   Ó Broin, Padráig. Rev. of *The Blur in Between*. *Canadian Poetry Magazine*, 27, No. 4 (Aug. 1964), 87-88.

Ó Broin sees Purdy as outwardly tough and uncompromising, but inwardly shy and sensitive. Purdy is not yet a major poet, but one in a major key, and, if he could control his forced, macabre humour, would be an even more significant poet. However, "when he is good, he is almost unbeatable."

Poems for All the Annettes (1962)

D17   Jones, B. W. Rev. of *Poems for All the Annettes* (1962), and *A Local Pride*, by Raymond Souster. *Queen's Quarterly*, 69, No. 4 (Winter 1962-63), 646-47.

Jones is not favourably impressed by this book. He finds Purdy too often "obtrusive and affected," and his language lacking in flexibility. Thus Purdy cannot pass on to the reader what might have been his own sensitive response.

D18   Webb, Phyllis. Rev. of *Poems for All the Annettes* (1962). *Canadian Literature*, No. 15 (Winter 1963), pp. 80-81.

Purdy is called one of the few important voices in Canadian poetry today. His method and tone are often criticized and found offensive. "Archaeology of Snow" is the central poem in the collection; although it seems at first clumsy and fragmented, the style reflects the theme of time and division. Purdy's weakness is clutter, lack of trimming.

D19   Bowering, George. Rev. of *Poems for All the Annettes* (1962). *Tish*, No. 17 (14 Jan. 1963), p. 11.

Even at this early stage of Purdy's work, Bowering sees him as the "leading poet of his generation in Canada." Although Purdy sometimes writes dead lines and bad phrases, his poetry is never boring, always interesting, and often exciting.

D20   Mandel, E. W. "Turning New Leaves." Rev. of *Poems for All the Annettes* (1962); *Twelve Letters to a Small*

Town, by James Reaney; *The Sun Is Axeman*, by D. G. Jones; and *The Things which Are*, by Alden Nowlan. *The Canadian Forum*, March 1963, pp. 278-80.

He discusses Purdy's syntax, which "threatens at any moment to tear itself to pieces simply out of spite at its own difficulties." Purdy lusts for something permanent, while sensing the elusiveness of experience, the patterns that never succeed. This book is Purdy's "big bang" and Mandel hopes that he writes a dozen more.

D21 Rev. of *Poems for All the Annettes* (1962). *Teanga-doir*, 2nd Ser., 1, No. 5 (15 May 1963), n. pag.

The reviewer feels that Purdy's "polysyllabic, polygot, polygamous, polygonal vocabulary" sometimes bogs you down. Purdy is very "Canadian" but unconsciously so; he believes that people of all times and places are coeval. The main criticism of the book itself is that it was cheaply printed by an American printer.

D22 Nowlan, Alden. Rev. of *Poems for All the Annettes* (1962), and *A Friction of Lights*, by Eldon Grier. *The Fiddlehead*, No. 57 (Summer 1963), pp. 67-68.

Purdy is praised for his gusto and insight, for being a whole and a real man. Nowlan feels that this is more important than his occasional weaknesses as a poet. "Alfred Purdy never bores me. Sometimes I think he stands on his head and rides his bicycle without using his hands a bit oftener than is good for him and occasionally I get a bit impatient with some of his smart aleckisms. But those are the kind of mistakes we all make."

D23 Wilson, Milton. "Letters in Canada: 1962." *University of Toronto Quarterly*, 32, No. 4 (July 1963), 379-81.

In these direct, intimate poems, Purdy makes poetry out of his quarrels with form, language, and selection, and finds humanity in his doubts of human identity and continuity. Wilson especially likes the poem "Archaeology of Snow," but writes that it works a bit too hard at its own undoing.

D24 Lochhead, Douglas. Rev. of *Poems for All the Annettes* (1962); *The Things which Are*, by Alden Nowlan; *Jawbreakers*, by Milton Acorn; *A Friction of Lights*, by Eldon Grier; *A Shifting Pattern*, by Peter Miller; and *A Local Pride*, by Raymond Souster. *Dalhousie Review*, 44, No. 2 (Summer 1964), 241-47.

Although this reviewer praises Souster for publishing all of the above books with his Contact Press, he does not like or appreciate Purdy's poetry, even though this is probably Purdy's first good book. Lochhead finds the urbanity and the journalistic trickery or opportunism of Purdy's poems annoying, and calls Purdy's strident bravado "perhaps . . . a kind of sickness." "Mr. Purdy is just not my kind of poet, clever, adroit, and prolific though he is."

D25 Blostein, David. Rev. of *Poems for All the Annettes* and *The Blur in Between. Alphabet*, No. 8 (June 1964), pp. 77-79.

This is not so much a review of the books as a statement of the general characteristics of Purdy's poetry. Purdy's poems express "the difficulty of grasping the blurred interval between birth and death," and the difficulty in expressing things. Purdy distrusts the fully articulated, possessing a kind of "negative capability"; he writes best when he is satisfied with hints rather than with sharp definitions. Too often, however, Purdy is self-conscious and embarrassed by his lack of answers.

The Cariboo Horses

D26 Colombo, John Robert. Rev. of *The Cariboo Horses. Canadian Literature*, No. 25 (Summer 1965), pp. 62-64.

Colombo realizes that Purdy has reached a higher plateau with this book, and has developed a personal and characteristic way of writing. Poetry is a process and a search. No pat answers can be found, and the connections between place and purpose are made only in the mind of the poet.

D27 McCarthy, Brian. "Poetry Chronicle." *The Tamarack Review*, No. 36 (Summer 1965), pp. 67-70.

This book is Purdy's first public success. McCarthy says that the poems are not social or psycho-analytical and should not be analyzed that way; Purdy deals with social and psychological problems but goes beyond them. Purdy's poems are sometimes too rambling or too prosy, but are very much alive. He "packs a poetical wallop that puts him among the first half-dozen heavyweight poetical talents in North America."

D28 Percy, H. R. Rev. of *The Cariboo Horses. Canadian Author & Bookman*, 40, No. 4 (Summer 1965), 10.

This is a general review, concentrating more on the impression of Purdy one gets from the book than on specific poems. Percy calls Purdy "a poet of considerable stature who has the virtue, all too rare in our day, of an independent mind, and who carries his erudition with a grace that his academic contemporaries would do well to emulate."

D29 Ó Broin, Padráig. Rev. of *The Cariboo Horses. Canadian Poetry Magazine*, 28, No. 4 (Aug. 1965), 77-78.

Ó Broin criticizes Purdy's sloppy writing and lack of discipline, but finds him an important poet, who is "distinctively and uncomplicatedly Canadian."

D30 Weaver, Robert. Rev. of *The Cariboo Horses. The Canadian Reader*, Aug. 1965, pp. 4-5.

This book shows that Al Purdy is now at the height of his powers, as is demonstrated by the fact that he does not need to show off and writes with "superb confidence."

D31 Stevens, Peter. "Two Kinds of Honesty." Rev. of *The Cariboo Horses*, and *Moving in Alone*, by John Newlove. *The Canadian Forum*, Sept. 1965, p. 139.

With this book Purdy is firmly in control of his method, and avoids the pitfalls of his earlier poems. Stevens' reservations about the book are minor when placed against the positive merits. Purdy's faults are: unnecessary adjectives, needless repetition, sprawling ideas, words for shock effect, and cheap wisecracks. However, Stevens finds Purdy's "an individual and important Canadian voice."

D32 MacCallum, Hugh. "Letters in Canada: 1965." *University of Toronto Quarterly*, 35, No. 4 (July 1966), 358-62.

Although MacCallum praises Purdy's new ease and precision of technique, his firmer sense of direction, his blending of myth and reality, and his drama and immediacy, he criticizes the poems for the lack of a finished structure which focusses and holds attention, for a voice that doesn't give us answers or solutions.

D33 Lacey, Edward A. [pseudonym]. Rev. of *The Cariboo Horses. Edge*, No. 5 (Fall 1966), pp. 105-07.

He dislikes the rhetoric, the sentimentality, the exaggerations of Purdy's style, but is aware of Purdy's importance as a poet, and thinks he may become "the most important Canadian poet of this generation."

D34 Hooper, A. G. Rev. of *The Cariboo Horses*, and *Selected Poems 1940-1966*, by Earle Birney. *Journal of Canadian Studies*, 3 (July 1967), 114-17.

The reviewer describes Purdy's style as colloquial and non-academic, and finds his poems vital and intelligent. However, he states that "Purdy will probably never be a popular poet."

North of Summer

D35　Barbour, Douglas. Rev. of *North of Summer. Quarry*, 17, No. 1 (Fall 1967), 45-47.

With this book, Purdy's best to date, he has found himself and his vision; his poems are consciously unpoetic, but provide a special view of life. Purdy does not patronize the Indians, but plays the bumbling outsider, accepting the Eskimos and seeing them as clearly as he can. All the poems are good; some are superb.

D36　Helwig, David. "Canadian Poetry: Seven Recent Books." Rev. of *North of Summer*; *Periods of the Moon*, by Irving Layton; *Abracadabra*, by John Robert Colombo; *The Silverthorn Bush*, by Robert Finch; *The Circle Game*, by Margaret Atwood; *The Danish Portraits*, by Heather Spears; and *The Dumbfounding*, by Margaret Avison. *Queen's Quarterly*, 74, No. 4 (Winter 1967), 754-61.

Purdy's book is a public event; it is journalism and a documentary report, with the facts and details often remaining just facts, with no conclusions drawn, as Purdy feels that some real facts cannot be reduced to literature. But the book as a whole makes all the bits add up; one should read the whole book.

D37　Gibbs, Robert. Rev. of *North of Summer. The Fiddlehead*, No. 74 (Winter 1968), pp. 84-86.

Gibbs finds this a handsome book, more carefully devised than at first appears. Purdy is criticized, however, for his complete informality when it becomes itself a mannerism leading Purdy to the vice of self-parody. "Purdy writes almost too much like Purdy."

D38　MacCallum, Hugh. "Letters in Canada: 1967." *University of Toronto Quarterly*, 37, No. 4 (July 1968), 360-62.

This book includes some of Purdy's best poems to date, with a new intensity and cohesiveness of themes, and complete mastery of technique. The reviewer appreciates Purdy's unpretentiousness as a traveller, his direct responses, and his curiosity and wonder. Purdy's warmth enables him to "bridge, momentarily, the gulf which separates him from the Eskimo."

Poems for All the Annettes (1968)

D39　Barbour, Douglas. Rev. of *Wild Grape Wine* and *Poems for All the Annettes* (1968); *Selected Poems 1956-1968*, by Leonard Cohen; *The Animals in That Country*, by Margaret Atwood; and *The Collected Poems of Anne Wilkinson*, ed. A. J. Smith. *The Dalhousie Review*, 48 (Winter 1968-69), 566-71.

Purdy is called the "dean of Canadian poets," but he is honest and humorous, never close to self-adulation. Both of these books contain many exciting poems, in which Purdy's imagination careens all over the universe. Although Purdy is undisciplined and wild, he has genuine talent; his imagination, honesty of vision, gusto, and bravura raise him "high above many minor craftsmen."

D40　Cogswell, Fred. Rev. of *Poems for All the Annettes* (1968), and *Winter of the Luna Moth*, by Joe Rosenblatt. *Canadian Literature*, No. 40 (Spring 1969), pp. 71-72.

This book is called as good as *The Cariboo Horses*, and better than *North of Summer* and *Wild Grape Wine*. Purdy's ability depends on: (1) the lively oral personality that he stamps on all his poems; (2) his "intellectuality," the curiosity and imagination by which he fuses elements that seem unfusable. Cogswell states that Purdy has perfected his voice, but that his intellectuality hasn't kept up with the development of his style and voice.

D41　Helwig, David. "The Winemaker." Rev. of *Poems for All the Annettes* and *Wild Grape Wine*. *Queen's Quarterly*, 76, No. 2 (Summer 1969), 340-44.

Helwig feels that Purdy is now the major Canadian poet, having taken over from Layton. The fact that Purdy is non-academic and self-educated is a virtue, as he has never debased his wide learning by using it to pass an exam. Both books are good, especially the *Annettes*, but some poems are better than others. A Purdy poem often starts out as autobiography, moves toward the comic, then down toward some final, often ironic, insight. Purdy's loose forms can be compared to those of Whitman, Rexroth, and Ginsberg, yet Purdy has a precision of language and emotional depth that those poets lack.

Wild Grape Wine

D42　Barbour, Douglas.
　　　See D39.

D43　Geddes, Gary. "No Brew Like Home-Brew." *Canadian Literature*, No. 40 (Spring 1969), pp. 87-89.
　　　Geddes calls Purdy "the most refreshing poet now writing in Canada," and this book "a superb achievement." Three different voices characterize these poems: the humorous, self-mocking Purdy; the more restrained, meditative Purdy; and Purdy the journalist. Sometimes Purdy is too chatty, which makes his poems less precise than they should be.

D44　Pacey, Desmond. Rev. of *Wild Grape Wine*. *The Fiddlehead*, No. 79 (March-April 1969), pp. 106-07.
　　　Pacey praises Purdy for his sense of humour, his hope and affirmation, his appetite for life. With this book, Purdy has mastered his medium and found his own voice, after moving from the rhetoric of his early poetry to the realism of his present poetry.

D45　Keyes, Mary. Rev. of *Wild Grape Wine*. *The Canadian Forum*, April 1969, pp. 17-18.
　　　Keyes is most concerned with Purdy's effect on his

audience, and is impressed that with Purdy, the poet and his audience "touch."

D46　Helwig, David.
　　　See D41.

D47　MacCallum, Hugh. "Letters in Canada: 1968." *University of Toronto Quarterly*, 38, No. 4 (July 1969), 342.
　　　Purdy's voice is "ebullient, extroverted, and volatile," but his candid manner sometimes seems only a mask. His mind responds both to the trivia of everyday life and to myth. MacCallum likes Purdy's witty, probing poems about politics.

D48　Fetherling, Doug. "Al Purdy's Recent Poetry." *Quarry*, 18, No. 2 (Winter 1969), 42-43.
　　　This is a flattering and laudatory review, rather than a critical one. Fetherling says that "Al Purdy knows more about writing poetry than anyone else I have ever met, heard or read about," and calls *Wild Grape Wine* "so shit-hot it is impossible to review." He does not review the book, but calls Purdy the most popular poet in Canada and the best.

The New Romans

D49　Duffy, Dennis. Rev. of *The New Romans*. *The Canadian Forum*, Nov. 1968, p. 181.
　　　Duffy concludes that this book contains the same type of criticisms that Americans make of their own society, but that the Americans do a much better job than do outsiders.

D50　Sherman, George. "Purdy's Romans." *The Tamarack Review*, No. 50 (Winter 1968), pp. 66-70.
　　　This very critical but very astute review contends that this book shows that English Canadian intellectuals are the most neurotic on the continent. The book lacks organization and depth, bores the reader, and says the same things that American intellectuals have been

saying for some time. Canadian intellectuals are "hooked" on the U.S. and cannot define themselves except in American terms; they would do better to deal with the much more important problem of relations with Quebec.

D51 Lane, Lauriat, Jr. Rev. of *The New Romans*. *The Fiddlehead*, No. 80 (May-June-July 1969), pp. 97-98.

The book is not anti-American or violent, yet is not a useful or original set of analyses, and is already dated. The poetry included does not do the poets justice, and deals indirectly with the topic. The book is interesting, however, in revealing what it is to be a Canadian. The main problem with the criticisms of America is — are the things criticized really American or did the Americans just happen to do first what has now been accepted everywhere?

D52 Angeles, Peter A. Rev. of *The New Romans*. *Alphabet*, No. 16 (Sept. 1969), pp. 52-57.

The reviewer finds the articles in this book all of good quality, displaying feelings from anti-Americanism to sympathetic attachment to the U.S. The main message is to *beware*. But Angeles believes that Canada is a potential giant that can learn from the U.S. He hopes that Canada will fulfil its potential, and not fall easy prey to bad imitation.

Love in a Burning Building

D53 Weaver, Robert. Rev. of *Love in a Burning Building*. *The Canadian Reader*, 11, No. 8 [1970-71?], 5-6.

This book is highly praised by Weaver for its reflective exploration of the human condition: of love, marriage, sex, and all human relationships. It is partially autobiographical, but Purdy often wears a mask and is "a poet who often watches the poet composing his autobiography." Purdy is a witty and very talented poet.

D54 Atwood, Margaret. "Love Is Ambiguous...Sex Is a Bully." *Canadian Literature*, No. 49 (Summer 1971), pp. 71-75.

Atwood likes this book, in spite of the flashy cover and the fact that the poems are all revised versions of earlier poems. She says that Purdy writes like "a cross between Shakespeare and a vaudeville comedian." She is one of surprisingly few critics who have recognized Purdy's similarities to the romantic poets, but observes that Purdy yearns for the ideal and eternal with no conviction that they exist. Purdy, as husband in these poems, sees marriage as both refuge and prison, is torn between home-life and adventure — but he always returns to his wife. Purdy's reflections on sex and love, as allaying his fear of death and vanishing, are personal and honest.

D55 Barbour, Douglas. Rev. of *Love in a Burning Building*, and *Rag & Bone Shop*, by Earle Birney. *The Dalhousie Review*, 51, No. 2 (Summer 1971), 289-90.

This book contains many old poems, and many worthwhile new poems. As an introduction to Purdy, it is a "gem." Purdy gives a "marvellously wide-ranging view of homo-sapiens engaged in his most profound and silly activity."

D56 Hornyansky, Michael. "Letters in Canada 1970." *University of Toronto Quarterly*, 40, No. 4 (Summer 1971), 379-80.

The review is much like a Purdy poem, in that the writer undergoes a process, changing his mind part way through the review. Hornyansky is at first skeptical of the book, due to its firelit, passionate cover. "Was this to be a non-stop swagger, with Purdy in his rangy dungfooted leering persona?" The reviewer believes that Purdy's image of surly vitality obtrudes and limits him. However, he finds the book good after all, as Purdy often changes to other personae who mock his "randy swaggerer," and has perfected his skill at craftsmanship. After reading the book, the reviewer was won over.

D57   Pokorny, Amy. Rev. of *Hiroshima Poems*, and *Theme and Variations for Sounding Brass*, by Ralph Gustafson. *Quarry*, 22, No. 2 (Spring 1973), 75-76.

Pokorny writes that Purdy has left the restrictions of traditional prosody behind him, and is now using form that allows him to express himself much better. Purdy's personal sympathy for the underdog is mentioned, and the book is seen as Purdy's expression of his sorrow over the suffering that took place at Hiroshima.

D58   Warkentin, Germaine. "Drifting to Oblivion." Rev. of *Hiroshima Poems*, and *Lies*, by John Newlove. *Canadian Literature*, No. 56 (Spring 1973), pp. 121-22. Rpt. (abridged) in *Contemporary Literary Criticism*. Ed. Carolyn Riley. Vol. III. Detroit: Gale, 1975, p. 408.

Purdy's response to a civilization that survived oblivion is uneven; he is sometimes too prosy, sometimes too sentimental. "Remembering Hiroshima" is an especially good poem, however.

Selected Poems

D59   Duffy, Dennis. Rev. of *Selected Poems*. *The Globe and Mail*, 1 April 1972, Sec. Entertainment-Travel, p. 23.

Purdy writes of "the stuff of one man's experience taking on a shape resembling those larger forces shaping us all." Duffy sees Purdy as a Loyalist, who from the tragic vision of Canada receives the inspiration to seek the truth and the sources of life. The danger to Purdy is that he could become institutionalized as the Canadian Nationalist. Although he describes the inner life that is timeless and cyclical, as opposed to the outer life that is historical and linear, Purdy's talents have not been "stretched to the fullest" in this book. Purdy needs to combine the anguish of some of his poems with the humour of the others and Duffy believes he can do it.

D60   Sherman, Joseph. Rev. of *Selected Poems*; *Intense Pleasure*, by David McFadden; and *The Armies of the Moon*, by Gwendolyn MacEwen. *The Fiddlehead*, No. 94 (Summer 1972), pp. 120-22.

The book is praised as a literary milestone in Purdy's career, but Purdy is criticized for the unnecessary revising which defeats the purpose of this sort of book. The reviewer emphasizes Purdy's Canadianism and calls him a "surface man."

D61   Keyes, Mary. Rev. of *Selected Poems*. *The Canadian Forum*, June 1972, pp. 42-43.

Keyes concentrates on praising Purdy for the honesty of his communication and his closeness to the reader.

D62   Helwig, David. "Four Poets." Rev. of *Selected Poems*; *Intense Pleasure*, by David McFadden; *Skydeck*, by Stuart MacKinnon; and *Our Man in Utopia*, by Doug Fetherling. *Queen's Quarterly*, 79, No. 3 (Autumn 1972), 404-07.

This review is a flattering one to Purdy, but very general. Helwig writes that Purdy's poems are "better medicine than booze," and that the central theme of the book is "the sense of the mystery of time by which things happen and are lost, happen and endure."

D63   Mundwiler, Leslie. Rev. of *Selected Poems*. *Open Letter*, 2nd Ser., No. 3 (Fall 1972), 75-78.

Mundwiler points out that Purdy, in his poems, is not stagnantly seeking Canadian identity, a metaphysical communion with landscape, or an idealized national character, but instead seeks a dynamic awareness, remaining filled with doubt and uncertainty in the process. Purdy makes no final conclusion or statement, but is concerned with the process and with the question itself. People who are aware of Purdy's purpose and of the identifications he makes can accept his grotesque juxtapositions and his intentional stylelessness.

D64 Weaver, Robert. "A Radical Romantic." *Books in Canada*, Oct. 1972, pp. 16-17.

Weaver describes Purdy well, as "a romantic disguised (thinly) as the anti-romantic plain man." He discusses Purdy's irony, and his open form, with special praise for "Lament for the Dorsets."

D65 Shucard, Alan R. Rev. of *Selected Poems*. *World Literature Written in English*, 11, No. 2 (Nov. 1972), 106-08.

Shucard calls Purdy "the most Canadian living poet," possibly "the best Canadian poet living," and one of the first-rate poets writing in English anywhere. The reviewer praises Purdy's ability to "yoke deep and disparate insights to basic and sometimes base things." This book is called "a rugged, beautiful, and important book," which is both Canadian and universal. Although the praise seems lavish, the reviewer shows deep insight into Purdy's poetry and backs up his praise with solid reasons.

D66 Aide, William. Rev. of *Selected Poems*. *Quarry*, 22, No. 1 (Winter 1973), 66-70.

Purdy's poems are "wine-bright," and this book "solid" and "subtle." Purdy's major themes, which blend together, are place, ancestral time, and historic change. However, Purdy, in his self-mockery, does not tell the whole truth and covers up something in him that he should express.

D67 Stevens, Peter. "The Beowulf Poet Is Alive and Well." *Canadian Literature*, No. 55 (Winter 1973), pp. 99-102. Rpt. (abridged) in *Contemporary Literary Criticism*. Ed. Carolyn Riley. Vol. III. Detroit: Gale 1975, p. 408.

Like the Beowulf poet, Purdy is the poet of an emerging nation; he welds together sharply contrasting states of mind and emotional moods, and he displays an ambivalent attitude towards his experiences in various places. The central polarity of Purdy's poetry is "the transcience yet persistence of man, the vitality of life in the face of inevitable death." Unlike the Beowulf poet, Purdy is self-conscious, focussing on men and on himself. The poet defines himself in relation to this country and the world and tells us something about ourselves. "If Purdy didn't exist, it would have been necessary for Canadians to invent him."

On the Bearpaw Sea

D68 Woodcock, George. "Purdy's Prelude and Other Poems." Rev. of *On the Bearpaw Sea, In Search of Owen Roblin*, and eight other books. *Canadian Literature*, No. 64 (Spring 1975), pp. 92-98.

Both these long poems are "used for a rather intensive elaboration of philosophic and moral and historic reflections on the nature and direction of human life, of all life." In *On the Bearpaw Sea*, the clowning and solemnity flow into each other. *Owen Roblin* is Purdy's search to recover a sense of himself, and is about time and death and the beauty of transient things. It is also about continuity, about being part of an enduring whole, and is therefore Purdy's *Prelude*.

Poems for All the Annettes (1973)

D69 Rev. of *Poems for All the Annettes* (1973), and *Hymn to Isis*, by Edmund Fancott. *The Canadian Reader*, 14, No. 6 (Dec. 1973), 13-14.

Purdy now writes "with a mature power undistorted by the popularity and praise that have properly come his way." Like other poets, his subjects are love, life, death, etc. but "he speaks Canadian." This is the third version of *Annettes*. The reviewer quotes from some poems, but does not evaluate the book.

Sex and Death

D70 Barbour, Douglas. Rev. of *Sex and Death*. *Quill & Quire*, Aug. 1973, p. 12.

In this flattering review, Barbour expresses his gratefulness that we have Purdy, and that he has shared with us his "eccentric but clear vision of the passing world." Barbour thinks this book to be possibly Purdy's best collection, as Purdy is now a whole being, and completely in control of his abilities. Purdy is called a time traveller and a space traveller, who moves through all history, galactic and human.

D71 Geddes, Gary. "A Victim in Darker Reality." *The Globe and Mail*, 20 Oct. 1973, Sec. Entertainment-Travel, p. 23.

This book includes all Purdy's "familiar faces" and adds a new one — that of the troubled modern man viewing twentieth-century politics. But his political poems are too personal and subjective, showing only himself as the victim. *Sex and Death* is called a transitional book, "a stage in Purdy's descent into a darker, more terrible reality." Although some of the poems are powerful, others show need of a good editor. Geddes criticizes Purdy for his dependence on collo-quialisms, throwaway lines, too much chattiness, and formlessness, and thinks that Purdy may be a "narrative poet who has been too long caught in lyrical suspenders." He should not publish everything he writes, in order to publish a book a year, but should take more care, if he wishes his reputation to continue to grow.

D72 Sutherland, Fraser. Rev. of *Sex and Death*. *Books in Canada*, Oct. 1973, pp. 4-5.

This review finds many joys, but some failures in the book. But Sutherland aptly describes the Purdy persona "groping through windy rhetoric and taut imagery toward some realization."

D73 Lee, Dennis. Rev. of *Sex and Death*. *Saturday Night*, Dec. 1973, p. 33. Rpt. (abridged) in *Contemporary Literary Criticism*. Ed. Carolyn Riley and Phyllis Carmel Mendelson. Vol. VI. Detroit: Gale, 1976, p. 428.

Lee calls Purdy "one of the best poets in the world," and *Sex and Death* "one of his very fine collections." Although the book has lapses and untidiness, ". . . finally who cares?"

D74 Stevens, Peter. "The Perils of Majority." *The University of Windsor Review*, 9, No. 2 (Spring 1974), 100-09.

Stevens feels that Purdy's book combines the attributes of Layton and Birney. But he finds some "disastrously bad poems" in this volume, especially the poems he has written about places that he finds uncongenial. Purdy's poems about South Africa, and some of the Hiroshima poems, fail, while his Canadian poems are best.

D75 Bowering, George. "Suitcase Poets." Rev. of *Sex and Death*, and *What's So Big about Green?*, by Earle Birney. *Canadian Literature*, No. 61 (Summer 1974), pp. 95-100. Rpt. (abridged) in *Contemporary Literary Criticism*. Ed. Carolyn Riley and Phyllis Carmel Mendelson. Vol. VI. Detroit: Gale, 1976, pp. 428-29.

Bowering is critical of Purdy for using his personality as the main organizing principle in his poetry, for making no innovations in his verse form since *The Cariboo Horses*, for distancing the reader by his form. His poetry is very prosy, or like diary entries. His poems succeed only when the personality and the story are interesting. The poems in this book are less ribald and exaggerated than in his other books; Purdy tries to get to the bare naked moment. The best poem here is "The Horseman of Agawa."

D76 Levinson, Christopher. Rev. of *Sex and Death*. *Queen's Quarterly*, 81, No. 2 (Summer 1974), 318-20.

This is an astute review, of Purdy in general, and of this book in particular. Levinson writes that this volume is more urban, social, and political than Purdy's others, and that it deepens and darkens the picture that Purdy has been giving us. Purdy should be respected for the range and solidity of his poems, for the manner in which he juxtaposes thoughts and fantasies, even though he doesn't always seem to take himself seriously. Purdy is only too aware of the multiplicity and complexity of various types of existence and of alternative actions open to him; sometimes his imaginative leaps include too much. His poems appear to have been written as he goes along, and he shows his distrust of neatness and completeness.

In Search of Owen Roblin

D77 David, Jack. Rev. of *In Search of Owen Roblin*. *Quill & Quire*, Oct. 1974, p. 24.

This book, which resembles a child's book with its photographs and large type, is "a meditation on Purdy's own locus." The purpose of this long poem is to explore a part of Canada in a distinctly Canadian way, to explore "the poet's and the locality's essence."

D78 Levinson, Christopher. Rev. of *In Search of Owen Roblin: Atlantic Crossings*, by David Helwig; and *Change-Up: New Poems*, by Raymond Souster. *Books in Canada*, Dec. 1974, pp. 26-27.

This long poem enables Purdy to use his historical imagination in a more sustained way. By interfusing present and past, Purdy transcends the local and personal, and shows the importance of communication with both past and future.

D79 Cameron, Barry. "The Motive for Fiction." Rev. of *In Search of Owen Roblin*, with mention of *Sex and Death*, *Hiroshima Poems*, *Poems for All the Annettes* (1973), and *On the Bearpaw Sea*. *The Canadian Forum*, Jan. 1975, pp. 47-48.

In *Owen Roblin*, Purdy seeks the adequate language and a psychic place that will yield meaning. His theme is man's motive for fiction, which is to shape life so that we can make sense of it, and so that the past can exist in the present. The poem shows the tension between fixity and open-endedness; the poet can never structure permanently any experience. *Sex and Death* is Purdy's best work technically, but *Owen Roblin* is the most valuable book in order to understand all his work. Cameron feels that it is unfortunate that the book is an expensive, coffee-table volume, as fewer people will read it.

D80 Gutteridge, Don. Rev. of *In Search of Owen Roblin*, and *Fire on Stone*, by Ralph Gustafson. *Queen's Quarterly*, 82, No. 1 (Spring 1975), 139-40.

This narrative of Purdy's ancestors and chronicle of his search for his roots brings together Purdy's strengths and minimizes his weaknesses. Gutteridge believes Purdy's tendency to circle around the truth with accumulated detail is a strength here. The accumulated detail helps the reader and Purdy know these ancestors fully in order to become human themselves.

D81 Woodcock, George.
See D68.

D82 Sandler, Linda. "Purdy on Owen Roblin." *The Tamarack Review*, No. 65 (March 1975), pp. 98-100. Rpt. in *The Canadian Reader*, 16, No. 3 (March 1975), 5-7.

Sandler calls this poem a "superbly varied 'documentary' poem," which acknowledges the past as a historical reality. Although it tells a powerful story, the poem does not quite work, according to Sandler, as we need to know more about the present to make the recovered past more convincing as a "compass point" for the future.

D83   Dragland, Stan. Rev. of *In Search of Owen Roblin*. *The Fiddlehead*, No. 110 (Summer 1976), pp. 138-42.

Dragland criticizes this book for its lack of tightness, finding some parts good, others slack. Although the reviewer likes the personal, down-to-earth approach of the Purdy persona, he finds the "I" sometimes an intruder in this long poem.

D84   Gibbs, Robert. "Presiding Voices: Purdy, Layton, and Gustafson." Rev. of *In Search of Owen Roblin*; *The Pole-Vaulter*, by Irving Layton; and *Fire on Stone*, by Ralph Gustafson. *The Dalhousie Review*, 56 (Summer 1976), 356-65.

This is a very intelligent discussion and comparison of these three books, with emphasis on the personae used by the three poets. Purdy's voice varies between that of the persona undergoing an intimate search and that of the more detached observer, who frames and distances the material. In the attempt to integrate the detached persona with the fully integrated poetic personality, Purdy's quest for self mostly succeeds.

D85   Stevens, Peter. "Explorer/Settler/Poet." *The University of Windsor Review*, 13, No. 1 (Fall-Winter 1977), 63-74.

Canadian writers have turned to early historical figures "as a basis for some mythic ground to construct a sense of a Canadian poetic or literary consciousness." Purdy's search for his ancestors in *In Search of Owen Roblin* is also a search for a poetic voice, which he finds. His poetry becomes more colloquial, more based on his roots, after he has settled at Roblin Lake. Thus, this book by Purdy tells the story of Purdy's own development as a poet.

Storm Warning 2: The New Canadian Poets

D86   Cogswell, Fred. Rev. of *Storm Warning 2*. *Books in Canada*, May 1976, p. 15.

Cogswell appreciates Purdy's encouragement to young poets, but finds this book a disappointment after the good quality of poems in *Storm Warning 1*. The poets in this volume are clever, but not exciting or original; in fact, Purdy tends to pick poets who sound like himself or appeal to his personal taste. The two types of poets in this book, those who respond to life in the urban subculture, and those who ruminate, like Purdy, are all imitative of others and have not found their own voices.

D87   Kishkan, Teresa. Rev. of *Storm Warning 2*. *The Malahat Review*, No. 42 (April 1977), pp. 138-39.

This book contains a variety of poetry and represents all regions of Canada. However, the good work is hidden amongst much "sloppy uninspired writing." Purdy's method of selection was based on his "personal taste," which is a very questionable method. Except for a few poems, the book doesn't predict much of a storm coming.

D88   Barbour, Douglas. "Poetry Chronicle IV." Rev. of *Storm Warning 2*, *Sundance at Dusk*, and *The Poems of Al Purdy*. *The Dalhousie Review*, 57, No. 2 (Summer 1977), 355-70.

Storm Warning 2 is said to be of a higher quality than the first one. *Sundance at Dusk* is a good book. The shadow of mortality looms darker than ever before, but Purdy's laughter always heals. *The Poems of Al Purdy* is "a superb collection," which shows how good Purdy is at his best.

D89   Abbey, Lloyd. Rev. of *Storm Warning 2*. *Canadian Literature*, No. 76 (Spring 1978), pp. 123-25.

Although this book contains many good poems, Purdy's influence is probably too pervasive. Abbey even wonders if this book is a put-on, and if Purdy is publishing his latest poems under other people's names. However, the book is "a total commitment to excellence."

The Poems of Al Purdy

D90   Harvey, Roderick W. Rev. of *The Poems of Al Purdy*. *Quill & Quire*, May 1976, p. 41.

        The reviewer is pleased to see Purdy's poems collected in an inexpensive paperback, and hopes that the book will be used as a course text. This is a good selection of Purdy's diverse poems. Purdy cannot be categorized; some think him a stylist, others a nationalist. These poems are all "philosophical explorations of identity in Canada."

D91   Barbour, Douglas.
        See D88.

Sundance at Dusk

D92   Wayman, Tom. "Let's Hear It for the Big P." *Books in Canada*, Oct. 1976, pp. 22-24.

        Wayman uses the opportunity to discuss his relationship with Purdy and to thank Purdy for playing the father-figure to him in helping him publish his poetry. Wayman also mentions Purdy's combination of anecdote with history in his poems; Purdy's open form; Purdy's insistence that a poem is not the beginning and end of existence, but that, even though a poem cannot change things, that is no reason not to write one. Wayman finds this book successful, and picks his favourite poems.

D93   Jewinski, Ed. Rev. of *Sundance at Dusk*. *Quill & Quire*, Dec. 1976, p. 30.

        This is a perceptive review, which looks at the book as a whole, and at individual poems. Jewinski praises the book, but finds weak, uncontrolled poems along with the powerful ones. The book is filled with a mood of lamentation and loss at man's fate, but also with energy, endurance despite everything, and "a kind of jubilation," as Purdy writes.

D94   Weaver, Robert. Rev. of *Sundance at Dusk*. *The Canadian Reader*, Feb. 1977, pp. 5-6.

        Weaver feels that Purdy's readers have overlooked his more recent books, such as *In Search of Owen Roblin*, because they think they have heard it all before; but this is far from true. Purdy *has* been walking in the shadow of his own reputation in recent years, but Weaver hopes that *Sundance at Dusk* won't be ignored, as Purdy is "more complex and various than he is now sometimes given credit for being."

D95   Barbour, Douglas.
        See D88.

D96   Scobie, Stephen. Rev. of *Sundance at Dusk*; *Octomi*, by Andrew Suknaski; and *Tecumseh*, by Don Gutteridge. *The Fiddlehead*, No. 114 (Summer 1977), pp. 139-40.

        This review shows excellent understanding of the Purdy persona and style. Purdy's style is ironic, yet affectionate; earthy yet educated; colloquial and controlled; localized yet widely travelled; rambling and discursive. The inevitable unevenness is part of his poetic verse and could not be removed without destroying the virtues as well. The poems in this book, however, are sometimes too strained and often flawed, when Purdy stretches things too far beyond their limits.

D97   McKay, Don. Rev. of *Sundance at Dusk*, and *The Catch* and *Poems and Other Baseballs*, by George Bowering. *The University of Windsor Review*, 13, No. 1 (Fall-Winter 1977), 99-104.

        Purdy has established an original voice and created his own kind of speech, which is rooted in experience rather than art. His voice, and poems, seem discovered rather than invented; he often revises his own views part way through a poem. In this book, there are many travel poems, but "Ameliasburg is still the navel of the world."

D98 McFadden, David. Rev. of *Sundance at Dusk. Queen's Quarterly*, 84, No. 4 (Winter 1977), 687-88.

Purdy writes at random, letting his thoughts flow onto the page, until something makes him stop. His "best poems, though rare, are on a par with the best of any poet at any time"; his worst are of interest because of his sincerity. McFadden praises the poem "At the Hot Gates," which he feels refutes those who say Purdy writes nothing but chopped-up prose, as Purdy completely effaces himself in this poem.

A Handful of Earth

D99 Farmiloe, Dorothy. Rev. of *A Handful of Earth. Quill & Quire*, 14 Nov. 1977, pp. 9-10.

Although Purdy admits that this is his bottom drawer stuff, these poems are worth reading, as they have the Purdy touch and the Purdy voice. These poems are mellower than most of his others; his theme is what we have learned or failed to learn from the past.

D100 Woodcock, George. Rev. of *A Handful of Earth*, and *Selected Strawberries*, by Susan Musgrave. *CV/II*, 3, No. 4 (Summer 1978), 6-7.

Poetry has room for two types of voices, Athens (like Purdy) and Delphi (Musgrave). The voice of Athens is that of man speaking to man, is discursive, conversational, and rational. Woodcock finds that Purdy's poetry is an excellent example of that type of voice, and finds this book very good, and even the old poems valuable. Purdy is read widely because of the kind of verse he writes rather than because of his "stature" as a poet, but those who read him for superficial reasons often go back to read him for deeper intents.

At Marsport Drugstore

D101 Dempster, Barry. Rev. of *At Marsport Drugstore. Quill & Quire*, July 1978, p. 12.

The book is called "playboy gone literary," a blend of literature and men's magazines. The poems are sometimes clumsy, and are crude, but crude in such a way as to create a different style of poetry.

No Other Country

D102 Christy, Jim. Rev. of *No Other Country. Books in Canada*, Oct. 1977, pp. 13-14.

This is a harshly critical review. Christy finds this book hackneyed and hack work, published only because Al Purdy is Al Purdy. The book is called depressing reading, sloppy, trite, boring, and bland; Purdy minimizes each place and whatever people he is in contact with.

D103 Barnes, Michael. Rev. of *No Other Country. Quill & Quire*, 14 Nov. 1977, p. 9.

Purdy writes well about Canadian landscape and people, according to Barnes, and his story about Roderick Haig-Brown is "pure gold."

Being Alive

D104 Helwig, David. Rev. of *Being Alive. The Toronto Star*, 23 Sept. 1978, Sec. D, p. 7.

Helwig appreciates this book, for it is the "best introduction to Purdy," fairly complete, and shows Purdy's development over twenty years. The poems are arranged in a "loosely chronological" fashion, according to Purdy, but also grouped according to theme and feeling. The book is diverse and "resists summary." It contains comic poems, love poems, intimate poems, and everyone's old favourites. Helwig especially likes "The Country North of Belleville," and finds it hard to believe that "anyone ever sat down in a chair and wrote it and then read it for the first time."

D105 Colombo, John Robert. Rev. of *Being Alive. The Globe and Mail*, 26 Sept. 1978, Sec. 1, p. 16.

Colombo calls this book, which marks the event of Purdy's sixtieth birthday, "vintage Purdy, the best possible introduction to the man and his world." One can see in this chronological arrangement of poems Purdy's movement from blunt statement of the world's contradictions to "a lyric and tentative appreciation of its subtleties."

D106 Trethewey, Eric. "Praising Water and Friendship, Praising Love." *The Fiddlehead*, No. 121 (Spring 1979), pp. 146-49.

The reviewer dislikes Purdy's sentimentality and thinks his humour is often flat but admires his "expansiveness and his generosity of spirit which find their expression in a uniquely Canadian idiom."

Moths in the Iron Curtain

D107 Bemrose, John. Rev. of *Moths in the Iron Curtain*. *Toronto Star*, 9 June 1979, p. F7.

Bemrose thinks this is a minor addition to Purdy's canon.

Selected Record Reviews

Canadian Poets I

D108 Colombo, John Robert. Rev. of *Canadian Poets*. *The Canadian Reader*, 7, No. 12 [1966?], 4-5.

Although none of the poets read as well as Dylan Thomas did, most of them give exciting performances. Colombo enjoys Purdy's "rambling, witty, occasionally coarse voice."

D109 Robertson, George. "Voices of Poets." *Canadian Literature*, No. 36 (Spring 1968), pp. 70-74.

Although Robertson does not usually like readings of poetry, he likes this, and especially the reading by Purdy, whose "rough, hectoring beer-parlour voice is surely the clinching argument in favour of hearing the poet as well as reading him." But his voice doesn't disguise his seriousness of purpose.

D110 Swan, Susan. Rev. of *Canadian Poets I*. *Books in Canada*, April-May-June 1973, pp. 19-20.

Swan thinks that Purdy reads best of all the poets on this album. His Ontario accent and idiom gives the sense of place to his poems, and his voice, which is nasal and flat, leads up to a flash of recognition and surprise.

Al Purdy's Ontario

D111 Wilde, Kelly. Rev. of *Al Purdy's Ontario*. *Books in Canada*, Oct. 1973, pp. 12-13.

Purdy's style of reading is criticized for its lack of passion and lack of electricity and involvement. Because he seems to be talking to himself, he loses his audience. Purdy sounds like "any one of a score of lesser talented poets at a Canlit jam session," moving among a prosy, anti-poetic tone, a self-conscious detachment, and a tough shell and tired sigh. He should make more effort with his reading and performance skills.

D112 Weaver, Robert. Rev. of *Al Purdy's Ontario*. *The Canadian Reader*, 12, No. 5 (n.d.), 5-6.

Weaver does not review the record, but discusses Al Purdy as an Ontario poet, and his concern with Eastern Ontario. Purdy is sometimes social historian, but often makes his region and its characters into myth.

Index to Critics Listed
in the Bibliography
